The New Answers Book 1

Over 25 Questions on Creation/Evolution and the Bible

Ken Ham General Editor

First printing: November 2006
Twenty-first printing: May 2014

ISBN: 978-0-89051-509-9
Library of Congress Number: 2006937546

Cover design by Left Coast Design, Portland, Oregon
Interior design by Diane King
Compiled by Bodie Hodge and Gary Vaterlaus

Please consider requesting that a copy of this volume be purchased by
your local library system.

Printed in the United States of America

Please visit our website for other great titles:
www.masterbooks.net

For information regarding author interviews, please contact the
publicity department at (870) 438-5288.

Master
Books®
A Division of New Leaf Publishing Group
www.masterbooks.net

Acknowledgments and special thanks

To Dr. John Baumgardner, Dr. John Whitmore, Dr. Don DeYoung, Dr. Larry Vardiman, Dr. Danny Faulkner, Dr. Bob Compton, Dr. Gary Parker, Dr. Jason Lisle, Dr. Georgia Purdom, Dr. Terry Mortenson, Ken Ham, Bodie Hodge, Mike Matthews, and Stacia McKeever for reviewing chapters of this book.

To Dan Lietha for many of the illustrations used in this book. To Dr. John Baumgardner for the illustrations in the chapter on plate tectonics. To Mike Oard for the illustrations in the chapter on the Ice Age. (All other illustrations are noted on the illustration, figure, or photograph.)

To Roger Patterson for developing the glossary of terms.

In the defining apologetic battle of the last 150 years, *The Answers Book*, (and now *The New Answers Book*) stands as one of the top introductory handbooks for those who love God's Word and aspire to wisely defend the faith against evolutionary scientism. It provides helpful, easy to understand, devastating arguments which will benefit students, pastors, and scientists.

— Douglas W. Phillips
President of Vision Forum

I would recommend that every person seeking the truth of God's Word read this book. *The New Answers Book* provides well-documented answers to tough questions asked by many unbelievers as well as Christians. It is a wealth of information that belongs in every library.

— John D. Morris
President, Institute for Creation Research

Even a young teen can read and understand the 27 different topics in this wonderful, eye-opening book. It is excellent for educational purposes or as a ministry resource.

— Ray Comfort
Living Waters Publications

Ken Ham is a gifted thinker and a gift to the Christian community. He is not only a biblical thinker, but a powerhouse communicator in the debate on creation v. evolution. Read this book, then train your children to have a biblical world view like Ken does.

— Dennis Rainey
President, FamilyLife

Contents

1

Is There Really a God?

KEN HAM & JASON LISLE

God—an Eternal, Uncreated Being?

In our everyday experience, just about everything seems to have a beginning. In fact, the laws of science show that even things which look the same through our lifetime, such as the sun and other stars, are, in reality, running down. The sun is using up its fuel at millions of tons each second—since the sun cannot last forever, it had to have a beginning. The same can be shown to be true for the entire universe.

So when Christians claim that the God of the Bible created all the basic entities of life and the universe, some will ask what seems to be a logical question: "Who created God?"

The very first verse in the Bible declares: "In the beginning God ... ." There is no attempt in these words to prove the existence of God or imply in any way that God had a beginning. In fact, the Bible makes it clear in many places that God is outside time. He is eternal, with no beginning or end. He also knows all things, being infinitely intelligent.[1]

Is it logical, though, to accept the existence of such an eternal being? Can modern science, which has produced our technology of computers, space shuttles, and medical advances, even allow for such a notion?

---

[1] Psalm 90:2; 106:48; 147:5. Notice that only things which have a beginning have to have a cause.

What Would We Look For?

What evidence would we expect to find if there really is an infinite God who created all things as the Bible claims? How would we even recognize the hand of such an omnipotent (all-powerful) Creator?

The Bible claims that God knows all things—He is omniscient! Therefore, He is infinitely intelligent. To recognize His handiwork, one would have to know how to recognize the evidence of the works of His intelligence.

How Do We Recognize the Evidence of Intelligence?

Why do scientists become so excited when they discover stone tools together with bones in a cave? The stone tools show signs of intelligence. The scientists recognize that these tools could not have designed themselves but that they are a product of intelligent input. Thus, the researchers rightly conclude that an intelligent creature was responsible for making these tools.

In a similar way, one would never look at the Great Wall of China, the U.S. Capitol building in Washington, D.C., or the Sydney Opera House in Australia and conclude that such structures were formed after explosions in a brick factory.

Neither would anyone believe that the presidents' heads on Mt. Rushmore were the products of millions of years of erosion. We *can* recognize design, the evidence of the outworkings of intelligence. We see man-made objects all around us— cars, airplanes, computers, stereos, houses, appliances, and so on. And yet, at no time would anyone ever suggest that such objects were just the products of time and chance. Design is everywhere. It would never enter our minds that metal, left to itself, would eventually form into engines, transmissions, wheels, and all the other intricate parts needed to produce an automobile.

This "design argument" is often associated with the name of William Paley, an Anglican clergyman who wrote on this topic in the late eighteenth century. He is particularly remembered for his example of the watch and the watchmaker. In discussing a comparison between a stone and a watch, he concluded that "the watch must have had a maker; that there must have existed, at some time and at some place or other, an artificer or artificers, who formed it for the purpose which we find it actually to answer; who comprehended its construction, and designed its use."[2]

Paley thus believed that, just as the watch implied a watchmaker, so too does design in living things imply a Designer. Although he believed in a God who created all things, his God was a Master Designer who is now remote from His Creation, not the personal God of the Bible.[3]

Today, however, a large proportion of the population, including many leading scientists, believe that all plants and creatures, including the intelligent engineers who make watches, cars, etc., were the product of an evolutionary process—not a Creator God.[4] But this is not a defensible position, as we will see.

Living Things Show Evidence of Design!

The late Isaac Asimov, an ardent anti-creationist, declared, "In man is a three-pound brain which, as far as we know, is the most complex and orderly arrangement of matter in the universe."[5] It is much more complex than the most complicated computer ever built. Wouldn't it be logical to assume that if man's highly intelligent brain designed the computer, then the human brain was also the product of design?

Scientists who reject the concept of a Creator God agree that all living

---

[2] W. Paley, *Natural Theology: or Evidences of the Existence and Attributes of the Deity, Collected from the Appearances of Nature*, reprinted in 1972 by St. Thomas Press, Houston, Texas, 3.

[3] I. Taylor, *In the Minds of Men*, TFE Publishing, Toronto, Canada, 1991, 121.

[4] This is the process by which life is supposed to have arisen spontaneously from nonlife. Over long periods of time, different kinds of animals and plants have then supposedly developed as a result of small changes, resulting in an increase in genetic information. For instance, evolutionists propose that fish developed into amphibians, amphibians into reptiles, reptiles evolved into birds and mammals. Man eventually evolved from an ancestor shared with apes.

[5] I. Asimov, In the game of energy and thermodynamics you can't even break even, *Smithsonian*, June 1970, 10.

things exhibit evidence of design. In essence, they accept the design argument of Paley, but not Paley's Designer. For example, Dr. Michael Denton, a non-Christian medical doctor and scientist with a doctorate in molecular biology, concludes:

> It is the sheer universality of perfection, the fact that everywhere we look, to whatever depth we look, we find an elegance and ingenuity of an absolutely transcending quality, which so mitigates against the idea of chance.

> Alongside the level of ingenuity and complexity exhibited by the molecular machinery of life, even our most advanced artifacts appear clumsy. We feel humbled, as neolithic man would in the presence of twentieth-century technology.

> It would be an illusion to think that what we are aware of at present is any more than a fraction of the full extent of biological design. In practically every field of fundamental biological research ever-increasing levels of design and complexity are being revealed at an ever-accelerating rate.[6]

Dr. Richard Dawkins, holder of the Charles Simonyi Chair of Public Understanding of Science at Oxford University, has become one of the world's leading evolutionist spokespersons. His fame has come as the result of the publication of books, including *The Blind Watchmaker*, which defend modern evolutionary theory and claim to refute once and for all the notion of a Creator God. He said, "We have seen that living things are too improbable and too beautifully 'designed' to have come into existence by chance."[7]

There is no doubt that even the most ardent atheist concedes that design is evident in the animals and plants that inhabit our planet. If Dawkins rejects "chance" in design, what does he put in place of "chance" if he does not accept a Creator God?

Who—or What—Is the Designer Then?

Design obviously implies a designer. To a Christian, the design we see all around us is totally consistent with the Bible's explanation: "In the beginning God created the heavens and the earth" (Genesis 1:1), and "For by him

---

[6] M. Denton, *Evolution: A Theory in Crisis*, Adler & Adler Publishers, Bethesda, Maryland, 1986, 32.
[7] R. Dawkins, *The Blind Watchmaker*, W.W. Norton & Co., New York, 1987, 43.

[Jesus Christ] all things were created that are in heaven and that are in earth, visible and invisible, whether thrones or dominions or principalities or powers. All things were created through him and for him" (Colossians 1:16).

However, evolutionists like Richard Dawkins, who admit the design in living things, reject the idea of any kind of a Designer/God. In reference to Paley, Dawkins states:

> Paley's argument is made with passionate sincerity and is informed by the best biological scholarship of his day, but it is wrong, gloriously and utterly wrong. The analogy between telescope and eye, between watch and living organism, is false.[8]

Why? It is because Dawkins attributes the design to what he calls "blind forces of physics" and the processes of natural selection. Dawkins writes:

> *All appearance to the contrary*, the only watchmaker in nature is the blind forces of physics, albeit deployed in a very special way. A true watchmaker has foresight: he designs his cogs and springs, and plans their interconnections, with future purpose in his mind's eye. Natural selection, the blind, unconscious, automatic process which Darwin discovered, and which we now know is the explanation for the existence and apparently purposeful form of all life, has no purpose in mind. It has no mind and no mind's eye. It does not plan for the future. It has no vision, no foresight, no sight at all. If it can be said to play the role of watchmaker in nature, it is the blind watchmaker [emphasis added].[9]

Dawkins does, however, concede that "the more statistically improbable a thing is, the less can we believe that it just happened by blind chance. Superficially the obvious alternative to chance is an Intelligent Designer."[10]

Nonetheless, he rejects the idea of an "Intelligent Designer" and instead offers this "answer":

[8] Ibid., 5.
[9] Ibid., 5.
[10] R. Dawkins, The necessity of Darwinism, *New Scientist* **94**:130, 1982.

The answer, Darwin's answer, is by gradual, step-by-step transformations from simple beginnings, from primordial entities sufficiently simple to have come into existence by chance. Each successive change in the gradual evolutionary process was simple enough, relative to its predecessor, to have arisen by chance.

But the whole sequence of cumulative steps constitutes anything but a chance process, when you consider the complexity of the final end product relative to the original starting point. The cumulative process is directed by nonrandom survival. The purpose of this chapter is to demonstrate the power of this cumulative selection as a fundamentally nonrandom process.[11]

Basically, then, Dawkins is doing nothing more than insisting that natural selection[12] and mutations[13] together provide the mechanism for the evolutionary process. He believes these processes are nonrandom and directed. In reality, this is just a sophisticated way of saying that evolution is itself the designer.

---

[11] Dawkins, *The Blind Watchmaker*, 43.

[12] Dr. Gary Parker, a creationist, argues that natural selection does occur, but operates as a "preservative" and has nothing to do with one organism changing into another. "Natural selection is just one of the processes that operates in our present corrupted world to insure that the created kinds can indeed spread throughout the Earth in all its ecologic and geographic variety (often, nowadays, in spite of human pollution)." G. Parker, *Creation: Facts of Life*, Master Books, Green Forest, Arkansas, 1994, 75.
"[Richard] Lewontin is an evolutionist and outspoken anticreationist, but he honestly recognizes the same limitations of natural selection that creation scientists do: '… natural selection operates essentially to enable the organisms to maintain their state of adaptation rather than to improve it.' Natural selection does not lead to continual improvement (evolution); it only helps to maintain features that organisms already have (creation). Lewontin also notes that extinct species seem to have been just as fit to survive as modern ones, so he adds: '… natural selection over the long run does not seem to improve a species' chances of survival, but simply enables it to "track," or keep up with, the constantly changing environment.'"
"It seems to me that natural selection works only because each kind was created with sufficient variety to multiply and fill the earth in all its ecologic and geographic variety." G. Parker, *Creation: Facts of Life*, 84–86.

[13] "After all, mutations are only changes in genes that already exist," G. Parker, *Creation: Facts of Life*, 103.
"In an article paradoxically titled 'The Mechanisms of Evolution,' Francisco Ayala defines a mutation as 'an error' in DNA." G. Parker, *Creation: Facts of Life*, 99.

Does Natural Selection Produce Design?

Life is built on information. A great amount of this information is contained in that molecule of heredity, DNA, which makes up the genes of an organism. Therefore, to argue that natural selection and mutations are the basic mechanisms of the evolutionary process, one must show that these processes produce the information responsible for the design that is evident in living things.

Anyone who understands basic biology recognizes, of course, as Darwin did, that natural selection is a logical process that one can observe. However, natural selection only operates on the information that is already contained in the genes—it does not produce new information.[14] Actually, this is consistent with the Bible's account of origins, in that God created distinct kinds of animals and plants, each to reproduce after its own kind.

It is true that one can observe great variation in a kind and see the results of natural selection. For instance, wolves, coyotes, and dingoes have developed over time as a result of natural selection operating on the

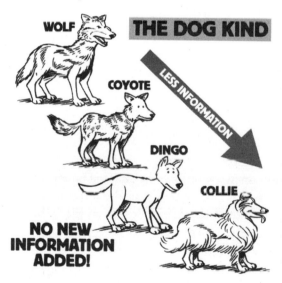

information found in the genes of the wolf/dog kind. But the point is that no new information was produced—these varieties of dogs have resulted from a rearrangement, sorting out, and separation of the information in the original dog kind. One kind has never been observed to change into a totally different kind with information that previously

---

[14] L.P. Lester and R.G. Bohlin, *The Natural Limits to Biological Change*, Probe Books, Dallas, 1989, 175–176.
E. Noble et al., *Parasitology: The Biology of Animal Parasites*, Lea & Febiger, Philadelphia, 1989. Chapter 6: "Evolution of Parasitism?" 516, states, "Natural selection can act only on those biologic properties that already exist; it cannot create properties in order to meet adaptational needs."

did not exist.[15] Without intelligent input to increase information, natural selection will not work as a mechanism for evolution.

Denton confirms this when he states:

> It cannot be stressed enough that evolution by natural selection is analogous to problem solving without any intelligent guidance, without any intelligent input whatsoever. No activity which involves an intelligent input can possibly be analogous to evolution by natural selection.[16]

Without a way to increase information, natural selection will not work as a mechanism for evolution. Evolutionists would agree with this, but they believe that mutations somehow provide the new information for natural selection to act upon.

Can Mutations Produce New Information?

Actually, scientists now know that the answer is "no!" Dr. Lee Spetner, a highly qualified scientist who taught information and communication theory at Johns Hopkins University, makes this abundantly clear in his scholarly and thoroughly researched book, *Not by Chance*:

> In this chapter I'll bring several examples of evolution, particularly mutations, and show that information is not increased. ... But in all the reading I've done in the life-sciences literature, I've never found a mutation that *added* information.[17]

> All point mutations that have been studied on the molecular level turn out to *reduce* the genetic information and not to increase it.[18]

> The NDT [neo-Darwinian theory] is supposed to explain how information of life has been built up by evolution. The essential biological difference between a human and a bacterium is in the information they contain. All other biological differences follow from that. The human genome has much more information than does the bacterial genome. *Information cannot be built up by mutations that lose it.*

---

[15] For instance, despite many unproved claims to the contrary by evolutionists, nobody has observed or documented a reptile changing into a bird. The classic example paraded by some evolutionists as an "in-between" creature, *Archaeopteryx*, has now been rejected by many evolutionists.

[16] M. Denton, *Evolution: A Theory in Crisis*, 317.

[17] L. Spetner, *Not By Chance*, The Judaica Press, Brooklyn, New York, 1997, 131–132.

[18] Ibid., 138.

A business can't make money by losing it a little at a time [emphasis added].[19]

Evolutionary scientists have no way around this conclusion that many scientists, including Dr. Spetner, have now come to. Mutations do not work as a mechanism for the evolutionary process. Spetner sums it all up as follows:

The neo-Darwinians would like us to believe that large evolutionary changes can result from a series of small events if there are enough of them. But if these events all *lose* information they can't be the steps in the kind of evolution the NDT is supposed to explain, no matter how many mutations there are. Whoever thinks macroevolution can be made by mutations that lose information is like the merchant who lost a little money on every sale but thought he could make it up in volume ... . Not even one mutation has been observed that adds a little information to the genome. That surely shows that there are not the millions upon millions of potential mutations the theory demands. There may well not be any. The failure to observe even one mutation that adds information is more than just a failure to find support for the theory. It is evidence *against* the theory. We have here a serious challenge to neo-Darwinian theory [emphasis added].[20]

This is also confirmed by Dr. Werner Gitt, a director and professor at the German Federal Institute of Physics and Technology. In answering the question, "Can new information originate through mutations?" he said:

This idea is central in representations of evolution, but mutations can only cause changes in *existing* information. There can be no increase in information, and in general the results are injurious. New blueprints for new functions or new organs cannot arise; mutations cannot be the source of new (creative) information [emphasis added].[21]

So if natural selection and mutations are eliminated as mechanisms to produce the information and design of living systems, then another source must be found.

But there are even more basic problems for those who reject the Creator God as the source of information.

---

[19] Ibid., 143.
[20] Ibid., 159–160.
[21] W. Gitt, *In the Beginning Was Information*, Master Books, Green Forest, Arkansas, 2006, 127.

More Problems!

Imagine yourself sitting in the seat of a 747 airplane, reading about the construction of this great plane. You are fascinated by the fact that this flying machine is made up of six million parts—but then you realize that not one part by itself flies. This realization can be rather disconcerting if you are flying along at 500 mph (805 km/h) at 35,000 feet (10,668 m).

You can be comforted, however, by the fact that even though not one part of an airplane flies on its own, when it is assembled as a completed machine, it does fly.

We can use the construction of an airplane as an analogy to understand the basic mechanisms of the biochemistry of cells that enable organisms to function.

Scientists have found that within the cell there are thousands of what can be called "biochemical machines." For example, one could cite the cell's ability to sense light and turn it into electrical impulses. But what scientists once thought was a simple process within a cell, such as being able to sense light and turn it into electrical impulses, is in fact a highly complicated event. For just this one example alone to work, numerous compounds must all be in the right place, at the right time, in the right

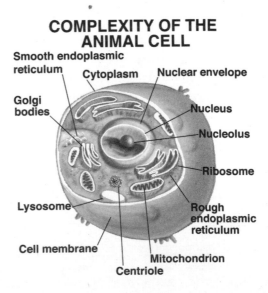

COMPLEXITY OF THE ANIMAL CELL

Smooth endoplasmic reticulum
Cytoplasm
Nuclear envelope
Golgi bodies
Nucleus
Nucleolus
Ribosome
Lysosome
Rough endoplasmic reticulum
Cell membrane
Mitochondrion
Centriole

concentration—or it just won't happen. In other words, just as all the parts of a 747 need to be assembled before it can fly, so all the parts of these "biochemical machines" in cells need to be in place, or they can't function. And there are literally thousands of such "machines" in a single cell that are vital for it to operate.

What does this mean? Quite simply, evolution from chemicals to a living system is impossible.

Scientists now know that life is built on these "machines." Dr. Michael Behe, Associate Professor of Biochemistry at Lehigh University in Pennsylvania, describes these "biochemical machines" as examples of "irreducible complexity":

> Now it's the turn of the fundamental science of life, modern biochemistry, to disturb. *The simplicity that was once expected to be the foundation of life has proven to be a phantom;* instead, systems of horrendous, irreducible complexity inhabit the cell. The resulting realization that life was designed by an intelligence is a shock to us in the twentieth century who have gotten used to thinking of life as the result of simple natural laws. But other centuries have had their shocks, and there is no reason to suppose that we should escape them [emphasis added].[22]

To illustrate this further, consider swatting a mosquito.

Then think about this question: Why did the mosquito die? You see, the squashed mosquito has all the chemicals for life that an evolutionist could ever hope for in some primordial soup. Yet we know that nothing is going to evolve from this mosquito "soup." So why did the mosquito die? Because by squashing it, you *disorganized* it.

Once the "machinery" of the mosquito has been destroyed, the organism can no longer exist. At a cellular level, literally thousands of "machines" need to exist before life

---

[22] M.J. Behe, *Darwin's Black Box*, The Free Press, New York, 1996, 252–253.

ever becomes possible. This means that evolution from chemicals is *impossible*. Evolutionist Dawkins recognizes this problem of needing "machinery" to start with when he states:

> A Xerox machine is capable of copying its own blueprints, but it is not capable of springing spontaneously into existence. Biomorphs readily replicate in the environment provided by a suitably written computer program, but they can't write their own program or build a computer to run it. The theory of the blind watchmaker is extremely powerful given that we are allowed to assume replication and hence cumulative selection. But if replication needs complex machinery, since the only way we know for complex machinery ultimately to come into existence is cumulative selection, we have a problem.[23]

A problem indeed! The more we look into the workings of life, the more complicated it becomes, and the more we see that life could *not* arise by itself. Not only does life require a source of information, but the complex "machines" of the chemistry of life must be in existence *right from the start*.

A Greater Problem Still!

Some scientists and educators have tried to get around the above problems by speculating that as long as all the chemicals that make up the molecule of heredity (and the information it contains) came together at some time in the past, then life could have begun.

Life is built upon information. In fact, in just one of the trillions of cells that make up the human body, the amount of information in its genes would fill at least 1,000 books of 500 pages of typewritten information. Scientists now think this is hugely underestimated.

Where did all this information come from? Some try to explain it this way: imagine a professor taking all the letters of the alphabet, A–Z, and placing them in a hat. He then passes the hat around to students of his class and asks each to randomly select a letter.

---

[23] Dawkins, *The Blind Watchmaker*, 139–140.

It is easy for us to see the possibility (no matter how remote it seems) of three students in a row selecting B then A and finally T. Put these three letters together and they spell a word—BAT. Thus, the professor concludes, given enough time, no matter how improbable it seems, there is always the possibility one could form a series of words that make a sentence, and eventually compile an encyclopedia. The students are then led to believe that no intelligence is necessary in the evolution of life from chemicals. As long as the molecules came together in the right order for such compounds as DNA, then life could have begun.

On the surface, this sounds like a logical argument. However, there is a basic, fatal flaw in this analogy. The sequence of letters, BAT, is a word to whom? Someone who speaks English, Dutch, French, German, or Chinese? It is a word only to someone who knows the language. In other words, the order of letters is meaningless unless there is a language system and a translation system already in place to make the order meaningful.

In the DNA of a cell, the order of its molecules is also meaningless, except that in the biochemistry of a cell, there is a language system (other molecules) that makes the order meaningful. DNA without the language system is meaningless, and the language system without the DNA wouldn't work either. The other complication is that the language system that reads the order of the molecules in the DNA is itself specified by the DNA. This is another one of those "machines" that must already be in existence and fully formed, or life won't work!

Can Information Arise from Noninformation?

We have already shown that information cannot come from mutations, a so-called mechanism of evolution, but is there any other possible way information could arise from matter?

Dr. Werner Gitt makes it clear that one of the things we know for sure from science is that information *cannot* arise from disorder by chance. It *always* takes (greater) information to produce information, and ultimately information is the result of intelligence:

A code system is always the result of a mental process (it requires an intelligent origin or inventor) ... . It should be emphasized that matter as such is unable to generate any code. All experiences indicate that a thinking being voluntarily exercising his own free will, cognition, and creativity, is required.[24]

There is no known natural law through which matter can give rise to information, neither is any physical process or material phenomenon known that can do this.[25]

"There is no known law of nature, no known process and no known sequence of events which can cause information to originate by itself in matter.[26]

What Then Is the Source of the Information?

We can therefore conclude that the huge amount of information in living things must originally have come from an intelligence, which had to have been far superior to ours. But then, some will say that such a source would have to be caused by something with even greater information/intelligence.

However, if they reason this way, one could ask where even this greater information/intelligence came from. And then where did that one come from? One could extrapolate to infinity, unless there was a source of infinite intelligence, beyond our finite understanding. But isn't this what the Bible indicates when we read, "In the beginning God..."? The God of the Bible is not bound by limitations of time, space, or anything else.

Even Richard Dawkins recognizes this:

Once we are allowed simply to postulate organized complexity, if only the organized complexity of the DNA/protein replicating engine, it is relatively easy to invoke it as a generator of yet more organized complexity. That, indeed, is what most of this book is about. But of course any God capable of intelligently designing something as complex as the DNA/protein replicating machine must have been at least as complex and organized as that machine itself.

Far more so if we suppose him additionally capable of such advanced functions as listening to prayers and forgiving sins. To explain the origin of the DNA/protein machine by invoking a supernatural Designer is

---

[24] Gitt, *In the Beginning Was Information*, 64–67.
[25] Ibid., 79.
[26] Ibid., 107.

to explain precisely nothing, for it leaves unexplained the origin of the Designer. You have to say something like, "God was always there," and if you allow yourself that kind of lazy way out, you might as well just say "DNA was always there," or "Life was always there," and be done with it.[27]

So what is the logically defensible position? Is it that matter has eternally existed (or came into existence by itself for no reason) and then that, by it-self, matter was arranged into information systems against everything observed in real science? Or did an eternal Be-ing, the God of the Bible, the source of infinite intelligence,[28] create information systems for life to exist, which *agrees* with real science?

If real science supports the Bible's claims about an eternal Creator God, then why isn't this readily accepted? Michael Behe answers with this:

What we see in God's world agrees with what we read in God's Word.

> The fourth and most powerful reason for science's reluctance to embrace a theory of intelligent design is also based on philosophical consider-ations. Many people, including many important and well-respected sci-entists, just don't want there to be anything beyond nature. They don't want a supernatural being to affect nature, no matter how brief or con-structive the interaction may have been. In other words ... they bring an *a priori* philosophical commitment to their science that restricts what kinds of explanations they will accept about the physical world. Some-times this leads to rather odd behavior.[29]

The crux of the matter is this: if one accepts there is a God who cre-ated us, then that God also owns us. If this God is the God of the Bible, He owns us and thus has a right to set the rules by which we must live. More important, He also tells us in the Bible that we are in rebellion against Him,

---

[27] Dawkins, *The Blind Watchmaker*, 141.
[28] Thus, it is capable of generating infinite information, and certainly the enormous, though finite, information of life.
[29] Behe, *Darwin's Black Box*, 243.

our Creator. Because of this rebellion (called sin), our physical bodies are sentenced to death; but we will live on forever, either with God or without Him in a place of judgment. But the good news is that our Creator provided a means of deliverance for our sin of rebellion, so that those who come to Him in faith and repentance for their sin can receive the forgiveness of a holy God and spend eternity with Him.

God Is the Foundation for Science and Reason

As stated before, the Bible takes God's existence as a given. It never attempts to prove the existence of God, and this for a very good reason. When we logically prove a particular thing, we show that it must be true because it follows logically from something *authoritative*. But there is nothing more authoritative than God and His Word. God knows absolutely everything. So it makes sense to base our worldview on what God has written in His Word.

Some people claim that it is unscientific to start from God's Word. But in reality, nothing could be further from the truth. A belief in God is actually foundational to logical thought and scientific inquiry. Think about it: why is logical reasoning possible? There are laws of logic that we use when we reason. For example, there is the law of noncontradiction, which states that you can't have "A" and "not-A" at the same time and in the same relationship. We all "know" that this is true. But *why* is it true, and *how* do we know it?

The Bible makes sense of this: God is self-consistent. He is noncontradictory, and so this law follows from God's nature. And God has made us in His image; so we instinctively know this law. It has been hard-wired into us. Logical reasoning is possible because God is logical and has made us in His image. (Of course, because of the Curse we sometimes make mistakes in logic.)

But if the universe were merely a chance accident, then why should logical reasoning be possible? If my brain is merely the product of mutations (guided only by natural selection), then why should I think that it can determine what is *true*? The secular, evolutionary worldview cannot account for the existence of logical reasoning.

Likewise, only a biblical worldview can really account for the existence of science—the study of the natural world. Science depends on the fact that the universe obeys orderly laws which do not arbitrarily change. But why should that be so? If the universe were merely an accident, why should it obey logical, orderly laws—or any laws at all for that matter? And why should these laws not be constantly changing, since so many other things change?

The Bible explains this. There are orderly laws because a logical Law-Giver upholds the universe in a logical and consistent way. God does not change; so He sustains the universe in a consistent way. Only a biblical worldview can account for the existence of science and technology.

Now, does this mean that a non-Christian is incapable of reasoning logically or doing science? Not at all. But he is being inconsistent. The non-Christian must "borrow" the above biblical principles in order to do science, or to think rationally. But this is inconsistent. The unbeliever must use *biblical ideas* in order to use science and reason, while he simultaneously denies that the Bible is true.

So Who Created God?

By very definition, an eternal Being has always existed—nobody created Him. God is the Self-Existent One—the great "I Am" of the Bible.[30] He is outside time; in fact, He created time. Think about it this way: everything that has a *beginning* requires a *cause*. The universe has a beginning and therefore requires a cause. But God has no beginning since He is beyond time. So God does not need a cause. There is nothing illogical about an eternal Being who has always existed even though it might be difficult to fully understand.

You might argue, "But that means I have to accept this by faith because I can't totally understand it."

We read in the book of Hebrews: "But without faith it is impossible to please Him, for he who comes to God must believe that He is, and that He is a rewarder of those who diligently seek Him" (11:6).

What kind of faith is Christianity then? It is not blind faith as some may think. In fact, it is the evolutionists who deny the Creator who have the blind "faith."[31] They have to believe in something (i.e., that information can arise from disorder by chance) which goes against real science.

But Christ, through the Holy Spirit, actually opens the eyes of

---

[30] See Exodus 3:14; Job 38:4; John 8:58; Revelation 1:18; Isaiah 44:6; Deuteronomy 4:39.
[31] See Matthew 13:15; John 12:40; Romans 11:8–10.

Christians so that they can see that their faith is real.[32] The Christian faith is a logically defensible faith. This is why the Bible makes it very clear that anyone who does not believe in God is without excuse: "For since the creation of the world His invisible *attributes* are clearly seen, being understood by the things that are made, *even* His eternal power and Godhead, so that they are without excuse" (Romans 1:20).

How Do We Know the Creator Is the God of the Bible?

You can believe fallible man's ideas that there is no God, or trust the perfect Word of God, the 66 books of the Bible, that says there is. The issue is simple; it is a matter of faith—God exists or God doesn't exist. The exciting thing about being a Christian is knowing that the Bible is not just another religious book, but it is the Word of the Creator God, as it claims.[33]

Only the Bible explains why there is beauty and ugliness; why there is life and death; why there is health and disease; why there is love and hate. Only the Bible gives the true and reliable account of the origin of all basic entities of life and the entire universe.

And over and over again, the Bible's historical account has been confirmed by archaeology, biology, geology, and astronomy. No contradiction or erroneous information has ever been found in its pages, even though it was written over hundreds of years by many different authors, each inspired by the Holy Spirit.

Scientists from many different fields have produced hundreds of books and tapes defending the Bible's accuracy and its claim that it is a revelation to us from our Creator. It not only tells us who we are and where we came from, but it also shares the good news of how we can spend eternity with our Lord and Savior. Take that first step and place your faith in God and His Word.

---

32 See Matthew 13:16; Acts 26:18; Ephesians 1:18; 1 John 1:1.
33 See Matthew 5:18; 2 Timothy 3:16; 2 Peter 1:21; Psalms 12:6; 1 Thessalonians 2:13.

2

Why Shouldn't Christians Accept Millions of Years?

TERRY MORTENSON

There is an intensifying controversy in the church all over the world regarding the age of the earth. For the first 18 centuries of church history the almost universal belief of Christians was that God created the world in six literal days roughly 4,000 years before Christ and destroyed the world with a global Flood at the time of Noah.

But about 200 years ago some scientists developed new theories of earth history, which proposed that the earth and universe are millions of years old. Over the past 200 years Christian leaders have made various attempts to fit the millions of years into the Bible. These include the day-age view, gap theory, local flood view, framework hypothesis, theistic evolution, and progressive creation.

A growing number of Christians (now called young-earth creationists), including many scientists, hold to the traditional view, believing it to be the only view that is truly faithful to Scripture and that fits

the scientific evidence far better than the reigning old-earth evolutionary theory.

Many Christians say that the age of the earth is an unimportant and divisive side issue that hinders the proclamation of the gospel. But is that really the case? Answers in Genesis and many other creationist organizations think not.

In this chapter, I want to introduce you to some of the reasons we think that Christians cannot accept the millions of years without doing great damage to the church and her witness in the world. Other chapters in this book will go into much more detail on these issues.

1. **The Bible clearly teaches that God created in six literal, 24-hour days a few thousand years ago.** The Hebrew word for day in Genesis 1 is *yom*. In the vast majority of its uses in the Old Testament it means a literal day; and where it doesn't, the context makes this clear.

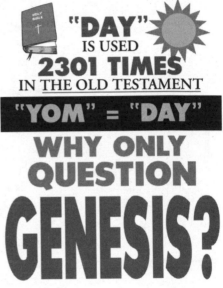

2. **The context of Genesis 1 clearly shows that the days of creation were literal days.** First, *yom* is defined the first time it is used in the Bible (Genesis 1:4–5) in its two literal senses: the light portion of the light/dark cycle and the whole light/dark cycle. Second, *yom* is used with "evening" and "morning." Everywhere these two words are used in the Old Testament, either together or separately and with or without *yom* in the context, they always mean a literal evening or morning of a literal day. Third, *yom* is modified with a number: one day, second day, third day, etc., which everywhere else in the Old Testament indicates literal days. Fourth, *yom* is defined literally in Genesis 1:14 in relation to the heavenly bodies.

3. **The genealogies of Genesis 5 and 11 make it clear that the creation days happened only about 6,000 years ago.** It is transparent from the genealogies of Genesis 5 and 11 (which give very detailed chronological information, unlike the clearly abbreviated genealogy in Matthew 1)

and other chronological information in the Bible that the Creation Week took place only about 6,000 years ago.

4. **Exodus 20:9–11 blocks all attempts to fit millions of years into Genesis 1.** "Six days you shall labor and do all your work, but the seventh day is a sabbath of the LORD your God; in it you shall not do any work, you or your son or your daughter, your male or your female servant or your cattle or your sojourner who stays with you. For in six days the LORD made the heavens and the earth, the sea and all that is in them, and rested on the seventh day; therefore the LORD blessed the sabbath day and made it holy" (Exodus 20:9-11).

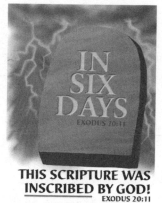

THIS SCRIPTURE WAS INSCRIBED BY GOD!
EXODUS 20:11

This passage gives the reason for God's command to Israel to work six days and then take a sabbath rest. *Yom* is used in both parts of the commandment. If God meant that the Jews were to work six days because He created over six long periods of time, He could have said that using one of three indefinite Hebrew time words. He chose the only word that means a literal day, and the Jews understood it literally (until the idea of millions of years developed in the early nineteenth century). For this reason, the day-age view or framework hypothesis must be rejected. The gap theory or any other attempt to put millions of years before the six days are also false because God says that in six days He made the heaven and the earth and the sea and *all* that is in them. So He made everything in those six literal days and nothing before the first day.

5. **Noah's Flood washes away millions of years.** The evidence in Genesis 6–9 for a global catastrophic flood is overwhelming. For example, the Flood was intended to destroy not only all sinful people but also all land animals and birds and the surface of the earth, which only a global flood could accomplish. The Ark's purpose was to save two of every kind of land animal and bird (and seven of some) to repopulate the earth after the Flood. The Ark was totally unnecessary if the Flood was only local. People, animals, and birds could have migrated out of the flood zone before it occurred, or the zone could have been populated from creatures outside the area after the Flood. The catastrophic nature of the Flood is seen in the nonstop rain for at least 40 days, which would have produced

massive erosion, mud slides, hurricanes, etc. The Hebrew words translated "the fountains of the great deep burst open" (Genesis 7:11) clearly point to tectonic rupturing of the earth's surface in many places for 150 days, resulting in volcanoes, earthquakes, and tsunamis. Noah's Flood would produce exactly the kind of complex geological record we see worldwide today: thousands of feet of sediments clearly deposited by water and later hardened into rock and containing billions of fossils. If the year-long Flood is responsible for most of the rock layers and fossils, then those rocks and fossils cannot represent the history of the earth over millions of years, as evolutionists claim.

6. **Jesus was a young-earth creationist.** Jesus consistently treated the miracle accounts of the Old Testament as straightforward, truthful, historical accounts (e.g., creation of Adam, Noah and the Flood, Lot and his wife in Sodom, Moses and the manna, and Jonah in the fish). He continually affirmed the authority of Scripture over men's ideas and traditions (Matthew 15:1–9). In Mark 10:6 we have the clearest (but not the only) statement showing that Jesus was a young-earth creationist. He teaches that Adam and Eve were made at the "*beginning* of creation," not billions of years after the beginning, as would be the case if the universe were really billions of years old. So, if Jesus was a young-earth creationist, then how can His faithful followers have any other view?

7. **Belief in millions of years undermines the Bible's teaching on death and on the character of God.** Genesis 1 says six times that God called the creation "good," and when He finished creation on Day 6, He called

everything "very good." Man and animals and birds were originally vegetarian (Gen. 1:29–30, plants are not "living creatures," as people and animals are, according to Scripture). But Adam and Eve sinned, resulting in the judgment of God on the whole creation. Instantly

Adam and Eve died spiritually, and after God's curse they began to die physically. The serpent and Eve were changed physically and the ground itself was cursed (Genesis 3:14–19). The whole creation now groans in bondage to corruption, waiting for the final redemption of Christians (Romans 8:19–25) when we will see the restoration of all things (Acts 3:21; Colossians 1:20) to a state similar to the pre-Fall world, when there will be no more carnivorous behavior (Isaiah 11:6–9) and no disease, suffering, or death (Revelation 21:3–5) because there will be no more Curse (Revelation 22:3). To accept millions of years of animal death before the

creation and Fall of man contradicts and destroys the Bible's teaching on death and the full redemptive work of Christ. It also makes God into a bumbling, cruel creator who uses (or can't prevent) disease, natural disasters, and extinctions to mar His creative work, without any moral cause, but still calls it all "very good."

8. **The idea of millions of years did not come from the scientific facts.** This idea of long ages was developed by deistic and atheistic geologists in the late eighteenth and early nineteenth centuries. These men used antibiblical philosophical and religious assumptions to interpret the geological observations in a way that plainly contradicted the biblical account of creation, the Flood, and the age of the earth. Most church leaders and

scholars quickly compromised using the gap theory, day-age view, local flood view, etc. to try to fit "deep time" into the Bible. But they did not understand the geological arguments and they did not defend their views by careful Bible study. The "deep time" idea flows out of naturalistic assumptions, not scientific observations.

9. **Radiometric dating methods do not prove millions of years.** Radiometric dating was not developed until the early twentieth century, by which time virtually the whole world had already accepted the millions of years. For many years creation scientists have cited numerous examples in the published scientific literature of these dating methods clearly giving erroneous dates (e.g., a date of millions of years for lava flows that occurred in the past few hundred years or even decades). In recent years creationists in the RATE project have done experimental, theoretical, and field research to uncover more such evidence (e.g., diamonds and coal, which the evolutionists say are millions of years old, were dated by carbon-14 to be only thousands of years old) and to show that decay rates were orders of magnitude faster in the past, which shrinks the millions of years to thousands of years, confirming the Bible.[1]

Conclusion

These are just some of the reasons why we believe that the Bible is giving us the true history of the world. God's Word must be the final authority on all matters about which it speaks—not just the moral and spiritual matters, but also its teachings that bear on history, archaeology, and science.

What is at stake here is the authority of Scripture, the character of God, the doctrine of death, and the very foundation of the gospel. If the early chapters of Genesis are not true literal history, then faith in the rest of the Bible is undermined, including its teaching about salvation and morality. I urge you to carefully read the other chapters in this book. The health of the church, the effectiveness of her mission to a lost world, and the glory of God are at stake.

---

[1] For the results of the RATE project, see Larry Vardiman, Andrew Snelling, and Eugene Chaffin, eds., *Radioisotopes and the Age of the Earth*, Vol. 2, Master Books, Green Forest, Arkansas, 2005; and Don DeYoung, *Thousands ... Not Billions*, Master Books, Green Forest, Arkansas, 2005.

3

Couldn't God Have Used Evolution?

KEN HAM

During the Scopes Trial in 1925, ACLU attorney Clarence Darrow placed William Jennings Bryan (seen as the man representing Christianity) on the stand and questioned him about his faith. In his questioning, Darrow pitted Bryan's faith in the Bible against his belief in modern scientific thinking. Darrow questioned Bryan about the meaning of the word "day" in Genesis. Bryan's answer rejected the clear teaching of Scripture, which indicates that the days of Genesis 1 are six actual days of approximately 24 hours. Bryan accepted modern evolutionary thinking instead when he said, "I think it would be just as easy for the kind of God we believe in to make the earth in six days as in six years or in six million years or in 600 million years. I do not think it important whether we believe one or the other."[1] This is not the first time a Christian has rejected the intended meaning of God's Word, and it certainly will not be the last.

Many Christians today claim that millions of years of earth history fit with the Bible and that God could have used evolutionary processes to create. This idea is not a recent invention. For over 200 years, many theologians have attempted such harmonizations in response to the work of people like Charles Darwin and Scottish geologist Charles Lyell, who helped popularize the idea of millions of years of earth history and slow geological processes.

---

[1] *The World's Most Famous Court Trial*, Second Reprint Edition, Bryan College, Dayton, Ohio,1990, 296, 302–303.

When we consider the possibility that God used evolutionary processes to create over millions of years, we are faced with serious consequences: the Word of God is no longer authoritative, and the character of our loving God is questioned.

SCRIPTURAL IMPLICATIONS

Already in Darwin's day, one of the leading evolutionists saw the compromise involved in claiming that God used evolution, and his insightful comments are worth reading again. Once you accept evolution and its implications about history, then man becomes free to pick and choose which parts of the Bible he wants to accept.

From an Evolutionist's Perspective

The leading humanist of Darwin's day, Thomas Huxley (1825–1895), eloquently pointed out the inconsistencies of reinterpreting Scripture to fit with popular scientific thinking. Huxley, an ardent evolutionary humanist, was known as "Darwin's bulldog," as he did more to popularize Darwin's ideas than Darwin himself. Huxley understood Christianity much more clearly than did compromising theologians who tried to add evolution and millions of years to the Bible. He used their compromise against them to help his cause in undermining Christianity.

In his essay "Lights of the Church and Science," Huxley stated,

I am fairly at a loss to comprehend how anyone, for a moment, can doubt that Christian theology must stand or fall with the historical trustworthiness of the Jewish Scriptures. The very conception of the Messiah, or Christ, is inextricably interwoven with Jewish history; the identification of Jesus of Nazareth with that Messiah rests upon the interpretation of the passages of the Hebrew Scriptures which have no evidential value unless they possess the historical character assigned to them. If the covenant with Abraham was not made; if circumcision and sacrifices were not ordained by Jahveh; if the 'ten words' were not written by God's hand on the stone tables; if Abraham is more or less a mythical hero, such as Theseus; the Story of the Deluge a fiction; that of the Fall a legend; and that of the Creation the dream of a seer; if all these definite and detailed narratives of apparently real events have no more value as history than have the stories of the regal period of Rome—what is to be said about the Messianic doctrine, which is so much less clearly enunciated: And what about the authority of the writers of the books of the New Testament, who, on this theory, have not merely accepted flimsy fictions for solid truths, but have built the very foundations of Christian dogma upon legendary quicksands?[2]

Huxley made the point that if we are to believe the New Testament doctrines, we must believe the historical account of Genesis as historical truth.

Huxley was definitely out to destroy the truth of the biblical record. When people rejected the Bible, he was happy. But when they tried to harmonize evolutionary ideas with the Bible and reinterpret it, he vigorously attacked this position.

> I confess I soon lose my way when I try to follow those who walk delicately among "types" and allegories. A certain passion for clearness forces me to ask, bluntly, whether the writer means to say that Jesus did not believe the stories in question or that he did? When Jesus spoke, as a matter of fact, that "the Flood came and destroyed them all," did he believe that the Deluge really took place, or not? It seems to me that, as the narrative mentions Noah's wife, and his sons' wives, there is good scriptural warranty for the statement that the antediluvians married and were given in marriage: and I should have thought that their eating and drinking might be assumed by the firmest believer in the literal truth of the story. Moreover, I venture to ask what sort of value, as an illustration of God's methods of dealing with sin, has an account of an event that never happened? If no Flood swept the careless people away, how is the warning of more worth than the cry of 'Wolf' when there is no wolf?[3]

Huxley then gave a lesson on New Testament theology. He quoted Matthew 19:4–5: "And He answered and said to them, 'Have you not read that He who made *them* at the beginning "made them male and female," and said, "For this reason a man shall leave his father and mother and be joined to his wife, and the two shall become one flesh"?'" Huxley commented, "If divine authority is not here claimed for the twenty-fourth verse of the second chapter of Genesis, what is the value of language? And again, I ask, if one may play fast and loose with the story of the Fall as a 'type' or 'allegory,' what becomes of the foundation of Pauline theology?"[4]

---

[2] T. Huxley, *Science and Hebrew Tradition*, D. Appleton and Company, New York, 1897, 207.

[3] Ibid., 232.

[4] Ibid., 235–236.

And to substantiate this, Huxley quoted 1 Corinthians 15:21–22: "For since by man *came* death, by Man also *came* the resurrection of the dead. For as in Adam all die, even so in Christ all shall be made alive."

Huxley continued, "If Adam may be held to be no more real a personage than Prometheus, and if the story of the Fall is merely an instructive 'type,' comparable to the profound Promethean mythos, what value has Paul's dialectic?"[5]

Thus, concerning those who accepted the New Testament doctrines that Paul and Christ teach but rejected Genesis as literal history, Huxley claimed "the melancholy fact remains, that the position they have taken up is hopelessly untenable."[6]

He was adamant that science (by which he meant evolutionary, long-age ideas about the past) had proven that one cannot intelligently accept the Genesis account of creation and the Flood as historical truth. He further pointed out that various doctrines in the New Testament are dependent on the truth of these events, such as Paul's teaching on the doctrine of sin, Christ's teaching on the doctrine of marriage, and the warning of future judgment. Huxley mocked those who try to harmonize evolution and millions of years with the Bible, because it requires them to give up a historical Genesis while still trying to hold to the doctrines of the New Testament.

What was Huxley's point? He insisted that the theologians had to accept evolution and millions of years, but he pointed out that, to be consistent, they had to give up the Bible totally. Compromise is impossible.

---

[5] Ibid., 236.
[6] Ibid., 236.

From the Teaching of Christian Leaders

B. B. Warfield and Charles Hodge, great leaders of the Christian faith during the 1800s, adopted the billions-of-years belief concerning the age of the earth and reinterpreted Genesis 1 accordingly. In regard to a discussion on Genesis 1 and the days of creation, Hodge said, "The Church has been forced more than once to alter her interpretation of the Bible to accommodate the discoveries of science. But this has been done without doing any violence to the Scriptures or in any degree impairing their authority."[7]

Even though much of Warfield's and Hodge's teachings were biblically sound, these two men helped unlock the door of compromise, which helped to begin to undermine biblical authority. Once Christians concede to the world that we don't have to take the words in Genesis as written but can use outside beliefs to reinterpret Scripture (e.g., concerning the age of earth), then the door has been unlocked to do this throughout the whole of Scripture. Once this door is unlocked, subsequent generations push it open even farther.

In a number of instances throughout the Bible, one sees compromise in one generation, and in the next, the compromise is usually much greater. It isn't long before the godly foundation is eroded (e.g., the kings of Israel; and idolatry in 2 Kings 14–16, especially in light of Exodus 20:4–6).

Warfield and Hodge taught that Scripture could and should be altered to agree with the newest "scientific" discoveries (which were really men's interpretations about the past) while they claimed that the authority of the other teachings in God's Word remained. But this thinking is faulty. How can one portion of God's Word be open to interpretation while the other portion is untouchable? It can't.

Adding evolution to God's creation has serious scriptural implications because it undermines and attacks the authority of the Word of God.

CHARACTER IMPLICATIONS

Another result of believing that God used evolution or that millions of years of earth history can fit into the Bible is that God's character comes into question.

---

[7] C. Hodge, *Systematic Theology*, Vol. 1, Wm. B. Eerdmans, Grand Rapids, Michigan, 1997, 573. Hodge was probably referring to the usual humanist spin-doctoring of the Galileo affair, but for a more accurate portrayal, see R. Grigg, The Galileo "twist," *Creation* **19**(4):30–32, 1997, and T. Schirrmacher, The Galileo affair: history or heroic hagiography? *TJ* **14**(1):91–100, 2000.

The book of Genesis teaches that death is the result of Adam's sin (Genesis 3:19; Romans 5:12, 8:18–22) and that all of God's creation was "very good" upon its completion (Genesis 1:31). All animals and humans were originally vegetarian (Genesis 1:29–30). But if we compromise on the history of Genesis by adding millions of years, we must believe that death and disease were part of the world before Adam sinned. You see, the (alleged) millions of years of earth history in the fossil record shows evidence of animals eating each other,[8] diseases like cancer in their bones,[9] violence, plants with thorns,[10] and so on. All of this supposedly takes place *before* man appears on the scene, and thus before sin (and its curse of death, disease, thorns, carnivory, etc.) entered the world.

Christians who believe in an old earth (billions of years) need to come to grips with the real nature of the god of an old earth—it is *not* the loving God of the Bible. Even many conservative, evangelical Christian leaders accept and actively promote a belief in millions and billions of years for the age of rocks. How could a God of love allow such horrible processes as disease, suffering, and death for millions of years as part of His "very good" creation?

Interestingly, the liberal camp points out the inconsistencies in holding to an old earth while trying to cling to evangelical Christianity. For instance, Bishop John Shelby Spong, the retired bishop of the Episcopal Diocese of Newark, states:

> The Bible began with the assumption that God had created a finished and perfect world from which human beings had fallen away in an act of cosmic rebellion. Original sin was the reality in which all life was presumed to live. Darwin postulated instead an unfinished and thus imperfect creation... . Human beings did not fall from perfection into sin as the Church had taught for centuries... . Thus the basic myth of Christianity that interpreted Jesus as a divine emissary who came to rescue the victims of the fall from the results of their original sin became inoperative.[11]

---

[8] E.g., ground up dinosaur bones were found in the fossil dung of another dinosaur. See *Nature* **393**(6686):680–682, 1998.

[9] D.H. Tanke and B.M. Rothschild, Paleopathology, P.J. Currie and K. Padian, eds., *Encyclopedia of Dinosaurs*, Academic Press, San Diego, 1997, 525–530.

[10] H.P. Banks, *Evolution and Plants of the Past*, Wadsworth Publishing Company, Belmont, California, 1970, 9–10.

[11] J.S. Spong, A call for a new Reformation, www.dioceseofnewark.org/jsspong/reform.html.

This is an obvious reference to the millions of years associated with the fossil record. The god of an old earth is one who uses death as part of creating. Death therefore can't be the penalty for sin and can't be described as the last enemy (1 Corinthians 15:26).

The god of an old earth cannot therefore be the God of the Bible who is able to save us from sin and death. Thus, when Christians compromise with the millions of years attributed by many scientists to the fossil record, they are, in that sense, seemingly worshipping a different god—the cruel god of an old earth.

People must remember that God created a perfect world; so when they look at this present world, they are not looking at the nature of God but at the results of our sin.

The God of the Bible, the God of mercy, grace, and love, sent His one and only Son to become a man (but God nonetheless), to become our sin-bearer so that we could be saved from sin and eternal separation from God. As 2 Corinthians 5:21 says, "For He has made Him who knew no sin, to be sin for us, that we might become the righteousness of God in Him."

There's no doubt—the god of an old earth destroys the gospel.

DOOR OF COMPROMISE

Now it is true that rejection of six literal days doesn't ultimately affect one's salvation, if one is truly born again. However, we need to stand back and look at the big picture.

In many nations, the Word of God was once widely respected and taken seriously. But once the door of compromise is unlocked, once Christian leaders concede that we shouldn't interpret the Bible as written in Genesis, why

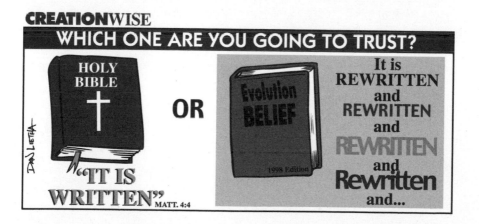

CREATIONWISE

WHICH ONE ARE YOU GOING TO TRUST?

HOLY BIBLE

OR

Evolution BELIEF

1998 Edition

It is REWRITTEN and REWRITTEN and REWRITTEN and Rewritten and...

"IT IS WRITTEN" MATT. 4:4

should the world take heed of God's Word in any area? Because the church has told the world that one can use man's interpretation of the world, such as billions of years, to reinterpret the Bible, this Book is seen as an outdated, scientifically incorrect holy book not intended to be believed as written.

As each subsequent generation has pushed this door of compromise open farther and farther, they are increasingly not accepting the morality or salvation of the Bible either. After all, if the history in Genesis is not correct, how can one be sure the rest is correct? Jesus said, "If I have told you earthly things, and you do not believe, how will you believe if I tell you of heavenly things?" (John 3:12).

The battle is not one of young earth vs. old earth, or billions of years vs. six days, or creation vs. evolution—the real battle is the authority of the Word of God vs. man's fallible opinions.

Why do Christians believe in the bodily Resurrection of Jesus Christ? Because of the words of Scripture ("according to the Scriptures").

And why should Christians believe in the six literal days of creation? Because of the words of Scripture ("In six days the Lord made ...").

The real issue is one of authority—is God's Word the authority, or is man's word the authority? So, couldn't God have used evolution to create? The answer is No. A belief in millions of years of evolution not only contradicts the clear teaching of Genesis and the rest of Scripture but also impugns the character of God. He told us in the book of Genesis that He created the whole universe and everything in it in six days by His word: "Then God said... ." His Word is the evidence of how and when God created, and His Word is incredibly clear.

4

Don't Creationists Deny the Laws of Nature?

JASON LISLE

The Word of God

Everything in the universe, every plant and animal, every rock, every particle of matter or light wave, is bound by laws, which it has no choice but to obey. The Bible tells us that there are laws of nature—"ordinances of heaven and earth" (Jeremiah 33:25). These laws describe the way God normally accomplishes His will in the universe.

God's logic is built into the universe, and so the universe is not haphazard or arbitrary. It obeys laws of chemistry which are logically derived from the laws of physics, many of which can be logically derived from other laws of physics and laws of mathematics. The most fundamental laws of nature exist only because God wills them to; they are the logical, orderly way that the Lord upholds and sustains the universe He has created. The atheist is unable to account for the logical orderly state of the universe. Why should the universe obey laws if there is no law-giver? But laws of nature are perfectly consistent with biblical creation. In fact, the Bible is the foundation for natural laws. So, of course, creationists do not deny these laws; laws of nature are exactly what a creationist would expect.

The Law of Life (Biogenesis)

There is one well-known law of life: the law of biogenesis. This law states simply that life always comes from life. This is what observational science tells us; organisms reproduce other organisms after their own kind. Historically, Louis Pasteur disproved one form of spontaneous generation; he showed that life comes from previous life. Since then, we have seen that this law is universal—with no known exceptions. This is, of course, exactly what we would expect from the Bible. According to Genesis 1, God supernaturally created the first diverse kinds of life on earth and made them to reproduce after their kind. Notice that molecules-to-man evolution violates the law of biogenesis. Evolutionists believe that life (at least once) spontaneously formed from non-living chemicals. But this is inconsistent with the law of biogenesis. Real science confirms the Bible.

The Laws of Chemistry

Life requires a specific chemistry. Our bodies are powered by chemical reactions and depend on the laws of chemistry operating in a uniform fashion. Every living being has information stored on a long molecule called DNA. Life as we know it would not be possible if the laws of chemistry were different. God created the laws of chemistry in just the right way so that life would be possible.

The laws of chemistry give different properties to the various elements (each made of one type of atom) and compounds (made up of two or more types of atoms that are bonded together) in the universe. For example, when given sufficient activation energy, the lightest element (hydrogen) will react

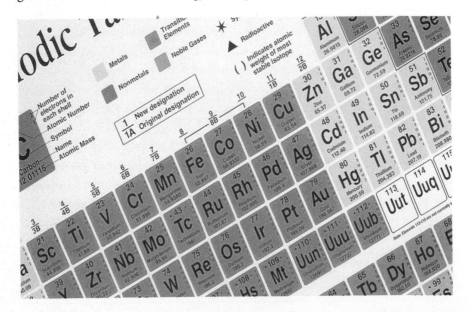

with oxygen to form water. Water itself has some interesting properties such as the ability to hold an unusually large amount of heat energy. When frozen, water forms crystals with six-sided symmetry (which is why snowflakes are generally six-sided). Contrast this with salt (sodium chloride) crystals which tend to form cubes. It is the six-fold symmetry of water-ice that causes "holes" in its crystal, making it less dense than its own liquid. That's why ice floats in water (whereas essentially all other frozen compounds sink in their own liquid.)

The properties of elements and compounds are not arbitrary. In fact, the elements can be logically organized into a periodic table based on their physical properties. Substances in the same column on the table tend to have similar properties. This follows because elements in a vertical column have the same outer electron structure. It is these outermost electrons which determine the physical characteristics of the atom. This periodic table did not happen by chance. Atoms and molecules have their various properties because their electrons are bound by the laws of quantum physics. In other words, chemistry is based on physics. If the laws of quantum physics were just a bit different, atoms might not even be possible. God designed the laws of physics *just right* so that the laws of chemistry would come out the way He wanted them to.

The Laws of Planetary Motion

The creation scientist Johannes Kepler discovered that the planets in our solar system obey three laws of nature. He found that planets orbit in ellipses (not perfect circles as had been previously thought) with the sun at one focus of the ellipse; thus, a given planet is sometimes closer to the sun than at other times. Kepler found that planets sweep out equal areas in equal times— in other words, planets speed up as they get closer to the sun within their orbit. And third, Kepler found the exact mathematical relationship between a planet's distance from the sun (a) as measured in AUs, and its orbital period (p) as measured in years; planets that are farther from the sun take much longer to orbit than planets that are closer (expressed as $p^2 = a^3$). Kepler's laws also apply to the orbits of moons around a given planet.[1]

As with the laws of chemistry, these laws of planetary motion are not fundamental. Rather, they are the logical derivation of other laws of nature. In fact, it was another creation scientist (Sir Isaac Newton) who discovered

---

[1] However, the constant of proportionality is different for the third law. This is due to the fact that the sun has a different mass than the planets.

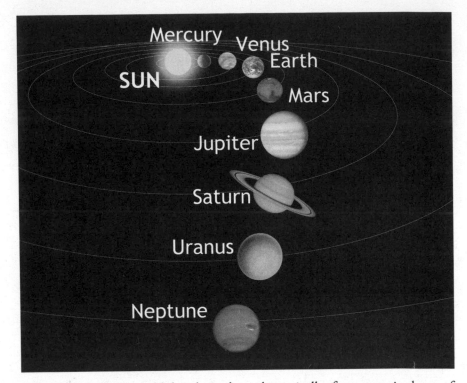

that Kepler's laws could be derived mathematically from certain laws of physics—specifically, the laws of gravity and motion (which Newton himself formulated).

The Laws of Physics

The field of physics describes the behavior of the universe at its most fundamental level. There are many different laws of physics. They describe the way in which the universe operates today. There are laws of physics that describe how light propagates, how energy is transported, how gravity operates, how mass moves through space, and many other phenomena. The laws of physics are usually mathematical in nature; some laws of physics can be described with a concise formula such as $E=mc^2$. The simple formula $F=ma$ shows how an object with mass (m) will accelerate (a) when a net force (F) is applied to it. It is amazing that every object in the universe consistently obeys these rules.

There is a hierarchy in physics: some laws of physics can be derived from other laws of physics. For example, Einstein's famous formula $E=mc^2$ can be derived from the principles and equations of special relativity. Conversely, there are many laws of physics that cannot be derived from other laws of physics; many of these are suspected to be derivative principles, but scientists have not yet deduced their derivation.

And some laws of physics may be truly fundamental (not based on other laws); they exist only because God wills them to. In fact, this *must* be the case for at least *one* law of physics (and perhaps several)—the most fundamental. (Logically, this is because if the most fundamental law were based on some other law, it would not be the most fundamental law.)

Universal Constants

Additionally, there are many physical constants of nature. These are parameters within the laws of physics which set the strengths of the fundamental forces (such as gravity), and the masses of fundamental particles (such as electrons). As with the laws of physics, some constants depend on others, whereas some constants are likely fundamental—God alone has set their value. These constants are essential for life. In many cases, if the fundamental constants had a slightly different value, life would not be possible. For example, if the strength of the electromagnetic coupling constant were slightly altered, molecules could not exist.

The Anthropic Principle

The laws of physics (along with their associated constants) are fine-tuned in just the right way so that life, particularly human life, is possible. This fact is called the "anthropic principle."[2] God created the fundamental laws of physics in just the right way, and gave the constants just the right values so that the other constants and derivative laws of physics would come out in just the right way, so that chemistry would work in the right way, so that the elements and compounds would have the right properties, so that life would be possible![3] It's an amazingly complex challenge—one that no mere human being has the intellectual capacity to solve.[4] In fact, there are many, many

---

[2] Anthropic comes from the Greek word for man: *anthropos*.

[3] Of course, there may be more than one possible solution. That is, it might be possible for God to create life that uses an entirely different chemistry, based on entirely different physics. God may have had considerable freedom in how He chose to create the universe. But it seems likely that there are many more possible (hypothetical) universes in which life is not possible than universes in which life is possible.

[4] A number of resources are available on the anthropic principle. See the secular book *The Anthropic Cosmological Principle* by J. Barrow, F. Tipler, and J. Wheeler, Oxford Univ. Press, New York, 1988.

aspects of this present universe that we still do not completely understand. The laws of nature which we have discovered and expressed mathematically are only imperfect models of reality. Our current understanding of the creation is imperfect. One is reminded of 1 Corinthians 13:12, which tells us that we now only "see through a glass darkly."

The Laws of Mathematics

Notice that the laws of physics are highly mathematical in nature. They would not work if there were not also laws of mathematics. Mathematical laws and principles include the rules of addition, the transitive property, the commutative properties of addition and multiplication, the binomial theorem, and many others. Like the laws of physics, some laws and properties of mathematics can be derived from other mathematical principles. But unlike the laws of physics, the laws of mathematics are abstract; they are not "attached" to any specific part of the universe. It is possible to imagine a universe where the laws of physics are different; but it is difficult to imagine a (consistent) universe where the laws of mathematics are different.[5]

The laws of mathematics are an example of a "transcendent truth." They *must* be true regardless of what kind of universe God created. This may be because God's nature is logical and mathematical. Thus, any universe He chose to create would necessarily be mathematical in nature. The secular naturalist cannot account for the laws of mathematics. Certainly, he would believe in mathematics and would use mathematics; but he is unable to account for the existence of mathematics within a naturalistic framework since mathematics is not a part of the physical universe. However, the Christian understands that there is a God beyond the universe and that mathematics reflects the thoughts of the Lord. Understanding math is in a sense "thinking God's thoughts after Him"[6] (though in a limited, finite way, of course).

Some have supposed that mathematics is a human invention; it is said that if human history had been different, an entirely different form of math would have been constructed—with alternate laws, theorems, axioms, etc. But such thinking is not consistent. Are we to believe that the universe did not obey mathematical laws before people discovered them? Did the planets

---

[5] Granted, there are different systems of starting definitions and axioms that allow for some variation in mathematical systems of thought (alternate geometries, etc.), but most of the basic principles remain unchanged.

[6] This phrase is attributed to the creation astronomer Johannes Kepler.

orbit differently before Kepler discovered that $p^2 = a^3$? Clearly, mathematical laws are something that human beings have *discovered*—not *invented*. The only thing that might have been different (had human history taken a different course) is the notation—the way in which we choose to express mathematical truths through symbols. But these truths exist regardless of how they are expressed. Mathematics is the "language of creation."

The Laws of Logic

All the laws of nature, from physics and chemistry to the law of biogenesis, depend on the laws of logic. Like mathematics, the laws of logic are transcendent truths. One cannot imagine that the laws of logic could be anything different than what they are. Take the law of noncontradiction as an example. This law states that you cannot have both "A" and "not A" at the same time and in the same relationship. Without the laws of logic, reasoning would be impossible. But where do the laws of logic come from?

The atheist cannot account for the laws of logic, even though he or she must accept that they exist in order to do any rational thinking. But according to the Bible, God is logical. Indeed, the law of noncontradiction is reflective of God's nature; God cannot lie (Numbers 23:19) or be tempted with evil (James 1:13) since these things contradict His perfect nature. Since we have been made in God's image, we instinctively know the laws of logic. We are able to reason logically (though because of finite minds and sin we don't always think entirely logically).

The Uniformity of Nature

The laws of nature are uniform. They do not change arbitrarily, and they apply throughout the whole cosmos. The laws of nature apply in the future just as they have applied in the past—this is one of the most basic assumptions in all of science. Without this assumption, science would be impossible. If the laws of nature suddenly and arbitrarily changed tomorrow, then past experimental results would tell us nothing about the future. Why is it that we can depend on the laws of nature to apply consistently throughout time? The secular scientist cannot justify this important assumption. But the Christian can; the Bible gives us the answer. God is Lord over all creation and sustains the universe in a consistent and logical way. God does not change, and so He upholds the universe in a consistent, uniform way throughout time (Jeremiah 33:25).

Conclusions

We have seen that the laws of nature depend on other laws of nature, which ultimately depend on God's will. Thus, God created the laws of physics in just the right way so that the laws of chemistry would be correct, so that life can exist. It is doubtful that any human would have been able to solve such a complex puzzle. Yet, God has done so. The atheist cannot account for these laws of nature, even though he agrees that they must exist, for such laws are inconsistent with naturalism. Yet they are perfectly consistent with the Bible. We expect the universe to be organized in a logical, orderly fashion and to obey uniform laws because the universe was created by the power of God.

5

What About the Gap & Ruin-Reconstruction Theories?

KEN HAM

Because of the accepted teachings of evolution, many Christians have tried to place a gap of indeterminate time between the first two verses of Genesis 1. Genesis 1:1–2 states: "In the beginning God created the heavens and the earth. The earth was without form, and void; and darkness was on the face of the deep. And the Spirit of God was hovering over the face of the waters."

There are many different versions as to what supposedly happened during this gap of time, but most versions of the gap theory place millions of years of geologic time (including billions of animal fossils) between the Bible's first two verses. This version of the gap theory is sometimes called the ruin-reconstruction theory.

Most ruin-reconstruction theorists have allowed the fallible theories of secular scientists to determine the meaning of Scripture and have, therefore, accepted the millions-of-years dates for the fossil record.

Some theorists also put the fall of Satan in this supposed period. But any rebellion of Satan during this gap of time contradicts God's description of His completed creation on Day 6 as all being "very good" (Genesis 1:31).

All versions of the gap theory impose outside ideas on Scripture and thus open the door for further compromise.

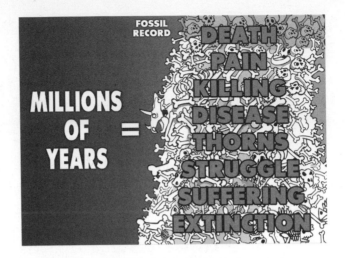

Where Did the Gap Theory Come From?

Christians have made many attempts over the years to harmonize the Genesis account of creation with accepted geology and its teaching of billions of years for the age of the earth. Examples of such attempts include the views of theistic evolution, progressive creation, and the gap theory.

This idea of the gap theory can be traced back to the rather obscure writings of the Dutchman Episcopius (1583–1643), but it was first recorded from one of the lectures of Thomas Chalmers.[1] Chalmers (1780–1847) was a notable Scottish theologian and the first modera-

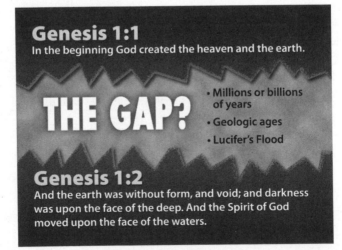

---

[1] I. Taylor, *In the Minds of Men: Darwin and the New World Order*, TFE Publishing, Toronto, Canada, 1984, 363.

tor of the Free Church of Scotland, and he was perhaps the man most responsible for the gap theory.[2] Rev. William Buckland, a geologist, also did much to popularize the idea.

Although Chalmers' writings give very little information about the gap theory,[3] many of the details are obtained from other writers, such as the nineteenth century geologist Hugh Miller, who quoted from Chalmers' lectures on the subject.[4]

The most notably influential nineteenth century writer to popularize this view was G. H. Pember, in his book *Earth's Earliest Ages*,[5] first published in 1884. Numerous editions of this work were published, the 15th edition appearing in 1942.[6]

The 20th-century writer who published the most academic defense of the gap theory was Arthur C. Custance in his work *Without Form and Void*.[7]

Bible study aids such as the Scofield Reference Bible, Dake's Annotated Reference Bible, and The Newberry Reference Bible also include the gap theory and have influenced many to accept this teaching. The basic reason for developing and promoting this view can be seen from the following very-telling quotes:

Scofield Study Bible: "Relegate fossils to the primitive creation, and no conflict of science with the Genesis cosmogony remains."[8]

Dake's Annotated Reference Bible: "When men finally agree on the age of the earth, then place the many years (over the historical 6,000) between Genesis 1:1 and 1:2, there will be no conflict between the Book of Genesis and science."[9]

These quotes are typical of the many compromise positions—accepting

---

[2] W.W. Fields, *Unformed and Unfilled*, Burgeners Enterprises, Collinsville, Illinois, 1976, 40.

[3] W. Hanna, ed., *Natural Theology*, Selected works of Thomas Chalmers, Vol. 5, Thomas Constable, Edinburgh, 1857, 146. The only thing Chalmers basically states concerning the gap theory in these writings is "The detailed history of creation in the first chapter of Genesis begins at the middle of the second verse."

[4] H. Miller, *The Testimony of the Rocks*, Boston, Gould and Lincoln, New York, 1867, 143.

[5] G.H. Pember, *Earth's Earliest Ages*, H. Revell Company, New York, 1900.

[6] Taylor, *In the Minds of Men*, 363.

[7] A.C. Custance, *Without Form and Void*, Brookville, Canada, 1970.

[8] C.I. Scofield, Ed., The Scofield Study Bible, Oxford University Press, New York, 1945. (Originally published as The Scofield Reference Bible; this edition is unaltered from the original of 1909.)

[9] F.H. Dake, Dake's Annotated Reference Bible, Dake Bible Sales, Lawrenceville, Georgia, 1961, 51.

so-called "science"[10] and its long ages for the earth, and incorporating them into Scripture.

A Testimony of Struggle

G. H. Pember's struggle with long geologic ages, recounted in *Earth's Earliest Ages*, has been the struggle of many Christians ever since the idea of millions of years for the fossil record became popular in the early nineteenth century. Many respected Christian leaders of today wrestle with this same issue.

Reading Pember's struggle helps us understand the implications of the gap theory. Pember, like today's conservative Christians, defended the authority of Scripture. He was adamant that one had to start *from* Scripture alone and *not* bring preconceived ideas *to* Scripture. He boldly chastened people who came to the Bible "filled with myths, philosophies, and prejudices, which they could not altogether throw off, but retained, in part at least, and mingled—quite unwillingly, perhaps—with the truth of God" (p. 5). He describes how the church is weakened when man's philosophies are used to interpret God's Word: "For, by skillfully blending their own systems with the truths of Scripture, they so bewildered the minds of the multitude that but few retained the power of distinguishing the revelation of God from the craftily interwoven teachings of men" (p. 7). He also said, "And the result is that inconsistent and unsound interpretations have been handed down from generation to generation, and received as if they were integral parts of the Scriptures themselves; while any texts which seemed violently opposed were allegorized, spiritualized, or explained away, till they ceased to be troublesome, or perchance, were even made subservient" (p. 8).

He then warns Christians, "For, if we be observant and honest, we must often ourselves feel the difficulty of approaching the sacred writings without bias, seeing that we bring with us a number of stereotyped ideas, which we have received as absolutely certain, and never think of testing, but only seek to confirm" (p. 8).

What happened to Pember should warn us that no matter how great a theologian we may be or how respected and knowledgeable a Christian leader, we, as finite, sinful human beings, cannot easily empty ourselves of preconceived

---

[10] Many people now equate the teaching of millions of years and evolution with science. However, these teachings are *not* science in the empirical (repeatable, testable) sense. Scientists have only the present to work with. To connect the present to the past involves interpretations based on unprovable assumptions.

ideas. Pember did exactly what he preached against, without realizing it. Such is the ingrained nature of the long-ages issue. He did not want to question Scripture (he accepted the six literal days of creation), but he did not question the long ages, either. So Pember struggled with what to do. Many of today's respected Christian leaders show the same struggle in their commentaries as they then capitulate to progressive creation or even theistic evolution.[11]

Pember said, "For, as the fossil remains clearly show not only were disease and death—inseparable companions of sin—then prevalent among the living creatures of the earth, but even ferocity and slaughter." He, therefore, recognized that a fossil record of death, decay, and disease before sin was totally inconsistent with the Bible's teaching. And he understood that there could be no carnivores before sin: "On the Sixth Day God pronounced every thing which He had made to be very good, a declaration which would seem altogether inconsistent with the present condition of the animal as well as the vegetable kingdom. Again: He gave the green herb alone for food 'to every beast of the field, and to every fowl of the air, and to every thing that creepeth upon the earth.' There were, therefore, no carnivora in the sinless world" (p. 35).

Pember taught from Isaiah that the earth will be restored to what it was like at first—no more death, disease, or carnivorous activity. However, because he had accepted the long ages for the fossil record, what was he to do with all this death, disease, and destruction in the record? He responded, "Since, then, the fossil remains are those of creatures anterior to Adam, and yet show evident tokens of disease, death, and mutual destruction, they must have belonged to another world, and have a sin-stained history of their own" (p. 35).

Thus, in trying to reconcile the long ages with Scripture, Pember justified the gap theory by saying, "There is room for any length of time between the first and second verses of the Bible. And again; since we have no inspired account of geological formations, we are at liberty to believe that they were developed just in the order which we find them. The whole process took place in pre-Adamite times, in connection, perhaps, with another race of beings, and, consequently, does not at present concern us" (p. 28).

With this background, let us consider this gap theory in detail. Basically, this theory incorporates three strands of thought:

1. A literal view of Genesis.

2. Belief in an extremely long but unidentified age for the earth.

---

[11] K. Ham, Millions of years and the "doctrine of Balaam," *Creation* **19**(3):15–17, 1997.

3. An obligation to fit the origin of most of the geologic strata and other geologic evidence between Genesis 1:1 and 1:2. (Gap theorists oppose evolution but believe in an ancient origin of the universe.)

There are many variations of the gap theory. According to the author Weston Fields, the theory can be summarized as follows, "In the far distant dateless past, God created a perfect heaven and perfect earth. Satan was ruler of the earth which was peopled by a race of 'men' without any souls. Eventually, Satan, who dwelled in a garden of Eden composed of minerals (Ezekiel 28), rebelled by desiring to become like God (Isaiah 14). Because of Satan's fall, sin entered the universe and brought on the earth God's judgment in the form of a flood (indicated by the water of 1:2), and then a global ice age when the light and heat from the sun were somehow removed. All the plant, animal, and human fossils upon the earth today date from this 'Lucifer's flood' and do not bear any genetic relationship with the plants, animals, and fossils living upon the earth today."[12]

Some versions of the gap theory state that the fossil record (geologic column) formed over millions of years, and then God destroyed the earth with a catastrophe (i.e., Lucifer's flood) that left it "without form and void."

Western Bible commentaries written before the eithteenth century (before the belief in a long age for the earth became popular) knew nothing of any gap between Genesis 1:1 and 1:2. Certainly some commentaries proposed intervals of various lengths of time for reasons relating to Satan's fall,[13] but none proposed a ruin-reconstruction situation or a pre-Adamite world. In the nineteenth century, it became popular to believe that the geological changes occurred slowly and roughly at the present rate (uniformitarianism[14]). With increased acceptance of uniformitarianism, many theologians urged

---

[12] Fields, *Unformed and Unfilled*, 7.

[13] Those who try to put the fall of Satan (not connected with millions of years) into this gap, need to consider that if all the angels were a part of the original creation, as Exodus 20:11 indicates and Colossians 1 seems to confirm, then *everything* God had created by the end of the sixth day was "very good." There could not have been *any* rebellion before this time. So Satan fell some time after Day 7.

[14] The term "uniformitarian" commonly refers to the idea that geological processes, such as erosion and sedimentation, have remained essentially the same throughout time, and so the present is the key to the past. But after the mid-nineteenth century, the application of the concept has been extended. Huxley said, "Consistent uniformitarianism postulates evolution as much in the organic as in the inorganic world." It is now assumed that a closed system exists, to which neither God nor any other nonhuman or nonnatural force has access (from J. Rendle-Short, *Man: Ape or Image*, Master Books, Green Forest, Arkansas, 1984, 20, note 4).

reinterpretation of Genesis (with ideas such as day-age, progressive creation, theistic evolution, and days-of-revelation).

Problems with the Gap Theory

Believing in the gap theory presents a number of problems and inconsistencies, especially for a Christian.

1. It is inconsistent with God creating *everything* in six days, as Scripture states.

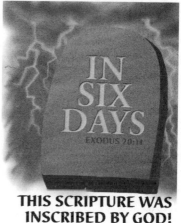

Exodus 20:11 says, "For in six days the LORD made the heavens and earth, the sea, and all that is in them, and rested the seventh day. Therefore the LORD blessed the Sabbath day, and hallowed it." Thus the creation of the heavens and the earth (Genesis 1:1) and the sea and *all that is in them* (the rest of the creation) was completed in six days.[15] Is there any time for a gap?

THIS SCRIPTURE WAS INSCRIBED BY GOD!
EXODUS 20:11

2. It puts death, disease, and suffering before the Fall, contrary to Scripture.

Romans 5:12 says, "Therefore, just as through one man [Adam] sin entered the world, and death through sin, and thus death spread to all men, because all sinned." From this we understand that there could not have been human sin or death before Adam. The Bible teaches in 1 Corinthians 15 that Adam was the first man, and as a result of his rebellion (sin), death and corruption (disease, bloodshed, and suffering) entered the universe. Before Adam sinned, there could not have been any animal *(nephesh[16])* or human death. Note also that there could not have been a race of men before Adam that died in Lucifer's flood because 1 Corinthians 15:45 tells us that Adam was the first man.

Genesis 1:29–30 teaches us that animals and man were originally created to eat plants, which is consistent with God's description of His creation as "very good." But how could a fossil record, which gives evidence of disease, violence, death, and decay (fossils have been found of animals

---

[15] See Chapter 8 for more details.

[16] The Bible speaks of animals and humans having or being *nephesh* (Hebrew), or soul-life, in various contexts suggesting conscious life. The death of a jellyfish, for example, may not be death of a *nephesh* animal.

apparently fighting and certainly eating each other), be described as "very good"? For this to be true, the death of billions of animals (and many humans) as seen in the fossil record must have occurred *after* Adam's sin. The historical event of the global Flood, recorded in Genesis, explains the presence of huge numbers of dead animals buried in rock layers, laid down by water all over the earth.

Romans 8:22 teaches that "the whole creation groans and travails in pain together until now." Clearly the whole of creation was, and is, subject to decay and corruption because of sin. When gap theorists believe that disease, decay, and death existed before Adam sinned, they ignore that this contradicts the teaching of Scripture.[17]

The version of the gap theory that puts Satan's fall at the end of the geological ages, just before the supposed Lucifer's flood that destroyed all pre-Adamic life, has a further problem—the death and suffering recorded in the fossils must have been God's fault. Since it happened before Satan's fall, Satan and sin cannot be blamed for it.[18]

3. The gap theory is logically inconsistent because it explains away what it is supposed to accommodate—supposed evidence for an old earth.

Gap theorists accept that the earth is very old—a belief based on geologic evidence interpreted with the assumption that the present is the key to the past. This assumption implies that in the past sediments containing fossils formed at basically the same rate as they do today. This process is also used by most geologists and biologists to justify belief that the geologic column represents billions of years of earth history. This geologic column has become the showcase of evolution because the fossils are claimed to show ascent from simple to complex life forms.

This places gap theorists in a dilemma. Committed to literal creation because of their acceptance of a literal view of Genesis, they cannot accept the conclusions of evolution based on the geologic column. Nor can they accept that the days in the Genesis record correspond to geologic periods. So they propose that God reshaped the earth and re-created all life in six literal days after Lucifer's flood (which produced the fossils); hence the name "ruin-reconstruction." Satan's sin supposedly caused this flood, and the resulting

---

[17] See chapter 26; also, K. Ham, *The Lie: Evolution,* Master Books, Green Forest, Arkansas, 1987, 71–82.
[18] H. Morris, Why the gap theory won't work, *Back to Genesis* No. 107, Institute for Creation Research, San Diego, California, 1997.

judgment upon that sin reduced the previous world to a state of being "without form and void."

While the gap theorist may think Lucifer's flood solves the problem of life before God's creation recorded in Genesis 1:2 and following, this actually removes the reason for the theory in the first place. If all, or most, of the sediments and fossils were produced quickly in one massive worldwide Lucifer's flood, then the main evidence that the earth is extremely old no longer exists, because the age of the earth is based on the assumed slow formation of earth's sediments.

Also, if the world was reduced to a shapeless, chaotic mess, as gap theorists propose, how could a reasonably ordered assemblage of fossils and sediments remain as evidence? Surely with such chaos the fossil record would have been severely disrupted, if not entirely destroyed. This argument also applies to those who say the fossil record formed over hundreds of millions of years before this so-called Lucifer's flood, which would have severely rearranged things.

4. The gap theory does away with the evidence for the historical event of the global Flood.

If the fossil record was formed by Lucifer's flood, then what did the global Flood of Noah's day do? On this point the gap theorist is forced to conclude that the global Flood must have left virtually no trace. To be consistent, the gap theorist would also have to defend that the global Flood was a local event. Custance, one of the major proponents of the gap theory, did just that, and he even published a paper defending a local flood.[19]

Genesis, however, depicts the global Flood as a judgment for man's sin (Genesis 6). Water flooded the earth for over a year (Genesis 6:17; 7:19–24) and only eight people, along with two of every kind (and seven of some) of air-breathing, land-dwelling animal survived (Genesis 7:23). It is more

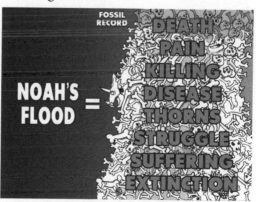

[19] A.C. Custance, The Flood: local or global? *The Doorway Papers*, Zondervan, Grand Rapids, Michigan, Vol. 9, 1970.

consistent with the whole framework of Scripture to attribute most fossils to the global Flood of Noah's day rather than to resort to a strained interpretation of the fall of Satan[20] and a totally speculative catastrophe that contributes nothing to biblical understanding or to science.

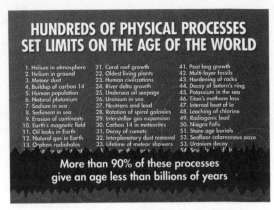

HUNDREDS OF PHYSICAL PROCESSES SET LIMITS ON THE AGE OF THE WORLD

1. Helium in atmosphere
2. Helium in ground
3. Meteor dust
4. Buildup of carbon 14
5. Human population
6. Natural plutonium
7. Sodium in sea
8. Sediment in sea
9. Erosion of continents
10. Earth's magnetic field
11. Oil leaks in Earth
12. Natural gas in Earth
13. Orphan radiohalos

21. Coral reef growth
22. Oldest living plants
23. Human civilizations
24. River delta growth
25. Undersea oil seepage
26. Uranium in sea
27. Neutrons and lead
28. Rotation of spiral galaxies
29. Interstellar gas expansion
30. Carbon 14 in meteorites
31. Decay of comets
32. Interplanetary dust removal
33. Lifetime of meteor showers

41. Peat bog growth
42. Multi-layer fossils
43. Hardening of rocks
44. Decay of Saturn's ring
45. Potassium in the sea
46. Titan's methane loss
47. Internal heat of Io
48. Leaching of chlorine
49. Radiogenic lead
50. Niagra Falls
51. Stone age burials
52. Seafloor calcareous ooze
53. Uranium decay

More than 90% of these processes give an age less than billions of years

Sadly, in relegating the fossil record to the supposed gap, gappists have removed the evidence of God's judgment in the Flood, which is the basis for God's warning of judgment to come (2 Peter 3:2–14).

5. The gap theorist ignores the evidence for a young earth.

The true gap theorist also ignores evidence consistent with an earth fewer than 10,000 years of age. There is much evidence for this—the decay and rapid reversals of the earth's magnetic field, the amount of salt in the oceans, the wind-up of spiral galaxies, and much more.[21]

6. The gap theory fails to accommodate standard uniformitarian geology with its long ages.

Today's uniformitarian geologists allow for no worldwide flood of any kind—the imaginary Lucifer's flood or the historical Flood of Noah's day. They also recognize no break between the supposed former created world and the current recreated world.

7. Most importantly, the gap theory undermines the gospel at its foundations.

By accepting an ancient age for the earth (based on the standard uniformitarian interpretation of the geologic column), gap theorists leave the evolutionary system intact (which by their own assumptions they oppose).

Even worse, they must also theorize that Romans 5:12 and Genesis 3:3 refer only to spiritual death. But this contradicts other scriptures, such as

---

[20] This also impinges upon the perspicuity of Scripture—that is, that the Bible is clear and understandable to ordinary Christians in all that's important.

[21] D.R. Humphreys, Evidence for a young world, *Creation* **13**(3):46–50, 1991; also available as a pamphlet. See also www.answersingenesis.org/go/young.

1 Corinthians 15 and Genesis 3:22–23. These passages tell us that Adam's sin led to *physical* death, as well as spiritual death. In 1 Corinthians 15 the death of the Last Adam (the Lord Jesus Christ) is compared with the death of the first Adam. Jesus suffered physical death for man's sin, because Adam, the first man, died physically because of sin.

In cursing man with physical death, God also provided a way to redeem man through the person of His Son Jesus Christ, who suffered the curse of death on the Cross for us. He tasted "death for everyone" according to Hebrews 2:9. He took the penalty that should rightly have been ours at the hands of the Righteous Judge, and bore it in His own body on the Cross. Jesus Christ tasted death for all mankind, and He defeated death when He rose from the grave three days later. Men can be free from eternal death in hell if they believe in Jesus Christ as Lord and Savior. They then are received back to God to spend eternity with Him. That is the message of Christianity.

To believe there was death before Adam's sin destroys the basis of the Christian message. The Bible states that man's rebellious actions led to death and the corruption of the universe, but the gap theory undermines the reason that man needs a Savior.

A Closer Look at Genesis 1:1–2

The earliest available manuscript of Genesis 1:1–2 is found in the Greek translation of the Old Testament, called the Septuagint (LXX), which was prepared about 250–200 B.C. The LXX does not permit the reading of any ruin-reconstruction scenario into these verses, as even Custance admitted. A closer look at these verses reveals that the gap theory imposes an interpretation upon Genesis 1:1–2 that is unnatural and grammatically unsound. Like many attempts to harmonize the Bible with uniformitarian geology, the gap theory involves a well-meant but misguided twisting of Scripture.

Below are the five major challenges to the gap theory in interpreting Scripture. For a much fuller analysis, we recommend the book *Unformed and Unfilled* by Weston Fields, published by Burgener Enterprises, 1997.

Creating and Making (Hebrew: *Bara* and *Asah*)

It is generally acknowledged that the Hebrew word *bara*, used with "God" as its subject, means "to create"—in the sense of the production of something which did not exist before.

However, according to Exodus 20:11, God "made" *(asah)* the heavens and the earth and everything in them in six days. If God made everything in six days, then there is clearly no room for a gap. To avoid this clear scriptural testimony against any gap, gap theorists have alleged that *asah* does not mean "to create," but "to form" or even "re-form." They claim that Exodus 20:11 refers not to six days of creation but to six days of re-forming a ruined world.

Is there such a difference between *bara* and *asah* in biblical usage? A number of verses show that, while *asah* may mean "to do" or "to make," it can also mean "to create," which is the same as *bara*. For example, Nehemiah 9:6 states that God made *(asah)* "heaven, the heaven of heavens, with all their host, the earth and everything on it, the seas and all that is in them." This reference is obviously to the original *ex nihilo* (out of nothing) creation, but the word *asah* is used. (We may safely assume that no gappist will want to say that Nehemiah 9:6 refers to the supposed reconstruction, because if the passage did, the gappist would have to include the geological strata in the reconstruction, thereby depriving the whole theory of any power to explain away the fossil record.)

The fact is that the words *bara* and *asah* are often used interchangeably in the Old Testament; indeed, in some places they are used in synonymous parallelism (e.g., Genesis 1:26–27, 2:4; Exodus 34:10; Isaiah 41:20, 43:7).

Applying this conclusion to Exodus 20:11, 31:17, and Nehemiah 9:6, we see that Scripture teaches that God created the universe (everything) in six days, as outlined in Genesis 1.

The Grammar of Genesis 1:1–2

Many adherents of the gap theory claim that the grammar of Genesis 1:1–2 allows, and even requires, a time-gap between the events in verse 1 and the events in verse 2. Into this gap—believed by many to be billions of years—they want to place all the major geological phenomena that have shaped the world.

This is an unnatural interpretation, not suggested by the plain meaning of the text. The most straightforward reading of the verses sees verse 1 as a subject-and-verb clause, with verse 2 containing three circumstantial clauses (i.e., three statements that further describe the circumstances introduced by the principal clause in verse 1).

This conclusion is reinforced by the grammarian Gesenius. He says that the Hebrew conjunction *waw*, meaning "and" at the beginning of verse 2, is a "*waw* copulative," which compares with the old English expression "to wit." This grammatical connection between verses 1 and 2 thus rules out the gap theory. Verse 2 is in fact a description of the state of the originally created earth: "*And* the earth was without form and void" (Genesis 1:2a).[22]

"Was" or "Became"?

Gappists translate "the earth *was* without form and void" to be "the earth *became* (or, *had become*) without form and void." At stake is the translation of the Hebrew word *hayetah* (a form of the Hebrew verb, *hayah*, meaning "to be").

Custance, a supporter of the gap theory, claims that out of 1,320 occurrences of the verb *hayah* in the Old Testament, only 24 can certainly be said to bear the meaning "to be." He concludes that in Genesis 1:2 *hayetah* must mean "became" and not simply "was."

However, we must note that the meaning of a word is controlled by its context, and that verse 2 is circumstantial to verse 1. Thus "was" is the most natural and appropriate translation for *hayetah*. It is rendered this way in most English versions (as well as in the LXX). Furthermore, in Genesis 1:2 *hayetah* is not followed by the preposition *le*, which would have removed any ambiguity in the Hebrew and required the translation "became."

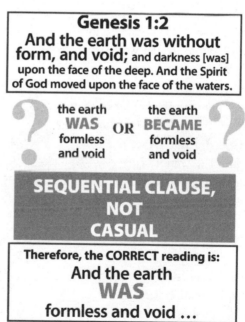

Genesis 1:2
And the earth was without form, and void; and darkness [was] upon the face of the deep. And the Spirit of God moved upon the face of the waters.

? the earth **WAS** formless and void **OR** the earth **BECAME** formless and void ?

SEQUENTIAL CLAUSE, NOT CASUAL

Therefore, the CORRECT reading is:
And the earth WAS formless and void ...

---

[22] The word "and" is included in the KJV translation but is translated "now" in the NIV and is not translated at all in the NKJV or the NASB.

Tohu and Bohu

The words *tohu* and *bohu*, usually translated "formless and void," are used in Genesis 1:2. They imply that the original universe was created unformed and unfilled and was, during six days, formed and filled by God's creative actions.

Gappists claim that these words imply a process of judgmental destruction and that they indicate a sinful, and therefore not an original, state of the earth. However, this brings interpretations from other parts of the Old Testament with very different contexts (namely, Isaiah 34:11 and Jeremiah 4:23) and imports them into Genesis 1.

Tohu and *bohu* appear together only in the three above-mentioned places in the Old Testament. However, *tohu* appears alone in a number of other places and in all cases simply means "formless." The word itself does not tell us about the cause of formlessness; this has to be gleaned from the context. Isaiah 45:18 (often quoted by gappists) is rendered in the KJV "he created it not in vain [*tohu*], he formed it to be inhabited." In the context, Isaiah is speaking about Israel, God's people, and His grace in restoring them. He did not choose His people in order to destroy them, but to be their God and for them to be His people. Isaiah draws an analogy with God's purpose in creation: He did not create the world for it to be empty. No, He created it to be formed and filled, a suitable abode for His creation. Gappists miss the point altogether when they argue that because Isaiah says God did not create the world *tohu*, it must have *become tohu* at some later time. Isaiah 45:18 is about God's *purpose* in creating, not about the original state of the creation.

Though the expression "*tohu* and *bohu*" in Isaiah 34:11 and Jeremiah 4:23 speaks of a formlessness and emptiness resulting from divine judgment for sin, this meaning is not implicit in the expression itself

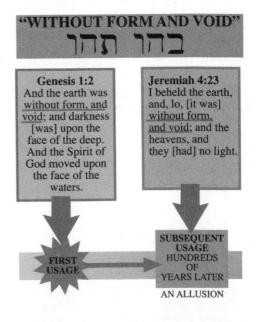

"WITHOUT FORM AND VOID"

בהו תהו

Genesis 1:2	**Jeremiah 4:23**
And the earth was without form, and void; and darkness [was] upon the face of the deep. And the Spirit of God moved upon the face of the waters.	I beheld the earth, and, lo, [it was] without form, and void; and the heavens, and they [had] no light.

FIRST USAGE

SUBSEQUENT USAGE HUNDREDS OF YEARS LATER

AN ALLUSION

but is gained from the particular contexts in which it occurs. It is not valid therefore to infer that same meaning from Genesis 1:2, where the context does not suggest any judgment. As an analogy, we might think of a word like "blank" in reference to a computer screen. It can be blank because nothing has been typed on the keyboard, or it can be blank because the screen has been erased. The word "blank" does not suggest, in itself, the reason why the screen is blank. Likewise with "formless and void"—the earth began that way simply because it was not yet formed and filled, or it was that way because of judgment.

Theologians call the form of use of *tohu* and/or *bohu* in Isaiah 34:11 and Jeremiah 4:23 a "verbal allusion." These passages on judgment allude to the formless and empty earth at the beginning of creation to suggest the extent of God's judgment to come. God's judgment will be so complete that the result will be like the earth before it was formed and filled—formless and empty. This does not imply that the state of the creation in Genesis 1:2 was arrived at by some sort of judgment or destruction as imagined by gappists. As theologian Robert Chisholm, Jr. wrote, "By the way, allusion only works one way. It is unwarranted to assume that Jeremiah's use of the phrase in a context of judgment implies some sort of judgment in the context of Genesis 1:2. Jeremiah is not interpreting the meaning of Genesis 1:2."[23]

"Replenish"

Many gappists have used the word "replenish" in the KJV translation of Genesis 1:28 to justify the gap theory on the basis that this word means "refill." Thus, they claim that God told Adam and Eve to refill the earth, implying it was once before filled with people (the pre-Adamites). However,

___
23 R.B. Chisholm, Jr., *From Exegesis to Exposition: A Practical Guide to Using Biblical Hebrew*, Baker Books, Grand Rapids, Michigan, 1998, 41.

this is wrong. The Hebrew word translated "replenish," *male*,[24] simply means "fill" (or "fulfill" or "be filled").

The English word "replenish" meant "fill" from the thirteenth to the seventeenth centuries; then it changed to mean "refill." When the KJV was published in 1611, the translators used the English word "replenish," which at that time meant only "fill," not "refill."[25]

The Straightforward Meaning of Genesis 1:1–2

The gap (or ruin-reconstruction) theory is based on a very tenuous interpretation of Scripture.

The simple, straightforward meaning of Genesis 1:1–2 is that, when God created the earth at the beginning, it was initially formless, empty, and dark, and God's Spirit was there above the waters. It was through His creative energy that the world was then progressively formed and filled during the six days of creation.

Consider the analogy of a potter making a vase. The first thing he does is gather a ball of clay. What he has is good, but it is unformed. Next, he shapes it into a vase, using his potter's wheel. Now the ball of clay is no longer formless. He then dries it, applies glaze, and fires it. Now it is ready to be filled—with flowers and water. At no time could one of the stages be considered evil or bad. It was just unfinished—unformed and unfilled. When the vase was finally formed and filled, it could be described as "very good."

Warning

Many sincere Christians have invented reinterpretations of Scripture to avoid intellectual conflicts with popular scientific ideas. The gap theory was one such reinterpretation designed to fit in with scientific concepts that arose in the early 1800s and are still popular today.

---

[24] *Strong's Concordance*, Hebrew word No. 4390.

[25] See C. Taylor, What does "replenish the earth" mean? *Creation* **18**(2):44–45, 1996, for more details on the history of the meaning of "replenish."

In reality, though, the gap theory was an effective anesthetic that put the church to sleep for over 100 years. When the children who learned this compromise position went on to higher education, they were shocked to discover that this theory explained nothing. Many of them then accepted the only remaining "respectable" theory—evolution—which went hand-in-hand with millions of years. The results were usually disastrous for their faith.

Today, other compromise positions, such as progressive creation or theistic evolution, have mostly replaced the gap theory.[26] The gappists, by attempting to maintain a literal Genesis but adhering to the long ages (millions of years), opened the door for greater compromise in the next generation—the reinterpretation of the days, God using evolution, etc.

But whether it is the gap theory, day-age/progressive creation, or theistic evolution, the results are the same. These positions may be acceptable in some churches, but the learned in the secular world will, with some justification, mock those who hold them because they see the inconsistencies.

In Martin Luther's day the church compromised what the Bible clearly

taught, and he nailed his *Ninety-Five Theses* to the door of the church to call them back to the authority of God's Word. In the same way, the church today has, by and large, neglected what the Bible clearly says in Genesis 1–11. It's time to call the church back to the authority of God's Word beginning with Genesis.

---

[26] A strange modern gap theory is found in *Genesis Unbound*, by J. Sailhamer, Multnomah Books, Sisters, Oregon, 1996. The author fits the supposed millions of years of geologic history into Genesis 1:1 and then claims the six days of creation relate to the Promised Land. He states his motivation for this novel approach on p. 29: "If billions of years really are covered by the simple statement, 'In the beginning God created the heavens and the earth,' then many of the processes described by modern scientists fall into the period covered by the Hebrew term 'beginning.' Within that 'beginning' would fit the countless geologic ages, ice ages, and the many global climatic changes on our planet. The many biological eras would also fit within 'the beginning' of Genesis 1:1, including the long ages during which the dinosaurs roamed the earth. By the time human beings were created on the sixth day of the week, the dinosaurs already could have flourished and become extinct—all during the 'beginning' recorded in Genesis 1:1." Many of the problems with the classical gap theory also apply to this attempt to fit millions of years into the Bible.

6

Cain's Wife—
Who Was She?

KEN HAM

Is She the Most-Talked-About Wife in History?

We don't even know her name, yet she was discussed at the Scopes Trial, mentioned in the movies *Inherit the Wind*[1] and *Contact*,[2] and talked about in countries all over the world for hundreds of years.

Skeptics of the Bible have used Cain's wife time and again to try to discredit the book of Genesis as a true historical record. Sadly, most Christians have not given an adequate answer to this question. As a result, the world sees them as not being able to defend the authority of Scripture and thus the Christian faith.

For instance, at the historic Scopes Trial in Tennessee in 1925, William Jennings Bryan, the prosecutor who stood for the Christian faith, failed to answer the question about Cain's wife posed by the ACLU lawyer Clarence Darrow. Consider the following excerpt from the trial record as Darrow interrogates Bryan:

Q—Did you ever discover where Cain got his wife?

A—No, sir; I leave the agnostics to hunt for her.

---

[1] This is a Hollywood version of the famous Scopes Trial. K. Ham, The wrong way round! *Creation* **8**(3):38-41, 1996; D. Menton, Inherit the Wind: an historical analysis, *Creation* **19**(1):35-38, 1997.
[2] *Contact*, Warner Bros., released July 11, 1997. Based on Carl Sagan's *Contact*, Pocket Books, New York, 1985.

Q—You have never found out?

A—I have never tried to find.

Q—You have never tried to find?

A—No.

Q—The Bible says he got one doesn't it? Were there other people on the earth at that time?

A—I cannot say.

Q—You cannot say. Did that ever enter your consideration?

A—Never bothered me.

Q—There were no others recorded, but Cain got a wife.

A—That is what the Bible says.

Q—Where she came from you do not know.[3]

The world's press was focused on this trial, and what they heard has affected Christianity to this day—Christians can't defend the biblical record!

In recent times, this same example was taken up by Carl Sagan in his book *Contact* [2] (which was on the *New York Times* best-seller list) and used in the movie of the same name based upon this work.

In the book, we read the fictional character Ellie's account of how she could not get answers from a minister's wife, who was the leader of a church discussion group:

> Ellie had never seriously read the Bible before ... . So over the weekend preceding her first class, she read through what seemed to be the important parts of the Old Testament, trying to keep an open mind. She at once recognized that there were two different and mutually contradictory stories of Creation ... and had trouble figuring out exactly who it was that Cain had married.[4]

Sagan cleverly listed a number of common questions (including Cain's wife) that are often directed at Christians in an attempt to supposedly

---

[3] *The World's Most Famous Court Trial, Tennessee Evolution Case* (a word-for-word report), Bryan College (reprinted from the original edition), p. 302, 1990.

[4] C. Sagan, *Contact*, Pocket Books, New York, 1985, 19–20.

prove the Bible is full of contradictions and can't be defended. The truth is—most Christians probably couldn't answer these questions. And yet there *are* answers. But since churches lack in the teaching of apologetics,[5] particularly in regard to the book of Genesis, most believers in the church are not able to be "always be ready to give a defense to everyone who asks you a reason for the hope that is in you, with meekness and fear" (1 Peter 3:15).

Why Is It Important?

Many skeptics have claimed that for Cain to find a wife, there must have been other "races" of people on the earth who were not descendants of Adam and Eve. To many people, this question is a stumbling block to accepting the creation account of Genesis and its record of only one man and woman at the beginning of history. Defenders of the gospel must be able to show that all human beings are descendants of one man and one woman (Adam and Eve) because only descendants of Adam and Eve can be saved. Thus, believers need to be able to account for Cain's wife and show clearly she was a descendant of Adam and Eve.

Our thinking in every area!

---

[5] Apologetics—from the Greek word, ἀπολογία *(apologia)*, meaning "to give a defense." The field of Christian apologetics covers the ability of Christians to give a defense of their faith in Jesus Christ and their hope in Him for salvation, as expressed in 1 Peter 3:15. This ability requires a thorough knowledge of Scripture, including the doctrines of the creation, Original Sin, Curse, Flood, Virgin Birth, life and ministry of Jesus of Nazareth, the Cross, Crucifixion, Resurrection, Ascension, promise of the Second Coming, and a new heaven and new earth. Then one needs to be able to explain logically and clearly these various doctrines in a way that justifies one's faith and hope in Jesus Christ.

In order to answer this question of where Cain got his wife, we first need to cover some background information concerning the meaning of the gospel.

The First Man

"Wherefore, as by one man sin entered into the world, and death by sin; and so death passed upon all men, for that all have sinned" (Romans 5:12).

We read in 1 Corinthians 15:45 that Adam was "the first man." God did not start by making a race of men.

The Bible makes it clear that *only* the descendants of Adam can be saved. Romans 5 teaches that we sin because Adam sinned. The death penalty, which Adam received as judgment for his sin of rebellion, has also been passed on to all his descendants.

Since Adam was the head of the human race, when he fell we who were in the loins of Adam fell also. Thus, we are all separated from God. The final consequence of sin would be separation from God in our sinful state forever. However, the good news is that there is a way for us to return to God.

Because a man brought sin and death into the world, the human race, who are all descendants of Adam, needed a sinless Man to pay the penalty for sin and the resulting judgment of death. However, the Bible teaches that "all have sinned" (Romans 3:23). What was the solution?

Jesus Christ "The Last Adam"
1 Cor. 15:45

For as in Adam all die, even so in Christ shall all be made alive.
1 Corinthians 15:22

"The First Adam"
1 Cor. 15:45

Which Adam is "non-essential" to the Gospel?

The Last Adam

God provided the solution—a way to deliver man from his wretched state. Paul explains in 1 Corinthians 15 that God provided another Adam. The Son of God became a man—a *perfect* Man—yet still our relation. He is called "the last Adam" (1 Corinthians 15:45) because he took the place of the first Adam. He became the new head and, because He was sinless, was able to pay the penalty for sin:

"For since by [a] man came death, by [a] Man also came the resurrection of the dead. For as in Adam all die, even so in Christ all shall be made alive" (1 Corinthians 15:21–22).

Christ suffered death (the penalty for sin) on the Cross, shedding His blood ("and without shedding of blood there is no remission," Hebrews 9:22) so that those who put their trust in His work on the Cross can come in repentance of their sin of rebellion (in Adam) and be reconciled to God.

Thus, only descendants of the first man Adam can be saved.

All Related

Since the Bible describes *all* human beings as sinners, and we are *all* related ("And He has made from one blood every nation of men to dwell on all the face of the earth," Acts 17:26), the gospel makes sense only on the basis that all humans alive and all that have ever lived (except for the first woman[6]) are descendants of the first man Adam. If this were not so, then the gospel could not be explained or defended.

Thus, there was only *one* man at the beginning—made from the dust of the earth (Genesis 2:7).

This also means that Cain's wife was a descendant of Adam. She couldn't have come from another race of people and must be accounted for from Adam's descendants.

The First Woman

In Genesis 3:20 we read, "And Adam called his wife's name Eve, because she was the mother of all living." In other words, all people other than Adam

---

[6] Eve, in a sense, was a descendant of Adam in that she was made from his flesh and thus had a direct biological connection to him (Genesis 2:21–23).

are descendants of Eve—she was the first woman.

Eve was made from Adam's side (Genesis 2:21–24)—this was a unique event. In the New Testament, Jesus (Matthew 19:4-6) and Paul (Ephesians 5:31) use this historical and one-time event as the foundation for the marriage of one man and one woman.

Also, in Genesis 2:20, we are told that when Adam looked at the animals, he couldn't find a mate—there was no one of his kind.

AFTER EDEN   by Dan Lietha

EVE, YOU'RE THE ONLY ONE FOR ME!

www.AnswersInGenesis.org

© 2000 AiG

In his first attempt to be romantic, Adam merely states the obvious.

All this makes it obvious that there was only *one* woman, Adam's wife, from the beginning. There could not have been a "race" of women.

Thus, if Christians cannot defend that all humans, including Cain's wife, can trace their ancestry ultimately to Adam and Eve, then how can they understand and explain the gospel? How can they justify sending missionaries to every tribe and nation? Therefore, one needs to be able to explain Cain's wife, to illustrate that Christians can defend the gospel and all that it teaches.

Who Was Cain?

Cain was the first child of Adam and Eve recorded in Scripture (Genesis 4:1). He and his brothers, Abel (Genesis 4:2) and Seth (Genesis 4:25), were part of the first generation of children ever born on this earth. Even though these three males are specifically mentioned, Adam and Eve had other children.

Cain's Brothers and Sisters

In Genesis 5:4 we read a statement that sums up the life of Adam and Eve: "After he begot Seth, the days of Adam were eight hundred years; and he had sons and daughters."

During their lives, Adam and Eve had a number of male and female children. In fact, the Jewish historian Josephus wrote, "The number of

Adam's children, as says the old tradition, was thirty-three sons and twenty-three daughters."[7]

Scripture doesn't tell us how many children were born to Adam and Eve, but considering their long life spans (Adam lived for 930 years—Genesis 5:5), it would seem logical to suggest there were many. Remember, they were commanded to "be fruitful, and multiply" (Genesis 1:28).

The Wife

If we now work totally from Scripture, without any personal prejudices or other extrabiblical ideas, then back at the beginning, when there was only the first generation, brothers would have had to marry sisters or there wouldn't have been any more generations!

We're not told when Cain married or many of the details of other marriages and children, but we can say for certain that Cain's wife was either his sister or a close relative.

A closer look at the Hebrew word for "wife" in Genesis reveals something readers may miss in translation. It was more obvious to those speaking Hebrew that Cain's wife was likely his sister. (There is a slim possibility that she was his niece, but either way, a brother and sister would have married in the beginning.) The Hebrew word for "wife" used in Genesis 4:17 (the first mention of Cain's wife) is *ishshah*, and it means "woman/wife/female."

> And Cain knew his wife [*ishshah*], and she conceived and bore Enoch. And he built a city, and called the name of the city after the name of his son—Enoch (Genesis 4:17).

The word *ishshah* is the word for "woman," and it means "from man." It is a derivation of the Hebrew word *iysh* and *enowsh,* which both mean "man." This can be seen in Genesis 2:23 where the name "woman" (*ishshah*) is given to one who came from Adam.

---

[7] F. Josephus, *The Complete Works of Josephus,* translated by W. Whiston, Kregel Publications, Grand Rapids, Michigan, 1981, 27.

And Adam said: "This is now bone of my bones and flesh of my flesh; She shall be called Woman [*ishshah*], because she was taken out of Man [*iysh*]" (Genesis 2:23).

Thus, Cain's wife is a descendant of Adam/man. Therefore, she had to be his sister (or possibly niece). Hebrew readers should be able to make this connection easier; however, much is lost when translated.

Objections

GOD'S LAWS

Many people immediately reject the conclusion that Adam and Eve's sons and daughters married each other by appealing to the law against brother-sister marriage. Some say that you can't marry your relation. Actually, if you don't marry your relation, you don't marry a human! A wife is related to her husband before they are married because all people are descendants of Adam and Eve—all are of *one blood*. This law forbidding *close* relatives marrying was not given until the time of Moses (Leviticus 18–20). Provided marriage was one man for one woman for life (based on Genesis 1–2), there was no disobedience to God's law originally (before the time of Moses) when close relatives (even brothers and sisters) married each other.

Remember that Abraham was married to his half-sister (Genesis 20:12).[8] God's law forbade such marriages,[9] but that was some four hundred years later at the time of Moses.

BIOLOGICAL DEFORMITIES

Today, brothers and sisters (and half brothers and half-sisters, etc.) are not currently permitted by law to marry and have children.

Now it is true that children produced in a union between brother and sister have a greater chance to be deformed. As a matter of fact, the closer the couple are in relationship, the *more* likely it is that any offspring will be deformed. It is very easy to understand this without going into all the technical details.

Each person inherits a set of genes from his or her mother and father. Unfortunately, genes today contain many mistakes (because of sin

---

[8] Another example would be Isaac's wife, Rebekah—she was Isaac's second cousin (Genesis 24:15).

[9] Leviticus 18–20.

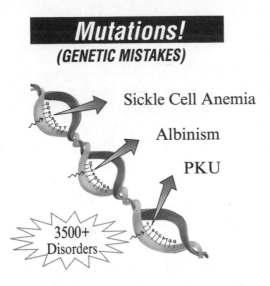

Mutations!
(GENETIC MISTAKES)

Sickle Cell Anemia

Albinism

PKU

3500+ Disorders

and the Curse), and these mistakes show up in a variety of ways. For instance, people let their hair grow over their ears to hide the fact that one ear is lower than the other. Or perhaps someone's nose is not quite in the middle of his or her face, or someone's jaw is a little out of shape. Let's face it, the main reason we call each other normal is because of our common agreement to do so!

The more closely related two people are, the more likely it is that they will have similar mistakes in their genes, inherited from the same parents. Therefore, brother and sister are likely to have similar mistakes in their genetic material. If there were to be a union between these two that produces offspring, children would inherit one set of genes from each of their parents. Because the genes probably have similar mistakes, the mistakes pair together and result in deformities in the children.

Conversely, the further away the parents are in relationship to each other, the more likely it is that they will have different mistakes in their genes. Children, inheriting one set of genes from each parent, are likely to end up with some of the pairs of genes containing only one bad gene in each pair. The good gene tends to override the bad so that a deformity (a serious one, anyway) does not occur. Instead of having totally deformed ears, for instance, a person may have only crooked ones. (Overall, though, the human race is slowly degenerating as mistakes accumulate generation after generation.)

However, this fact of present-day life did not apply to Adam and Eve. When the first two people were created, they were perfect. Everything God made was "very good" (Genesis 1:31). That means their genes were perfect— no mistakes. But when sin entered the world because of Adam (Genesis 3:6), God cursed the world so that the perfect creation then began to degenerate, that is, suffer death and decay (Romans 8:22). Over a long period of time, this degeneration would have resulted in all sorts of mistakes occurring in the genetic material of living things.

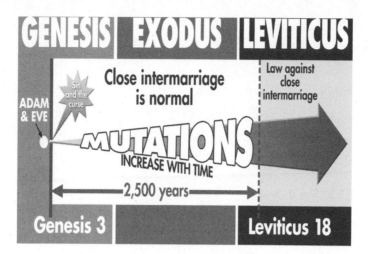

But Cain was in the first generation of children ever born. He, as well as his brothers and sisters, would have received virtually no imperfect genes from Adam or Eve, since the effects of sin and the Curse would have been minimal to start with. In that situation, brother and sister could have married (provided it was one man for one woman, which is what marriage is all about, Matthew 19:4–6) without any potential to produce deformed offspring.

By the time of Moses (about 2,500 years later), degenerative mistakes would have accumulated to such an extent in the human race that it would have been necessary for God to bring in the laws forbidding brother-sister (and close relative) marriage (Leviticus 18–20).[10]

(Also, there were plenty of people on the earth by now, and there was no reason for close relations to marry.)

In all, there appear to be three interrelated reasons for the introduction of laws forbidding close intermarriage:

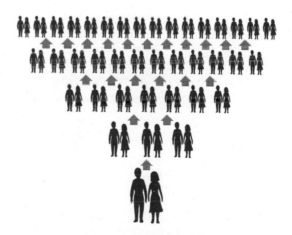

---

[10] Some have claimed this means God changed His mind by changing the laws. But God didn't change His mind—because of the changes that sin brought and because God never changes, He introduced new laws for our sake.

1. As we have already discussed, there was the need to protect against the increasing potential to produce deformed offspring.

2. God's laws were instrumental in keeping the Jewish nation strong, healthy, and within the purposes of God.

3. These laws were a means of protecting the individual, the family structure, and society at large. The psychological damage caused by incestuous relationships should not be minimized.

Cain and the Land of Nod

Some claim that the passage in Genesis 4:16–17 means that Cain went to the land of Nod and found a wife. Thus, they conclude there must have been another race of people on the earth who were not descendants of Adam, who produced Cain's wife.

> Then Cain went out from the presence of the LORD and dwelt in the land of Nod on the east of Eden. And Cain knew his wife, and she conceived and bore Enoch. And he built a city, and called the name of the city after the name of his son—Enoch.

From what has been stated above, it is clear that *all* humans, Cain's wife included, are descendants of Adam. However, this passage does not say that Cain went to the land of Nod and found a wife. John Calvin in commenting on these verses states:

> From the context we may gather that Cain, before he slew his brother, had married a wife; otherwise Moses would now have related something respecting his marriage.[11]

Cain was married *before* he went to the land of Nod. He didn't find a wife there but "knew" (had sexual relations with) his wife.[12]

This makes sense in light of what Nod is, too. Nod means "wandering" in Hebrew. So when Cain went to the land of Nod, he was literally going to the land of wandering, not a place full of people.

---

[11] J. Calvin, *Commentaries on The First Book of Moses Called Genesis*, Vol. 1, reprinted, Baker House, Grand Rapids, Michigan, 1979, 215.

[12] Even if Calvin's suggestion concerning this matter is not correct, there was still plenty of time for numerous descendants of Adam and Eve to move out and settle areas such as the land of Nod.

Who was Cain Fearful of (Genesis 4:14)?

Some claim that there had to be lots of people on the earth other than Adam and Eve's descendants; otherwise Cain wouldn't have been fearful of people wanting to slay him because he killed Abel.

First of all, one reason that someone would want to harm Cain for killing Abel is if that person was a close relation of Abel!

Secondly, Cain and Abel were born quite some time before the event of Abel's death. Genesis 4:3 states:

> And in the process of time it came to pass that Cain brought an offering of the fruit of the ground to the LORD.

Note the phrase "in the process of time." We know Seth was born when Adam was 130 years old (Genesis 5:3), and Eve saw him as a replacement for Abel (Genesis 4:25). Therefore, the time period from Cain's birth to Abel's death may have been 100 years or more—allowing plenty of time for other children of Adam and Eve to marry and have children. By the time Abel was killed, there may have been a considerable number of descendants of Adam and Eve involving several generations.

Where Did the Technology Come From?

Some claim that for Cain to go to the land of Nod and build a city, he would have required a lot of technology that must have already been in that land, presumably developed by other races.

Adam and Eve's descendants were very intelligent people. We are told that Jubal made musical instruments, such as the harp and organ (Genesis 4:21), and Tubal-cain worked with brass and iron (Genesis 4:22).

Because of intense evolutionary indoctrination, many people today have the idea that their generation is the most advanced that has ever been on this planet. Just because we have jet airplanes and computers doesn't mean we are the most intelligent or advanced. This modern technology is really a result of the accumulation of knowledge.

We must remember that our brains have suffered from 6,000 years of the Curse. We have greatly degenerated compared to people many generations ago. We may be nowhere near as intelligent or inventive as Adam and Eve's children. Scripture gives us a glimpse of what appears to be advanced technology almost from the beginning.

Cain had the knowledge and talent to know how to build a city!

Conclusion

One of the reasons many Christians cannot answer the question about Cain's wife is that they tend to look at today's world and the problems that would be associated with close relations marrying, and they do not look at the clear historical record God has given to us.

They try to interpret Genesis from our present situation rather than understand the true biblical history of the world and the changes that have occurred because of sin. Because they are not building their worldview on Scripture but taking a secular way of thinking to the Bible, they are blinded to the simple answers.

Genesis is the record of the God who was there as history happened. It is the Word of One who knows everything and who is a reliable Witness from the past. Thus, when we use Genesis as a basis for understanding history, we can make sense of evidence which would otherwise be a real mystery. You see, if evolution is true, science has an even bigger problem than Cain's wife to explain—namely, how could man ever evolve by mutations (mistakes) in the first place, since that process would have made everyone's children deformed? The mere fact that people can produce offspring that are *not* largely deformed is a testimony to creation, not evolution.

7

Doesn't Carbon-14 Dating Disprove the Bible?

MIKE RIDDLE

Scientists use a technique called radiometric dating to estimate the ages of rocks, fossils, and the earth. Many people have been led to believe that radiometric dating methods have proved the earth to be billions of years old. This has caused many in the church to reevaluate the biblical creation account, specifically the meaning of the word "day" in Genesis 1. With our focus on one particular form of radiometric dating—carbon dating—we will see that carbon dating strongly supports a young earth. Note that, contrary to a popular misconception, carbon dating is not used to date rocks at millions of years old.

Basics

Before we get into the details of how radiometric dating methods are used, we need to review some preliminary concepts from chemistry. Recall that atoms are the basic building blocks of matter. Atoms are made up of much smaller particles called protons, neutrons, and electrons. Protons and neutrons make up the center (nucleus) of the atom, and electrons form shells around the nucleus.

The number of protons in the nucleus of an atom determines the

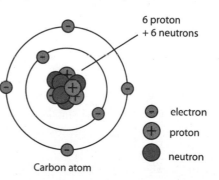

6 proton + 6 neutrons

electron

proton

neutron

Carbon atom

element. For example, all carbon atoms have 6 protons, all atoms of nitrogen have 7 protons, and all oxygen atoms have 8 protons. The number of neutrons in the nucleus can vary in any given type of atom. So, a carbon atom might have six neutrons, or seven, or possibly eight—but it would always have six protons. An "isotope" is any of several different forms of an element, each having different numbers of neutrons. The illustration below shows the three isotopes of carbon.

The atomic number corresponds to the number of protons in an atom.
Atomic mass is a combination of the number of protons and neutrons
in the nucleus. (The electrons are so much lighter that they do
not contribute significantly to the mass of an atom.)

Some isotopes of certain elements are unstable; they can spontaneously change into another kind of atom in a process called "radioactive decay." Since this process presently happens at a known measured rate, scientists attempt to use it like a "clock" to tell how long ago a rock or fossil formed. There are two main applications for radiometric dating. One is for potentially dating fossils (once-living things) using carbon-14 dating, and the other is for dating rocks and the age of the earth using uranium, potassium and other radioactive atoms.

Carbon-14 Dating

Carbon-14 (^{14}C), also referred to as radiocarbon, is claimed to be a reliable dating method for determining the ages of fossils up to 50,000 to 60,000 years. If this claim is true, the biblical account of a young earth (about 6,000 years) is in question, since ^{14}C dates of tens of thousands of years are common.[1]

When a scientist's interpretation of data does not match the clear meaning of the text in the Bible, we should never reinterpret the Bible. God knows just what He meant to say, and His understanding of science is infallible, whereas ours is fallible. So we should never think it necessary to modify His Word. Genesis 1 defines the days of creation to be literal days (a number with the word "day" always means a normal day in the Old Testament, and the

---

[1] *Earth Science* (Teachers Edition), Prentice Hall, 2002, p. 301.

phrase "evening and morning" further defines the days as literal days). Since the Bible is the inspired Word of God, we should examine the validity of the standard interpretation of ^{14}C dating by asking several questions:

1. Is the explanation of the data derived from empirical, observational science, or an interpretation of past events (historical science)?

2. Are there any assumptions involved in the dating method?

3. Are the dates provided by ^{14}C dating consistent with what we observe?

4. Do all scientists accept the ^{14}C dating method as reliable and accurate?

All radiometric dating methods use scientific procedures in the present to interpret what has happened in the past. The procedures used are not necessarily in question. The interpretation of past events is in question. The secular (evolutionary) worldview interprets the universe and world to be billions of years old. The Bible teaches a young universe and earth. Which worldview does science support? Can carbon-14 dating help solve the mystery of which worldview is more accurate?

The use of carbon-14 dating is often misunderstood. Carbon-14 is mostly used to date once-living things (organic material). It cannot be used directly to date rocks; however, it can potentially be used to put time constraints on some inorganic material such as diamonds (diamonds could contain carbon-14). Because of the rapid rate of decay of ^{14}C, it can only give dates in the thousands-of-year range and not millions.

There are three different naturally occurring varieties (isotopes) of carbon: ^{12}C, ^{13}C, and ^{14}C. Carbon-14 is used for dating because it is unstable (radioactive), whereas ^{12}C and ^{13}C are stable. Radioactive means that ^{14}C will decay (emit radiation) over time and become a different element. During this process (called "beta decay") a neutron in the ^{14}C atom will be converted into a proton and an electron. By losing one neutron and gaining one proton, ^{14}C is changed into nitrogen-14 (^{14}N = 7 protons and 7 neutrons).

If ^{14}C is constantly decaying, will the earth eventually run out of ^{14}C? The answer is no. Carbon-14 is constantly being added to the atmosphere. Cosmic rays from outer space, which contain high levels of energy, bombard the earth's upper atmosphere.

C-12 Stable   C-13 Stable   C-14 Unstable

These cosmic rays collide with atoms in the atmosphere and can cause them to come apart. Neutrons that come from these fragmented atoms collide with ^{14}N atoms (the atmosphere is made mostly of nitrogen and oxygen) and convert them into ^{14}C atoms (a proton changes into a neutron).

Once ^{14}C is produced, it combines with oxygen in the atmosphere (^{12}C behaves like ^{14}C and also combines with oxygen) to form carbon dioxide (CO_2). Because CO_2 gets incorporated into plants (which means the food we eat contains ^{14}C and ^{12}C), all living things should have the same ratio of ^{14}C and ^{12}C in them as in the air we breathe.

HOW THE CARBON-14 DATING PROCESS WORKS

Once a living thing dies, the dating process begins. As long as an organism is alive it will continue to take in ^{14}C; however, when it dies, it will stop. Since ^{14}C is radioactive (decays into ^{14}N), the amount of ^{14}C in a dead organism gets less and less over time. Therefore, part of the dating process involves measuring the amount of ^{14}C that remains after some has been lost (decayed). Scientists now use a device called an "Accelerator Mass Spectrometer" (AMS) to determine the ratio of ^{14}C to ^{12}C, which increases the assumed accuracy to about 80,000 years. In order to actually do the dating, other things need to be known. Two such things include the following questions:

At death, carbon intake STOPS!

^{14}C in bone at the time of death

The amount of ^{14}C becomes less with time

Many years later

1. How fast does ^{14}C decay?

2. What was the starting amount of ^{14}C in the creature when it died?

The decay rate of radioactive elements is described in terms of half-life. The half-life of an atom is the amount of time it takes for half of the atoms in a sample to decay. The half-life of ^{14}C is 5,730 years. For example, a jar starting full of ^{14}C atoms at time zero will contain half ^{14}C atoms and half ^{14}N atoms at the end of 5,730 years (one half-life). At the end of 11,460 years (two half-lives) the jar will contain one-quarter ^{14}C atoms and three-quarter ^{14}N atoms.

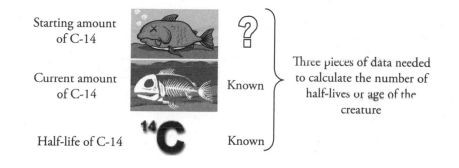

Starting amount of C-14

Current amount of C-14 — Known

Half-life of C-14 — Known

Three pieces of data needed to calculate the number of half-lives or age of the creature

Since the half-life of ^{14}C is known (how fast it decays), the only part left to determine is the starting amount of ^{14}C in a fossil. If scientists know the original amount of ^{14}C in a creature when it died, they can measure the current amount and then calculate how many half-lives have passed. Since no one was there to measure the amount of ^{14}C when a creature died, scientists need to find a method to determine how much ^{14}C has decayed.

To do this, scientists use the main isotope of carbon, called carbon-12 (^{12}C). Because ^{12}C is a stable isotope of carbon, it will remain constant; however, the amount of ^{14}C will decrease after a creature dies. All living things take in carbon (^{14}C and ^{12}C) from eating and breathing. Therefore, the ratio of ^{14}C to ^{12}C in living creatures will be the same as in the atmosphere. This ratio turns out to be about one ^{14}C atom for every 1 trillion ^{12}C atoms. Scientists can use this ratio to help determine the starting amount of ^{14}C.

When an organism dies, this ratio (1 to 1 trillion) will begin to change. The amount of ^{12}C will remain constant, but the amount of ^{14}C will become less and less. The smaller the ratio, the longer the organism has been dead. The following illustration demonstrates how the age is estimated using this ratio.

Percent ^{14}C Remaining	Percent ^{12}C Remaining	Ratio	Number of Half-Lives	Years Dead (Age of Fossil)
100	100	1 to 1T	0	0
50	100	1 to 2T	1	5,730
25	100	1 to 4T	2	11,460
12.5	100	1 to 8T	3	17,190
6.25	100	1 to 16T	4	22,920
3.125	100	1 to 32T	5	28,650

T = Trillion

A Critical Assumption

A critical assumption used in carbon-14 dating has to do with this ratio. It is assumed that the ratio of ^{14}C to ^{12}C in the atmosphere has always been the same as it is today (1 to 1 trillion). If this assumption is true, then the AMS ^{14}C dating method is valid up to about 80,000 years. Beyond this number, the instruments scientists use would not be able to detect enough remaining ^{14}C to be useful in age estimates. This is a critical assumption in the dating process. If this assumption is not true, then the method will give incorrect dates. What could cause this ratio to change? If the production rate of ^{14}C in the atmosphere is not equal to the removal rate (mostly through decay), this ratio will change. In other words, the amount of ^{14}C being produced in the atmosphere must equal the amount being removed to be in a steady state (also called "equilibrium"). If this is not true, the ratio of ^{14}C to ^{12}C is not a constant, which would make knowing the starting amount of ^{14}C in a specimen difficult or impossible to accurately determine.

Dr. Willard Libby, the founder of the carbon-14 dating method, assumed this ratio to be constant. His reasoning was based on a belief in evolution, which assumes the earth must be billions of years old. Assumptions in the scientific community are extremely important. If the starting assumption is false, all the calculations based on that assumption might be correct but still give a wrong conclusion. In Dr. Libby's original work, he noted that the atmosphere did not appear to be in equilibrium. This was a troubling idea for Dr. Libby since he believed the world was billions of years old and enough time had passed to achieve equilibrium. Dr. Libby's calculations showed that if the earth started with no ^{14}C in the atmosphere, it would take up to 30,000 years to build up to a steady state (equilibrium).

If the cosmic radiation has remained at its present intensity for 20,000 or 30,000 years, and if the carbon reservoir has not changed appreciably in this time, then there exists at the present time a complete balance between the rate of disintegration of radiocarbon atoms and the rate of assimilation of new radiocarbon atoms for all material in the life-cycle.[2]

Dr. Libby chose to ignore this discrepancy (nonequilibrium state), and he attributed it to experimental error. However, the discrepancy has turned out to be very real. The ratio of $^{14}C / ^{12}C$ is not constant.

The Specific Production Rate (SPR) of C-14 is known to be 18.8 atoms per gram of total carbon per minute. The Specific Decay Rate (SDR) is known to be only 16.1 disintegrations per gram per minute.[3]

What does this mean? If it takes about 30,000 years to reach equilibrium and ^{14}C is still out of equilibrium, then maybe the earth is not very old.

Magnetic Field of the Earth

Other factors can affect the production rate of ^{14}C in the atmosphere. The earth has a magnetic field around it which helps protect us from harmful radiation from outer space. This magnetic field is decaying (getting weaker). The stronger the field is around the earth, the fewer the number of cosmic rays that are able to reach the atmosphere. This would result in a smaller production of ^{14}C in the atmosphere in earth's past.

The cause for the long term variation of the C-14 level is not known. The variation is certainly partially the result of a change in the cosmic ray production rate of radiocarbon. The cosmic-ray flux, and hence the production rate of C-14, is a function not only of the solar activity but also of the magnetic dipole moment of the Earth.[4]

Though complex, this history of the earth's magnetic field agrees with Barnes' basic hypothesis, that the field has always freely decayed … . The field has always been losing energy despite its variations, so it cannot be more than 10,000 years old.[5]

[2] W. Libby, *Radiocarbon Dating*, Univ. of Chicago Press, Chicago, Illinois, 1952, 8.
[3] C. Sewell, "Carbon-14 and the Age of the Earth," 1999, www.rae.org/pdf/bits23.pdf.
[4] M. Stuiver and H. Suess, On the relationship between radiocarbon dates and true sample ages, *Radiocarbon* vol. 8, 1966, 535.
[5] D.R. Humphreys, The mystery of earth's magnetic field, ICR *Impact #292*, Feb 1, 1989. www.icr.org/article/292.

Earth's magnetic field is fading. Today it is about 10 percent weaker than it was when German mathematician Carl Friedrich Gauss started keeping tabs on it in 1845, scientists say.[6]

If the production rate of ^{14}C in the atmosphere was less in the past, dates given using the carbon-14 method would incorrectly assume that more ^{14}C had decayed out of a specimen than what has actually occurred. This would result in giving older dates than the true age.

Genesis Flood

What role might the Genesis Flood have played in the amount of carbon? The Flood would have buried large amounts of carbon from living organisms (plant and animal) to form today's fossil fuels (coal, oil, etc.). The amount of fossil fuels indicates there must have been a vastly larger quantity of vegetation in existence prior to the Flood than exists today. This means that the biosphere just prior to the Flood might have had 500 times more carbon in living organisms than today. This would further dilute the amount of ^{14}C and cause the ^{14}C /^{12}C ratio to be much smaller than today.

> If that were the case, and this C-14 were distributed uniformly throughout the biosphere, and the total amount of biosphere C were, for example, 500 times that of today's world, the resulting C-14/C-12 ratio would be 1/500 of today's level ... .[7]

When the Flood is taken into account, along with the decay of the magnetic field, it is reasonable to believe that the assumption of equilibrium is a false assumption. Because of this false assumption, any age estimates using ^{14}C on organic material that dates from prior to the Flood will give much older dates than the true ages. Pre-Flood organic materials would be dated at perhaps ten times the true age.

The RATE Group Findings

In 1997 an eight-year research project was started to investigate the age of the earth. The group was called the RATE group (Radioisotopes and the Age of The Earth). The team of scientists included:

---

[6] J. Roach, *National Geographic News*, September 9, 2004.
[7] J.R. Baumgarder, C-14 evidence for a recent global Flood and a young earth, in L. Vardiman, A.A. Snelling, and E.F. Chaffin (Eds.), *Radioisotopes and the Age of the Earth: Results of a Young-Earth Creationist Research Initiative*, Institute for Creation Research, Santee, California, and Creation Research Society, Chino Valley, Arizona, 2005, 618.

Larry Vardiman, PhD Atmospheric Science
Russell Humphreys, PhD Physics
Eugene Chaffin, PhD Physics
Donald DeYoung, PhD Physics
John Baumgardner, PhD Geophysics
Steven Austin, PhD Geology
Andrew Snelling, PhD Geology
Steven Boyd, PhD Hebraic and Cognate Studies

The objective was to gather data commonly ignored or censored by evolutionary standards of dating. The scientists reviewed the assumptions and procedures used in estimating the ages of rocks and fossils. The results of the carbon-14 dating demonstrated serious problems for long geologic ages. For example, a series of fossilized wood samples that conventionally have been dated according to their host strata to be from Tertiary to Permian (40-250 million years old) all yielded significant, detectable levels of carbon-14 that would conventionally equate to only 30,000-45,000 years "ages" for the original trees.[8] Similarly, a survey of the conventional radiocarbon journals resulted in more than forty examples of supposedly ancient organic materials, including limestones, that contained carbon-14, as reported by leading laboratories.[9]

Samples were then taken from ten different coal layers that, according to evolutionists, represent different time periods in the geologic column (Cenozoic, Mesozoic, and Paleozoic). The RATE group obtained these ten coal samples from the U.S. Department of Energy Coal Sample Bank, from samples collected from major coalfields across the United States. The chosen coal samples, which dated millions to hundreds of millions of years old based on standard evolution time estimates, all contained measurable amounts of ^{14}C. In all cases, careful precautions were taken to eliminate any possibility of contamination from other sources. Samples, in all three "time periods," displayed

---

[8] A.A. Snelling, Radioactive "dating" in conflict! Fossil wood in ancient lava flow yields radiocarbon, *Creation Ex Nihilo* **20**(1):24–27, 1997; A.A. Snelling, Stumping old-age dogma: Radiocarbon in an "ancient" fossil tree stump casts doubt on traditional rock/fossil dating, *Creation Ex Nihilo* **20**(4):48–51, 1998; A.A. Snelling, Dating dilemma: Fossil wood in ancient sandstone: *Creation Ex Nihilo* **21**(3):39–41, 1992; A.A. Snelling, Geological conflict: Young radiocarbon date for ancient fossil wood challenges fossil dating, *Creation Ex Nihilo* **22**(2):44–47, 2000; A.A. Snelling, Conflicting "ages" of Tertiary basalt and contained fossilized wood, Crinum, central Queensland, Australia, *Creation Ex Nihilo Technical Journal* **14**(2):99–122, 2000.

[9] P. Giem, Carbon-14 content of fossil carbon, *Origins* **51**:6–30, 2001.

significant amounts of ^{14}C. This is a significant discovery. Since the half-life of ^{14}C is relatively short (5,730 years), there should be no detectable ^{14}C left after about 100,000 years. The average ^{14}C estimated age for all the layers from these three time periods was approximately 50,000 years. However, using a more realistic pre-Flood ^{14}C /^{12}C ratio reduces that age to about 5,000 years.

These results indicate that the entire fossil-bearing geologic column is much less than 100,000 years old—and even much younger. This confirms the Bible and challenges the evolutionary idea of long geologic ages.

> Because the lifetime of C-14 is so brief, these AMS [Accelerator Mass Spectrometer] measurements pose an obvious challenge to the standard geological timescale that assigns millions to hundreds of millions of years to this part of the rock layer. [10]

Another noteworthy observation from the RATE group was the amount of ^{14}C found in diamonds. Secular scientists have estimated the ages of diamonds to be millions to billions of years old using other radiometric dating methods. These methods are also based on questionable assumptions and are discussed elsewhere.[11] Because of their hardness, diamonds (the hardest known substance) are extremely resistant to contamination through chemical exchange. Since diamonds are considered to be so old by evolutionary

---

[10] J.R. Baumgardner, ibid., 587.
[11] M. Riddle, Does radiometric dating prove the earth is old?, in K.A. Ham (Ed.), *The New Answers Book*, Master Books, Green Forest, Arkansas, pp. 113–124, 2006.

standards, finding any ^{14}C in them would be strong support for a recent creation.

The RATE group analyzed twelve diamond samples for possible carbon-14 content. Similar to the coal results, all twelve diamond samples contained detectable, but lower levels of ^{14}C. These findings are powerful evidence that coal and diamonds cannot be the millions or billions of years old that evolutionists claim. Indeed, these RATE findings of detectable ^{14}C in diamonds have been confirmed independently.[12] Carbon-14 found in fossils at all layers of the geologic column, in coal and in diamonds, is evidence which confirms the biblical timescale of thousands of years and not billions.

Because of C-14's short half-life, such a finding would argue that carbon and probably the entire physical earth as well must have a recent origin.[13]

Conclusion

All radiometric dating methods are based on assumptions about events that happened in the past. If the assumptions are accepted as true (as is typically done in the evolutionary dating processes), results can be biased toward a desired age. In the reported ages given in textbooks and other journals, these evolutionary assumptions have not been questioned, while results inconsistent with long ages have been censored. When the assumptions are evaluated and shown to be faulty, the results support the biblical account of a global Flood and young earth. Thus Christians should not be afraid of radiometric dating methods. Carbon-14 dating is really the friend of Christians, because it supports a young earth.

The RATE scientists are convinced that the popular idea attributed to geologist Charles Lyell from nearly two centuries ago, "The present is the key to the past," is simply not valid for an earth history of millions or billions of years. An alternative interpretation of the carbon-14 data is that the earth experienced a global flood catastrophe which laid down most of the rock strata and fossils … . Whatever the source of the carbon-14, its presence in nearly every sample tested worldwide is a strong challenge to an ancient age. Carbon-14 data is now firmly on the side of the young-earth view of history.[14]

---

[12] R.E. Taylor, and J. Southon, Use of natural diamonds to monitor ^{14}C AMS instrument backgrounds, *Nuclear Instruments and Methods in Physics Research B* **259**:282–287, 2007.
[13] J.R. Baumgardner, ibid., 609.
[14] D. DeYoung, *Thousands…Not Billions*, Master Books, Green Forest, Arkansas, 2005, 61.

8

Could God Really Have Created Everything in Six Days?

KEN HAM

Why Is It Important?

If the days of creation are really geologic ages of millions of years, then the gospel message is undermined at its foundation because it puts death, disease, thorns, and suffering *before* the Fall. The effort to define "days" as "geologic ages" results from an erroneous approach to Scripture—reinterpreting the Word of God on the basis of the fallible theories of sinful people.

It is a good exercise to read Genesis 1 and try to put aside outside influences that may cause you to have a predetermined idea of what the word "day" may mean. Just let the words of the passage speak to you.

Taking Genesis 1 in this way, at face value, without doubt it says that God created the universe, the earth, the sun, moon and stars, plants and animals, and the first two people within six ordinary (approximately 24-hour) days. Being really honest, you would have to admit that you could never get the idea of millions of years from reading this passage.

The majority of Christians (including many Christian leaders) in the Western world, however, do not insist that these days of creation were ordinary-length days, and many of them accept and teach, based on outside influences, that they must have been long periods of time—even millions or billions of years.

How Does God Communicate to Us?

God communicates through language. When He made the first man, Adam, He had already "programmed" him with a language, so there could be communication. Human language consists of words used in a specific context that relates to the entire reality around us.

Thus, God can reveal things to man, and man can communicate with God, because words have meaning and convey an understandable message. If this were not so, how could any of us communicate with each other or with God?

Why "Long Days"?

Romans 3:4 declares: "Let God be true, and every man a liar."

In *every* instance where someone has not accepted the "days" of creation to be ordinary days, they have *not* allowed the words of Scripture to speak to them in context, as the language requires for communication. They have been influenced by ideas from *outside* of Scripture. Thus, they have set a precedent that could allow any word to be reinterpreted by the preconceived ideas of the person reading the words. Ultimately, this will lead to a communication breakdown, as the same words in the same context could mean different things to different people.

The Church Fathers

Most church fathers accepted the days of creation as ordinary days.[1] It is true that some of the early church fathers did not teach the days of creation as

---

[1] M. Van Bebber and P. Taylor, *Creation and Time: A Report on the Progressive Creationist Book by Hugh Ross,* Films for Christ, Mesa, Arizona, 1994.

ordinary days—but many of them had been influenced by Greek philosophy, which caused them to interpret the days as allegorical. They reasoned that the creation days were related to God's activities, and God being timeless meant that the days could not be related to human time.[2] In contrast to today's allegorizers, they could not accept that God took *as long as* six days.

Thus, the non-literal days resulted from extrabiblical influences (i.e., influences from *outside* the Bible), not from the words of the Bible.

This approach has affected the way people interpret Scripture to this day. As the man who started the Reformation said,

> The days of creation were ordinary days in length. We must understand that these days were actual days *(veros dies),* contrary to the opinion of the Holy Fathers. Whenever we observe that the opinions of the Fathers disagree with Scripture, we reverently bear with them and acknowledge them to be our elders. Nevertheless, we do not depart from the authority of Scripture for their sake.[3]

Today's Church Leaders

Many church leaders today do *not* accept the creation days as ordinary earth-rotation days. However, when their reasons are investigated, we find that influences from *outside* of Scripture (particularly belief in a billions-of-years-old universe) are the ultimate cause.

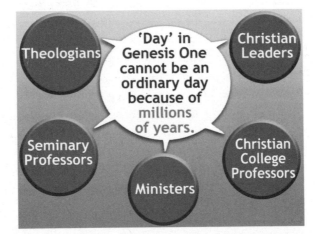

[2] G. Hasel, The "days" of creation in Genesis 1: literal "days" or figurative "periods/epochs" of time? *Origins* **21**(1):5–38, 1994.
[3] Martin Luther as cited in E. Plass, *What Martin Luther Says: A Practical In-Home Anthology for the Active Christian,* Concordia Publishing House, St. Louis, Missouri, 1991, 1523.

Again and again, such leaders admit that Genesis 1, taken in a straightforward way, seems to teach six ordinary days. But they then say that this cannot be because of the age of the universe or some other extrabiblical reason.

Consider the following representative quotes from Bible scholars who are considered to be conservative yet who do not accept the days of creation as ordinary-length days:

> From a superficial reading of Genesis 1, the impression would seem to be that the entire creative process took place in six twenty-four-hour days. ... This seems to run counter to modern scientific research, which indicates that the planet Earth was created several billion years ago.[4]

> We have shown the possibility of God's having formed the Earth and its life in a series of creative days representing long periods. In view of the apparent age of the Earth, this is not only possible—it is probable.[5]

It is as if these theologians view "nature" as a "67th book of the Bible," albeit with more authority than the 66 written books. Rather, we should consider the words of Charles Haddon Spurgeon, the renowned "prince of preachers," in 1877:

> We are invited, brethren, most earnestly to go away from the old-fashioned belief of our forefathers because of the supposed discoveries of science. What is science? The method by which man tries to conceal his ignorance. It should not be so, but so it is. You are not to be dogmatical in theology, my brethren, it is wicked; but for scientific men it is the correct thing. You are never to assert anything very strongly; but scientists may boldly assert what they cannot prove, and may demand a faith far more credulous than any we possess. Forsooth, you and I are to take our Bibles and shape and mould our belief according to the ever-shifting teachings of so-called scientific men. What folly is this! Why, the march of science, falsely so called, through the world may be traced by exploded fallacies and abandoned theories. Former explorers once adored are now ridiculed; the continual wreckings of false hypotheses is a matter of universal notoriety. You may tell where the learned have encamped by the debris left behind of suppositions and theories as plentiful as broken bottles.[6]

---

[4] G. Archer, *A Survey of Old Testament Introduction,* Moody Press, Chicago, 1994, 196–197.
[5] J. Boice, *Genesis: An Expositional Commentary,* Vol. 1, Genesis 1:1–11, Zondervan Publishing House, Grand Rapids, 1982, 68.
[6] C.H. Spurgeon, *The Sword and the Trowel,* 1877, 197.

Those who would use historical science (as propounded by people who, by and large, ignore God's written revelation) to interpret the Bible, to teach us things about God, have matters front to back. Because we are fallen, fallible creatures, we need God's written Word, illuminated by the Holy Spirit, to properly understand natural history. The respected systematic theologian Berkhof said:

> Since the entrance of sin into the world, man can gather true knowledge about God from His general revelation only if he studies it in the light of Scripture, in which the elements of God's original self-revelation, which were obscured and perverted by the blight of sin, are republished, corrected, and interpreted. ... Some are inclined to speak of God's general revelation as a second source; but this is hardly correct in view of the fact that nature can come into consideration here only as interpreted in the light of Scripture.[7]

In other words, Christians should build their thinking on the Bible, not on science.

The "Days" of Genesis 1

What does the Bible tell us about the meaning of "day" in Genesis 1? A word can have more than one meaning, depending on the context. For instance, the English word "day" can have perhaps 14 different meanings. For example, consider the following sentence: "Back in my grandfather's day, it took 12 days to drive across the country during the day."

Here the first occurrence of "day" means "time" in a general sense. The second "day," where a number is used, refers to an ordinary day, and the third refers to the daylight portion of the 24-hour period. The point is that words can have more than one meaning, depending on the context.

To understand the meaning of "day" in Genesis 1, we

Back in my grandfather's **day**, it took 12 **days** to drive across the country during the **day**.

ARE WE THERE YET?

---

7   L. Berkhof, Introductory volume to *Systematic Theology*, Wm. B. Eerdmans, Grand Rapids, Michigan, 1946, 60, 96.

need to determine how the Hebrew word for "day," *yom,* is used in the context of Scripture. Consider the following:

- A typical concordance will illustrate that *yom* can have a range of meanings: a period of light as contrasted to night, a 24-hour period, time, a specific point of time, or a year.

- A classic, well-respected Hebrew-English lexicon[8] (a dictionary) has seven headings and many subheadings for the meaning of *yom*—but it defines the creation days of Genesis 1 as ordinary days under the heading "day as defined by evening and morning."

- A number and the phrase "evening and morning" are used with each of the six days of creation (Gen. 1:5, 8, 13, 19, 23, 31).

- Outside Genesis 1, *yom* is used with a number 359 times, and each time it means an ordinary day.[9] Why would Genesis 1 be the exception?[10]

- Outside Genesis 1, *yom* is used with the word "evening" or "morning"[11] 23 times. "Evening" and "morning" appear in association, but without *yom,* 38 times. All 61 times the text refers to an ordinary day. Why would Genesis 1 be the exception?[12]

- In Genesis 1:5, *yom* occurs in context with the word "night." Outside of Genesis 1, "night" is used with *yom* 53 times, and each time it means an ordinary day. Why would Genesis 1 be the exception? Even the usage of the word "light" with *yom* in this passage determines the meaning as ordinary day.[13]

- The plural of *yom,* which does not appear in Genesis 1, *can* be used to communicate a longer time period, such as "in those days."[14] Adding a

---

8 F. Brown, S. Driver, and C. Briggs, *A Hebrew and English Lexicon of the Old Testament,* Clarendon Press, Oxford, 1951, 398.

9 Some say that Hosea 6:2 is an exception to this because of the figurative language. However, the Hebrew idiomatic expression used, "After two days ... in the third day," meaning "in a short time," makes sense only if "day" is understood in its normal sense.

10 J. Stambaugh, The days of creation: a semantic approach, *TJ* 5(1):70–78, April 1991. Available online at www.answersingenesis.org/go/days.

11 The Jews start their day in the evening (sundown followed by night), obviously based on the fact that Genesis begins the day with the "evening."

12 Stambaugh, The days of creation: a semantic approach, 75.

13 Ibid., 72.

14 Ibid., 72–73.

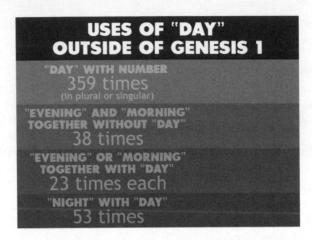

**USES OF "DAY"
OUTSIDE OF GENESIS 1**

"DAY" WITH NUMBER
359 times
(in plural or singular)

"EVENING" AND "MORNING"
TOGETHER WITHOUT "DAY"
38 times

"EVENING" OR "MORNING"
TOGETHER WITH "DAY"
23 times each

"NIGHT" WITH "DAY"
53 times

number here would be nonsensical. Clearly, in Exodus 20:11, where a number is used with "days," it unambiguously refers to six earth-rotation days.

- There are words in biblical Hebrew (such as *olam* or *qedem*) that are very suitable for communicating long periods of time, or indefinite time, but *none* of these words are used in Genesis 1.[15] Alternatively, the days or years could have been compared with grains of sand if long periods were meant.

Dr. James Barr (Regius Professor of Hebrew at Oxford University), who himself does not believe Genesis is true history, nonetheless admitted as far as the language of Genesis 1 is concerned that

> So far as I know, there is no professor of Hebrew or Old Testament at any world-class university who does not believe that the writer(s) of Gen. 1–11 intended to convey to their readers the ideas that (a) creation took place in a series of six days which were the same as the days of 24 hours we now experience (b) the figures contained in the Genesis genealogies provided by simple addition a chronology from the beginning of the world up to later stages in the biblical story (c) Noah's Flood was understood to be worldwide and extinguish all human and animal life except for those in the ark.[16]

---

[15] Stambaugh, The days of creation: a semantic approach, 73–74.
[16] J. Barr, personal letter to David Watson, April 23, 1984.

In like manner, nineteenth century liberal Professor Marcus Dods, New College, Edinburgh, said,

> If, for example, the word "day" in these chapters does not mean a period of twenty-four hours, the interpretation of Scripture is hopeless.[17]

Conclusion About "Day" in Genesis 1

If we are prepared to let the words of the language speak to us in accord with the context and normal definitions, without being influenced by outside ideas, then the word for "day" found in Genesis 1—which is qualified by a number, the phrase "evening and morning" and for Day 1 the words "light and darkness"—*obviously* means an ordinary day (about 24 hours).

In Martin Luther's day, some of the church fathers were saying that God created everything in only one day or in an instant. Martin Luther wrote,

> When Moses writes that God created Heaven and Earth and whatever is in them in six days, then let this period continue to have been six days, and do not venture to devise any comment according to which six days were one day. But, if you cannot understand how this could have been done in six days, then grant the Holy Spirit the honor of being more learned than you are. For you are to deal with Scripture in such a way that you bear in mind that God Himself says what is written. But since God is speaking, it is not fitting for you wantonly to turn His Word in the direction you wish to go.[18]

Similarly, John Calvin stated, "Albeit the duration of the world, now declining to its ultimate end, has not yet attained six thousand years. ... God's work was completed not in a moment but in six days."[19]

Luther and Calvin were the backbone of the Protestant Reformation that called the church back to Scripture—*Sola Scriptura* (Scripture alone). Both of these men were adamant that Genesis 1 taught six ordinary days of creation—only thousands of years ago.

---

[17] M. Dods, *Expositor's Bible*, T & T Clark, Edinburgh, 1888, 4, as cited by D. Kelly, *Creation and Change*, Christian Focus Publications, Fearn, Scotland, 1997, 112.
[18] Plass, *What Martin Luther Says: A Practical In-Home Anthology for the Active Christian*, 1523.
[19] J. McNeil, Ed., *Calvin: Institutes of the Christian Religion 1*, Westminster Press, Louisville, Kentucky, 1960, 160–161, 182.

Why Six Days?

Exodus 31:12 says that God commanded Moses to say to the children of Israel:

> Six days may work be done, but on the seventh is the sabbath of rest, holy to the Lord. Whoever does any work in the Sabbath day, he shall surely be put to death. Therefore the sons of Israel shall keep the Sabbath, to observe the Sabbath throughout their generations, for an everlasting covenant. It is a sign between me and the sons of Israel forever. For in six days the Lord made the heavens and the earth, and on the seventh day He rested, and was refreshed (Exodus 31:15–17).

Then God gave Moses two tablets of stone upon which were written the commandments of God, written by the finger of God (Exodus 31:18).

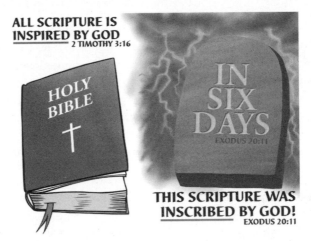

ALL SCRIPTURE IS INSPIRED BY GOD
—————— 2 TIMOTHY 3:16

HOLY BIBLE

IN SIX DAYS
EXODUS 20:11

THIS SCRIPTURE WAS INSCRIBED BY GOD!
—————— EXODUS 20:11

Because God is infinite in power and wisdom, there's no doubt He could have created the universe and its contents in no time at all, or six seconds, or six minutes, or six hours—after all, with God nothing shall be impossible (Luke 1:37).

However, the question to ask is, "Why did God take so long? Why as long as six days?" The answer is also given in Exodus 20:11, and that answer is the basis of the Fourth Commandment:

> For *in* six days the LORD made the heavens and the earth, the sea, and all that *is* in them, and rested the seventh day. Therefore the LORD blessed the Sabbath day and hallowed it.

The seven-day week has no basis outside of Scripture. In this Old Testament passage, God commands His people, Israel, to work for six days and rest for one—thus giving us a reason why He deliberately took as long as six days to create everything. He set the example for man. Our week is patterned after this principle. Now if He created everything in six thousand (or six million) years, followed by a rest of one thousand or one million years, then we would have a very interesting week indeed.

Some say that Exodus 20:11 is only an analogy in the sense that man is to work and rest—not that it was to mean six literal ordinary days followed by one literal ordinary day. However, Bible scholars have shown that this commandment "does not use analogy or archetypal thinking but that its emphasis is 'stated in terms of the imitation of God or a divine precedent that is to be followed.'"[20] In other words, it was to be six literal days of work, followed by one literal day of rest, just as God worked for six literal days and rested for one.

Some have argued that "the heavens and the earth" is just earth and perhaps the solar system, not the whole universe. However, this verse clearly says that God made *everything* in six days—six consecutive ordinary days, just like the commandment in the previous verse to work for six consecutive ordinary days.

The phrase "heaven(s) and earth" in Scripture is an example of a figure of speech called a *merism*, where two opposites are combined into an all-encompassing single concept, in this case the totality of creation. A linguistic analysis of the words "heaven(s) and earth" in Scripture shows that they refer to the totality of all creation (the Hebrews did not have a word for "universe"). For example, in Genesis 14:19 God is called "Creator of heaven and earth." In Jeremiah 23:24 God speaks of Himself as filling "heaven and earth." See also Genesis 14:22; 2 Kings 19:15; 2 Chronicles 2:12; Psalms 115:15, 121:2, 124:8, 134:3, 146:6; and Isaiah 37:16.

---

[20] G. Hasel, The "days" of creation in Genesis 1: literal "days" or figurative "periods/epochs" of time? *Origins* **21**(1):29, 1994.

Thus, there is no scriptural warrant for restricting Exodus 20:11 to earth and its atmosphere or the solar system alone. So Exodus 20:11 does show that the whole universe was created in six ordinary days.

Implication

As the days of creation are ordinary days in length, then by adding up the years in Scripture (assuming no gaps in the genealogies[21]), the age of the universe is only about six thousand years.[22]

Refuting Common Objections to Six Literal Days

OBJECTION 1

"Science" has shown the earth and universe are billions of years old; therefore the "days" of creation must be long periods (or indefinite periods) of time.

ANSWER

a. The age of the earth, as determined by man's fallible methods, is based on unproven assumptions, so it is not proven that the earth is billions of years old.[23]

b. This unproven age is being used to force an interpretation on the language of the Bible. Thus, man's fallible theories are allowed to interpret the Bible. This ultimately undermines the use of language to communicate.

---

[21] J. Whitcomb and H. Morris, *The Genesis Flood,* Presbyterian and Reformed Publ., Phillipsburg, New Jersey, 1961, 481–483, Appendix II. They allow for the possibility of gaps in the genealogies because the word "begat" can skip generations. However, they point out that even allowing for gaps would give a maximum age of around 10,000 years.

[22] L. Pierce, The forgotten archbishop, *Creation* **20**(2):42–43, 1998. Ussher carried out a very scholarly work in adding up all the years in Scripture to obtain a date of creation of 4004 BC. Ussher has been mocked for stating that creation occurred on October 23—he obtained this date by working backward using the Jewish civil year and accounting for how the year and month were derived over the years. Thus, he didn't just pull this date out of the air but gave a scholarly mathematical basis for it. This is not to say this is the correct date, as there are assumptions involved, but the point is, his work is not to be scoffed at. Ussher did *not* specify the hour of the day for creation, as some skeptics assert. Young's *Analytical Concordance,* under "creation," lists many other authorities, including extrabiblical ones, who all give a date for creation of less than 10,000 years ago.

[23] See chapters 7 and 9 on these dating methods to see the assumptions involved. See also H. Morris and J. Morris, *Science, Scripture, and the Young Earth,* Institute for Creation Research, El Cajon, California, 1989, 39–44; J. Morris, *The Young Earth,* Master Books, Green Forest, Arkansas, 1996, 51–67; S. Austin, *Grand Canyon: Monument to Catastrophe,* Institute for Creation Research, El Cajon, California, pp. 1994, 111–131; L. Vardiman, ed., *Radio Isotopes and the Age of the Earth,* Vol. 2, Master Books, Green Forest, Arkansas, 2005.

c. Evolutionary scientists claim the fossil layers over the earth's surface date back hundreds of millions of years. As soon as one allows millions of years for the fossil layers, then one has accepted death, bloodshed, disease, thorns, and suffering before Adam's sin.

The Bible makes it clear[24] that death, bloodshed, disease, thorns, and suffering are a *consequence* of sin.[25] In Genesis 1:29–30, God gave Adam and Eve and the animals plants to eat (this is reading Genesis at face value, as literal history, as Jesus did in Matthew 19:3–6). In fact, there is a theological distinction made between animals and plants. Human beings and higher animals are described in Genesis 1 as having a *nephesh,* or life principle. (This is true of at least the vertebrate land animals as well as the birds and fish: Genesis 1:20, 24.) Plants do not have this *nephesh*—they are not "alive" in the same sense animals are. They were given for food.

Man was permitted to eat meat only after the Flood (Genesis 9:3). This makes it obvious that the statements in Genesis 1:29–30 were meant to inform us that man and the animals were vegetarian to start with. Also, in Genesis 9:2, we are told of a change God apparently made in the way animals react to man.

God warned Adam in Genesis 2:17 that if he ate of the "tree of the knowledge of good and evil" he would "die." The Hebrew grammar actually means, "dying, you will die." In other words, it would be the commencement of a process of physical dying (see Genesis 3:19). It also clearly involved spiritual death (separation from God).

After Adam disobeyed God, the Lord clothed Adam and Eve with "coats of skins" (Genesis 3:21).[26] To do this He must have killed and shed the blood of at least one animal. The reason for this can be summed up by Hebrews 9:22:

---

[24] K. Ham, *The Lie: Evolution,* Master Books, Green Forest, Arkansas, Introduction, 1987, xiii–xiv; K. Ham, The necessity for believing in six literal days, *Creation* 18(1):38–41, 1996; K. Ham, The wrong way round! *Creation* 18(3):38–41, 1996; K. Ham, Fathers, promises and vegemite, *Creation* 19(1):14–17, 1997; K. Ham, The narrow road, *Creation* 19(2):47–49, 1997; K. Ham, Millions of years and the "doctrine of Balaam," *Creation* 19(3):15–17, 1997.

[25] J. Gill, *A Body of Doctrinal and Practical Divinity,* 1760. Republished by Primitive Baptist Library, Carthage, Illinois, 1980, 191. This is not just a new idea from modern scholars. In 1760 John Gill, in his commentaries, insisted there was no death, bloodshed, disease, or suffering before sin.

[26] All Eve's progeny, except the God-man Jesus Christ, were born with original sin (Romans 5:12, 18–19), so Eve could not have conceived when she was sinless. So the Fall must have occurred fairly quickly, before Eve had conceived any children (they were told to "be fruitful and multiply").

And according to the law almost all things are purified with blood, and without shedding of blood there is no remission.

God requires the shedding of blood for the remission of sins. What happened in the garden was a picture of what was to come in Jesus Christ, who shed His blood on the Cross as the Lamb of God who took away the sin of the world (John 1:29).

Now if the Garden of Eden were sitting on a fossil record of dead things millions of years old, then blood was shed *before* sin. This would destroy the foundation of the Atonement. The Bible is clear: the sin of Adam brought death and suffering into the world. As Romans 8:19–22 tells us, the whole of creation "groans" because of the effects of the fall of Adam, and the creation will be liberated "from the bondage of corruption into the glorious liberty of the children of

God" (Rom. 8:21). Also, bear in mind that thorns came into existence after the Curse. Because there are thorns in the fossil record, it had to be formed after Adam and Eve sinned.

The pronouncement of the death penalty on Adam was both a curse and a blessing. A curse because death is horrible and continually reminds us of the ugliness of sin; a blessing because it meant the consequences of sin—separation from fellowship with God—need not be eternal. Death stopped Adam and his descendants from living in a state of sin, with all its consequences, forever. And because death was the just penalty for sin, Jesus Christ suffered physical death, shedding His blood, to release Adam's descendants from the consequences of sin. The Apostle Paul discusses this in depth in Romans 5 and 1 Corinthians 15.

Revelation 21–22 makes it clear that there will be a "new heavens and a new earth" one day, where there will be "no more death" and "no more

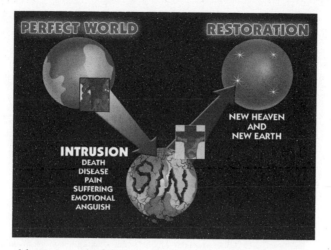

curse"—just like it was before sin changed everything. If there are to be animals as part of the new earth, obviously they will not be dying or eating each other, nor eating the redeemed people!

Thus, adding the supposed millions of years to Scripture destroys the foundations of the message of the Cross.

OBJECTION 2

According to Genesis 1, the sun was not created until Day 4. How could there be day and night (ordinary days) without the sun for the first three days?

ANSWER

a. Again, it is important for us to let the language of God's Word speak to us. If we come to Genesis 1 without any outside influences, as has been shown, each of the six days of creation appears with the Hebrew word *yom* qualified by a number and the phrase "evening and morning." The first three days are written the *same* way as the next three. So if we let the language speak to us, all six days were ordinary earth days.

b. The sun is not needed for day and night. What is needed is light and a rotating earth. On the first day of creation, God made light (Genesis 1:3). The phrase "evening and morning" certainly implies a rotating earth. Thus, if we have light from one direction, and a spinning earth, there can be day and night.

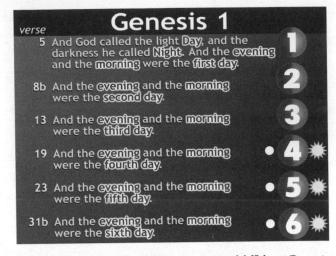

Genesis 1

verse

5 And God called the light **Day**, and the darkness he called **Night**. And the **evening** and the **morning** were the **first day**.

8b And the **evening** and the **morning** were the **second day**.

13 And the **evening** and the **morning** were the **third day**.

19 And the **evening** and the **morning** were the **fourth day**.

23 And the **evening** and the **morning** were the **fifth day**.

31b And the **evening** and the **morning** were the **sixth day**.

Where did the light come from? We are not told,[27] but Genesis 1:3 certainly indicates it was a created light to provide day and night until God made the sun on Day 4 to rule the day. Revelation 21:23 tells us that one day the sun will not be needed because the glory of God will light the heavenly city.

Perhaps one reason God did it this way was to illustrate that the sun did not have the priority in the creation that people have tended to give it. The sun did not give birth to the earth as evolutionary theories postulate; the sun was God's created tool to rule the day that God had made (Genesis 1:16).

Down through the ages, people such as the Egyptians have worshiped the sun. God warned the Israelites, in Deuteronomy 4:19, not to worship the sun as the pagan cultures around them did. They were commanded to worship the God who made the sun—not the sun that was *made* by God.

Evolutionary theories (the "big bang" hypothesis for instance) state that the sun came before the earth and that the sun's energy on the earth eventually gave rise to life. Just as in pagan beliefs, the sun is, in a sense, given credit for the wonder of creation.

It is interesting to contrast the speculations of modern cosmology with the writings of the early church father Theophilus:

On the fourth day the luminaries came into existence. Since God has foreknowledge, he understood the nonsense of the foolish philosophers

---

[27] Some people ask why God did not tell us the source of this light. However, if God told us everything, we would have so many books we would not have time to read them. God has given us all the information we need to come to the right conclusions about the things that really matter.

who were going to say that the things produced on Earth came from the stars, so that they might set God aside. In order therefore that the truth might be demonstrated, plants and seeds came into existence before stars. For what comes into existence later cannot cause what is prior to it.[28]

OBJECTION 3

2 Peter 3:8 states that "one day is with the Lord as a thousand years," therefore the days of creation could be long periods of time.

ANSWER

a. This passage has *no* creation context—it is *not* referring to Genesis or the six days of creation.

b. This verse has what is called a "comparative article"—"as" or "like"—which is not found in Genesis 1. In other words, it is *not* saying a day *is* a thousand years; it is comparing a real, literal day to a real, literal thousand years. The context of this passage is the Second Coming of Christ. It is saying that, to God, a day is *like* a thousand years, because God is outside of time. God is not limited by natural processes and time as humans are. What may seem like a long time to us (e.g., waiting for the Second Coming), or a short time, is nothing to God, either way.

c. The second part of the verse reads "and a thousand years as one day," which, in essence, cancels out the first part of the verse for those who

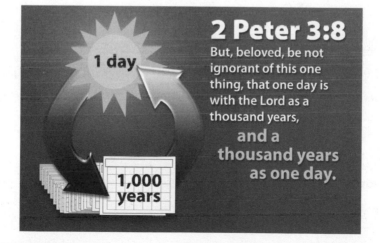

---

[28] L. Lavallee, The early church defended creation science, *Impact*, No. 160, p. ii, 1986. Quotation from *Theophilus "To Autolycus,"* 2.8, Oxford Early Christian Texts.

want to equate a day with a thousand years. Thus, it cannot be saying a day is a thousand years or vice versa.

d. Psalm 90:4 states, "For a thousand years in your sight are as yesterday when it is past, and as a watch in the night." Here a thousand years is being compared with a "watch in the night" (four hours[29]). Because the phrase "watch in the night" is joined in a particular way to "yesterday," it is saying that a thousand years is being compared with a short period of time—not simply to a day.

e. If one used this passage to claim that "day" in the Bible means a thousand years, then, to be consistent, one would have to say that Jonah was in the belly of the fish three thousand years, or that Jesus has not yet risen from the dead after two thousand years in the grave.

OBJECTION 4

Insisting on six solar days for creation limits God, whereas allowing God billions of years does not limit Him.

ANSWER

Actually, insisting on six ordinary earth-rotation days of creation is not limiting *God*, but limiting *us* to believing that God actually did what He tells us in His Word. Also, if God created everything in six days, as the Bible says, then surely this reveals the power and wisdom of God in a profound way—Almighty God did not *need* eons of time. However, the billions-of-years scenarios diminish God by suggesting that mere chance could create things or that God needed huge amounts of time to create things—this would be limiting God's power by reducing it to naturalistic explanations.

OBJECTION 5

Adam could not have accomplished all that the Bible states in one day (Day 6). He could not have named all the animals, for instance; there was not enough time.

ANSWER

Adam did not have to name *all* the animals—only those God brought to him. For instance, Adam was commanded to name "every beast of the field" (Genesis 2:20), not "beast of the earth" (Genesis 1:25). The phrase "beast of

---

[29] The Jews had three watches during the night (sunset to 10 pm; 10 pm to 2 am; 2 am to sunrise), but the Romans had four watches, beginning at 6 pm.

the field" is most likely a subset of the larger group "beast of the earth." He did not have to name "everything that creeps upon the earth" (Genesis 1:25) or any of the sea creatures. Also, the number of "kinds" would be much less than the number of species in today's classification.

When critics say that Adam could not name the animals in less than one day, what they really mean is they do not understand how *they* could do it, so Adam could not. However, our brain has suffered from 6,000 years of the Curse—it has been greatly affected by the Fall. Before sin, Adam's brain was perfect.

When God made Adam, He must have programmed him with a perfect language. Today we program computers to "speak" and "remember." How much more could our Creator God have created Adam as a mature human (he was not born as a baby needing to learn to speak), having in his memory a perfect language with a perfect understanding of each word. (That is why Adam understood what God meant when he said he would "die" if he disobeyed, even though he had not seen any death.) Adam may also have had a "perfect" memory  (something like a photographic memory, perhaps).

It would have been no problem for this first perfect man to make up words and name the animals God brought to him and remember the names—in far less than one day.[30]

OBJECTION 6

Genesis 2 is a different account of creation, with a different order, so how can the first chapter be accepted as teaching six literal days?

---

[30] Andrew Kulikovsky, How Could Adam Have Named All the Animals in a Single Day? Answers in Genesis, www.answersingenesis.org/docs2002/1112animals.asp.

ANSWER

Actually, Genesis 2 is not a *different* account of creation. It is a *more detailed* account of Day 6 of creation. Chapter 1 is an overview of the whole of creation; chapter 2 gives details surrounding the creation of the garden, the first man, and his activities on Day 6.[31]

Between the creation of Adam and the creation of Eve, the King James Version says, "Out of the ground the Lord God formed every beast of the field and every fowl of the air" (Genesis 2:19). This seems to say that the land beasts and birds were created between the creation of Adam and Eve. However, Jewish scholars did not recognize any such conflict with the account in chapter 1, where Adam and Eve were both created after the beasts and birds (Genesis 1:23–25). There is no contradiction, because in Hebrew the precise tense of a verb is determined by the context. It is clear from chapter 1 that the beasts and birds were created before Adam, so Jewish scholars would have understood the verb "formed" to mean "had formed" or "having formed" in Genesis 2:19 If we translate verse 19, "Now the Lord God had formed out of the ground all the beasts of the field," the apparent disagreement with Genesis 1 disappears completely.

Regarding the plants and herbs in Genesis 2:5 and the trees in Genesis 2:9 (compare with Genesis 1:12), the plants and herbs are described as "of the field" and they needed a man to tend them. These are clearly cultivated plants, not just plants in general (Genesis 1). Also, the trees (Genesis 2:9) are only the trees planted in the garden, not trees in general.

In Matthew 19:3–6 Jesus Christ quotes from both Genesis 1:27 and Genesis 2:24 when referring to the *same man and woman* in teaching the doctrine of marriage. Clearly, Jesus saw them as *complementary* accounts, *not* contradictory ones.

OBJECTION 7

There is no "evening and morning" for the seventh day of the Creation Week (Genesis 2:2). Thus, we must still be in the "seventh day," so none of the days can be ordinary days.

---

[31] Paul Taylor, Isn't the Bible Full of Contradictions? chapter 27 in Ken Ham, ed., *The New Answers Book 2* (Green Forest, AR: Master Books, 2008), 288–291; M. Kruger, An understanding of Genesis 2:5, *CEN Technical Journal* **11**(1):106–110, 1997.

ANSWER

Look again at the section entitled "Why Six Days?" on page 97. Exodus 20:11 is clearly referring to seven literal days—six for work and one for rest.

Also, God stated that He *"rested"* from His work of creation (not that He *is resting!*). The fact that He rested from His work of creation does not preclude Him from continuing to rest from this activity. God's work now is different—it is a work of sustaining His creation and of reconciliation and redemption because of man's sin.

The word *yom* is qualified by a number (Genesis 2:2–3), so the context still determines that it is an ordinary solar day. Also, God blessed this seventh day and made it holy. In Genesis 3:17–19 we read of the Curse on the earth because of sin. Paul refers to this in Romans 8:22. It does not make sense that God would call this day holy and blessed if He cursed the ground on this "day." We live in a sin-cursed earth—we are not in the seventh blessed holy day!

Note that in arguing that the seventh day is not an ordinary day because it is not associated with "evening and morning," proponents are tacitly agreeing that the other six days are ordinary days because they are defined by an evening and a morning.

Some have argued that Hebrews 4:3–4 implies that the seventh day is continuing today:

> For we who have believed do enter that rest, as He has said: "So I swore in My wrath, 'They shall not enter My rest,'" although the works were finished from the foundation of the world. For He has spoken in a certain place of the seventh day in this way: "And God rested on the seventh day from all His works... ."

However, verse 4 reiterates that God rested (past tense) on the seventh day. If someone says on Monday that he rested on Friday and is still resting, this would not suggest that Friday continued through to Monday! Also, only those who have believed in Christ will enter that rest, showing that it is a spiritual rest, which is compared with God's rest since the Creation Week. It is not some sort of continuation of the seventh day (otherwise *everyone* would be "in" this rest).[32]

Hebrews does *not* say that the seventh day of Creation Week is continuing today, merely that the rest He instituted is continuing.

---

[32] Tim Chaffey and Jason Lisle, *Old Earth Creationism on Trial* (Green Forest, AR: Master Books, 2008), 51–52.

OBJECTION 8

Genesis 2:4 states, "In the day that the Lord God made the earth and the heavens." As this refers to all six days of creation, it shows that the word "day" does not mean an ordinary day.

ANSWER

The Hebrew word *yom* as used here is *not* qualified by a number, the phrase "evening and morning," or light or darkness. In this context, the verse really means "in the time God created" (referring to the Creation Week) or "when God created."

Other Problems with Long Days and Similar Interpretations

- If the plants made on Day 3 were separated by millions of years from the birds and nectar bats (created Day 5) and insects (created Day 6) necessary for their pollination, then such plants could not have survived. This problem would be especially acute for species with complex symbiotic relationships (each depending on the other; e.g., the yucca plant and the associated moth[33]).

- Adam was created on Day 6, lived through Day 7, and then died when he was 930 years old (Genesis 5:5). If each day were a thousand years or millions of years, this would make no sense of Adam's age at death.

- Some have claimed that the word for "made" (*asah*) in Exodus 20:11 actually means "show." They propose that God showed or revealed the information about creation to Moses during a six-day period. This allows for the creation itself to have occurred over millions of years. However, "showed" is not a valid translation for *asah*. Its meaning covers "to make, manufacture, produce, do," etc., but not "to show" in the sense of reveal.[34] Where *asah* is translated as "show"—for example, "show kindness" (Genesis 24:12)—it is in the sense of "to do" or "make" kindness.

---

[33] F. Meldau, *Why We Believe in Creation Not in Evolution,* Christian Victory Publ., Denver, Colorado, 1972, 114–116.

[34] Nothing in Gesenius's *Lexicon* supports the interpretation of *asah* as "show"; See Charles Taylor's "Days of Revelation or creation?" (1997) found at www.answersingenesis.org/docs/188.asp.

- Some have claimed that because the word *asah* is used for the creation of the sun, moon, and stars on Day 4, and not the word *bara,* which is used in Genesis 1:1 for "create," this means God only revealed the sun, moon, and stars at this stage. They insist the word *asah* has the meaning of "revealed." In other words, the luminaries were supposedly already in existence and were only revealed at this stage. However, *bara* and *asah* are used in Scripture to describe the same event. For example, *asah* is used in Exodus 20:11 to refer to the creation of the heavens and the earth, but *bara* is used to refer to the creation of the heavens and the earth in Genesis 1:1. The word *asah* is used concerning the creation of the first people in Genesis 1:26—they did not previously exist. And then they are said to have been created *(bara)* in Genesis 1:27. There are many other similar examples. *Asah* has a broad range of meanings involving "to do" or "to make," which includes *bara* creation.

- Some accept that the days of creation are ordinary days as far as the language of Genesis is concerned but not as literal days of history as far as man is concerned. This is basically the view called the "framework hypothesis."[35] This is a very complex and contrived view which has been thoroughly refuted by scholars.[36]

The real purpose of the framework hypothesis can be seen in the following quote from an article by one of its proponents:

> To rebut the literalist interpretation of the Genesis creation "week" propounded by the young-earth theorists is a central concern of this article.[37]

- Some people want the days of creation to be long periods in an attempt to harmonize evolution or billions of years with the Bible's account of origins. However, the order of events according to long-age beliefs does not agree with that of Genesis. Consider the following table:

---

[35] M. Kline, Because it had not rained, *Westminster Theological Journal* **20**:146–157, 1957–1958.

[36] Kruger, An understanding of Genesis 2:5, 106–110; J. Pipa, From chaos to cosmos: a critique of the framework hypothesis, presented at the Far-Western Regional Annual Meeting of the Evangelical Theological Society, USA, April 26, 1996; Wayne Grudem's *Systematic Theology,* InterVarsity Press, Downers Grove, Illinois, 1994, 302–305, summarizes the framework hypothesis and its problems and inconsistencies.

[37] M. Kline, Space and time in the Genesis cosmology, *Perspectives on Science & Christian Faith* **48**(1), 1996.

CONTRADICTIONS BETWEEN THE ORDER OF CREATION IN THE BIBLE AND EVOLUTION/LONG-AGES

Biblical account of creation	Evolutionary/long-age speculation
Earth before the sun and stars	Stars and sun before earth
Earth covered in water initially	Earth a molten blob initially
Oceans first, then dry land	Dry land, then the oceans
Life first created on the land	Life started in the oceans
Plants created before the sun	Plants came long after the sun
Land animals created after birds	Land animals existed before birds
Whales before land animals	Land animals before whales

Clearly, those who do not accept the six literal days are the ones reading their own preconceived ideas into the passage.

Long-Age Compromises

Other than the "gap theory" (the belief that there is a gap of indeterminate time between the first two verses of Genesis 1), the major compromise positions that try to harmonize long ages and/or evolution with Genesis fall into two categories:

1. "theistic evolution" wherein God supposedly directed the evolutionary process of millions of years, or even just set it up and let it run, and

2. "progressive creation" where God supposedly intervened in the processes of death and struggle to create millions of species at various times over millions of years.

All long-age compromises reject Noah's Flood as global—it could only be a local event because the fossil layers are accepted as evidence for millions of years. A global Flood would have destroyed this record and produced another. Therefore, these positions cannot allow a catastrophic global Flood that would form layers of fossil-bearing rocks over the earth. This, of course, goes against Scripture, which obviously teaches a global Flood (Genesis 6–9).[38] Sadly, most theologians years ago simply tried to add this belief to the Bible instead of realizing that these layers were laid down by Noah's Flood.

---

[38] M. Van Bebber and P. Taylor, *Creation and Time: A Report on the Progressive Creationist Book by Hugh Ross*, 55–59; Whitcomb and Morris, *The Genesis Flood*, 212–330.

Does It Really Matter?

Yes, it does matter what a Christian believes concerning the days of creation in Genesis 1. Most importantly, all schemes which insert eons of time into, or before, creation undermine the gospel by putting death, bloodshed, disease, thorns, and suffering before sin and the Fall, as explained above (see answer to Objection 1). Here are two more reasons:

1. It is really a matter of how one approaches the Bible, in principle. If we do not allow the language to speak to us in context, but try to make the text fit ideas outside of Scripture, then ultimately the meaning of any word in any part of the Bible depends on man's interpretation, which can change according to whatever outside ideas are in vogue.

2. If one allows science (which has wrongly become synonymous with evolution and materialism) to determine our understanding of Scripture, then this can lead to a slippery slope of unbelief through the rest of Scripture. For instance, science would proclaim that a person cannot be raised from the dead. Does this mean we should interpret the Resurrection of Christ to reflect this? Sadly, some do just this, saying that the Resurrection simply means that Jesus' teachings live on in His followers.

When people accept at face value what Genesis is teaching and accept the days as ordinary days, they will have no problem accepting and making sense of the rest of the Bible.

Martin Luther once said:

> I have often said that whoever would study Holy Scripture should be sure to see to it that he stays with the simple words as long as he can and by no means departs from them unless an article of faith compels him to understand them differently. For of this we must be certain: no clearer speech has been heard on Earth than what God has spoken.[39]

Pure Words

God's people need to realize that the Word of God is something very special. It is not just the words of men. As Paul said in 1 Thessalonians 2:13, "You received it not as the word of men, but as it is, truly the word of God."

Proverbs 30:5–6 states that "every word of God is pure … . Do not add to His words, lest He reprove you and you be found a liar." The Bible cannot

---

[39] Plass, *What Martin Luther Says: A Practical In-Home Anthology for the Active Christian*, 93.

be treated as just some great literary work. We need to "tremble at his word" (Isaiah 66:2) and not forget:

> All Scripture is given by inspiration of God, and is profitable for doctrine, for reproof, for correction, for instruction in righteousness, that the man of God may be complete, thoroughly equipped for every good work (2 Timothy 3:16–17).

In the original autographs, every word and letter in the Bible is there because God put it there. Let us listen to God speaking to us through His Word and not arrogantly think we can tell God what He really means!

9

Does Radiometric Dating Prove the Earth Is Old?

MIKE RIDDLE

The presupposition of long ages is an icon and foundational to the evolutionary model. Nearly every textbook and media journal teaches that the earth is billions of years old.

> Using radioactive dating, scientists have determined that the Earth is about 4.5 billion years old, ancient enough for all species to have been formed through evolution.[1]

> The earth is now regarded as between 4.5 and 4.6 billion years old.[2]

The primary dating method scientists use for determining the age of the earth is radioisotope dating. Proponents of evolution publicize radioisotope dating as a reliable and consistent method for obtaining absolute ages of rocks and the age of the earth. This apparent consistency in textbooks and the media has convinced many Christians to accept an old earth (supposedly 4.6 billion years old).

What Is Radioisotope Dating?

Radioisotope dating (also referred to as radiometric dating) is the process of estimating the ages of rocks from the decay of radioactive elements in

---

[1] *Biology: Visualizing Life*, Holt, Rinehart, and Winston, Austin, Texas, 1998, 117.
[2] C. Plummer, D. Carlson, and D. McGeary, *Physical Geology*, McGraw Hill, New York, 2006, 216.

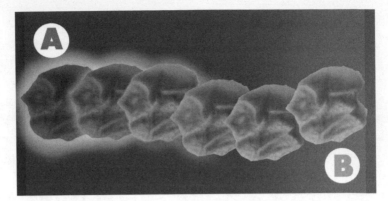

them. There are certain kinds of atoms in nature that are unstable and spontaneously change (decay) into other kinds of atoms. For example, uranium will radioactively decay through a series of steps until it becomes the stable element lead. Likewise, potassium decays into the element argon. The original element is referred to as the parent element (in these cases uranium and potassium), and the end result is called the daughter element (lead and argon).

The Importance of Radioisotope Dating

The straightforward reading of Scripture reveals that the days of creation (Genesis 1) were literal days and that the earth is just thousands of years old, and not billions. There appears to be a fundamental conflict between the Bible and the reported ages given by radioisotope dating. Since God is the Creator of all things (including the human ability to do science), and His Word is true ("Sanctify them by Your truth. Your word is truth," John 17:17), the true age of the earth must agree with His Word. However, rather than accept the biblical account of creation, many Christians have accepted the radioisotope dates of billions of years and attempted to fit long ages into the Bible. The implications of doing this are profound and affect many parts of the Bible.

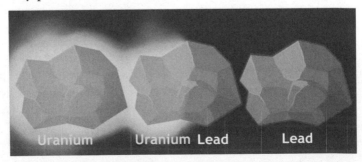

How Radioisotope Dating Works

Radioisotope dating is commonly used to date igneous rocks. These are rocks which form when hot, molten material cools and solidifies. Types of igneous rocks include granite and basalt (lava). Sedimentary rocks, which contain most of the world's fossils, are not commonly used in radioisotope dating. These types of rocks are comprised of particles from many preexisting rocks which were transported (mostly by water) and redeposited somewhere else. Types of sedimentary rocks include sandstone, shale, and limestone.

The radioisotope dating clock starts when a rock cools. During the molten state it is assumed that the intense heat will force any gaseous daughter elements like argon to escape. Once the rock cools it is assumed that no more atoms can escape and any daughter element found in a rock will be the result of radioactive decay. The dating process then requires measuring how much daughter element is in a rock sample and knowing the decay rate (i.e., how long it takes the parent element to decay into the daughter element—uranium into lead or potassium

Uranium-238 (^{238}U) is an isotope of uranium. Isotopes are varieties of an element that have the same number of protons but a different number of neutrons within the nucleus. For example, carbon-14 (^{14}C) is a particular isotope. All carbon atoms have 6 protons but can vary in the number of neutrons. ^{12}C has 6 protons and 6 neutrons in its nucleus. ^{13}C has 6 protons and 7 neutrons. ^{14}C has 6 protons and 8 neutrons. Extra neutrons often lead to instability, or radioactivity. Likewise, all isotopes (varieties) of uranium have 92 protons. ^{238}U has 92 protons and 146 neutrons. It is unstable and will radioactively decay first into ^{234}Th (thorium-234) and finally into ^{206}Pb (lead-206). Sometimes a radioactive decay will cause an atom to lose 2 protons and 2 neutrons (called alpha decay). For example, the decay of ^{238}U into ^{234}Th is an alpha decay process. In this case the atomic mass changes (238 to 234). Atomic mass is the heaviness of an atom when compared to hydrogen, which is assigned the value of one. Another type of decay is called beta decay. In beta decay, either an electron is lost and a neutron is converted into a proton (beta minus decay) or an electron is added and a proton is converted into a neutron (beta plus decay). In beta decay the total atomic mass does not change significantly. The decay of ^{234}Th into ^{234}Pa (protactinium-234) is an example of beta decay.

Uranium-238

Thorium-234

Protactinium-234

Uranium-234

Thorium-230

Radium-226

Radon-222

Polonium-218

Lead-214

Bismuth-214

Polonium-214

Lead-210

Bismuth-210

Polonium-210

Lead-206 (stable)

Uranium to lead decay sequence

into argon). The decay rate is measured in terms of half-life. Half-life is defined as the length of time it takes half of the remaining atoms of a radioactive parent element to decay. For example, the remaining radioactive parent material will decrease by 1/2 during the passage of each half-life (1‡1/2‡1/4‡1/8‡1/16, etc.). Half-lives as measured today are very accurate, even the extremely slow half-lives. That is, billion-year half-lives can be measured statistically in just hours of time. The following table is a sample of different element half-lives.

Parent	Daughter	Half-life
Polonium-218	Lead-214	3 minutes
Thorium-234	Protactinium-234	24 days
Carbon-14	Nitrogen-14	5,730 years
Potassium-40	Argon-40	1.25 billion years
Uranium-238	Lead-206	4.47 billion years
Rubidium-87	Strontium-87	48.8 billion years

Science and Assumptions

Scientists use observational science to measure the amount of a daughter element within a rock sample and to determine the present observable decay rate of the parent element. Dating methods must also rely on another kind of science called historical science. Historical science cannot be observed. Determining the conditions present when a rock first formed can only be studied through historical science. Determining how the environment might have affected a rock also falls under historical science. Neither condition is directly observable. Since radioisotope dating uses both types of science, we can't directly measure the age of something. We can use scientific techniques in the present, combined with assumptions about historical events, to estimate the age. Therefore, there are several assumptions that must be made in radioisotope dating. Three critical assumptions can affect the results during radioisotope dating:

1. The initial conditions of the rock sample are accurately known.

2. The amount of parent or daughter elements in a sample has not been altered by processes other than radioactive decay.

3. The decay rate (or half-life) of the parent isotope has remained constant since the rock was formed.

The Hourglass Illustration

Radioisotope dating can be better understood using an illustration with an hourglass. If we walk into a room and observe an hourglass with sand at the top and sand at the bottom, we could calculate how long the hourglass has been running. By estimating how fast the sand is falling and measuring the amount of sand at the bottom, we could calculate how much time has elapsed since the hourglass was turned over. All our calculations could be correct (observational science), but the result could be wrong. This is because we failed to take into account some critical assumptions.

1. Was there any sand at the bottom when the hourglass was first turned over (initial conditions)?

2. Has any sand been added or taken out of the hourglass? (Unlike the open-system nature of a rock, this is not possible for a sealed hourglass.)

3. Has the sand always been falling at a constant rate?

Since we did not observe the initial conditions when the hourglass time started, we must make assumptions. All three of these assumptions can affect our time calculations. If scientists fail to consider each of these three critical assumptions, then radioisotope dating can give incorrect ages.

The Facts

We know that radioisotope dating does not always work because we can test it on rocks of known age. In 1997, a team of eight research scientists known as the RATE group (Radioisotopes and the Age of The Earth) set out to investigate the assumptions commonly made in standard radioisotope dating practices (both single-sample and multiple-samples radioisotope dating). Their findings were significant and directly impact the evolutionary dates of millions of years.[3]

---

[3] L. Vardiman, A.A. Snelling and E.F. Chaffin (eds.), *Radioisotopes and the Age of the Earth: A Young-Earth Creationist Research Initiative*, Institute for Creation Research, Santee, California, and Creation Research Society, St. Joseph, Missouri, 2000; L. Vardiman, A.A. Snelling and E.F. Chaffin (eds.), *Radioisotopes and the Age of the Earth: Results of a Young-Earth Creationist Research Initiative*, Institute for Creation Research, Santee, California, and Creation Research Society, Chino Valley, Arizona, 2005; D. DeYoung, *Thousands ... Not Billions*, Master Books, Green Forest, Arkansas, 2005.

A rock sample from the newly formed 1986 lava dome from Mount St. Helens was dated using Potassium-Argon dating. The newly formed rock gave ages for the different minerals in it of between 0.5 and 2.8 million years.[4] These dates show that significant argon (daughter element) was present when the rock solidified (assumption 1 is false).

Mount Ngauruhoe is located on the North Island of New Zealand and is one of the country's most active volcanoes. Eleven samples were taken from solidified lava and dated. These rocks are known to have formed from eruptions in 1949, 1954, and 1975. The rock samples were sent to a respected commercial laboratory (Geochron Laboratories in Cambridge, Massachusetts). The "ages" of the rocks ranged from 0.27 to 3.5 million years old.[5] Because these rocks are known to be less than 70 years old, it is apparent that assumption #1 is again false. When radioisotope dating fails to give accurate dates on rocks of known age, why should we trust it for rocks of unknown age? In each case, the ages of the rocks were greatly inflated.

Isochron Dating

There is another form of dating called isochron dating, which involves analyzing four or more samples from the same rock unit. This form of dating attempts to eliminate one of the assumptions in single-sample radioisotope dating by using ratios and graphs rather than counting atoms present. It does not depend on the initial concentration of the daughter element being zero. The isochron dating technique is thought to be infallible, because it supposedly eliminates the assumption about starting conditions. However, this

---

[4] S.A. Austin, Excess argon within mineral concentrates from the new dacite lava dome at Mount St Helens volcano, *Creation Ex Nihilo Technical Journal* **10**(3): 335–343, 1996.
[5] A.A. Snelling, The cause of anomalous potassium-argon "ages" for recent andesite flows at Mt Ngauruhoe, New Zealand, and the implications for potassium-argon "dating," in R.E. Walsh (ed.), *Proceedings of the Fourth International Conference on Creationism*, Creation Science Fellowship, Pittsburgh, Pennsylvania, pp. 503–525, 1998.

method has a different assumption about starting conditions and can also give incorrect dates.

If single-sample and isochron dating methods are objective and reliable they should agree. However, they frequently do not. When a rock is dated by more than one method it may yield very different ages. For example, the RATE group obtained radioisotope dates from ten different locations. To omit any potential bias, the rock samples were analyzed by several commercial laboratories. In each case, the isochron dates differed substantially from the single-sample radioisotope dates. In some cases the range was more than 500 million years.[6] Two conclusions drawn by the RATE group include:

1. The single-sample potassium-argon dates showed a wide variation.

2. A marked variation in ages was found in the isochron method using different parent-daughter analyses.

If different methods yield different ages and there are variations with the same method, how can scientists know for sure the age of any rock or the age of the earth?

In one specific case, samples were taken from the Cardenas Basalt, which is among the oldest strata in the eastern Grand Canyon. Next, samples from the western canyon basalt lava flows, which are among the youngest formations in the canyon, were analyzed. Using the rubidium-strontium isochron dating

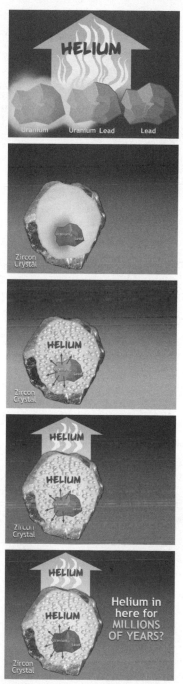

[6] A.A. Snelling, Isochron discordances and the role of inheritance and mixing of radioisotopes in the mantle and crust, in Vardiman et al., *Radioisotopes and the Age of the Earth*, pp. 393–524, 2005; D. DeYoung, *Thousands … Not Billions*, pp. 123–139, 2005.

method, an age of 1.11 billion years was assigned to the oldest rocks and a date of 1.14 billion years to the youngest lava flows. The youngest rocks gave a billion year age the same as the oldest rocks! Are the dates given in textbooks and journals accurate and objective? When assumptions are taken into consideration and discordant (disagreeing or unacceptable) dates are not omitted, radioisotope dating often gives inconsistent and inflated ages.

Two Case Studies

The RATE team selected two locations to collect rock samples to conduct analyses using multiple radioisotope dating methods. Both sites are understood by geologists to date from the Precambrian (supposedly 543–4,600 million years ago). The two sites chosen were the Beartooth Mountains of northwest Wyoming near Yellowstone National Park, and the Bass Rapids sill in the central portion of Arizona's Grand Canyon. All rock samples (whole rock and separate minerals within the rock) were analyzed using four radioisotope methods. These included the isotopes potassium-argon (K-Ar), rubidium-strontium (Rb-Sr), samarium-neodymium (Sm-Nd), and lead-lead (Pb-Pb). In order to avoid any bias, the dating procedures were contracted out to commercial laboratories located in Colorado, Massachusetts, and Ontario, Canada.

In order to have a level of confidence in dating, different radioisotope methods used to date a rock sample should closely coincide in age. When this occurs, the sample ages are said to be concordant. In contrast, if multiple results for a rock disagree with each other in age they are said to be discordant.

Beartooth Mountains Sample Results

Geologists believe the Beartooth Mountains rock unit to contain some of the oldest rocks in the United States, with an estimated age of 2,790 million years. The following table summarizes the RATE results.[7]

The results show a significant scatter in the ages for the various minerals and also between the isotope methods. In some cases, the whole rock age is greater than the age of the minerals, and for others, the reverse occurs. The potassium-argon mineral results vary between 1,520 and 2,620 million years (a difference of 1,100 million years).

---

[7] S.A. Austin, Do radioisotope clocks need repair? Testing the assumptions of isochron dating using K-Ar, Rb-Sr, Sm-Nd, and Pb-Pb isotopes, in Vardiman et al., *Radioisotopes and the Age of the Earth*, pp. 325–392, 2005; D. DeYoung, *Thousands ... Not Billions*, pp. 109-121, 2005.

Dating Isotopes	Millions of Years	Type of Data (whole rock or separate mineral within the rock)
Potassium-Argon	1,520	Quartz-plagioclase mineral
(single-sample)	2,011	Whole rock
	2,403	Biotite mineral
	2,620	Hornblende mineral
Rubidium-Strontium (isochron)	2,515	5 minerals
	2,790	Previously published result based on 30 whole rock samples (1982)
Samarium-Neodymium (isochron)	2,886	4 minerals
Lead-Lead (isochron)	2,689	5 minerals

Bass Rapids Sill Sample Results

The 11 Grand Canyon rock samples were also dated commercially using the most advanced radioisotope technology. The generally accepted age for this formation is 1,070 million years. The RATE results are summarized in the table on the following page.[8]

The RATE results differ considerably from the generally accepted age of 1,070 million years. Especially noteworthy is the multiple whole rocks potassium-argon isochron age of 841.5 million years while the samarium-neodymium isochron gives 1,379 million years (a difference of 537.5 million years).

Possible Explanations for the Discordance

There are three possible explanations for the discordant isotope dates.

1. There may have been a mixing of isotopes between the molten rock and the rocks into which it intruded. There are ways to determine if this has occurred and can be eliminated as a possible explanation.

2. Some of the minerals have crystallized at different times as the rock formed and cooled. However, there is no evidence that molten rock

---

[8] A.A. Snelling, S.A. Austin, and W.A. Hoesch, Radioisotopes in the diabase sill (Upper Precambrian) at Bass Rapids, Grand Canyon, Arizona: an application and test of the isochron dating methods, in R.L. Ivey, Jr. (ed.), *Proceedings of the Fifth International Conference on Creationism*, Creation Science Fellowship, Pittsburgh, Pennsylvania, pp. 269–284, 203; S.A. Austin, in Vardiman et al., 2005, 325–392; D. DeYoung, 2005, 109–121.

Dating Isotopes	Millions of Years	Type of data (whole rock or separate mineral within the rock)
Potassium-Argon	841.5	11 whole rock samples (isochron)
	665 to 1,053	Model ages from single-sample whole rocks
Rubidium-Strontium (isochron)	1,007	Magnetite mineral grains from 7 rock samples
	1,055	11 whole rocks
	1,060	7 minerals
	1,070	Previously published age based on 5 whole rock samples (1982)
	1,075	12 minerals
Lead-Lead (isochron)	1,250	11 whole rocks
	1,327	6 minerals
Samarium-Neodymium (isochron)	1,330	8 minerals
	1,336	Magnetite mineral grains from 7 rock samples
	1,379	6 minerals

crystallizes and cools in the same place at such an incredibly slow pace. Rather, molten rocks crystallize and cool relatively rapidly, so therefore this explanation can be eliminated.

3. The radioactive decay rates have been different in the past than they are today. The following section will show that this provides the best explanation for the discordant ages.

New Studies

New studies by the RATE group have provided evidence that radioactive decay supports a young earth. One of their studies involved the amount of helium found in granite rocks. Granite contains tiny zircon crystals, which contain radioactive uranium (^{238}U), which decays into lead (^{206}Pb). During this process, for each atom of ^{238}U decaying into ^{206}Pb, eight helium atoms are formed and migrate out of the zircons and granite rapidly.

> Within the zircon[9] crystals, any helium atoms generated by nuclear decay in the distant past should have long ago migrated outward and escaped from these crystals. One would expect the helium gas to eventually diffuse upward out of the ground and then disappear into the atmosphere. To everyone's surprise, however, large amounts of helium have been found trapped inside zircons.[10]

The decay of ^{238}U into lead (^{206}Pb) is a slow process (half-life of 4.47 billion years). Since helium migrates out of rocks rapidly, there should be very little to no helium remaining in the zircon crystals.

Why is so much helium still in the zircons? One likely explanation is that sometime in the past the radioactive decay rate was greatly accelerated. The decay rate was accelerated so much that helium was being produced faster than it could have escaped, causing an abundant amount of helium to remain in the zircons in the granite. The RATE group has gathered evidence that at some time in history nuclear decay was greatly accelerated.

> The experiments the RATE project commissioned have clearly confirmed the numerical predictions of our Creation model.... The data and our analysis show that over a billion years worth of nuclear decay has occurred very recently, between 4000 and 8000 years ago.[11]

Confirmation of this accelerated nuclear decay having occurred is provided by adjacent uranium and polonium radiohalos that formed at the same time in the same biotite flakes in granites.[12] Radiohalos result from the physical damage caused by radioactive decay of uranium and intermediate daughter atoms of polonium, so they are observable evidence that a lot of radioactive decay has occurred during the earth's history. However, because the

---

[9] L. Vardiman, A. Snelling, and E. Chaffin, eds., *Radioisotopes and the Age of the Earth*, vol. 2, El Cajon, California, Institute of Creation Research and Chino Valley, Arizona: Creation Research Society, 2005, 74.

[10] DeYoung, *Thousands ... Not Billions*, 2005, 68.

[11] R. Humphreys, Young helium diffusion age of zircons supports accelerated nuclear decay, in Vardiman et al., *Radioisotopes and the Age of the Earth*, 2005, 74.

[12] A.A. Snelling, Radiohalos in granites: evidence of accelerated nuclear decay, in Vardiman et al., *Radioisotopes and the Age of the Earth*, 2005, 101–207; D. DeYoung, *Thousands ... Not Billions*, 2005, 81–97.

daughter polonium atoms are only short-lived (for example, polonium-218 decays within 3 minutes, compared to 4.47 billion years for uranium-238), the polonium radiohalos had to form within hours to a few days. But in order to supply the needed polonium atoms to produce these polonium radiohalos within that timeframe, the nearby uranium atoms had to decay at an accelerated rate. Thus hundreds of millions of years worth of uranium decay (compared to today's slow decay rate) had to have occurred within hours to a few days to produce these adjacent uranium and polonium radiohalos in granites.

The RATE group has suggested that this accelerated decay took place early during the Creation Week and then again during the Flood. Accelerated decay of this magnitude would result in immense amounts of heat being generated in rocks. Determining how this heat was dissipated presents a new and exciting opportunity for creation research.

Conclusion

The best way to learn about history and the age of the earth is to consult the history book of the universe—the Bible. Many scientists and theologians accept a straightforward reading of Scripture and agree that the earth is about 6,000 years old. It is better to use the infallible Word of God for our scientific assumptions than to change His Word in order to compromise with "science" that is based upon man's fallible assumptions. True science will always support God's Word.

> Based on the measured helium retention, a statistical analysis gives an estimated age for the zircons of 6,000 ± 2,000 years. This age agrees with literal biblical history and is about 250,000 times shorter than the conventional age of 1.5 billion years for zircons. The conclusion is that helium diffusion data strongly supports the young-earth view of history.[13]

It must also be concluded, therefore, that because nuclear decay has been shown to have occurred at grossly accelerated rates when molten rocks were forming, crystallizing and cooling, the radiometric methods cannot possibly date these rocks accurately based on the false assumption of constant decay through earth history at today's slow rates. Thus the radiometric dating methods are highly unreliable and don't prove the earth is old.

---

[13] DeYoung, *Thousands … Not Billions*, 2005, 76.

10

Was There Really a Noah's Ark & Flood?

KEN HAM & TIM LOVETT

The account of Noah and the Ark is one of the most widely known events in the history of mankind. Unfortunately, like other Bible accounts, it is often taken as a mere fairy tale.

The Bible, though, is the true history book of the universe, and in that light, the most-asked questions about the Ark and Flood of Noah can be answered with authority and confidence.

How Large Was Noah's Ark?

> The length of the ark shall be three hundred cubits, its width fifty cubits, and its height thirty cubits (Genesis 6:15).

Unlike many whimsical drawings that depict the Ark as some kind of overgrown houseboat (with giraffes sticking out the top), the Ark described in the Bible was a huge vessel. Not until the late 1800s was a ship built that exceeded the capacity of Noah's Ark.

The dimensions of the Ark are convincing for two reasons: the proportions are like that of a modern cargo ship, and it is about as large as a wooden ship can be built. The cubit gives us a good indication of size.[1] With the

---

[1] The cubit was defined as the length of the forearm from elbow to fingertip. Ancient cubits vary anywhere from 17.5 inches (45 cm) to 22 inches (56 cm), the longer sizes dominating the major ancient constructions. Despite this, even a conservative 18 inch (46 cm) cubit describes a sizeable vessel.

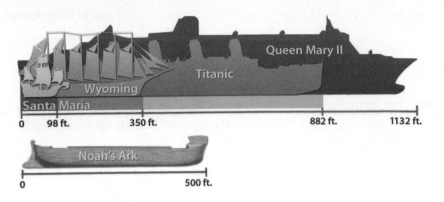

cubit's measurement, we know that the Ark must have been at least 450 feet (137 m) long, 75 feet (23 m) wide, and 45 feet (14 m) high. In the Western world, wooden sailing ships never got much longer than about 330 feet (100 m), yet the ancient Greeks built vessels at least this size 2,000 years earlier. China built huge wooden ships in the 1400s that may have been as large as the Ark. The biblical Ark is one of the largest wooden ships of all time—a mid-sized cargo ship by today's standards.

How Could Noah Build the Ark?

The Bible does not tell us that Noah and his sons built the Ark by themselves. Noah could have hired skilled laborers or had relatives, such as Methuselah and Lamech, help build the vessel. However, nothing indicates that they could not—or that they did not—build the Ark themselves in the time allotted. The physical strength and mental processes of men in Noah's day was at least as great (quite likely, even superior) to our own.[2] They certainly would have had efficient means for harvesting and cutting timber, as well as for shaping, transporting, and erecting the massive beams and boards required.

If one or two men today can erect a large house in just 12 weeks, how much more could three or four men do in a few years? Adam's descendants were making complex musical instruments, forging metal, and building cities—their tools, machines, and techniques were not primitive.

History has shown that technology can be lost. In Egypt, China, and the Americas the earlier dynasties built more impressive buildings or had finer art

---

[2] For the evidence, see Dr. Donald Chittick, *The Puzzle of Ancient Man*, Creation Compass, Newberg, Oregon, 1998. This book details evidence of man's intelligence in early post-Flood civilizations.

or better science. Many so-called modern inventions turn out to be re-inventions, like concrete, which was used by the Romans.

Even accounting for the possible loss of technology due to the Flood, early post-Flood civilizations display all the engineering know-how necessary for a project like Noah's Ark. People sawing and drilling wood in Noah's day, only a few centuries before the Egyptians were sawing and drilling granite, is very reasonable! The idea that more primitive civilizations are further back in time is an evolutionary concept.

In reality, when God created Adam, he was perfect. Today, the individual human intellect has suffered from 6,000 years of sin and decay. The sudden rise in technology in the last few centuries has nothing to do with increasing intelligence; it is a combination of publishing and sharing ideas, and the spread of key inventions that became tools for investigation and manufacturing. One of the most recent tools is the computer, which compensates a great deal for our natural decline in mental performance and discipline, since it permits us to gather and store information as perhaps never before.

How Could Noah Round Up So Many Animals?

Of the birds after their kind, of animals after their kind, and of every creeping thing of the earth after its kind, two of every kind will come to you, to keep them alive (Genesis 6:20).

This verse tells us that Noah didn't have to search or travel to far away places to bring the animals on board. The world map was completely different before the Flood, and on the basis of Genesis 1, there may have been only one continent. The animals simply arrived at the Ark as if called by a "homing instinct" (a behavior implanted in the animals by their Creator) and marched up the ramp, all by themselves.

Though this was probably a supernatural event (one that cannot be explained by our understanding of nature), compare it to the impressive migratory behavior we see in some animals today. We are still far from understanding all the marvelous animal behaviors exhibited in God's creation: the migration of Canada geese and other birds, the amazing flights of Monarch butterflies, the annual travels of whales and fish, hibernation instincts, earthquake sensitivity, and countless other fascinating capabilities of God's animal kingdom.

Were Dinosaurs on Noah's Ark?

The history of God's creation (told in Genesis 1 and 2) tells us that all the land-dwelling creatures were made on Day 6 of Creation Week—the same day God made Adam and Eve. Therefore, it is clear that dinosaurs (being land animals) were made with man.

Also, two of every kind (seven of some) of land animal boarded the Ark. Nothing indicates that any of the land animal kinds were already extinct before the Flood. Besides, the description of "behe-

AFTER EDEN   by Dan Lietha

HOW COULD NOAH HAVE POSSIBLY FIT **DINOSAURS** IN THE ARK?

HOW WAS IT POSSIBLE FOR YOUR MOTHER TO GIVE BIRTH TO **YOU**?

www.AnswersInGenesis.org

© 2001 AiG

Even the largest full-grown creatures were once small!

moth" in chapter 40 of the book of Job (Job lived after the Flood) only fits with something like a sauropod dinosaur. The ancestor of "behemoth" must have been on board the Ark.[3]

We also find many dinosaurs that were trapped and fossilized in Flood sediment. Widespread legends of encounters with dragons give another indication that at least some dinosaurs survived the Flood. The only way this could happen is if they were on the Ark.

Juveniles of even the largest land animals do not present a size problem, and, being young, they have their full breeding life ahead of them. Yet most dinosaurs were not very large at all—some were the size of a chicken (although absolutely no relation to birds, as many evolutionists are now saying). Most scientists agree that the average size of a dinosaur is actually the size of a sheep.

For example, God most likely brought Noah two young adult sauropods (e.g., apatosaurs), rather than two full-grown sauropods. The same goes for elephants, giraffes, and other animals that grow to be very large. However, there was adequate room for most fully grown adult animals anyway.

---

[3] For some remarkable evidence that dinosaurs have lived until relatively recent times, see chapter 12, "What Really Happened to the Dinosaurs?" Also read *The Great Dinosaur Mystery Solved*, New Leaf Press, Green Forest, Arkansas, 2000. Also visit www. answersingenesis.org/go/dinosaurs.

As far as the number of different types of dinosaurs, it should be recognized that, although there are hundreds of names for different varieties (species) of dinosaurs that have been discovered, there are probably only about 50 actual different kinds.

How Could Noah Fit All the Animals on the Ark?

And of every living thing of all flesh you shall bring two of every sort into the ark, to keep them alive with you; they shall be male and female (Genesis 6:19).

In the book *Noah's Ark: A Feasibility Study*[4], creationist researcher John Woodmorappe suggests that, at most, 16,000 animals were all that were needed to preserve the created kinds that God brought into the Ark.

The Ark did not need to carry every kind of animal—nor did God command it. It carried only air-breathing, land-dwelling animals, creeping things, and winged animals such as birds. Aquatic life (fish, whales, etc.) and many amphibious creatures could have survived in sufficient numbers outside the Ark. This cuts down significantly the total number of animals that needed to be on board.

Another factor which greatly reduces the space requirements is the fact that the tremendous variety in species we see today did not exist in the days of Noah. Only the parent "kinds" of these species were required to be on board in order to repopulate the earth.[5] For example, only two dogs were needed to give rise to all the dog species that exist today.

Creationist estimates for the maximum number of animals that would have been necessary to come on board the Ark have ranged from a few thousand to 35,000, but they may be as few as two thousand if the biblical kind is approximately the same as the modern family classification.

---

[4] J. Woodmorappe, *Noah's Ark: A Feasibility Study*, Institute for Creation Research, Santee, California, 2003.

[5] Here's one example: more than 200 different breeds of dogs exist today, from the miniature poodle to the St. Bernard—all of which have descended from one original dog "kind" (as have the wolf, dingo, etc.). Many other types of animals—cat kind, horse kind, cow kind, etc.—have similarly been naturally and selectively bred to achieve the wonderful variation in species that we have today. God "programmed" this variety into the genetic code of all animal kinds—even humankind! God also made it impossible for the basic "kinds" of animals to breed and reproduce with each other. For example, cats and dogs cannot breed to make a new type of creature. This is by God's design, and it is one fact that makes evolution impossible.

As stated before, Noah wouldn't have taken the largest animals onto the Ark; it is more likely he took juveniles aboard the Ark to repopulate the earth after the Flood was over. These younger animals also require less space, less food, and have less waste.

Using a short cubit of 18 inches (46 cm) for the Ark to be conservative, Woodmorappe's conclusion is that "less than half of the cumulative area of the Ark's three decks need to have been occupied by the animals and their enclosures."[6] This meant there was plenty of room for fresh food, water, and even many other people.

How Did Noah Care for All the Animals?

Just as God brought the animals to Noah by some form of supernatural means, He surely also prepared them for this amazing event. Creation scientists suggest that God gave the animals the ability to hibernate, as we see in many species today. Most animals react to natural disasters in ways that were designed to help them survive. It's very possible many animals did hibernate, perhaps even supernaturally intensified by God.

Whether it was supernatural or simply a normal response to the darkness and confinement of a rocking ship, the fact that God told Noah to build rooms ("*qen*"—literally in Hebrew "nests") in Genesis 6:14 implies that the animals were subdued or nesting. God also told Noah to take food for them (Genesis 6:21), which tells us that they were not in a year-long coma either.

Were we able to walk through the Ark as it was being built, we would undoubtedly be amazed at the ingenious systems on board for water and food storage and distribution. As Woodmorappe explains in *Noah's Ark: A Feasibility Study*, a small group of farmers today can raise thousands of cattle and other animals in a very small space. One can easily imagine all kinds of devices on the Ark that would have enabled a small number of people to feed and care for the animals, from watering to waste removal.

As Woodmorappe points out, no special devices were needed for eight people to care for 16,000 animals. But if they existed, how would these devices be powered? There are all sorts of possibilities. How about a plumbing system for gravity-fed drinking water, a ventilation system driven by wind or wave motion, or hoppers that dispense grain as the animals eat it? None of these require higher technology than what we know existed in ancient cultures.

---

[6] Woodmorappe, *Noah's Ark: A Feasibility Study*, 16.

And yet these cultures were likely well-short of the skill and capability of Noah and the pre-Flood world.

How Could a Flood Destroy Every Living Thing?

> And all flesh died that moved on the earth: birds and cattle and beasts and every creeping thing that creeps on the earth, and every man. All in whose nostrils was the breath of the spirit of life, all that was on the dry land, died (Genesis 7:21–22).

Noah's Flood was much more destructive than any 40-day rainstorm ever could be. Scripture says that the "fountains of the great deep" broke open. In other words, earthquakes, volcanoes, and geysers of molten lava and scalding water were squeezed out of the earth's crust in a violent, explosive upheaval. These fountains were not stopped until 150 days into the Flood—so the earth was literally churning underneath the waters for about five months! The duration of the Flood was extensive, and Noah and his family were aboard the Ark for over a year.

Relatively recent local floods, volcanoes, and earthquakes—though clearly devastating to life and land   are tiny in comparison to the worldwide catastrophe that destroyed "the world that then existed" (2 Peter 3:6). All land animals and people not on board the Ark were destroyed in the floodwaters—billions of animals were preserved in the great fossil record we see today.

How Could the Ark Survive the Flood?

The description of the Ark is very brief—Genesis 6:14–16. Those three verses contain critical information including overall dimensions, but Noah was almost certainly given more detail than this. Other divinely specified constructions in the Bible are meticulously detailed, like the descriptions of Moses' Tabernacle or the temple in Ezekiel's vision.

The Bible does not say the Ark was a rectangular box. In fact, Scripture gives no clue about the shape of Noah's Ark other than the proportions—length, width, and depth. Ships have long been described like this without ever implying a block-shaped hull.

Moses used the obscure term *tebah*, a word that is only used again for the basket that carried baby Moses (Exodus 2:3). One was a huge wooden ship and the other a tiny wicker basket. Both float, both rescue life, and both are covered. But the similarity ends there. We can be quite sure that the baby basket did not have the same proportions as the Ark, and Egyptian baskets of the time were typically rounded. Perhaps *tebah* means "lifeboat."

For many years biblical creationists have simply depicted the Ark as a rectangular box. This shape helped illustrate its size while avoiding the distractions of hull curvature. It also made it easy to compare volume. By using a short cubit and the maximum number of animal "kinds," creationists, as we've seen, have demonstrated how easily the Ark could fit the payload.[7] At the time, space was the main issue; other factors were secondary.

However, the next phase of research investigated sea-keeping (behavior and comfort at sea), hull strength, and stability. This began with a Korean study performed at the world-class ship research center (KRISO) in 1992.[8] The team of nine KRISO researchers was led by Dr. Hong, who is now director-general of the research center.

The study confirmed that the Ark could handle waves as high as 98 feet (30 m), and that the proportions of the biblical Ark are near optimal—an interesting admission from Dr. Hong, who believes evolutionary ideas, openly claiming "life came from the sea."[9] The study combined analysis, model wave testing, and ship standards, yet the concept was simple: compare the biblical Ark with 12 other vessels of the same volume but modified in length, width, or depth. Three qualities were measured—stability, hull strength, and comfort.

Ship Qualities Measured in the 1992 Korean Study

While Noah's Ark was an average performer in each quality, it was among the best designs overall. In other words, the proportions show a careful design balance that is easily lost when proportions are modified the wrong way. It is no surprise that modern ships have similar proportions—those proportions work.

Interesting to note is the fact that this study makes nonsense of the claim that Genesis was written only a few centuries before Christ and was based on flood legends such as the Epic of Gilgamesh. The Babylonian ark is a cube shape, something so far from reality that even the shortest hull in the Korean

---

[7] To read a thorough study on this research, see *Noah's Ark: A Feasibility Study* by John Woodmorappe (see Ref. 5).

[8] Hong, et al., Safety Investigation of Noah's Ark in a seaway, *TJ* 8(1):26–36, April 1994. www.answersingenesis.org/tj/v8/i1/noah.asp.

[9] Seok Won Hong, Warm greetings from the Director-General of MOERI (former KRISO), Director-General of MOERI/KORDI, www.moeri.re.kr/eng/about/about.htm.

study was not even close. But we would expect mistakes from other flood accounts, like that of Gilgamesh, as the account of Noah would have been distorted as it was passed down through different cultures.

Yet one mystery remained. The Korean study did not hide the fact that some shorter hulls slightly outperformed the biblical Noah's Ark. Further work by Tim Lovett, one author of this chapter, and two naval architects, Jim King and Dr. Allen Magnuson, focused attention on the issue of broaching—being turned sideways by the waves.

How do we know what the waves were like? If there were no waves at all, stability, comfort, or strength would be unimportant, and the proportions would not matter. A shorter hull would then be a more efficient volume, taking less wood and less work. However, we can take clues from the proportions of the Ark itself. The Korean study had assumed waves came from every direction, giving shorter hulls an advantage. But real ocean waves usually have a dominant direction due to the wind, favoring a short, wide hull even more.

Another type of wave may also have affected the Ark during the Flood—tsunamis. Earthquakes can create tsunamis that devastate coastlines. However, when a tsunami travels in deep water it is imperceptible to a ship. During the Flood, the water would have been very deep—there is enough water in today's oceans to cover the earth to a depth of about 1.7 miles (2.7 km). The Bible states that the Ark rose "high above the earth" (Genesis 7:17). Launched from high ground by the rising floodwaters, the Ark would have  avoided the initial devastation of coastlines and low-lying areas, and remained safe from tsunamis throughout the voyage.

After several months at sea, God sent a wind (Genesis 8:1), which could have produced very large waves since these waves can be produced by a strong, steady wind. Open-water testing confirms that any drifting vessel will naturally turn side-on to the waves (broach). With waves approaching the side of the vessel (beam sea), a long vessel like the Ark would be trapped in an uncomfortable situation; in heavy weather it could become dangerous. This could be overcome, however, by the vessel catching the wind (Genesis 8:1) at the bow and catching the water at the stern—aligning itself like a wind

vane. These features appear to have inspired a number of ancient ship designs. Once the Ark points into the waves, the long, ship-like proportions create a more comfortable and controlled voyage. Traveling slowly with the wind, it had no need for speed, but the Bible does say the Ark moved about on the surface of the waters (Genesis 7:18).

Compared to a ship-like bow and stern, blunt ends are not as strong, have edges that are vulnerable to damage during launch and beaching, and give a rougher ride. Since the Bible gives proportions like that of a true ship, it makes sense that it should look and act ship-like. The above design is an attempt to flesh out the biblical outline using real-life experiments and archeological evidence of ancient ships.

A proposed design for Noah's Ark, passively avoiding broaching in wind-generated waves

While Scripture does not point out a wind-catching feature at the bow, the abbreviated account we are given in Genesis makes no mention of drinking water, the number of animals, or the way they got out of the Ark either.

Nothing in this newly depicted Ark contradicts Scripture; in fact, it shows how accurate Scripture is!

Where Did All the Water Come From?

In the six hundredth year of Noah's life, in the second month, the seventeenth day of the month, on that day all the fountains of the great deep were broken up, and the windows of heaven were opened. And the rain was on the earth forty days and forty nights (Genesis 7:11–12).

The Bible tells us that water came from two sources: below the earth and above the earth. Evidently, the source for water below the ground was in great subterranean pools, or "fountains" of fresh water, which were broken open by volcanic and seismic (earthquake) activity.[10]

Where Did All the Water Go?

And the waters receded continually from the earth. At the end of the hundred and fifty days the waters decreased (Genesis 8:3).

Simply put, the water from the Flood is in the oceans and seas we see today. Three-quarters of the earth's surface is covered with water.

As even secular geologists observe, it does appear that the continents were at one time "together" and not separated by the vast oceans of today. The forces involved in the Flood were certainly sufficient to change all of this.

Scripture indicates that God formed the ocean basins, raising the land out of the water, so that the floodwaters returned to a safe place. (Some theologians believe Psalm 104 may refer to this event.) Some creation scientists believe this breakup of the continent was part of the mechanism that ultimately caused the Flood.[11]

Some have speculated, because of Genesis 10:25, that the continental break occurred during the time of Peleg. However, this division is mentioned in the context of the Tower of Babel's language division of the whole earth (Genesis 10–11). So the context points to a dividing of the languages and people groups, not the land breaking apart.

If there were a massive movement of continents during the time of Peleg, there would have been another worldwide flood. The Bible indicates that the mountains of Ararat existed for the Ark to land in them (Genesis 8:4); so

[10] For deeper study on this, please see Nozomi Osanai, *A Comparison of Scientific Reliability*, A comparative study of the flood accounts in the Gilgamesh Epic and Genesis, www.answersingenesis.org/go/gilgamesh.
[11] See chapter 14 by Dr. Andrew Snelling for more details on this subject.

135

the Indian-Australian Plate and Eurasian Plate had to have already collided, indicating that the continents had already shifted prior to Peleg.

Was Noah's Flood Global?

> And the waters prevailed exceedingly on the earth, and all the high hills under the whole heaven were covered. The waters prevailed fifteen cubits upward, and the mountains were covered (Genesis 7:19–20).

Many Christians today claim that the Flood of Noah's time was only a local flood. These people generally believe in a local flood because they have accepted the widely believed evolutionary history of the earth, which interprets fossil layers as the history of the sequential appearance of life over millions of years.[12]

Scientists once understood the fossils, which are buried in water-carried sediments of mud and sand, to be mostly the result of the great Flood. Those who now accept millions of years of gradual accumulation of fossils have, in their way of thinking, explained away the evidence for the global Flood. Hence, many compromising Christians insist on a local flood.

Secularists deny the possibility of a worldwide Flood at all. If they would think from a biblical perspective, however, they would see the abundant evidence for the global Flood. As someone once quipped, "I wouldn't have seen it if I hadn't believed it."

Those who accept the evolutionary timeframe, with its fossil accumulation, also rob the Fall of Adam of its serious consequences. They put the fossils, which testify of disease, suffering, and death, before Adam and Eve sinned and brought death and suffering into the world. In doing this, they also undermine the meaning of the death and resurrection of Christ. Such a scenario also robs all meaning from God's description of His finished creation as "very good."

If the Flood only affected the area of Mesopotamia, as some claim, why did Noah have to build an Ark? He could have walked to the other side of the mountains and escaped. Most importantly, if the Flood were local, people not living in the vicinity of the Flood would not have been affected by it. They would have escaped God's judgment on sin.

---

[12] For compelling evidence that the earth is not billions of years old, read *The Young Earth* by Dr. John Morris and *Thousands, not Billions* by Dr. Don DeYoung; also see www. answersingenesis.org/go/young.

A local Flood?

In addition, Jesus believed that the Flood killed every person not on the Ark. What else could Christ mean when He likened the coming world judgment to the judgment of "all" men in the days of Noah (Matthew 24:37–39)?

In 2 Peter 3, the coming judgment by fire is likened to the former judgment by water in Noah's Flood. A partial judgment in Noah's day, therefore, would mean a partial judgment to come.

If the Flood were only local, how could the waters rise to 20 feet (6 m) above the mountains (Genesis 7:20)? Water seeks its own level; it could not rise to cover the local mountains while leaving the rest of the world untouched.

Even what is now Mt. Everest was once covered with water and uplifted afterward.[13] If we even out the ocean basins and flatten out the mountains, there is enough water to cover the entire earth by about 1.7

---

[13] Mount Everest is more than 5 miles (8 km) high. How, then, could the Flood have covered "all the mountains under the whole heaven?" Before the Flood, the mountains were not so high. The mountains today were formed only towards the end of, and after, the Flood by collision of the tectonic plates and the associated up-thrusting. In support of this, the layers that form the uppermost parts of Mt. Everest are themselves composed of fossil-bearing, water-deposited layers. For more on this, see Chapter 14 on catastrophic plate tectonics.

miles (2.7 km).[14] Also important to note is that, with the leveling out of the oceans and mountains, the Ark would not have been riding at the height of the current Mt. Everest, thus no need for such things as oxygen masks either.

There's more. If the Flood were a local flood, God would have repeatedly broken His promise never to send such a flood again. God put a rainbow in the sky as a covenant between God and man and the animals that He would never repeat such an event. There have been huge local floods in recent times (e.g., in Bangladesh); but never has there been another global Flood that killed all life on the land.

Where Is the Evidence in the Earth for Noah's Flood?

For this they willingly forget: that by the word of God the heavens were of old, and the earth standing out of water and in the water, by which the world that then existed perished, being flooded with water (2 Peter 3:5–6).

Evidence of Noah's Flood can be seen all over the earth, from seabeds to mountaintops. Whether you travel by car, train, or plane, the physical features of the earth's terrain clearly indicate a catastrophic past, from canyons and craters to coal beds and caverns. Some layers of strata extend across continents, revealing the effects of a huge catastrophe.

---

14 A.R. Wallace, *Man's Place in the Universe*, McClure, Phillips & Co, New York, 1903, 225–226; www.wku.edu/~smithch/wallace/S728-3.htm.

The earth's crust has massive amounts of layered sedimentary rock, sometimes miles (kilometers) deep! These layers of sand, soil, and material—mostly laid down by water—were once soft like mud, but they are now hard stone. Encased in these sedimentary layers are billions of dead things (fossils of plants and animals) buried very quickly. The evidence all over the earth is staring everyone in the face.

Where Is Noah's Ark Today?

> Then the ark rested in the seventh month, the seventeenth day of the month, on the mountains of Ararat (Genesis 8:4).

The Ark landed in mountains. The ancient name for these mountains could refer to several areas in the Middle East, such as Mt. Ararat in Turkey or other mountain ranges in neighboring countries.

Mt. Ararat has attracted the most attention because it has permanent ice, and some people report to have seen the Ark. Many expeditions have searched for the Ark there. There is no conclusive evidence of the Ark's location or survival; after all, it landed on the mountains about 4,500 years ago. Also it could easily have deteriorated, been destroyed, or been used as lumber by Noah and his descendants.

Some scientists and Bible scholars, though, believe the Ark could indeed be preserved—perhaps to be providentially revealed at a future time as a reminder of the past judgment and the judgment to come, although the same could be said for things like the Ark of the Covenant or other biblical icons. Jesus said, "If they do not hear Moses and the prophets, neither will they be persuaded though one rise from the dead" (Luke 16:31).

The Ark is unlikely to have survived without supernatural intervention, but this is neither promised nor expected from Scripture. However, it is a good idea to check if it still exists.

Why Did God Destroy the Earth That He Had Made?

> Then the Lord saw that the wickedness of man was great in the earth, and that every intent of the thoughts of his heart was only evil continually. But Noah found grace in the eyes of the Lord (Genesis 6:5, 8).

These verses speak for themselves. Every human being on the face of the earth had turned after the wickedness in their own hearts, but Noah, because of his righteousness before God, was spared from God's judgment, along with his wife, their sons, and their wives. As a result of man's wickedness, God sent judgment on all mankind. As harsh as the destruction was, no living person was without excuse.

God also used the Flood to separate and to purify those who believed in Him from those who didn't. Throughout history and throughout the Bible, this cycle has taken place time after time: separation, purification, judgment, and redemption.

Without God and without a true knowledge and understanding of Scripture, which provides the true history of the world, man is doomed to repeat the same mistakes over and over again.

How Is Christ like the Ark?

> For the Son of Man has come to save that which was lost (Matthew 18:11).

As God's Son, the Lord Jesus Christ is like Noah's Ark. Jesus came to seek and to save the lost. Just as Noah and his family were saved by the Ark, rescued by God from the floodwaters, so anyone who believes in Jesus as Lord and Savior will be spared from the coming final judgment of mankind, rescued by God from the fire that will destroy the earth after the last days (2 Peter 3:7).

Noah and his family had to go through a doorway into the Ark to be saved, and the Lord shut the door behind them (Genesis 7:16). So we too have to go through a "doorway" to be saved so that we won't be eternally separated from God. The Son of God, Jesus, stepped into history to pay the penalty for our sin of rebellion. Jesus said, "I am the door. If anyone enters by Me, he will be saved, and will go in and out and find pasture" (John 10:9).

11

How Did Animals Spread All Over the World from Where the Ark Landed?

PAUL F. TAYLOR

An issue often used in an attempt to beat biblical creationists over the head is the worldwide distribution of animals. Such a distribution, say critics, proves that there could never have been a global Flood or an Ark. If the Ark landed somewhere in the Middle East, then all the animals would have disembarked at that point, including animals that we do not find in the Middle East today, or in the fossil record in that area. How did kangaroos get to Australia, or kiwis to New Zealand? How did polar bears get to North America and penguins to Antarctica?

Not a Science Textbook

Skeptics often claim, "The Bible is not a science textbook." This, of course, is true—because science textbooks change every year, whereas the Bible is the unchanging Word of God—the God who cannot lie. Nevertheless, the Bible can be relied upon when it touches on every scientific issue, including ecology. It is the Bible that gives us the big picture. Within this big picture, we can build scientific models that help us explain how past events may have come about. Such models should be held to lightly, but the Scripture to which they refer is inerrant. That is to say future research may cast doubt on an actual model, without casting doubt on Scripture.

With this in mind, the question needs to be asked, "Is there a Bible-based model that we can use to help explain how animals might have migrated from where the Ark landed to where they live today?" The answer is yes.

The Hard Facts

A biblical model of animal migration obviously must start with the Bible. From Genesis we can glean the following pertinent facts:

1. "And of every living thing of all flesh you shall bring two of every sort into the ark, to keep them alive with you; they shall be male and female. Of the birds after their kind, of animals after their kind, and of every creeping thing of the earth after its kind, two of every kind will come to you to keep them alive" (Genesis 6:19–20). The Bible is clear that representatives of all the *kinds* of air-breathing land animals and birds were present on the Ark. A technical term used by some creation scientists for these *kinds* is *baramin*—derived from the Hebrew words for *created kind*. Within these baramins is all the information necessary to produce all current species. For example, it is unlikely that the Ark contained two lions and two tigers. It is more likely that it contained two feline animals, from which lions, tigers, and other cat-like creatures have developed.

2. Another lesson from Genesis 6:20 is that the animals came to Noah. He did not have to go and catch them. Therefore, this preservation of the world's fauna was divinely controlled. It was God's intention that the fauna be preserved. The animals' recolonization of the land masses was therefore determined by God, and not left to chance.

3. "Then the ark rested in the seventh month, the seventeenth day of the month, on the mountains of Ararat" (Genesis 8:4). The Bible is clear that the Ark landed in the region of Ararat, but much debate has ensued over whether this is the same region as the locality of the present-day mountain known as Ararat. This issue is of importance, as we shall see. The Bible uses the plural "mountains." It is unlikely that the Ark rested on a point on the top of a mountain, in the manner often illustrated in children's picture books. Rather, the landing would have been among the mountainous areas of western Turkey, where present-day Mount Ararat is located, and eastern Iran, where the range extends.

4. It was God's will that the earth be recolonized. "Then God spoke to Noah, saying, 'Go out of the ark, you and your wife, and your sons and your

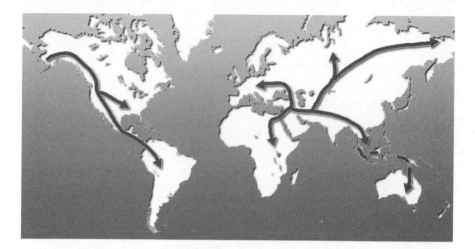

sons' wives with you. Bring out with you every living thing of all flesh that is with you: birds and cattle and every creeping thing that creeps on the earth, so that they may abound on the earth, and be fruitful and multiply on the earth.' So Noah went out, and his sons and his wife and his sons' wives with him. Every animal, every creeping thing, every bird, and whatever creeps on the earth, according to their families, went out of the ark" (Genesis 8:15–19). The abundance and multiplication of the animals was also God's will.

The biblical principles that we can establish then are that, after the Flood, God desired the ecological reconstruction of the world, including its vulnerable animal kinds, and the animals must have spread out from a mountainous region known as Ararat.

The construction of any biblical model of recolonization must include these principles. The model suggested on the following pages is constructed in good faith, to explain the observed facts through the "eyeglasses" of the Bible. The Bible is inspired, but our scientific models are not. If we subsequently find the model to be untenable, this would not shake our commitment to the absolute authority of Scripture.

The model uses the multiplication of dogs as an example of how animals could have quickly repopulated the earth. Two dogs came off Noah's Ark and began breeding more dogs. Within a relatively short time period, there would be an incredible number of dogs of all sorts of different shapes and sizes.

These dogs then began to spread out from the Ararat region to all parts of the globe.

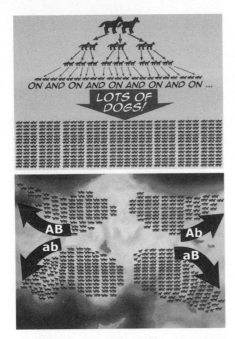

ON AND ON AND ON AND ON AND ON ...

LOTS OF DOGS!

AB

ab

Ab

aB

As these dogs spread around the world, variations within the dog kind led to many of the varieties we find today. But it is important to note that they are still dogs. This multiplication of variations within a kind is the same with the many other kinds of animals.

One final comment must be made in this section. As I have used the word recolonization several times, I must emphasize that I am not referring to the so-called *Recolonization Theory*. This theory will be discussed later.

Modern Recolonizations

One accusation thrown at biblical creationists is that kangaroos could not have hopped to Australia, because there are no fossils of kangaroos on the way. But the expectation of such fossils is a presuppositional error. Such an expectation is predicated on the assumption that fossils form gradually and inevitably from animal populations. In fact, fossilization is by no means inevitable. It usually requires sudden, rapid burial. Otherwise the bones would decompose before permineralization. One ought likewise to ask why it is that, despite the fact that millions of bison used to roam the prairies of North America, hardly any bison fossils are found there. Similarly, lion fossils are not found in Israel even though we know that lions once lived there.

Comparisons can be made with more modern recolonizations. For example, the *Encyclopædia Britannica* has the following to say about Surtsey Island and Krakatoa and the multiplication of species.

Six months after the eruption of a volcano on the island of Surtsey off the coast of Iceland in 1963, the island had been colonized by a few bacteria, molds, insects, and birds. Within about a year of the eruption of a volcano on the island of Krakatoa in the tropical Pacific in 1883, a few grass species, insects, and vertebrates had taken hold. On both Surtsey and Krakatoa, only a few decades had elapsed before hundreds of species reached the islands. Not all species are able to take hold and become permanently established, but eventually the island communities stabilize into a dynamic equilibrium.[1]

There is little secret, therefore, how nonflying animals may have travelled to the outer parts of the world after the Flood. Many of them could have floated on vast floating logs, left-overs from the massive pre-Flood forests that were ripped up during the Flood and likely remained afloat for many decades on the world's oceans, transported by world currents. Others could later have been taken by people. Savolainen et al., have suggested, for example, that all Australian dingoes are descended from a single female domesticated dog from Southeast Asia.[2] A third explanation of possible later migration is that animals could have crossed land bridges. This is, after all, how it is supposed by evolutionists that many animals and people migrated from Asia to the Americas—over a land bridge at the Bering Straits. For such land bridges to have existed, we may need to assume that sea levels were lower in the post-Flood period—an assumption based on a biblical model of the Ice Age.

Ice Age

As Michael Oard, a retired meteorologist and Ice Age researcher, has suggested in chapter 16, an Ice Age may have followed closely after the Flood. In his detailed analysis, Oard proposed a mechanism of how the rare conditions required to form an Ice Age may have been triggered by the Flood, and shows how this explains the field evidence for an Ice Age.[3]

Severe climatic changes could have been the catalyst that encouraged certain species to migrate in certain directions. These severe changes could also have accounted for some of the many extinctions that occurred. Additionally, Oard's studies provide a model for how land bridges could have developed.

Oard has pointed out that certain observed features from the Ice Age cause problems for the evolutionist, not the creationist. Thus, a creationist explanation of the Ice Age better explains the facts. An example of such an issue is that of disharmonious associations of fossils—

---

[1] *Encyclopædia Britannica*, www.britannica.com/eb/article-70601.

[2] P. Savolainen et al., A detailed picture of the origin of the Australian dingo, obtained from the study of mitochondrial DNA, *PNAS* (Proceedings of the National Academy of Sciences of the United States of America) **101**:12387–12390, August 2004.

[3] Oard has published many articles in journals and on the AiG and ICR websites on these issues. For a detailed account of his findings, see his book: M. Oard, *An Ice Age Caused by the Genesis Flood*, Institute for Creation Research, El Cajon, California, 2002.

fossils of creatures normally associated with different conditions (such as creatures with a preference for hot and cold climates) being found in close proximity.

> One of the more puzzling problems for uniformitarian theories of the ice age is disharmonious associations of fossils, in which species from different climatic regimes are juxtaposed. For example, a hippopotamus fossil found together with a reindeer fossil.[4]

Oard suggests that even with present topography, a number of significant land bridges would have existed to facilitate migrations if the sea level were only 180 ft (55 m) below current levels. However, there is even evidence that the land in some places where land bridges would be necessary could have been higher still. Thus, land bridges facilitated by the Ice Age constitute a serious model to explain how some migrations could have been possible.

Some still remain skeptical about the idea of land bridges all the way to Australia. Nevertheless, by a combination of methods that we see today, including land bridges, there are rational explanations as to how animals may have reached the far corners of the world. Of course, we were not there at the time to witness how this migration may have happened, but those adhering to a biblical worldview can be certain that animals obviously did get to far places, and that there are rational ways in which it could have happened.

We should therefore have no problem accepting the Bible as true. Creationist scientific models of animal migration are equally as valid as evolutionary models, if not more so. The reason such models are rejected is that they do not fit in with the orthodox, secular evolutionary worldview.

It is not a problem for us to rationalize why certain animals do not appear in certain parts of the world. Why, for example, does Australia have such an unusual fauna, including so many marsupials? Marsupials are, of course, known elsewhere in the world. For example, opossums are found in North and South America, and fossilized marsupials have been found elsewhere. But in many places, climatic changes and other factors could lead to their extinction.

The lack of great marsupials in other continents need be no more of a problem than the lack of dinosaurs. As with many species today, they just died out—a reminder of a sin-cursed world. One proposed theory is that marsupials—because they bore their young in pouches—were able to travel farther and faster than mammals that had to stop to care for their young.

---

[4] Ibid, p. 80.

They were able to establish themselves in far-flung Australia before competitors reached the continent.

Similar statements could be made about the many unusual bird species in New Zealand, on islands from which mammals were absent until the arrival of European settlers.

Recolonization Theory

The most logical interpretation of the biblical record of the Flood and its aftermath would seem to suggest that the animals disembarked and then recolonized the planet. Comparisons with modern migrations and incidents such as Surtsey have suggested that this recolonization need not have taken long. A plain reading of Scripture suggests that the Ark landed in the mountains of Ararat, most likely in the region of modern Turkey and Central Asia. It is also our contention that the significant quantity of death represented by the fossil record is best understood by reference to the Genesis Flood (i.e., the majority of fossils formed as a result of the Flood).

More recently, a theory has developed among certain creationists in the UK and Europe which suggests that the fossil record is actually a record not of catastrophe but of processes occurring during recolonization. This theory is called the Recolonization Theory.[5]

Proponents of this theory suggest that the Flood completely obliterated the earth's previous crust so that none of the present fossils were caused by it. To accommodate fossilization processes, Recolonization Theory suggests that the age of the earth be stretched by a few thousand years. Some advocates of this view suggest an age of about 8,000 years for the earth, while others suggest figures as high as 20,000 years.

A detailed criticism of Recolonization Theory has previously been published by McIntosh, Edmondson, and Taylor,[6] and another by Holt.[7]

---

[5] Spelled "Recolonisation" in the UK, which is where the theory began.

[6] A.C. McIntosh, T. Edmondson, and S. Taylor, Flood Models: The need for an integrated approach, *TJ* 14(1):52–59, April 2000; A.C. McIntosh, T. Edmondson, and S. Taylor, Genesis and Catastrophe, *TJ* 14(1):101–109, April 2000. Recolonizers' disagreements with these article were answered in A.C. McIntosh, T. Edmondson, and S. Taylor, McIntosh, Taylor, and Edmondson reply to Flood Models, *TJ* 14(3):80–82, 2000, available online at www.answersingenesis.org/tj/v14/i3/flood_reply.asp.

[7] R. Holt, *Evidence for a Late Cainozoic Flood/post-Flood Boundary*, *TJ* 10(1):128–168, April 1996.

The principal error of this view is that it starts from supposed scientific anomalies, such as the fossil record, rather than from Scripture. This has led to the proposals among some Recolonizers, but not all, that there must be gaps in the genealogies recorded in Genesis 5 and 11, even though there is no need for such gaps. Indeed the suggestion of gaps in these genealogies causes further doctrinal problems.[8]

Even the views of those Recolonizers who do not expand the genealogies contain possible seeds of compromise. Because the Recolonizers accept the geologic column, and because the Middle East has a great deal of what is called Cretaceous rock, it follows that the Middle East would need to be submerged after the Flood, at the very time of the Tower of Babel events in Genesis 11. This has led some of the Recolonizers to speculate that the Ark actually landed in Africa, and therefore, that continent was the host to the events of Genesis 11 and 12. This would seem to be a very weak position exegetically and historically. Such exegetical weaknesses led Professor Andy McIntosh and his colleagues to comment, "Their science is driving their interpretation of Scripture, and not the other way round."[9]

Conclusions

We must not be downhearted by critics and their frequent accusations against the Bible. We must not be surprised that so many people will believe all sorts of strange things, whatever the logic.

Starting from our presupposition that the Bible's account is true, we have seen that scientific models can be developed to explain the post-Flood migration of animals. These models correspond to observed data and are consistent with the Bible's account. It is notable that opponents of biblical creationism use similar models in their evolutionary explanations of animal migrations. While a model may eventually be superseded, it is important to note that such biblically consistent models exist. In any event, we have confidence in the scriptural account, finding it to be accurate and authoritative.[10] The fact of animal migration around the world is illustrative of the goodness and graciousness of God, who provided above and beyond our needs.

---

[8] For more on this, see www.answersingenesis.org/articles/am/v1/n2/who-begat-whom.

[9] A.C. McIntosh, T. Edmondson, and S. Taylor, McIntosh, Taylor, and Edmondson reply to Flood Models, *TJ* 14(3):80–82, 2000.

[10] John Woodmorappe has documented various detailed scientific models pertaining to the Ark, pre-Flood, and post-Flood issues in his book *Noah's Ark: A Feasibility Study*, Institute for Creation Research, El Cajon, California, 1996.

12

What Really Happened to the Dinosaurs?

KEN HAM

Dinosaurs are used more than almost anything else to indoctrinate children and adults in the idea of millions of years of earth history. However, the Bible gives us a framework for explaining dinosaurs in terms of thousands of years of history, including the mystery of when they lived and what happened to them. Two key texts are Genesis 1:24–25 and Job 40:15–24.

Are Dinosaurs a Mystery?

Many think that the existence of dinosaurs and their demise is shrouded in such mystery that we may never know the truth about where they came from, when they lived, and what happened to them. However, dinosaurs are only a mystery *if* you accept the evolutionary story of their history.

According to evolutionists: Dinosaurs first evolved around 235 million years ago, long before man evolved.[1] No human being ever lived with dinosaurs. Their history is recorded in the fossil layers on earth, which were deposited over millions of years. They were so successful as a group of animals that they eventually ruled the earth. However, around 65 million years ago,

---

[1] J. Horner and D. Lessem, *The Complete T. Rex,* Simon & Schuster, New York, 1993, 18; M. Norell, E. Gaffney and L. Dingus, *Discovering Dinosaurs in the American Museum of Natural History,* Nevraumont Publ., New York, 1995, 17, says that the oldest dinosaur fossil is dated at 228 million years.

something happened to change all of this—the dinosaurs disappeared. Most evolutionists believe some sort of cataclysmic event, such as an asteroid impact, killed them. But many evolutionists claim that some dinosaurs evolved into birds, and thus they are not extinct but are flying around us even today.[2]

There is no mystery surrounding dinosaurs if you accept the Bible's totally different account of dinosaur history.

According to the Bible: Dinosaurs first existed around 6,000 years ago.[3] God made the dinosaurs, along with the other land animals, on Day 6 of the Creation Week (Genesis 1:20–25, 31). Adam and Eve were also made on Day 6—so dinosaurs lived at the same time as people, not separated by eons of time.

Dinosaurs could not have died out before people appeared because dinosaurs had not previously existed; and death, bloodshed, disease, and suffering are a result of Adam's sin (Genesis 1:29–30; Romans 5:12, 14; 1 Corinthians 15:21–22).

---

[2] D. Gish, *Evolution: the Fossils Still Say No!* Institute for Creation Research, El Cajon, California, 1995, 129ff, discusses evolutionists' views from a creationist position; Norell et al., *Discovering Dinosaurs in the American Museum of Natural History,* 2: "Dinosaurs belong to a group called Archosauria ... . The living Archosauria are the twenty-one extant crocodiles and alligators, along with the more than ten thousand species of living theropod dinosaurs (birds)."

[3] J. Morris, *The Young Earth,* Master Books, Green Forest, Arkansas, 1994; H. Morris, *The Genesis Record,* Baker Book House, Grand Rapids, Michigan, 1976, 42–46. On the biblical chronology, see J. Ussher, *The Annals of the World,* Master Books, Green Forest, Arkansas, 2003; original published in 1658.

Representatives of all the *kinds* of air-breathing land animals, including the dinosaur kinds, went aboard Noah's Ark. All those left outside the Ark died in the cataclysmic circumstances of the Flood, and many of their remains became fossils.

After the Flood, around 4,300 years ago, the remnant of the land animals, including dinosaurs, came off the Ark and lived in the present world, along with people. Because of sin, the judgments of the Curse and the Flood have greatly changed earth. Post-Flood climatic change, lack of food, disease, and man's activities caused many types of animals to become extinct. The dinosaurs, like many other creatures, died out. Why the big mystery about dinosaurs?

Why Such Different Views?

How can there be such totally different explanations for dinosaurs? Whether one is an evolutionist or accepts the Bible's account of history, the evidence for dinosaurs is *the same*. All scientists have the same facts— they have the same world, the same fossils, the same living creatures, the same universe.

If the "facts" are the same, then how can the explanations be so different? The reason is that scientists have only the present—dinosaur fossils exist only in the present—but scientists are trying to connect the fossils in the present to the past. They ask, "What happened in history to bring dinosaurs into existence, wipe them out, and leave many of them fossilized?"[4]

The science that addresses such issues is known as *historical* or *origins science*, and it differs from the *operational science* that gives us computers, inexpensive food, space exploration, electricity, and the like. Origins science deals with the past, which is not accessible to direct experimentation, whereas operational science deals with how the world works in the here and now, which, of course, is open to repeatable experiments. Because of difficulties in reconstructing the past, those who study fossils (paleontologists) have diverse views on dinosaurs.[5] As has been said, "Paleontology (the study of fossils) is much like politics: passions run high, and it's easy to draw very different conclusions from the same set of facts."[6]

---

[4] M. Benton, *Dinosaurs: An A–Z Guide,* Derrydale Books, New York, 1988, 10–11.

[5] Benton, *Dinosaurs: An A–Z Guide.* See also D. Lambert and the Diagram Group, *The Dinosaur Data Book,* Avon Books, New York, 1990, 10–35; Norell, *et al., Discovering Dinosaurs in the American Museum of Natural History,* 62–69; V. Sharpton and P. Ward, Eds., *Global Catastrophes in Earth History,* The Geological Society of America, Special Paper 247, 1990.

[6] M. Lemonick, Parenthood, dino-style, *Time,* p. 48, January 8, 1996.

A paleontologist who believes the record in the Bible, which claims to be the Word of God,[7] will come to different conclusions than an atheist who rejects the Bible. Willful denial of God's Word (2 Peter 3:3–7) lies at the root of many disputes over historical science.

Many people think the Bible is just a book about religion or salvation. It is much more than this. The Bible is the History Book of the

The History Book of the Universe

Universe and tells us the future destiny of the universe as well. It gives us an account of when time began, the main events of history, such as the entrance of sin and death into the world, the time when the *whole* surface of the globe was destroyed by water, the giving of different languages at the Tower of Babel, the account of the Son of God coming as a man, His death and Resurrection, and the new heavens and earth to come.

Ultimately, there are only two ways of thinking: starting with the revelation from God (the Bible) as foundational to *all* thinking (including biology, history, and geology), resulting in a *Christian worldview;* or starting with man's beliefs (for example, the evolutionary story) as foundational to all thinking, resulting in a *secular worldview.*

Most Christians have been indoctrinated through the media and education system to think in a secular way. They tend to take secular thinking *to* the Bible, instead of using the Bible to *build* their thinking (Romans 12:1–2; Ephesians 4:20–24).

---

[7] Psalm 78:5; 2 Timothy 3:14–17; and 2 Peter 1:19–21. God, who inspired the writing, has always existed, is perfect and never lies (Titus 1:2).

The Bible says, "The fear of the Lord is the beginning of knowledge" (Proverbs 1:7) and "the fear of the Lord is the beginning of wisdom" (Proverbs 9:10).

If one begins with an evolutionary view of history (for which there were no witnesses or written record), then this way of thinking will be used to explain the evidence that exists in the present. Thus, we have the evolutionary explanation for dinosaurs above.

But if one begins with the biblical view of history from the written record of an eyewitness (God) to all events of history, then a totally different way of thinking, based on this, will be used to explain the *same* evidence. Thus, we have the biblical explanation given above.

Dinosaur History

Fossil bones of dinosaurs are found around the world. Many of these finds consist of just fragments of bones, but some nearly complete skeletons have been found. Scientists have been able to describe many different types of dinosaurs based on distinctive characteristics, such as the structure of the skull and limbs.[8]

Where Did Dinosaurs Come From?

The Bible tells us that God created different kinds of land animals on Day 6 of Creation Week (Genesis 1:24–25). Because dinosaurs were land animals, this must have included the dinosaur kinds.[9]

Secular history · Dinosaurs · Biblical history

[8]   D. Lambert, *A Field Guide to Dinosaurs,* Avon Books, New York, 1983, 17.
[9]   If some dinosaurs were aquatic, then these would have been created on Day 5 of Creation Week.

Evolutionists claim that dinosaurs evolved from some reptile that had originally evolved from amphibians. But they cannot point to any clear transitional (in-between) forms to substantiate their argument. Dinosaur family trees in evolutionary books show many distinct types of dinosaurs, but only hypothetical lines join them up to some common ancestor. The lines are dotted because there is *no* fossil evidence. Evolutionists simply cannot prove their belief in a nondinosaur ancestor for dinosaurs.

What Did Dinosaurs Look Like?

Scientists generally do not dig up a dinosaur with all its flesh intact. Even if they found *all* the bones, they still would have less than 40 percent of the animal to work out what it originally looked like. The bones do not tell the color of the animal, for example, although some fossils of skin impressions have been found, indicating the skin texture. As there is some diversity of color among reptiles living today, dinosaurs may have varied greatly in color, skin texture, and so on.

When reconstructing dinosaurs from bony remains, scientists make all kinds of guesses and often disagree. For example, debate has raged about whether dinosaurs were warm- or cold-blooded. It is even difficult to tell whether a dinosaur was male or female from its bones. There is much speculation about such things.

Sometimes scientists make mistakes in their reconstructions, which need correction when more bones are found. For instance, the famous *Brontosaurus* is not in newer dinosaur dictionaries. The original "discoverer" put the wrong head on a skeleton of a dinosaur that had already been named *Apatosaurus*.[10]

Who Discovered Dinosaurs?

Secular books would tell you that the first discovery of what later were called dinosaurs was in 1677 when Dr. Robert Plot found bones so big they were thought to belong to a giant elephant or a giant human.[11]

In 1822, Mary Anne Mantell went for a walk along a country road in

---

[10] S. West, Dinosaur head hunt, *Science News* **116**(18):314–315, 1979. Originally assembled wrongly with the head of a *Camarasaurus*-type dinosaur on an *Apatosaurus* skeleton and later corrected with the right head, which was from "the same family as its nearly identical cousin, *Diplodocus,*" p. 314.

[11] Benton, *Dinosaurs: An A-Z Guide*, 14.

Sussex, England. According to tradition, she found a stone that glittered in the sunlight and showed it to her fossil-collecting husband. Dr. Mantell, a physician, noticed that the stone contained a tooth similar to, but much larger than, that of modern reptiles. He concluded that it belonged to some extinct giant plant-eating reptile with teeth like an iguana. In 1825 he named the owner of the tooth *Iguanodon* (iguana tooth). It was Dr. Mantell who began to popularize the "age of reptiles."[12]

From a biblical perspective, however, the time of the above discoveries was actually the time when dinosaurs were *rediscovered*. Adam discovered dinosaurs when he first observed them.

When Did Dinosaurs Live?

Evolutionists claim dinosaurs lived millions of years ago. But it is important to realize that when they dig up a dinosaur bone it does not have a label attached showing its date. Evolutionists obtain their dates by *indirect* dating methods that other scientists question, and there is much evidence against the millions of years.[13]

Does God tell us when He made *Tyrannosaurus rex*? Many would say no. But the Bible states that God made all things in six normal days. He made the land animals, including dinosaurs, on Day 6 (Genesis 1:24–25), so they date from around 6,000 years ago—the approximate date of creation obtained by

---

12 Lambert et al., *The Dinosaur Data Book*, 279.
13 Morris, *The Young Earth*, 51–67.

adding up the years in the Bible.[14] So, since *T. rex* was a land animal and God made all the land animals on Day 6, then God made *T. rex* on Day 6.

DAY 6

LAND ANIMALS & MAN

Furthermore, from the Bible we see that there was no death, bloodshed, disease, or suffering before sin.[15] If one approaches Genesis to Revelation consistently, interpreting Scripture with Scripture, then death and bloodshed of man and animals came into the world only *after* Adam sinned. The first death of an animal occurred when God shed an animal's blood in the Garden of Eden and clothed Adam and Eve (Genesis 3:21). This was also a picture of the Atonement—foreshadowing Christ's blood that was to be shed for us. Thus, there could *not* have been bones of dead animals before sin—this would undermine the gospel.

This means that the dinosaurs must have died after sin entered the world, not before. Dinosaur bones could *not* be millions of years old because Adam lived only thousands of years ago.

Does the Bible Mention Dinosaurs?

If people saw dinosaurs, you would think that ancient historical writings, such as the Bible, should mention them. The King James Version was first translated in 1611.[16] Some people think that because the word "dinosaur" is not found in this or other translations, the Bible does not mention dinosaurs.

---

[14] Morris, *The Genesis Record*, 44–46.

[15] J. Stambaugh, Creation, suffering and the problem of evil, *CEN Technical Journal* **10**(3):391–404, 1996.

[16] The KJV most often used today is actually the 1769 revision by Benjamin Blayney of Oxford.

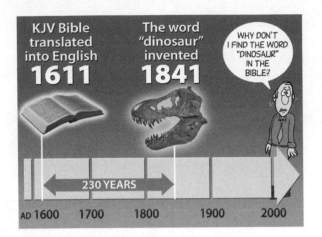

It was not until 1841, however, that the word "dinosaur" was invented.[17] Sir Richard Owen, a famous British anatomist and first superintendent of the British Museum (and a staunch anti-Darwinist), on viewing the bones of *Iguanodon* and *Megalosaurus*, realized these represented a unique group of reptiles that had not yet been classified. He coined the term "dinosaur" from Greek words meaning "terrible lizard."[18]

Thus, one would not expect to find the word "dinosaur" in the King James Bible—the word did not exist when the translation was done.

Is there another word for "dinosaur"? There are *dragon* legends from around the world. Many dragon descriptions fit the characteristics of specific dinosaurs. Could these actually be accounts of encounters with what we now call dinosaurs?

Dragons of Old
Dinosaurs in History

---

[17] D. Dixon et al., *The Macmillan Illustrated Encyclopedia of Dinosaurs and Prehistoric Animals*, Macmillan Publishing Co., New York, 1998, 92.

[18] D. Norman, *The Illustrated Encyclopedia of Dinosaurs*, Salamander Books Limited, London, 1985, 8. The meaning of "terrible lizard" has helped popularize the idea that dinosaurs were all gigantic savage monsters. This is far from the truth. Had Owen known about the *smaller* dinosaurs, he may never have coined the word.

Just as Flood legends are based on a real global Flood (Flood of Noah)—dragon legends are possibly based on actual encounters with real animals that today we call dinosaurs. Many of these land-dragon descriptions do fit with what we know about dinosaurs.

In Genesis 1:21, the Bible says, "And God created the great sea monsters and every living creature that moves, with which the waters swarmed, after their kind." The Hebrew word here for "sea monsters" ("whales" in KJV) is the word translated elsewhere as "dragon" (Hebrew: *tannin*). So, in the first chapter of the first book of the Bible, God may be describing the great sea dragons (sea-dwelling, dinosaur-type animals) that He created.

There are other Bible passages about dragons that lived in the sea: "the dragons in the waters" (Psalm 74:13), "and he shall slay the dragon that is in the sea" (Isaiah 27:1). Though the word "dinosaur" strictly refers to animals that lived on the land, the sea reptiles and flying reptiles are often grouped with the dinosaurs. The sea dragons could have included dinosaur-type animals such as the *Mosasaurus*.[19]

Job 41 describes a great animal that lived in the sea, Leviathan, that even breathed fire. This "dragon" may have been something like the mighty 40 ft. (12 m) *Sarcosuchus imperator* (Super Croc),[20] or the 82 ft. (25 m) *Liopleurodon*.

There is also mention of a flying serpent in the Bible: the "fiery flying serpent" (Isaiah 30:6). This could be a reference to one of the pterodactyls, which are popularly thought of as flying dinosaurs, such as the *Pteranodon, Rhamphorhynchus,* or *Ornithocheirus*.[21]

Not long after the Flood, God was showing a man called Job how great He was as Creator, by reminding Job of the largest land animal He had made:

---

[19] The Hebrew words have a range of meanings, including "sea monster" (Gen. 1:21; Job 7:12; Psa. 148:7; Isa. 27:1; Ezek. 29:3, 32:2) and "serpent" (Exod. 7:9; cf. Exod. 4:3 and Hebrew parallelism of Deut. 32:33). *Tannin/m* are fearsome creatures, inhabiting remote, desolate places (Isa. 34:13, 35:7; Jer. 49:33, 51:37; Mal. 1:8), difficult to kill (Isa. 27:1, 51:9) and/or serpentine (Deut. 32:33; cf. Psa. 91:13) and/or having feet (Ezek. 32:2). However, *tannin* are referred to as suckling their young (Lam. 4:3), which is not a feature of reptiles, but of whales (sea monsters?), for example. The word(s) seems to refer to large, fearsome creatures that dwelled in swampy areas or in the water. The term could include reptiles and mammals. Modern translators often render the words as "jackals," but this seems inappropriate because jackals are not particularly fearsome or difficult to kill and don't live in swamps.

[20] S. Czerkas and S. Czerkas, *Dinosaurs: A Global View,* Barnes and Noble Books, Spain, 1996, 179; P. Booker, A new candidate for Leviathan? *TJ* 19(2):14–16, 2005.

[21] D. Norman, *The Illustrated Encyclopedia of Dinosaurs,* Gramercy, New York, 1988, 170–172; P. Wellnhofer, *Pterosaurs: The Illustrated Encyclopedia of Prehistoric Flying Reptiles,* Barnes and Noble, New York, 1991, 83–85, 135–136.

Look now at the behemoth, which I made along with you; he eats grass like an ox. See now, his strength is in his hips, and his power is in his stomach muscles. He moves his tail like a cedar; the sinews of his thighs are tightly knit. His bones are like beams of bronze, his ribs like bars of iron. He is the first of the ways of God; only He who made him can bring near His sword (Job 40:15–19).

The phrase "first of the ways of God" suggests this was the largest land animal God had made. So what kind of animal was "behemoth"?

Bible translators, not being sure what this beast was, often transliterated the Hebrew, and thus the word *behemoth* (e.g., KJV, NKJV, NASB, NIV). However, in many Bible commentaries and Bible footnotes, "behemoth" is said to be "possibly the hippopotamus or elephant."[22] Some Bible versions actually translate "behemoth" this way.[23] Besides the fact that the elephant and hippo were *not* the largest land animals God made (some of the dinosaurs far eclipsed these), this description does not make sense, since the tail of behemoth is compared to the large cedar tree (verse 17).

Now an elephant's tiny tail (or a hippo's tail that looks like a flap of skin) is quite unlike a cedar tree. Clearly, the elephant and the hippo could not possibly be "behemoth."

No *living* creature comes close to this description. However, behemoth is very much like *Brachiosaurus*, one of the large dinosaurs.

---

22 E.g., NIV Study Bible, Zondervan, Grand Rapids, Michigan, 1985.
23 New Living Translation: Holy Bible, Tyndale House Publishers, Wheaton, Illinois, 1996. Job 40:15: "Take a look at the mighty hippopotamus."

BRACHIOSAUR

Are There Other Ancient Records of Dinosaurs?

In the film *The Great Dinosaur Mystery*,[24] a number of dragon accounts are presented:

- A Sumerian story dating back to 2000 BC or earlier tells of a hero named Gilgamesh, who, when he went to fell cedars in a remote forest, encountered a huge vicious dragon that he slew, cutting off its head as a trophy.

- When Alexander the Great (c. 330 BC) and his soldiers marched into India, they found that the Indians worshipped huge hissing reptiles that they kept in caves.

- China is renowned for its dragon stories, and dragons are prominent on Chinese pottery, embroidery, and carvings.

- England and several other cultures retains the story of St. George, who slew a dragon that lived in a cave.

- There is the story of a tenth-century Irishman who wrote of his encounter with what appears to have been a *Stegosaurus*.

- In the 1500s, a European scientific book, *Historia Animalium*, listed several living animals that we would call dinosaurs. A well-known naturalist of the time, Ulysses Aldrovandus, recorded an encounter between a peasant

---

[24] P. Taylor, *The Great Dinosaur Mystery,* Films for Christ, Mesa, Arizona, 1991. See also P. Taylor, *The Great Dinosaur Mystery and the Bible*, Accent Publications, Denver, Colorado, 1989.

named Baptista and a dragon whose description fits that of the small dinosaur *Tanystropheus*. The encounter was on May 13, 1572, near Bologna in Italy, and the peasant killed the dragon.

Petroglyphs (drawings carved on rock) of dinosaur-like creatures have also been found.[25]

Saint George (Sankt Goran) and the dragon in Gamla Stan (Old Town) of Stockholm, Sweden

In summary, people down through the ages have been very familiar with dragons. The descriptions of these animals fit with what we know about dinosaurs. The Bible mentions such creatures, even ones that lived in the sea and flew in the air. There is a tremendous amount of other historical evidence that such creatures have lived beside people.

What Do the Bones Say?

There is also physical evidence that dinosaur bones are not millions of years old. Scientists from the University of Montana found *T. rex* bones that were not totally fossilized. Sections of the bones were like fresh bone and contained what seems to be blood cells and hemoglobin. If these bones really were tens of millions of years old, then the blood cells and hemoglobin would have totally disintegrated. A report by these scientists stated the following:

> A thin slice of *T. rex* bone glowed amber beneath the lens of my microscope ... . The lab filled with murmurs of amazement, for I had focused on something inside the vessels that none of us had ever noticed before: tiny round objects, translucent red with a dark center ... . Red blood cells? The shape and location suggested them, but blood cells are mostly water and couldn't possibly have stayed preserved in the 65-million-year-old *tyrannosaur* ... . The bone sample that had us so excited came from a beautiful, nearly complete specimen of *Tyrannosaurus rex* unearthed in 1990 ... . When the team brought the dinosaur into the lab, we noticed that some parts

25 D. Swift, Messages on stone, *Creation* **19**(2):20–23, 1997.

deep inside the long bone of the leg had not completely fossilized … . So far, we think that all of this evidence supports the notion that our slices of *T. rex* could contain preserved heme and hemoglobin fragments. But more work needs to be done before we are confident enough to come right out and say, "Yes, this *T. rex* has blood compounds left in its tissues."[26]

Unfossilized duck-billed dinosaur bones have been found on the North Slope in Alaska.[27] The bones could not have survived for the millions of years unmineralized. This is a puzzle to those who believe in an "age of dinosaurs" millions of years ago, but not to someone who builds his thinking on the Bible.

What Did Dinosaurs Eat and How Did They Behave?

Movies like *Jurassic Park* and *The Lost World* portray most dinosaurs as aggressive meat-eaters. But the mere presence of sharp teeth does *not* tell you how an animal behaved or necessarily what food it ate—only what kind of teeth it had (for ripping food and the like). However, by studying fossil dinosaur dung (coprolite), scientists have been able to determine the diet of some dinosaurs.[28]

Originally, before sin, *all* animals, including the dinosaurs, were vegetarian. Genesis 1:30 states, "And to every beast of the earth, and to every bird of the air, and to every thing that creeps upon the earth, which has life, I have given every green herb for food: and it was so."

This means that even *T. rex*, before sin entered the world, ate only plants. Some people object to this by pointing to the big teeth that a large *T. rex* had, insisting they must have been used for attacking animals. However, just because an animal has big, sharp teeth does not mean it eats meat. It just means it has big, sharp teeth![29]

Many animals today have sharp teeth but are basically vegetarian. The giant panda has sharp teeth like a meat-eater, but it eats bamboo. Perhaps

---

[26] M. Schweitzer and T. Staedter, The real Jurassic Park, *Earth*, pp. 55–57, June 1997. See report in *Creation* 19(4):42–43, which describes the careful testing that showed that hemoglobin was present.

[27] K. Davies, Duckbill dinosaurs (Hadrosauridae, Ornithischia) from the North Slope of Alaska, *Journal of Paleontology* 61(1):198–200, 1987.

[28] S. Lucas, *Dinosaurs: The Textbook*, Wm. C. Brown Publishers, Dubuque, IA, 1994, 194–196.

[29] D. Marrs and V. Kylberg, *Dino Cardz*, 1991. *Estemmenosuchus* was a large mammal-like reptile. "Despite having menacing-looking fangs it apparently was a plant-eater." The authors possibly concluded this from its rear teeth.

the panda's teeth were beautifully designed to eat bamboo. To explain why a giant panda has teeth like a meat-eaters today, yet eats bamboo, evolutionists have to say that the giant panda evolved as a meat eater, and then switched to bamboo.[30]

Different species of bats variously eat fruit, nectar, insects, small animals, and blood, but their teeth do not clearly indicate what they eat.[31] Bears have teeth with carnivore features, but some bears are vegetarian, and many, if not most, are mainly vegetarian.

Before sin, God described the world as "very good" (Genesis 1:31). Some cannot accept this concept of perfect harmony because of the food chain that they observe in today's world. However, one cannot look at the sin-cursed world and the resultant death and struggle, and use this to reject the Genesis account of history. Everything has changed because of sin. That's why Paul describes the present creation as "groaning" (Romans 8:22). One must look through the Bible's "eyes" to understand the world.[32]

Some argue that people or animals would have been hurt even in an ideal world. They contend that even before sin, Adam or an animal could have stood on small creatures or scratched himself on a branch. Now these sorts of situations are true of today's fallen world—the present world is not perfect; it is suffering from the effects of the Curse (Romans 8:22). One cannot look at the Bible through the world's eyes and insist that the world before sin was just like the world we see today. We do not know what a perfect world, continually restored and totally upheld by God's power (Colossians 1:17; Hebrews 1:3), would have been like—we have never experienced perfection (only Adam and Eve did before sin).

We do get little glimpses from Scripture, however; in Deuteronomy 8:4, 29:5 and Nehemiah 9:21, we are told that when the Israelites wandered in the desert for 40 years, their clothes and shoes did not wear out, nor did their feet swell. When God upholds things perfectly, wearing out or being hurt in any way is not even an option.

Think of Shadrach, Meshach, and Abednego (Daniel 3:26–27). They came out of the fire without even the smell of smoke on them. Again, when the Lord upholds perfectly, being hurt is not possible. In a perfect world, before sin and the Curse, God would have upheld everything, but in this cursed world, things run down. Many commentators believe the description in Isaiah 11:6–9 of the

---

[30] K. Brandes, *Vanishing Species*, Time-Life Books, New York, 1974, 98.
[31] P. Weston, Bats: sophistication in miniature, *Creation* 21(1):28–31, 1999.
[32] Morris, *The Genesis Record*, 78.

wolf and lamb, and the lion that eats straw like an ox, is a picture of the new earth in the future restoration (Acts 3:21) when there will be no more curse or death (Revelation 21:1, 22:3). The animals described are living peacefully as vegetarians (this is also the description of the animal world before sin—Genesis 1:30). Today's world has been changed dramatically because of sin and the Curse. The present food chain and animal behavior (which also changed after the Flood—Genesis 9:2–3) cannot be used as a basis for interpreting the Bible—the Bible explains why the world is the way it is.

In the beginning, God gave Adam and Eve dominion over the animals: "Then God blessed them, and God said to them, 'Be fruitful and multiply; fill the earth and subdue it; have dominion over the fish of the sea, over the birds of the air, and over every living thing that moves on the earth'" (Genesis 1:28). Looking at today's world, we are reminded of Hebrews 2:8: "For in that He put all in subjection under him, He left nothing that is not put under him. But now we do not yet see all things put under him." Man's relationship with all things changed because of sin—they are not "under him" as they were originally.

Most people, including most Christians, tend to observe the world as it is today, with all its death and suffering, and then take that observation to the Bible and interpret it in that light. But we are sinful, fallible human beings, observing a sin-cursed world (Romans 8:22); and thus, we need to start with divine revelation, the Bible, to begin to understand.

So how did fangs and claws come about? Dr. Henry Morris, a founding figure in the modern creation movement, states:

> Whether such structures as fangs and claws were part of their original equipment, or were recessive features which only became dominant due to selection processes later, or were mutational features following the Curse, or exactly what, must await further research.[33]

After sin entered the world, everything changed. Maybe some animals started eating each other at this stage. By the time of Noah, God described what had happened this way: "So God looked upon the earth, and indeed it was corrupt; for all flesh had corrupted their way on the earth" (Genesis 6:12).

Also, after the Flood, God changed the behavior of animals. We read, "And the fear of you and the dread of you shall be on every beast of the earth, on

---

[33] See chapter 21 for more on the possible origin of defense-attack structures.

every bird of the air, on all that move on the earth, and on all the fish of the sea. They are given into your hand" (Genesis 9:2). Thus, man would find it much more difficult to carry out the dominion mandate given in Genesis 1:28.

Why Do We Find Dinosaur Fossils?

Fossil formation requires a sudden burial. When an animal dies, it usually gets eaten or decays until there is nothing left. To form a fossil, unique conditions are required to preserve the animal and replace it with minerals, etc.

Evolutionists once claimed that the fossil record was formed slowly as animals died and were gradually covered by sediment. But they have acknowledged more recently that the fossil record must involve catastrophic processes.[34] To form the billions of fossils worldwide, in layers sometimes kilometers thick, the organisms, by and large, must have been buried quickly. Many evolutionists now say the fossil record formed quickly, in spurts interspersed by millions of years.

According to the Bible, as time went on, earth became full of wickedness, so God determined that He would send a global Flood "to destroy from under heaven all flesh in which is the breath of life" (Genesis 6:17).

God commanded Noah to build a very large boat into which he would take his family and representatives of every kind of land-dwelling, air-breathing animal (that God Himself would choose and send to Noah, Genesis 6:20). This must have included two of each kind of dinosaur.

How Did Dinosaurs Fit on the Ark?

Many people think of dinosaurs as large creatures that would never have fit into the Ark.

But the average size of a dinosaur, based on the skeletons found over the earth, is about the size of a sheep.[35] Indeed, many dinosaurs were relatively small. For instance, *Struthiomimus* was the size of an ostrich, and *Compsognathus* was no bigger than a rooster. Only a few dinosaurs grew to extremely

---

[34] For example, D. Ager, *The New Catastrophism,* Cambridge University Press, Cambridge, UK, 1993.

[35] M. Crichton, *The Lost World*, Ballantine Books, New York, 1995, 122. "Dinosaurs were mostly small ... . People always think they were huge, but the average dinosaur was the size of a sheep or a small pony." According to Horner and Lessem, *The Complete T. Rex*, 1993, 124: "Most dinosaurs were smaller than bulls."

large sizes (e.g., *Brachiosaurus* and *Apatosaurus)*, but even they were not as large as the largest animal in the world today, the blue whale. (Reptiles have the potential to grow as long as they live. Thus, the large dinosaurs were probably very old ones.)

Dinosaurs laid eggs, and the biggest fossil dinosaur egg found is about the size of a football.[36] Even the largest dinosaurs were very small when first hatched. Remember that the animals that came off the boat were to repopulate the earth. Thus, it would have been necessary to choose young adults, which would soon be in the prime of their reproductive life, to go on the Ark. Recent research suggests that dinosaurs underwent rapid adolescent growth spurts.[37] So it is realistic to assume that God would have sent young adults to the Ark, not fully grown creatures.

Some might argue that the 600 or more named species of dinosaurs could not have fit on the Ark. But Genesis 6:20 states that representative *kinds* of land animals boarded the Ark. The question then is, what is a "kind" (Hebrew: *min*)? Biblical creationists have pointed out that there can be many species descended from a kind. For example, there are many types of cats in the world, but all cat species probably came from only a few kinds of cats originally.[38] The cat varieties today have developed by natural and artificial selection acting on the original variation in the information (genes) of the

[36] D. Lambert, *A Field Guide to Dinosaurs*, Avon Books, New York, 1983, 127.
[37] G.M. Erickson, K.C. Rogers, and S.A. Yerby, Dinosaurian growth patterns and rapid avian growth rates, *Nature* **412**(6845):405–408, 429–433, July 26, 2001.
[38] W. Mehlert, On the origin of cats and carnivores, *CEN Technical Journal*, **9**(1):106–120, 1995.

original cats. This has produced different combinations and subsets of information, and thus different types of cats.

Mutations (errors in copying of the genes during reproduction) can also contribute to the variation, but the changes caused by mutations are "downhill," causing loss of the original information.

Even speciation could occur through these processes. This speciation is *not* "evolution," since it is based on the created information *already present* and is thus a limited, downhill process, not involving an upward increase in complexity. Thus, only a few feline pairs would have been needed on Noah's Ark.

Dinosaur names have tended to proliferate, with new names being given to just a few pieces of bone, even if the skeleton looks similar to one that is a different size or found in a different country. There were probably fewer than 50 distinct groups or kinds of dinosaurs that had to be on the Ark.[39]

Also, it must be remembered that Noah's Ark was extremely large and quite capable of carrying the number of animals needed, including dinosaurs.

The land animals that were not on the Ark, including dinosaurs, drowned. Many were preserved in the layers formed by the Flood—thus the millions of fossils. Presumably, many of the dinosaur fossils were buried at this time, around 4,500 years ago. Also, after the Flood, there would have been considerable catastrophism, including such events as the Ice Age, resulting in some post-Flood formation of fossils, too.

The contorted shapes of these animals preserved in the rocks, the massive numbers of them in fossil graveyards, their wide distribution, and some whole

ONLY ABOUT 50 DINOSAUR "KINDS"

---

[39] Norell et al., *Discovering Dinosaurs in the American Museum of Natural History,* figure 56, pp. 86–87. See Czerkas and Czerkas, *Dinosaurs: A Global View,* 151.

skeletons, all provide convincing evidence that they were buried rapidly, testifying to massive flooding.[40]

Why Don't We See Dinosaurs Today?

At the end of the Flood, Noah, his family, and the animals came out of the Ark (Genesis 8:15–17). The dinosaurs thus began a new life in a new world. Along with the other animals, the dinosaurs came out to breed and repopulate the earth. They would have left the landing place of the Ark and spread over the earth's surface. The descendants of these dinosaurs gave rise to the dragon legends.

But the world they came out to repopulate differed from the one they knew before Noah's Flood. The Flood had devastated it. It was now a much more difficult world in which to survive.

After the Flood, God told Noah that from then on, the animals would fear man, and that animal flesh could be food for man (Genesis 9:1–7). Even for man, the world had become a harsher place. To survive, the once easily obtained plant nutrition would now have to be supplemented by animal sources.

Both animals and man would find their ability to survive tested to the utmost. We can see from the fossil record, from the written history of man, and from experience over recent centuries, that many forms of life on this planet have not survived that test.

We need to remember that many plants and air-breathing, land-dwelling animals have become extinct *since* the Flood—either due to man's action or competition with other species, or because of the harsher post-Flood environment. Many groups are still becoming extinct. Dinosaurs seem to be numbered among the extinct groups.

Why then are people so intrigued about dinosaurs and have little interest in the extinction of the fern *Cladophebius,* for example? It's the dinosaurs' appeal as monsters that excites and fascinates people.

Evolutionists have capitalized on this fascination, and the world is awash with evolutionary propaganda centered on dinosaurs. As a result, evolutionary philosophy has permeated modern thinking, even among Christians.

---

[40] For example, reptiles drowned in a flash flood 200 million years ago, according to the interpretation put upon the reptile fossils discovered in Lubbock Quarry, Texas (*The Weekend Australian,* p. 32, November 26–27, 1983).

If you were to ask the zoo why they have endangered species programs, you would probably get an answer something like this: "We've lost lots of animals from this earth. Animals are becoming extinct all the time. Look at all the animals that are gone forever. We need to act to save the animals." If you then asked, "Why are animals becoming extinct?" you might get an answer like this: "It's obvious! People killing them, lack of food, man destroying the environment, diseases, genetic problems, catastrophes like floods—there are lots of reasons."

If you then asked, "Well, what happened to the dinosaurs?" the answer would probably be, "We don't know! Scientists have suggested dozens of possible reasons, but it's a mystery."

Maybe one of the reasons dinosaurs are extinct is that we did not start our endangered species programs early enough. The factors that cause extinction today, which came about because of man's sin—the Curse, the aftermath of the Flood (a judgment), etc.—are the same factors that caused the dinosaurs to become extinct.

Are Dinosaurs Really Extinct?

One cannot prove an organism is extinct without having knowledge of every part of the earth's surface simultaneously. Experts have been embarrassed when, after having declared animals extinct, they were discovered alive and well. For example, in the 1990s explorers found elephants in Nepal that have many features of mammoths.[41]

---

41 Elephants take mammoth step out of an ancient past, *The Sunday Mail* (Brisbane, Australia), December 17, 1995.

Scientists in Australia found some living trees that they thought had become extinct with the dinosaurs. One scientist said, "It was like finding a 'live dinosaur.'"[42] When scientists find animals or plants that they thought were extinct long ago, they call them "living fossils." There are hundreds of living fossils, a big embarrassment for those who believe in millions of years of earth history.

Explorers and natives in Africa have reported sighting dinosaur-like creatures, even in the twentieth century.[43] These have usually been confined to out-of-the-way places such as lakes deep in the Congo jungles. Descriptions certainly fit those of dinosaurs.

Cave paintings by native Americans seem to depict a dinosaur.[44] Scientists accept the mammoth drawings in the cave, so why not the dinosaur drawings? Evolutionary indoctrination that man did not live at the same time as dinosaurs stops most scientists from even considering that the drawings are of dinosaurs.

It certainly would be no embarrassment to a creationist if someone discovered a dinosaur living in a jungle. However, this should embarrass evolutionists.

And no, we cannot clone a dinosaur, as in the movie *Jurassic Park*, even if we had dinosaur DNA. An egg from a living female dinosaur would also be a must to employ the cloning techniques currently used by scientists to clone a wide variety of animals.

Birdosaurs?

Many evolutionists do not really think dinosaurs are extinct anyway. In 1997, at the entrance to the bird exhibit at the zoo in Cincinnati, Ohio, we read the following on a sign:

> Dinosaurs went extinct millions of years ago—or did they? No, birds are essentially modern short-tailed feathered dinosaurs.

In the mid-1960s, Dr. John Ostrom from Yale University began to popularize the idea that dinosaurs evolved into birds.[45] However, not all

---

[42] See Anon., *Melbourne Sun*, February 6, 1980. More than 40 people claimed to have seen *plesiosaurs* off the Victorian coast (Australia) over recent years.

[43] Anon., Dinosaur hunt, *Science Digest* **89**(5):21, 1981. See H. Regusters, Mokele-mbembe: an investigation into rumors concerning a strange animal in the Republic of Congo, 1981, *Munger Africana Library Notes*, **64**: 2–32, 1982; M. Agmagna, Results of the first Congolese mokele-mbembe expedition, *Cryptozoology* **2**:103, 1983, as cited in *Science Frontiers* **33**, 1983.

[44] D. Swift, Messages on stone, *Creation*, **19**(2):20–23, 1997.

[45] Norell, *Discovering Dinosaurs in the American Museum of Natural History*, 13.

evolutionists agree with this. "It's just a fantasy of theirs," says Alan Feduccia, an ornithologist at the University of North Carolina at Chapel Hill, and a leading critic of the dino-to-bird theory. "They so much want to see living dinosaurs that now they think they can study them vicariously at the backyard bird feeder."[46]

There have been many attempts to indoctrinate the public to believe that modern birds are really dinosaurs. *Time* magazine, on April 26, 1993, had a front page cover of a "birdosaur," now called *Mononykus*, with feathers (a supposed transitional form between dinosaurs and birds) based on a fossil find that had *no* feathers.[47] In the same month, *Science News* had an article suggesting this animal was a digging creature more like a mole.[48]

In 1996, newspapers reported a find in China of a reptile fossil that supposedly had feathers.[49] Some of the media reports claimed that, if it were confirmed, it would be "irrefutable evidence that today's birds evolved from dinosaurs." One scientist stated, "You can't come to any conclusion other than that they're feathers."[50] However, in 1997 the Academy of Natural Sciences in Philadelphia sent four leading scientists to investigate this find. They concluded that they were *not* feathers. The media report stated, concerning one of the scientists, "He said he saw 'hair-like' structures—not hairs—that could have supported a frill, or crest, like those on iguanas."[51]

No sooner had this report appeared than another media report claimed that 20 fragments of bones of a reptile found in South America showed that dinosaurs were related to birds.[52]

Birds are warm-blooded and reptiles are cold-blooded, but evolutionists who believe dinosaurs evolved into birds would like to see dinosaurs as warm-blooded to support their theory. But Dr. Larry Martin, of the University of Kansas, opposes this idea:

> Recent research has shown the microscopic structure of dinosaur bones was "characteristic of cold-blooded animals," Martin said. "So we're back to cold-blooded dinosaurs."[53]

[46] V. Morell, Origin of birds: the dinosaur debate, *Audubon*, March–April 1997, p. 38.
[47] Anon., New "birdosaur" not missing link! *Creation* 15(3):3, 1993.
[48] Anon., "Birdosaur" more like a mole, *Creation* 15(4):7, 1993.
[49] M. Browne, Downy dinosaur reported, *Cincinnati Enquirer*, p. A13, October 19, 1996.
[50] Anon., Remains of feathered dinosaur bolster theory on origin of birds, Associated Press, New York, October 18, 1996.
[51] B. Stieg, Bones of contention, *Philadelphia Inquirer*, March 31, 1997.
[52] P. Recer, Birds linked to dinosaurs, *Cincinnati Enquirer*, p. A9, May 21, 1997.
[53] Stieg, Did birds evolve from dinosaurs? *The Philadelphia Inquirer*, March 1997.

Sadly, the secular media have become so blatant in their anti-Christian stand and pro-evolutionary propaganda that they are bold enough to make such ridiculous statements as, "Parrots and hummingbirds are also dinosaurs."[54]

Several more recent reports have fueled the bird/dinosaur debate among evolutionists. One concerns research on the embryonic origins of the "fingers" of birds and dinosaurs, showing that birds could *not* have evolved from dinosaurs.[55] A study of the so-called feathered dinosaur from China revealed that the dinosaur had a distinctively reptilian lung and diaphragm, which is distinctly different from the avian lung.[56] Another report said that the frayed edges that some thought to be "feathers" on the Chinese fossil are similar to the collagen fibers found immediately beneath the skin of sea snakes.[57]

There is *no* credible evidence that dinosaurs evolved into birds.[58] Dinosaurs have always been dinosaurs and birds have always been birds.

What if a dinosaur fossil *was* found with feathers on it? Would that prove that birds evolved from dinosaurs? No, a duck has a duck bill and webbed feet, as does a platypus, but nobody believes that this proves that platypuses evolved from ducks. The belief that reptiles or dinosaurs evolved into birds requires reptilian scales on the way to becoming feathers, that is, transitional scales, not fully formed feathers. A dinosaur-like fossil with feathers would just be another curious mosaic, like the platypus, and part of the pattern of similarities placed in creatures to show the hand of the one true Creator God who made everything.[59]

Why Does It Matter?

Although dinosaurs are fascinating, some readers may say, "Why are dinosaurs such a big deal? Surely there are many more important issues to deal with in today's world, such as abortion, family breakdown, racism, promiscuity, dishonesty, homosexual behavior, euthanasia, suicide, lawlessness,

---

[54] P. Recer, Birds linked to dinosaurs, 1997.

[55] A. Burke and A. Feduccia, Developmental patterns and the identification of homologies in the avian hand, *Science* **278**:666–668, 1997; A. Feduccia and J. Nowicki, The hand of birds revealed by early bird embryos, *Naturwissenschaften* **89**:391–393, 2002.

[56] J. Ruben et al., Lung structure and ventilation in theropod dinosaurs and early birds, *Science* **278**:1267–1270, 1997.

[57] A. Gibbons, Plucking the feathered dinosaur, *Science* **278**:1229, 1997.

[58] See chapter 24.

[59] For more on the problems with dinosaur-to-bird evolution, see chapter 24.

pornography, and so on. In fact, we should be telling people about the gospel of Jesus Christ, not worrying about side issues like dinosaurs."

Actually, the evolutionary teachings on dinosaurs that pervade society *do* have a great bearing on why many will not listen to the gospel, and thus why social problems abound today. If they don't believe the history in the Bible, why would anyone trust its moral aspects and message of salvation?

The Implications

If we accept the evolutionary teachings on dinosaurs, then we must accept that the Bible's account of history is false. If the Bible is wrong in this area, then it is not the Word of God and we can ignore everything else it says that we find inconvenient.

If everything made itself through natural processes—without God—then God does not own us and has no right to tell us how to live. In fact, God does not really exist in this way of thinking, so there is no absolute basis for morality. Without God, anything goes—concepts of right and wrong are just a matter of opinion. And without a basis for morality, there is no such thing as sin. And no sin means that there is no need to fear God's judgment and there is no need for the Savior, Jesus Christ. The history in the Bible is vital for properly understanding why one needs to accept Jesus Christ.

Millions of Years and the Gospel

The teaching that dinosaurs lived and died millions of years before man directly attacks the foundations of the gospel in another way. The fossil record,

I have spoken to you of earthly things and you do not believe; how then will you believe if I speak of heavenly things? John 3:12

BIBLICAL HISTORY

Earthly things

of which dinosaurs form a part, documents death, disease, suffering, cruelty, and brutality. It is a very ugly record. Allowing for millions of years in the fossil layers means accepting death, bloodshed, disease, and suffering *before* Adam's sin.

But the Bible makes it clear that death, bloodshed, disease, and suffering are a *consequence of sin*. As part of the Curse, God told Adam in Genesis 3:19 that he would return to the dust from which he was made, showing that the sentence of death was not only spiritual, but physical as well.

After Adam disobeyed God, the Lord clothed Adam and Eve with "coats of skins" (Genesis 3:21). To do this He must have killed and shed the blood of at least one animal. The reason for this can be summed up by Hebrews 9:22:

> And according to the law almost all things are purified with blood, and without shedding of blood there is no remission.

God required the shedding of blood for the forgiveness of sins. What happened in the Garden of Eden was a picture of what was to come in Jesus Christ, who shed His blood on the Cross as "the Lamb of God, who takes away the sin of the world" (John 1:29).

If the shedding of blood occurred before sin, as would have happened if the garden was sitting on a fossil record of dead things millions of years old, then the foundation of the Atonement would be destroyed.

This big picture also fits with Romans 8, which says that the whole creation "groans" because of the effects of the Fall of Adam—it was not "groaning" with death and suffering before Adam sinned. Jesus Christ suffered physical death and shed His blood because death was the penalty for sin. Paul discusses this in detail in Romans 5 and 1 Corinthians 15.

Revelation chapters 21 and 22 make it clear that there will be a "new heaven and a new earth" one day where there will be "no more death" and "no more curse"—just as it was before sin changed everything. Obviously, if there are going to be animals in the new earth, they will not die or eat each other or eat the redeemed people.

Thus, the teaching of millions of years of death, disease, and suffering before Adam sinned is a direct attack on the foundation of the message of the Cross.

Conclusion

If we accept God's Word, beginning with Genesis, as being true and authoritative, then we can explain dinosaurs and make sense of the evidence we observe in the world around us. In doing this, we are helping people see that Genesis is absolutely trustworthy and logically defensible, and is what it claims to be—the true account of the history of the universe and mankind. And what one believes concerning the book of Genesis will ultimately determine what one believes about the rest of the Bible. This, in turn, will affect how a person views himself or herself, fellow human beings, and what life is all about, including their need for salvation.

13

Why Don't We Find Human & Dinosaur Fossils Together?

BODIE HODGE

B iblical creationists believe that man and dinosaurs lived at the same time because God, a perfect eyewitness to history, said that He created man and land animals on Day 6 (Genesis 1:24–31). Dinosaurs are land animals, so logically they were created on Day 6.

In contrast, those who do not believe the plain reading of Genesis, such as many non-Christians and compromised Christians, believe the rock and fossil layers on earth represent millions of years of earth history and that man and dinosaurs did not live at the same time.

Old-earth proponents often argue that if man and dinosaurs lived at the same time, their fossils should be found in the same layers. Since no one has found definitive evidence of human remains in the same layers as dinosaurs (Cretaceous, Jurassic, and Triassic), they say that humans and dinosaurs are separated by millions of years of time and, therefore, didn't live together. So, old-earth proponents ask a very good question: Why don't we find human fossils with dinosaur fossils, if they lived at the same time?

We find human fossils in layers that most creationists consider post-Flood. Most of these were probably buried after the Flood and after the scattering of humans from Babel. So it is true that human and dinosaur fossils have yet to be found in the same layers, but does that mean that long-age believers are correct?

What Do We Find in the Fossil Record?

The first issue to consider is what we actually find in the fossil record.

- ~95% of all fossils are shallow marine organisms, such as corals and shell-fish.

- ~95% of the remaining 5% are algae and plants.

- ~95% of the remaining 0.25% are invertebrates, including insects.

- The remaining 0.0125% are vertebrates, mostly fish. (95% of land vertebrates consist of less than one bone, and 95% of mammal fossils are from the Ice Age after the Flood.)[1]

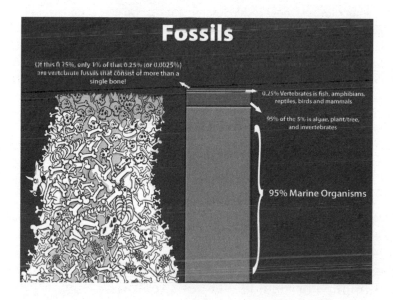

The number of dinosaur fossils is actually relatively small, compared to other types of creatures. Since the Flood was a marine catastrophe, we would expect marine fossils to be dominant in the fossil record. And that is the case.

Vertebrates are not as common as other types of life forms. This makes sense of these percentages and helps us understand why vertebrates, including dinosaurs, are so rare and even overwhelmed by marine organisms in the record.

---

[1] A. Snelling, Where are all the human fossils? *Creation* 14(1):28–33, December, 1991; J. Morris, *The Young Earth*, Master Books, Green Forest, Arkansas, 2002, 71.

Yet that still does not explain why there are no fossilized humans *found to date* in Flood sediments.

Were Pre-Flood Humans Completely Obliterated?

In Genesis 6:7 and 7:23, God says He will "blot out" man from the face of the earth using the Flood. Some have suggested that this phrase means to completely obliterate all evidence of man. However, this is not completely accurate. After a lengthy study, Fouts and Wise make it clear that the Hebrew word מחה (māhâ), translated as "blot out" or "destroy," can still leave evidence behind. They say,

> Although māhâ is properly translated "blot out," "wipe," or even "destroy," it is not to be understood to refer to the complete obliteration of something without evidence remaining. In every Biblical use of māhâ where it is possible to determine the fate of the blotted, wiped, or destroyed, the continued existence of something is terminated, but evidence may indeed remain of the previous existence and/or the blotting event itself. Even the theological consideration of the "blotting out" of sin suggests that evidence usually remains (e.g., consequences, scars, sin nature, etc.).[2]

In light of this, it is possible that human fossils from the Flood could still exist but just haven't been found yet.

So, should we find human fossils in layers that contain dinosaur fossils? To answer this further, we need to understand what we actually find in the fossil record, what the likelihood is that humans would have been fossilized, what is unusual about their distribution, and how much Flood sediment there was.

Do Humans Fossilize like Other Creatures?

Fossilization is a rare event, especially of humans who are very mobile. Since the rains of Noah's Flood took weeks to cover the earth, many people could have made it to boats, grabbed on to floating debris, and so on. Some may have made it to higher ground. Although they wouldn't have lasted that long and would have eventually perished, they might not fossilize.

---

[2] D. Fouts and K. Wise, Blotting out and breaking up: miscellaneous Hebrew studies in geocatastrophism, Proceedings of the Fourth International Conference on Creationism, Creation Science Fellowship, Pittsburgh, 1998, 219.

In most cases, dead things decompose or get eaten. They just disappear and nothing is left. The 2004 tsunami in Southeast Asia was a shocking reminder of the speed with which water and other forces can eliminate all trace of bodies, even when we know where to look. According to the United Nation's Office of the Special Envoy for Tsunami Recovery, nearly 43,000 tsunami victims were never found.[3]

Even if rare, it would still be possible to fossilize a human body. In fact, we do find fossils of humans, such as Neanderthals, in the post-Flood sediments. So why don't we find humans in pre-Flood sediments?

One suggestion has been that the human population was relatively small. Let's see how that possibility bears out.

Were Pre-Flood Humans Few in Number?

Estimates for the pre-Flood population are based on very little information, since Genesis 1 doesn't give extensive family size or population growth information. We know that Noah was in the tenth generation of his line, and he lived about 1,650 years after creation. Genesis also indicates that in Noah's lineage children were being born to fathers between the ages of 65 and more than 500 (when Noah bore his three sons).

How many generations were there in other lineages? We don't know. We know that those in the line from Adam to Noah were living upwards of 900 years each, but we can't be certain everyone lived that long. How many total children were born? Again, we don't know. What were the death rates? We simply don't know. Despite this lack of information, estimates have been done. One estimate puts the number as high as 17 billion people.[4] These estimates are based on various population growth rates and numbers of generations. Recall that Noah was in the tenth generation from Adam, however, so these estimates may be too high.

It seems doubtful that there were many hundreds of millions of people before the Flood. If the world was indeed bad enough for God to judge with a Flood, then people were probably blatantly disobedient to God's command to be fruitful and fill the earth. Moreover, the Bible says that violence filled the earth, so death rates may have been extraordinarily high.

---

[3] The Human Toll, www.tsunamispecialenvoy.org/country/humantoll.asp.
[4] T. Pickett, Population of the Pre-Flood World, www.ldolphin.org/pickett.html; H. Morris, *Biblical Cosmology and Modern Science*, Baker Book House, Grand Rapids, Michigan, 1970, 77–78; Morris, *The Young Earth*, 71.

In light of this, the population of humans in the pre-Flood world could have been as low as hundreds of thousands. Even if we make a generous assumption of 200 million people at the time of the Flood, there would be just over one human fossil per cubic mile of sediment laid down by the Flood!

Were Humans Concentrated in High Density Pockets that Have Not Been Discovered?

Today, humans tend to clump together in groups in towns, villages, and cities. In the same way, people were probably not evenly distributed before the Flood. The first city is recorded in Genesis 4:17, long before the Flood. We know that most of the population today lives within 100 miles (160 km) of the coastline. One report states, "Already nearly two-thirds of humanity—some 3.6 billion people—crowd along a coastline, or live with 150 kilometers of one."[5]

This is strong evidence that the pre-Flood civilizations probably were not evenly distributed on the landmass. If man wasn't evenly distributed, then the pockets of human habitation possibly were buried in places that have not yet been discovered.

Not only is fossilization a rare event, but fossils are also difficult to find. Just consider how much sediment was laid down by the Flood, compared to the area that has actually been exposed for us to explore.

John Woodmorappe's studies indicate that there are about 168 million cubic miles (700 million km^3) of Flood sediment.[6] John Morris estimates that there is about 350 million cubic miles of Flood sediment.[7] The latter may be high because the total volume of water on the earth is estimated at about 332.5 million cubic miles, according to the U.S. Geological Survey.[8] But even so, there is a lot of sediment left to sift through. Having such a massive amount of sediment to study is a major reason why we have not found human fossils yet.

So, a small human population and massive amounts of sediment are two prominent factors why we haven't found human fossils in pre-Flood sediments. It also may simply be that we haven't found the sediment where humans were living and were buried.

5 D. Hinrichsen, "Coasts in Crisis," www.aaas.org/international/ehn/fisheries/hinrichs.htm.
6 J. Woodmorappe, *Studies in Flood Geology,* Institute for Creation Research, El Cajon, California, 1999, 59. This number actually comes from A.B. Ronov, "The earth's sedimentary shell," *International Geology Review* 24(11):1321–1339, 1982.
7 Morris, *The Young Earth,* 71.
8 "Where is the earth's water located?" U.S. Geological Survey, ga.water.usgs.gov/edu/earthwherewater.html.

Think about It—Would You Want to Live with Dinosaurs?

Often, people believe that if human bones aren't found with dinosaur bones, then they didn't live at the same time. Actually, all we know for sure is that they weren't buried together. It is very easy for creatures to live at the same time on earth, but never even cross paths. Have you ever seen a tiger or a panda in the wild? Just because animals are not found together does not mean they do not live in the same world at the same time.

A great example is the coelacanth. Coelacanth fossils are found in marine deposits below dinosaurs and in other marine layers that "date" about the same age as dinosaurs.[9] It was once thought the coelacanth became extinct about 70 million years ago because their fossils are not found in any deposits higher than this. However, in 1938 living populations were found in the Indian Ocean.[10] It appears that coelacanths were buried with other sea creatures during the Flood—as we would expect. The example of the coelacanth shows that animals are not necessarily buried in the same place as other animals from different environments. We don't find human bones buried with coelacanths, either, but we live together today and people are enjoying them for dinner in some parts of the world.

Coelacanths aren't the only example. We find many examples like this, even with creatures that did not live in the sea. One popular example is the Wollemi Pine, which was fossilized in Jurassic deposits, supposedly 150 million years ago.[11] However, we find these trees living today. Another great living fossil is the Ginkgo tree, which supposedly thrived 240 million years ago, prior to the dinosaurs.[12] Yet, they are not found in layers with dinosaurs or post-Flood humans, even though they exist today. The list of "living fossils" goes on. Because animals and plants aren't buried together, it is no indication that things didn't live together.

In fact, based on human nature, we can assume that humans probably chose not to live in the same place with dinosaurs. So, the real issue is what happened to the local environment where humans lived.

---

[9] L. Dicks, The creatures time forgot, *New Scientist*, **164**(2209): 36–39, October 23, 1999.

[10] R. Driver, Sea monsters…more than a legend? *Creation* **19**(4):38–42, September 1997, www.answersingenesis.org/creation/v19/i4/seamonsters.asp.

[11] www.answersingenesis.org/docs2/4416livingfossil_tree12-25-2000.asp.

[12] www.pbs.org/wgbh/nova/fish/other.html.

What Can We Conclude?

If human and dinosaur bones are ever found in the same layers, it would be a fascinating find to both creationists and evolutionists. Those who hold a biblical view of history wouldn't be surprised but would consider several logical possibilities, such as human parties invading dinosaur lands for sport or for food, or merely humans and dinosaurs being washed up and buried together.

Evolutionists, on the other hand, who believe the geologic layers represent millions of years of time, would have a real challenge. In the old-earth view, man isn't supposed to be the same age as dinosaurs. Yet we can be sure that this finding would not overturn their starting assumptions—they would simply try to develop a hypothesis consistent with their preconceived view of history. For example, they might search for the possibility that the fossils were moved and redeposited.

So, ultimately, the debate is not about the evidence itself—where we find human fossils and dinosaur fossils. Nobody was there to actually observe humans and dinosaurs living together outside of written revelation, which is very limited pre-Flood. We are forced to reconstruct that history based on our existing assumptions about time and history, as well as our limited fossil evidence from the rocks.

As biblical creationists, we don't require that human and dinosaur fossils be found in the same layers. Whether they are found or not, does not affect the biblical view of history.

The fundamental debate is really about the most trustworthy source of information about history. Do we start with the Bible, which God says is true in every detail, including its history, or do we start with the changing theories of imperfect man? God tells Christians to walk by faith and that "without faith it is impossible to please Him" (Hebrews 11:6). But this is not a blind faith. God has filled the world with clear evidences that confirm the truth of His Word and the certainty of the Christian faith. The fossil record itself is an incredible testimony to the truth of God's Word and His promise to "blot out" all land dwelling, air-breathing animals and humans in a worldwide catastrophe.

14

Can Catastrophic Plate Tectonics Explain Flood Geology?

ANDREW A. SNELLING

What Is Plate Tectonics?

The earth's thin rocky outer layer (3–45 mi [5–70 km] thick) is called "the crust." On the continents it consists of sedimentary rock layers—some containing fossils and some folded and contorted—together with an underlying crystalline rocky basement of granites and metamorphosed sedimentary rocks. In places, the crystalline rocks are exposed at the earth's surface, usually as a result of erosion. Beneath the crust is what geologists call the mantle, which consists of dense, warm-to-hot (but solid) rock that extends to a depth of 1,800 mi (2,900 km). Below the mantle lies the earth's core, composed mostly of iron. All but the innermost part of the core is molten (see Figure 1).

Investigations of the earth's surface have revealed that it has been divided globally by past geologic processes into what today is a mosaic of rigid blocks called "plates." Observations indicate that these plates have moved large distances relative to one another in the past and that they are still moving very slowly today. The word "tectonics" has to do with earth movements; so the study of the movements and interactions among these plates is called "plate tectonics." Because almost all the plate motions occurred in the past, plate tectonics is, strictly speaking, an interpretation, model, or theoretical description of what geologists envisage happened to these plates through earth's history.

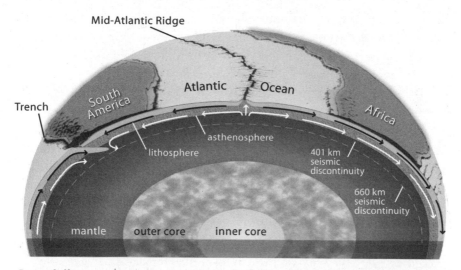

Figure 1. Cross-sectional view through the earth. The two major divisions of the planet are its mantle, made of silicate rock, and its core, comprised mostly of iron. Portions of the surface covered with a low-density layer of continental crust represent the continents. Lithospheric plates at the surface, which include the crust and part of the upper mantle, move laterally over the asthenosphere. The asthenosphere is hot and also weak because of the presence of water within its constituent minerals. Oceanic lithosphere, which lacks the continental crust, is chemically similar on average to the underlying mantle. Because oceanic lithosphere is substantially cooler, its density is higher, and it therefore has an ability to sink into the mantle below. The sliding of an oceanic plate into the mantle is known as "subduction," as shown here beneath South America. As two plates pull apart at a mid-ocean ridge, material from the asthenosphere rises to fill the gap, and some of this material melts to produce basaltic lava to form new oceanic crust on the ocean floor. The continental regions do not participate in the subduction process because of the buoyancy of the continental crust.

The general principles of plate tectonics theory may be stated as follows: deformation occurs at the edges of the plates by three types of horizontal motion—extension (rifting or moving apart), transform faulting (horizontal slippage along a large fault line), and compression, mostly by subduction (one plate plunging beneath another).[1]

Extension occurs where the seafloor is being pulled apart or split along rift zones, such as along the axes of the Mid-Atlantic Ridge and the East Pacific Rise. This is often called "seafloor spreading," which occurs where two

---

[1] S.E. Nevins and S.A. Austin, Continental drift, plate tectonics, and the Bible; in D.R. Gish and D.H. Rohrer, eds., *Up With Creation!* Creation-Life Publishers, San Diego, California, 1978, 173–180.

oceanic plates move away from each other horizontally, with new molten material from the mantle beneath rising between them to form new oceanic crust. Similar extensional splitting of a continental crustal plate can also occur, such as along the East African Rift Zone.

Transform faulting occurs where one plate is sliding horizontally past another, such as along the well-known San Andreas Fault of California.

Compressional deformation occurs where two plates move toward one another. If an oceanic crustal plate is moving toward an adjacent continental crustal plate, then the former will usually subduct (plunge) beneath the latter. Examples are the Pacific and Cocos Plates that are subducting beneath Japan and South America, respectively. When two continental crustal plates collide, the compressional deformation usually crumples the rock in the collision zone to produce a mountain range. For example, the Indian-Australian Plate has collided with the Eurasian Plate to form the Himalayas.

History of Plate Tectonics

The idea that the continents had drifted apart was first suggested by a creationist, Antonio Snider.[2] He observed from the statement in Genesis 1:9–10 about God's gathering together the seas into one place that at that point in earth history there may have been only a single landmass. He also noticed the close fit of the coastlines of western Africa and eastern South America. So he proposed that the breakup of that supercontinent with subsequent horizontal movements of the new continents to their present positions occurred catastrophically during the Flood.

However, his theory went unnoticed, perhaps because Darwin's book, which was published the same year, drew so much fanfare. The year 1859 was a bad year for attention to be given to any other new scientific theory, especially one that supported a biblical view of earth history. And it also didn't help that Snider published his book in French.

It wasn't until the early twentieth century that the theory of continental drift was acknowledged by the scientific community, through a book by Alfred Wegener, a German meteorologist.[3] However, for almost 50 years the overwhelming majority of geologists spurned the theory, primarily because a handful of seismologists claimed the strength of the mantle rock was too high to allow continents to drift in the manner Wegener had proposed. Their

[2] A. Snider, *Le Création et ses Mystères Devoilés*, Franck and Dentu, Paris, 1859.
[3] A. Wegener, *Die Entstehung der Kontinente und Ozeane*, 1915.

estimates of mantle rock strength were derived from the way seismic waves behave as they traveled through the earth at that time.

For this half-century the majority of geologists maintained that continents were stationary, and they accused the handful of colleagues who promoted the drift concept of indulging in pseudo-scientific fantasy that violated basic principles of physics. Today that persuasion has been reversed—plate tectonics, incorporating continental drift, is the ruling perspective.

What caused such a dramatic about-face? Between 1962 and 1968 four main lines of independent experiments and measurements brought about the birth of the theory of plate tectonics:[4]

1. Mapping of the topography of the seafloor using echo depth-sounders;

2. Measuring the magnetic field above the seafloor using magnetometers;

3. "Timing" of the north-south reversals of the earth's magnetic field using the magnetic memory of continental rocks and their radioactive "ages;" and

4. Determining very accurately the location of earthquakes using a world-wide network of seismometers.

An important fifth line of evidence was the careful laboratory measurement of how mantle minerals deform under stress. This measurement can convincingly demonstrate that mantle rock can deform by large amounts on timescales longer than the few seconds typical of seismic oscillations.[5]

Additionally, most geologists became rapidly convinced of plate tectonics theory because it elegantly and powerfully explained so many observations and lines of evidence:

1. The jigsaw puzzle fit of the continents (taking into account the continental shelves);

2. The correlation of fossils and fossil-bearing strata across the ocean basins (e.g., the coal beds of North America and Europe);

3. The mirror image zebra-striped pattern of magnetic reversals in the volcanic rocks of the seafloor parallel to the mid-ocean rift zones in the plates on either side of the zone, consistent with a moving apart of the plates (seafloor spreading);

---

[4] A. Co, ed., *Plate Tectonics and Geomagnetic Reversals*, W.H. Freeman and Co., San Francisco, California, 1973.

[5] S.H. Kirby, Rheology of the lithosphere, *Reviews of Geophysics and Space Physics* **25**(1): 219–1244, 1983.

4. The location of most of the world's earthquakes at the boundaries between the plates, consistent with earthquakes being caused by two plates moving relative to one another;

5. The existence of the deep seafloor trenches invariably located where earthquake activity suggests an oceanic plate is plunging into the mantle beneath another plate;

6. The oblique pattern of earthquakes adjacent to these trenches (subduction zones), consistent with an oblique path of motion of a subducting slab into the mantle;

7. The location of volcanic belts (e.g., the Pacific "ring of fire") adjacent to deep sea trenches and above subducting slabs, consistent with subducted sediments on the tops of down-going slabs encountering melting temperatures in the mantle; and

8. The location of mountain belts at or adjacent to convergent plate boundaries (where the plates are colliding).

Slow-and-Gradual or Catastrophic?

Because of the scientific community's commitment to the uniformitarian assumptions and framework for earth history, most geologists take for granted that the movement of the earth's plates has been slow and gradual over long eons. After all, if today's measured rates of plate drift—about 0.5–6 in (2–15 cm) per year—are extrapolated uniformly back into the past, it requires about 100 million years for the ocean basins and mountain ranges to form. And this rate of drift is consistent with the estimated 4.8 mi³ (20 km³) of molten magma that currently rises globally each year to create new oceanic crust.[6]

On the other hand, many other observations are incompatible with slow-and-gradual plate tectonics. While the seafloor surface is relatively smooth, zebra-stripe magnetic patterns are obtained when the ship-towed instrument (magnetometer) observations average over mile-sized patches. Drilling into the oceanic crust of the mid-ocean ridges has also revealed that those smooth patterns are not present at depth in the actual rocks.[7] Instead, the magnetic polarity changes rapidly

---

[6] J. Cann, Subtle minds and mid-ocean ridges. *Nature* 393:625–627, 1998.
[7] J.M. Hall and P.T. Robinson, Deep crustal drilling in the North Atlantic Ocean, *Science* **204:**573–576, 1979.

and erratically down the drill-holes. This is contrary to what would be expected with slow-and-gradual formation of the new oceanic crust accompanied by slow magnetic reversals. But it is just what is expected with extremely rapid formation of new oceanic crust and rapid magnetic reversal during the Flood, when rapid cooling of the new crust occurred in a highly nonuniform manner because of the chaotic interaction with ocean water.

Furthermore, slow-and-gradual subduction should have resulted in the sediments on the floors of the trenches being compressed, deformed, and thrust-faulted, yet the floors of the Peru-Chile and East Aleutian Trenches are covered with soft, flat-lying sediments devoid of compressional structures.[8] These observations are consistent, however, with extremely rapid subduction during the Flood, followed by extremely slow plate velocities as the floodwaters retreated from the continents and filled the trenches with sediment.

If uniformitarian assumptions are discarded, however, and Snider's original biblical proposal for continental "sprint" during the Genesis Flood is adopted, then a catastrophic plate tectonics model explains everything that slow-and-gradual plate tectonics does, plus most everything it can't explain.[9] Also, a 3-D supercomputer model of processes in the earth's mantle has demonstrated that tectonic plate movements can indeed be rapid and catastrophic when a realistic deformation model for mantle rocks is included.[10] And, even

---

[8] D.W. Scholl et al., Peru-Chile trench sediments and seafloor spreading, *Geological Society of America Bulletin* **81**:1339–1360, 1970; R. Von Huene, Structure of the continental margin and tectonism at the Eastern Aleutian Trench. *Geological Society of America Bulletin* **83**:3613–3626, 1972.

[9] S.A. Austin et al., Catastrophic plate tectonics: a global Flood model of earth history; in R.E. Walsh, ed., *Proceedings of the Third International Conference on Creationism*, Creation Science Fellowship, Pittsburgh, Pennsylvania, pp. 609–621, 1994.

[10] J.R. Baumgardner, Numerical simulation of the large-scale tectonic changes accompanying the Flood; in R.E. Walsh, C.L. Brooks, and R.S. Crowell, eds., *Proceedings of the First International Conference on Creationism*, Vol. 2, Pittsburgh, Pennsylvania, pp. 17–30, 1986; J.R. Baumgardner, 3-D finite element simulation of the global tectonic changes accompanying Noah's Flood; in R.E. Walsh, C.L. Brooks, and R.S. Crowell, eds., *Proceedings of the Second International Conference on Creationism*, Vol. 2, Creation Science Fellowship, Pittsburgh, Pennsylvania, pp. 35–45, 1990; J.R. Baumgardner, Computer modeling of the large-scale tectonics associated with the Genesis Flood; in R.E. Walsh, ed., *Proceedings of the Third International Conference on Creationism*, Creation Science Fellowship, Pittsburgh, Pennsylvania, pp. 49–62, 1994; J.R. Baumgardner, Runaway subduction as the driving mechanism for the Genesis Flood, in R.E. Walsh, ed., *Proceedings of the Third International Conference on Creationism*, Creation Science Fellowship, Pittsburgh, Pennsylvania, pp. 63–75, 1994; J.R. Baumgardner, The physics behind the Flood, in R.L. Ivey, Jr., ed., *Proceedings of the Fifth International Conference on Creationism*, Creation Science Fellowship, Pittsburgh, Pennsylvania, pp. 113–126, 2003.

though it was developed by a creation scientist, this supercomputer 3-D plate tectonics modeling is acknowledged as the world's best.[11]

The catastrophic plate tectonics model of Austin et al.[12] begins with a pre-Flood supercontinent surrounded by cold ocean-floor rocks that were denser than the warm mantle rock beneath. To initiate motion in the model, some sudden trigger "cracks" the ocean floors adjacent to the supercontinental crustal block, so that zones of cold ocean-floor rock start penetrating vertically into the upper mantle along the edge of most of the supercontinent.[13]

These vertical segments of ocean-floor rock correspond to the leading edges of oceanic plates. These vertical zones begin to sink in conveyor-belt fashion into the mantle, dragging the rest of the ocean floor with them. The sinking slabs of ocean plates produce stresses in the surrounding mantle rock, and these stresses, in turn, cause the rock to become more deformable and allow the slabs to sink faster. This process causes the stress levels to increase and the rock to become even weaker. These regions of rock weakness expand to encompass the entire mantle and result in a catastrophic runaway of the oceanic slabs to the bottom of the mantle in a matter of a few weeks.[14]

The energy for driving this catastrophe is the gravitational potential energy of the cold, dense rock overlying the less dense mantle beneath it at the beginning of the event. At its peak, this runaway instability allows the subduction rates of the plates to reach amazing speeds of feet-per-second. At the same time the pre-Flood seafloor was being catastrophically subducted into the mantle, the resultant tensional stress tore apart (rifted) the pre-Flood supercontinent (see Figure 2). The key physics responsible for the runaway instability is the fact that mantle rocks weaken under stress, by factors of a billion or more, for the sorts of stress levels that can occur in a planet the size of the earth—a behavior verified by many laboratory experiments over the past forty years.[15]

The rapidly sinking ocean-floor slabs forcibly displace the softer mantle rock into which they are subducted, which causes large-scale convectional flow throughout the entire mantle. The hot mantle rock displaced by these subducting slabs wells up elsewhere to complete the flow cycle, and in particular rises into the seafloor rift zones to form new ocean floor. Reaching the

---

[11] J. Beard, How a supercontinent went to pieces, *New Scientist* **137**:19, January 16, 1993.
[12] Ref. 9.
[13] Ibid.
[14] Ibid.
[15] Ref. 5.

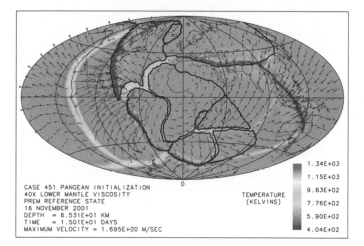

CASE 451 PANGEAN INITIALIZATION
40X LOWER MANTLE VISCOSITY
PREM REFERENCE STATE
16 NOVEMBER 2001
DEPTH = 6.531E+01 KM
TIME   = 1.501E+01 DAYS
MAXIMUM VELOCITY = 1.695E+00 M/SEC

TEMPERATURE
(KELVINS)

1.34E+03
1.15E+03
9.63E+02
7.76E+02
5.90E+02
4.04E+02

Figure 2(a). Snapshot of 3-D modeling solution after 15 days. The upper plot is an equal area projection of a spherical mantle surface 40 mi (65 km) below the earth's surface in which grayscale denotes absolute temperature. Arrows denote velocities in the plane of the cross-section. The dark lines denote plate boundaries where continental crust is present or boundaries between continent and ocean where both exist on the same plate. The lower plot is an equatorial cross-section in which the grayscale denotes temperature deviation from the average at a given depth.

surface of the ocean floor, this hot mantle material vaporizes huge volumes of ocean water with which it comes into contact to produce a linear curtain of supersonic steam jets along the entire 43,500 miles (70,000 km) of the seafloor rift zones stretching around the globe (perhaps the "fountains of the great deep" of Genesis 7:11 and 8:2). These supersonic steam jets capture large amounts of liquid water as they "shoot" up through the ocean above the seafloor where they form. This water is catapulted high above the earth and then falls back to the surface as intense global rain ("and the floodgates of heaven were opened"). The rain persisted for "40 days and nights" (Genesis 7:11–12) until all the pre-Flood ocean floor had been subducted.

This catastrophic plate tectonics model for earth history[16] is able to explain geologic data that slow-and-gradual plate tectonics over many millions of years cannot. For example, the new rapidly formed ocean floor would have initially been very hot. Thus, being of lower density than the pre-Flood ocean floor, it would have risen some 3,300 ft. (1,000 m) higher than its predecessor, causing a dramatic rise in global sea level. The ocean waters would

---

[16] Ref. 10.

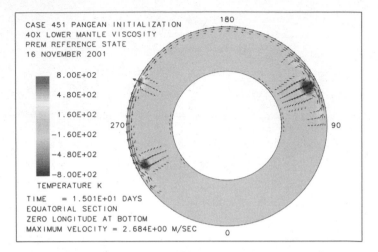

CASE 451 PANGEAN INITIALIZATION
40X LOWER MANTLE VISCOSITY
PREM REFERENCE STATE
16 NOVEMBER 2001

8.00E+02
4.80E+02
1.60E+02
-1.60E+02
-4.80E+02
-8.00E+02
TEMPERATURE K

TIME   = 1.501E+01 DAYS
EQUATORIAL SECTION
ZERO LONGITUDE AT BOTTOM
MAXIMUM VELOCITY = 2.684E+00 M/SEC

Figure 2(b). Snapshot of the modeling solution after 25 days. Grayscale and arrows denote the same quantities as in Figure 2(a). For a detailed explanation of this calculation, see Baumgardner, 2003.

thus have swept up onto and over the continental land surfaces, carrying vast quantities of sediments and marine organisms with them to form the thick, fossiliferous sedimentary rock layers we now find blanketing large portions of today's continents. This laterally extensive layer-cake sequence of sedimentary rocks is magnificently exposed, for example, in the Grand Canyon region of the southwestern U.S.[17] Slow-and-gradual plate tectonics simply cannot account for such thick, laterally extensive sequences of sedimentary strata containing marine fossils over such vast interior continental areas—areas which are normally well above sea level.

Furthermore, the whole mantle convectional flow resulting from runaway subduction of the cold ocean-floor slabs would have suddenly cooled the mantle temperature at the core-mantle boundary, thus greatly accelerating convection in, and heat loss from, the adjacent outer core. This rapid cooling of the surface of the core would result in rapid reversals of the earth's magnetic field.[18]

---

[17] S.A. Austin, ed., *Grand Canyon: Monument to Catastrophe*, Institute for Creation Research, Santee, California, 1994.
[18] R.E. Walsh, C.L. Brooks, and R.S. Crowell, eds., *Proceedings of the First International Conference on Creationism*, Vol. 2, Creation Science Fellowship, Pittsburgh, Pensylvania, 1986.

These magnetic reversals would have been expressed at the earth's surface and been recorded in the zebra-shaped magnetic stripes in the new ocean-floor rocks. This magnetization would have been erratic and locally patchy, laterally as well as at depth, unlike the pattern expected in the slow-and-gradual version. It was predicted that similar records of "astonishingly rapid" magnetic reversals ought to be present in thin continental lava flows, and such astonishingly rapid reversals in continental lava flows were subsequently found.[19]

This catastrophic plate tectonics model thus provides a powerful explanation for how the cold, rigid crustal plates could have moved thousands of miles over the mantle while the ocean floor subducted. It predicts relatively little plate movement today because the continental "sprint" rapidly decelerated when all the pre-Flood ocean floor had been subducted.

Also, we would thus expect the trenches adjacent to the subduction zones today to be filled with undisturbed late-Flood and post-Flood sediments. The model provides a mechanism for the retreat of the floodwaters from off the continents into the new ocean basins, when at the close of the Flood, as plate movements almost stopped, the dominant tectonic forces resulted in vertical earth movements (Psalm 104:8). Plate interactions at plate boundaries during the cataclysm generated mountains, while cooling of the new ocean floor increased its density, which caused it to sink and thus deepen the new ocean basins to receive the retreating floodwaters.

Aspects of modeling the phenomenon of runaway behavior in the mantle[20] have been independently duplicated and verified.[21] The same modeling predicts that since runaway subduction of the cold ocean-floor slabs occurred only a few thousand years ago during the Flood, those cold slabs would not have had sufficient time since the catastrophe to be fully "digested" into the surrounding mantle. Evidence for these relatively cold slabs just above the

---

[19] Ibid.; R.S. Coe and M. Prévot, Evidence suggesting extremely rapid field variation during a geomagnetic reversal, *Earth and Planetary Science Letters* **92**:292–298, 1989; A.A. Snelling "Fossil" magnetism reveals rapid reversals of the earth's magnetic field, *Creation* **13**(3):46–50, 1991; R.S. Coe, M. Prévot, and P. Camps, New evidence for extraordinary rapid change of the geomagnetic field during a reversal, *Nature* **374**:687–692, 1995; A.A. Snelling, The "principle of least astonishment"! *TJ* **9**(2):138–139, 1995.

[20] Ref. 9; Ref. 10.

[21] P.J. Tackley et al., Effects of an endothermic phase transition at 670 km depth on spherical mantle convection, *Nature* **361**:699–704, 1993; S.A. Weinstein, Catastrophic overturn of the earth's mantle driven by multiple phase changes and internal heat generation, *Geophysical Research Letters* **20**:101, 104, 1993; L. Moresi and Solomatov, Mantle convection with a brittle lithosphere: thoughts on the global tectonic styles of the earth and Venus, *Geophysical Journal International* **133**:669–682, 1998.

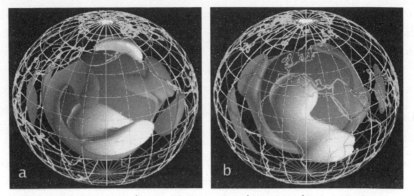

Figure 3. Distribution of hot (light-shaded surfaces) and cold (darker-shaded surfaces) regions in today's lower mantle as determined observationally by seismic tomography (imaging using recordings of seismic waves), viewed from (a) 180° longitude and (b) 0° longitude. The very low temperature inferred for the ring of colder rock implies that it has been subducted quite recently from the earth's surface. The columnar blobs of warmer rock have been squeezed together and pushed upward as the colder and denser rock settled over the core. (Figure courtesy of Alexandro Forte)

core-mantle boundary, to which they would have sunk, therefore should still be evident today, and it is (see Figure 3).[22]

Moreover, whether at the current rate of movement—only 4 in (10 cm) per year—the force and energy of the collision between the Indian-Australian and Eurasian Plates could have been sufficient to push up the Himalayas (like two cars colliding, each only traveling at .04 in/h [1 mm/h]) is questionable. In contrast, if the plate movements were measured as feet-per-second, like two cars each traveling at 62 mph (100 km/h), the resulting catastrophic collision would have rapidly buckled rock strata to push up those high mountains.

Is Catastrophic Plate Tectonics Biblical?

The Bible does not directly mention either continental drift or plate tectonics. However, if the continents were once joined together, as suggested by Genesis 1:9–10, and are now apart, then the only possibility is continental division and "sprint" during the Flood. Some have suggested this continental division

---

[22] S.P. Grand, Mantle shear structure beneath the Americas and surrounding oceans, *Journal of Geophysical Research* **99**:11591–11621, 1994; J.E. Vidale, A snapshot of whole mantle flow, *Nature* **370**:16–17, 1994.

occurred after the Flood during the days of Peleg when "the earth was divided" (Genesis 10:25). However, this Hebrew expression can be also translated to mean "lands being divided among peoples," which, according to the context, refers to the results of the Tower of Babel judgment. Furthermore, the destruction at the earth's surface, where people and animals were then living during such a rapid continental "sprint," would have been as utterly devastating as the Flood itself.

Therefore, using catastrophic plate tectonics as a model, mechanism, and framework to describe and understand the Genesis Flood event is far more reasonable and is also consistent with the Bible. Early skepticism about the slow-and-gradual plate tectonics model has largely evaporated because it has such vast explanatory power. When applied to the Flood, however, the catastrophic plate tectonics model not only explains those elements in a more consistent way, but it also provides a powerful explanation for the dramatic evidences of massive flooding and catastrophic geologic processes on the continents.

From the late eighteenth century to the present, most scientists, including creationists, rejected the Genesis Flood to explain the fossil-bearing portion of the geological record because it lacked an adequate mechanism to produce such a vast amount of geological change in such a short time. Only now are we beginning to understand at least part of the means God may have used to bring this world-destroying judgment to pass, including catastrophic plate tectonics.

Conclusion

Many creationist geologists now believe the catastrophic plate tectonics concept is very useful as the best explanation for how the Flood event occurred within the biblical framework for earth's history. Even though the Bible does not specifically mention this concept, it is consistent with the biblical account, which implies an original supercontinent that broke up during the Flood, with the resultant continents obviously then having to move rapidly ("sprint") into their present positions.

This concept is still rather new, and of course radical, but its explanatory power makes it compelling. Additional work is now being done to further detail this geologic model for the Flood event, especially to show that it provides a better explanation for the order and distribution of the fossils and strata globally than the failed slow-and-gradual belief. Of course, future discoveries may require adjustments in our thinking and understanding, but such is the nature of the human scientific enterprise. In contrast, "the word of the Lord endures forever" (1 Peter 1:25).

15

Don't Creationists Believe Some "Wacky" Things?

BODIE HODGE

When answering questions about the creation/evolution issue, I have often been accused of believing some strange things. Some accuse me of believing, for example, that the earth is flat, that animals don't change, or that the earth literally sits on several pillars.

When I tell these people I don't believe these things, they are sometimes shocked. I suspect these rumors exist to convince unsuspecting people that the Bible isn't true. With a little research, we can easily debunk some of these myths.

1. Claim: Biblical Creationists Believe the Earth Is Flat.

This charge is often leveled at biblical creationists the moment the Bible is brought up. As far as I'm aware, no biblical creationists believe this. The Bible doesn't teach a flat earth, and this belief was never widespread.[1] In fact, the Bible plainly teaches the earth isn't flat, so it shouldn't be an issue:

> It is He who sits above the *circle of the earth*, and its inhabitants are like grasshoppers, who stretches out the heavens like a curtain and spreads them out like a tent to dwell in (Isaiah 40:22, emphasis added).

> He drew a *circular horizon* on the face of the waters, at the boundary of light and darkness (Job 26:10, emphasis added).

---

[1] Who invented a flat earth? *Creation* **16**(2):48-49, March 1994. Found online at www.answersingenesis.org/creation/v16/i2/flatearth.asp.

Flat-earth beliefs were rather common in ancient Greece before 500 BC. This belief resurfaced in the early AD 300s with Lactantius; few others throughout history, though, have held to it. The humanists later revived this strange belief during the Renaissance and tried to imply that Christians, for the most part, believed this view. However, this simply wasn't the case.[1] Instead, the humanists took some biblical passages out of context. One such example is Revelation 7:1, which prophetically

The earth is circular as indicated by the Bible, not flat.

refers to the four corners of the earth. Instead of understanding the figurative nature of the verse, the humanists attempted to impose a strictly literal meaning on the passage. This passage is obviously referring to the directions of North, South, East, and West. Expositor John Gill comments on this verse:

> Four angels are mentioned, in allusion to the four spirits of the heavens, in Zec 6:5; and though the earth is not a plain square with angles, but round and globular, yet it is said to have four corners, with respect to the four points of the heavens; and though there is but one wind, which blows sometimes one way, and sometimes another, yet four are named with regard to the above points, east, west, north, and south, from whence it blows.[2]

Poetic passages, such as Psalm 75:3, which refers to the "pillars" of the earth, were also used to discredit Christians. Commentators such as John Gill[3] and Matthew Henry[4] rightly point out the figurative nature of these passages.

Recommended reading: *Taking Back Astronomy* (Chapter 2)

---

[2] J. Gill, *Exposition of the Old Testament*, Notes on Revelation 7:1, 1748–1763. Found online at eword.gospelcom.net/comments/revelation/gill/revelation7.htm.

[3] J. Gill, *Exposition of the Old Testament*, Notes on Psalm 75:3, 1748–1763. Found online at eword.gospelcom.net/comments/psalm/gill/psalm75.htm.

[4] M. Henry, *Matthew Henry Bible Complete Commentary*, notes on Psalms 75:3. Found online at eword.gospelcom.net/comments/psalm/mh/psalm75.htm.

2. Claim: Biblical Creationists Don't Believe There Are "Beneficial" Mutations.

Mutations in and of themselves are usually harmful and we would expect this because of the Curse. Most of the other mutations are static, meaning they don't really affect the organism as a whole. However, there are a few cases of *beneficial* mutations that have been observed—these are different from mutations that cause the alleged gain of *new* genetic information. In fact, they should be referred to as mutations with beneficial outcomes—you'll see why in a moment.

A mutation that causes a beetle to lose its wings would be considered beneficial if the beetle lived on a windy island. It would be beneficial because it might keep the beetle from blowing out to sea to die. However, this mutation causes a loss of genetic information since the beetle no longer has the information to make wings. It could also be considered a harmful mutation since it can't get away from predators as easily.

The mutation that causes sickle cell anemia could be considered beneficial because it protects against malaria. However, the person with this mutation has lost the information to make proper, efficient blood cells, and sickled blood cells cause many problems.

Normal blood cell   Sickle blood cell

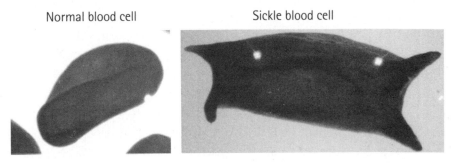

Both of these mutations were beneficial to the individual but were the result of a loss of information. This means mutations, even beneficial ones, are going in the opposite direction for molecules-to-man evolution, which requires a gain of new genetic information, even though there may have been a beneficial outcome.

Consider chickens that lost the information to produce feathers.[5] This can be considered "beneficial" because we no longer have to pluck them! But

---

[5] E. Young, Featherless chicken creates a flap, May 21, 2002, www.newscientist.com/article. ns?id=dn2307.

the chickens can't fly and have trouble keeping warm. Often, people confuse gains of new information with beneficial mutations, but they are different. For molecules-to-man evolutionary changes, the mutation needs to be beneficial *and* cause a gain of new information.

Recommended reading: *The New Answers Book 2*, chapter 7: Are mutations part of the "engine" of evolution?

3. Claim: You Can't Be a Christian If You Don't Believe in a Young Earth.

Answers in Genesis has continually claimed that one *can* be a Christian regardless of one's stance on the age of the earth or evolution. However, as AiG has also pointed out, these Christians are not being consistent.

Believing in a younger age of the earth (about 6,000 years) is a corollary of trusting the Bible. First, we start with the first five days of creation, then Adam was made on the sixth day, then adding ages given in the genealogies from Adam to Abraham we get about 2,000 years.[6] Both secular historians and Christians place Abraham at about 2,000 BC, so "the beginning" would be about 6,000 years ago. So the earth is about 6,000 years old—which is old—but much younger than the billions of years that are commonly touted.

	Time	Total Time
First 5 days of creation	5 days	5 days
Adam on Day 6 to Abraham	~2000 years	Still ~2000 years
Abraham to Christ	~2000 years	~4000 years
Christ until today	~2000 years	~6000 years

Believing in an approximately 6,000-year-old earth sets a proper foundation for believing Jesus Christ because you are letting God speak through His Word, without taking ideas to the Bible. In the same way, by trusting the Bible first, we realize that sin and death are intrusions into the world that go back to Genesis 3—which is the foundation for the gospel. Jesus came to save us from sin and death. If you give up this foundation of starting with the Bible and you insert evolutionary/millions-of-years ideas for the past history

---

[6] Bodie Hodge, "Ancient Patriarchs in Genesis," Answers in Genesis, www.answersingenesis. org/articles/2009/01/20/ancient-patriarchs-in-genesis.

of the world over the Bible's teachings in Genesis, it is inconsistent to believe the rest of the Bible—particularly the gospel. Sadly, people do it, and it is wrong, but it won't negate their salvation.

See other chapters in this book:

Chapter 8: Could God Have Created Everything in Six Days?

Chapter 9: Does Radiometric Dating Prove the Earth Is Old?

Chapter 19: Does Distant Starlight Prove the Universe Is Old?

4. Claim: Biblical Creationists Take the Whole Bible Literally.

It is better to say that creationists read and understand the Bible according to the grammatical-historical approach to Scripture. That is, we understand a biblical passage by taking into account its context, author, readership, literary style, etc. In other words, we read and understand the Bible in a plain or straightforward manner. This is usually what people mean when they say "literal interpretation of the Bible." This method helps to eliminate improper interpretations of the Bible.

> But we have renounced the hidden things of shame, not walking in craftiness nor handling the word of God deceitfully, but by manifestation of the truth commending ourselves to every man's conscience in the sight of God (2 Corinthians 4:2).

> All the words of my mouth are with righteousness; nothing crooked or perverse is in them. They are all plain to him who understands, and right to those who find knowledge (Proverbs 8:8–9).

Reading the Bible "plainly" means understanding which passages are written as historical narrative, which are written as poetry, which are written as parable, which are written as prophecy, and so on. The Bible is written in many different literary styles and should be read accordingly. Genesis records actual historical events; it was written as historical narrative, and there is no reason to read it as any other literary style, such as allegory or poetry.

For example, a non-Christian once claimed, "The Bible clearly says 'there is no God' in Psalms 14:1." However, this verse in context says:

> The fool has said in his heart, "There is no God." They are corrupt, they have done abominable works, there is none who does good (Psalm 14:1).

The context helps determine the proper interpretation—that a *fool* claims there is no God.

Someone else claimed, "To interpret the days in Genesis, you need to read 2 Peter 3:8, which indicates the days are each a thousand years." Many people try to use this passage to support the idea that the earth is millions or billions of years old, but let's read it in context:

> But, beloved, do not forget this one thing, that with the Lord one day is as a thousand years, and a thousand years as one day. The Lord is not slack concerning His promise, as some count slackness, but is longsuffering toward us, not willing that any should perish but that all should come to repentance (2 Peter 3:8–9).

This passage employs a literary device called a simile. Here, God compares a day to a thousand years in order to make the point that time doesn't bind Him, in this case specifically regarding His patience. God is eternal and is not limited to the time He created.

Also, this verse does not reference the days in Genesis, so it is not warranted to apply this to the length of the days in Genesis 1. When read plainly, these verses indicate that God is patient when keeping His promises. The gentleman that spoke to me had preconceived beliefs based on man's ideas that the earth was millions of years old. Those beliefs led him to this strange interpretation as opposed to using the historical-grammatical method.

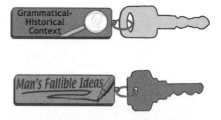

So, biblical Christians read the Bible plainly, or straightforwardly, and in context. Accordingly, we learn from what God says and means, and we don't apply strange literalistic (in the strict sense) meanings on metaphorical or allegorical passages, and vice versa.

Recommended reading: *The New Answers Book 3*, chapter 8: Did Bible Authors Believe in a Literal Genesis?

5. Claim: Biblical Creationists Don't Have Any Evidence for Their Position.

In fact, we have the same evidence that evolutionists have, whether bones, fossils, or rocks. The difference is the *interpretation* of the evidence. Creationists and evolutionists begin with different starting points when looking at the same evidence, which is why they arrive at different conclusions.

As biblical Christians, we trust as our axiom, or starting point, that God exists and that His Word is truth. From there, we use the Bible to explain the evidence we see in the world around us. Evolutionists commonly use their axiom (naturalism/materialism and a belief that molecules-to-man evolution is true) to interpret evidence. When carefully analyzing the two interpretations, the biblical interpretation is vastly superior—it explains the evidence and is confirmed by operational science.

> Recommended reading: *The New Answers Book 2*, chapter 2: What's the Best "Proof" of Creation?

> See chapter 1 in this book: Is There Really a God?

6. Claim: Biblical Creationists Believe the Earth Is the Same Now as It Was at the Beginning of Creation.

Biblical creationists believe that significant changes have happened to the earth in its 6,000-year history—two very catastrophic ones: the Fall and the Flood.

The Fall was when Adam and Eve disobeyed God. Prior to this, the earth and all of creation was perfect (Genesis 1:31; Deuteronomy 32:4). Adam was given precious few commands in this perfect world, one of which was to not eat from the fruit of the Tree of the Knowledge of Good and Evil. If he ate, his punishment would be death (Genesis 2:17).

But Adam ate, and he died (Genesis 3:19, 5:5), and now we die because we too sin (disobey God). Death and suffering entered the creation as an intrusion.

Secular history · Biblical history

There were also other results of Adam's disobedience (Genesis 3). One was that the ground was cursed. Another was thorns and thistles. There were changes to the animals and humans.

The Fall was a significant event that definitely caused the earth to change (Romans 8:18–22).

The Flood was God's judgment on the people of the world who had turned their back on Him (Genesis 6–8). God said He would destroy them with a Flood, and He did.

This Flood was a global Flood that demolished everything. Many biblical creationists believe there was initially only one continent (Genesis 1:9). This original continent broke apart and was rearranged catastrophically during the Flood and the following years and finally became what we have today.

This massive Flood buried many animals, plants, and marine life, and many became fossils. A vast portion of the sedimentary rock layers we find throughout the world today is a testimony to this global Flood.

The Flood also caused ocean basins to sink down, mountains to be pushed up, etc. Major geological features resulted. Additional after-effects of the Flood were the Ice Age, plate fault lines, etc.

Biblical creationists believe the world has changed. The real question is, in what way? This is an exciting part of creationist research today.

See other chapters in this book:

Chapter 10: Was There Actually a Noah's Ark and Flood?

Chapter 14: Can Catastrophic Plate Tectonics Explain Flood Geology?

Chapter 26: Why Does God's Creation Include Death and Suffering?

7. Claim: Biblical Creationists Are Anti-Science and Anti-Logic.

Biblical creationists love science! In fact, most fields of science were developed by men who believed the Bible, such as Isaac Newton (dynamics, gravitation, calculus), Michael Faraday (electromagnetics, field theory), Robert Boyle (chemistry), Johannes Kepler (astronomy), and Louis Pasteur (bacteriology, immunization). Francis Bacon, a Bible-believing Christian, developed the scientific method.

The reason such fields of science developed was the belief that God created the universe and that He instituted laws that we could investigate. Even today, many great scientists believe the Bible and use good observational science on a daily basis.[7]

Even logic flows naturally from a biblical worldview. Since we are created in the image of a logical God, we would expect to have logical faculties. However, logic is not a material entity, so it becomes a problem for the materialist atheist who denies the immaterial realm. From a materialistic perspective, a logical thought is the same as an illogical thought—merely a chemical reaction in the brain. From a materialistic point of view, then, the perception of logic is due to random processes and has nothing to do with absolute truth, which is also immaterial.

So in a biblical worldview, logic exists and so does truth, both of which are immaterial. But in a purely materialistic worldview, there is no basis for logic or truth to exist, since they are immaterial. And if our brains are the result of random mutations and natural selection, how do we know that our brains have evolved in a way that allows us to think and reason according to truth?

To state that logic *can* yield a truthful result means that absolute truth must exist, hence God. This does not mean that atheists and evolutionists cannot use logic or do science. But when they do, they must borrow from the above Christian principles, an action which is not consistent with their professed worldview.

Recommended reading: *The New Answers Book 2*, chapter 14: Can Creationists Be "Real" Scientists?

See chapter 4 in this book: Don't Creationists Deny the Laws of Nature?

---

[7] To read about creation scientists and other biographies of interest, see www.answersingenesis.org/go/bios.

16

Where Does the Ice Age Fit?

MICHAEL OARD

If you ask a youngster the question, "Was there really an ice age?" they might say rather quickly that there was. Then they may tell you that there were two of them. Of course, if you listen much longer, they will tell you that they saw both of those movies in the theater.

The ice age is a popular topic that is often discussed in school, at home, or in Hollywood. Sadly, most people hear the secular/uniformitarian view and don't look at this subject from a biblical perspective. This is where it gets interesting, though. The secular view has no good mechanism to cause a single ice age, let alone the many they propose. But the Bible does have a mechanism. Let's take a closer look.

Before I get too deep, let me define a few words you'll need to know to help clarify this chapter:

Glacier: a large mass of ice that has accumulated from snow over the years and is slowly moving from a higher place.

Moraines: stones, boulders, and debris that have been carried and dropped by a glacier.

Uniformitarianism: the belief that rates today are the same as they were in the past, without the possibility of major catastrophes like worldwide floods.

Interglacial: a short period of warming between glacier growth/movement that caused glaciers to melt away.

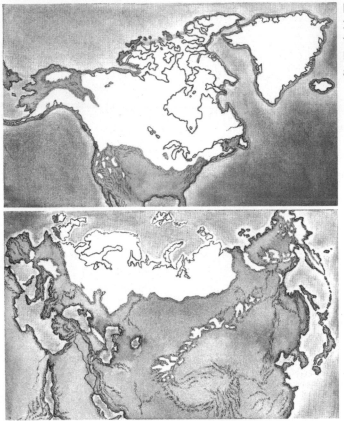

Figures 1 and 2. The extent of the Ice Age over North America and Eurasia.

Ice cores: cores of ice that have been drilled down into a glacier.

Ice Age: when seen in capital letters, refers to the biblical post-Flood Ice Age.

An ice age is defined as a time of extensive glacial activity in which substantially more of the land is covered by ice. During the Ice Age that ended several thousand years ago, 30 percent of the land surface of the earth was covered by ice (Figures 1 and 2). In North America an ice sheet covered almost all of Canada and the northern United States.

We know the extent of the Ice Age in the recent past because similar features, as observed around glaciers today, are also found in formerly glaciated areas, such as lateral and terminal moraines. A *lateral moraine* is a mound of rocks of all sizes deposited on the side of a moving glacier, while a *terminal,* or *end, moraine* is a mound of rocks bulldozed in front of the glacier.

Figure 3 shows a horseshoe-shaped moraine from a glacier that spread out from a valley in the Wallowa Mountains of northeast Oregon. The two

Figure 3. Horseshoe-shaped lateral and end moraines plowed up by a glacier moving out of a valley in the northern Wallowa Mountains of northeast Oregon. Beautiful Wallowa Lake fills the depression within the moraines.

lateral moraines are 600 feet (183 m) high, while the end moraine is 100 feet (30 m) high, enclosing beautiful Wallowa Lake. Scratched bedrock and boulders are telltale signs of previous glaciation (Figures 4 and 5), which are similar to such features found around glaciers today (Figures 6 and 7).

Figures 4 and 5. Striated bedrock and boulders from an ice cap in the northern Rocky Mountains that spread through the Sun River Canyon out onto the high plains, west of Great Falls, Montana.

Figures 6 and 7. Scratched bedrock and boulder from the Athabasca Glacier in the Canadian Rocky Mountains.

Secular/Uniformitarian Belief

Secular/uniformitarian scientists used to believe that there were four ice ages during the past few million years. However, the idea of four ice ages was rejected in the 1970s in favor of thirty or more ice ages separated by interglacials.[1] Such a switch was forced by a paradigm change in glaciology toward belief in the astronomical model of the ice ages (or "Milankovitch mechanism," as it is called). The idea of four ice ages still lingers in public museum displays, though (Figure 8).

The astronomical model postulates regularly repeating ice ages caused by the changing orbital geometry of the earth. Secular glaciologists believe that over the past 800,000 years there were, allegedly, eight ice ages, each lasting about 100,000 years.[2] The glacial phase supposedly dominated for 90,000 years, while the interglacial phase lasted only 10,000 years. Accordingly, the

---

[1] J. Kennett, *Marine Geology*, Prentice-Hall, Englewood Cliffs, New Jersey, 1982, 747.
[2] D. Paillard, Glacial cycles: toward a new paradigm, *Reviews of Geophysics,* **39**(3):325–346, 2001.

Figure 8. Display of four ice ages at the College of Eastern Utah Prehistoric Museum at Price, Utah, taken in 2006.

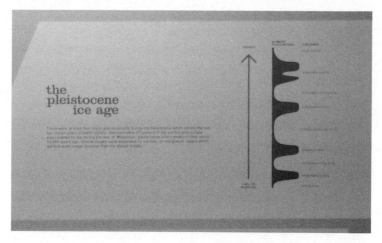

story continues that beyond 800,000 years, the ice ages are believed to have cycled every 40,000 years or so.

The secular/uniformitarian model now holds that the Antarctic Ice Sheet developed around 40 million years ago and reached general equilibrium about 15 million years ago.[3] The Greenland Ice Sheet, they say, is younger, having developed only a few million years ago.

Uniformitarian scientists further believe four "ancient ice ages" occurred during geological time (Table 1). These ice ages supposedly occurred hundreds of millions to several billion years ago, with each ice age lasting tens to hundreds of millions of years. Ancient ice ages are deduced from features in the rock that seem to indicate glaciation.

Geological Period	Secular Approximate Age Range (million years ago)
Late Paleozoic	256–338
Late Ordovician	429–445
Late Proterozoic	520–950
Early Proterozoic	2200–2400

Table 1. The four main "ancient ice ages" within the uniformitarian paradigm and their inferred age range in millions of years before the present. The age ranges for the earliest "ice ages" are admittedly rough estimates.[4]

[3] M.J. Oard, *The Frozen Record: Examining the Ice Core History of the Greenland and Antarctic Ice Sheets*, Institute for Creation Research, El Cajon, California, 2005, 31–34.
[4] J.C. Crowell, *Pre-Mesozoic Ice Ages: Their Bearing on Understanding the Climate System*, Geological Society of America Memoir 192, Boulder, Colorado, 1999, 3.

Severe Difficulties with Secular/Uniformitarian Beliefs

Secular/uniformitarian scientists have great difficulty explaining any recent ice ages based on rates they observe today. They have proposed dozens of hypotheses, but all have serious flaws. One problem is that the summer temperatures in the northern United States would have to cool more than 50°F (28°C) accompanied by a huge increase in snow. What would trigger or sustain such a dramatic climate change that would persist for thousands of years? David Alt of the University of Montana in Missoula recently admitted, "Although theories abound, no one really knows what causes ice ages."[5]

Ancient ice ages have been somewhat controversial over the years, but recently some uniformitarian scientists have come out with the shocking belief that some Proterozoic ice ages were global.[6] This belief is based on paleomagnetic data that supposedly shows certain rocks, believed to be from ancient ice ages, were marine and equatorial. Because of the reflection of sunlight from a white surface, it is likely that a glaciated earth would never melt. However, advocates of "snowball earth" state not only that such a glaciation completely melted but also that temperatures following glaciation ended up much warmer than today. Such a "freeze-fry" hypothesis indicates that the concept of ancient ice ages is unsound.

Did the Flood Trigger the Ice Age?

If uniformitarian scientists have severe difficulties accounting for ice ages, how would creationists explain an ice age or multiple ice ages? Let's start with the recent ice age.

When attempting to account for ice ages, the uniformitarian scientists do not consider one key element—the Genesis Flood. What if there truly were a worldwide Flood? How would it have affected the climate? A worldwide Flood would have caused major changes in the earth's crust, as well as earth movements and tremendous volcanism. It would have also greatly disturbed the climate.

A shroud of volcanic dust and aerosols (very small particles) would have been trapped in the stratosphere for several years following the Flood. These volcanic effluents would have then reflected some of the sunlight back to space

---

[5] D. Alt, *Glacial Lake Missoula and its Humongous Floods*, Mountain Press Publishing Company, Missoula, Montana, 2001, 180.

[6] M.J. Oard, Another tropical ice age? *Journal of Creation* 11(3):259–261, 1997; M.J. Oard, Snowball Earth—a problem for the supposed origin of multicellular animals, *Journal of Creation* 16(1):6–9, 2002.

and caused cooler summers, mainly over large landmasses of the mid and high latitudes. Volcanoes would have also been active during the Ice Age and gradually declined as the earth settled down. Abundant evidence shows substantial Ice Age volcanism, which would have replenished the dust and aerosols in the stratosphere.[7] The Greenland and Antarctic ice sheets also show abundant volcanic particles and acids in the Ice Age portion of the ice cores.[8]

An ice age also requires huge amounts of precipitation. The Genesis account records the "fountains of the great deep" bursting forth during the Flood. Crustal movements would have released hot water from the earth's crust along with volcanism and large underwater lava flows, which would have added heat to the ocean. Earth movement and rapid Flood currents would have then mixed the warm water, so that after the Flood the oceans would be warm from pole to pole. There would be no sea ice. A warm ocean would have had much higher evaporation than the present cool ocean surface. Most of this evaporation would have occurred at mid and high latitudes, close to the developing ice sheets, dropping the moisture on the cold continent. This is a recipe for powerful and continuous snowstorms that can be estimated using basic meteorology.[9] Therefore, to cause an ice age, rare conditions are required—warm oceans for high precipitation, and cool summers for lack of melting the snow. Only then can it accumulate into an ice sheet.

The principles of atmospheric science can also estimate areas of high oceanic evaporation, the eventual depth of the ice, and even the timing of the Ice Age. Numerical simulations of precipitation in the polar regions using conventional climate models with warm sea surface temperatures have demonstrated that ice sheets thousands of feet thick could have accumulated in less than 500 years.[10]

A Rapid Ice Age

Most creationists agree that there was one major Ice Age following the Flood. The timing of the Ice Age is quite significant, since uniformitarians claim that each ice age over the past 800,000 years lasted about 100,000 years. To estimate the time for a post-Flood Ice Age, we need to know how long the volcanism lasted and the cooling time of the oceans. Once these two

---

[7] M.J. Oard, *An Ice Age Caused by the Genesis Flood*, Institute for Creation Research, El Cajon, California, 1990, 33–38.
[8] Oard, *The Frozen Record*.
[9] Oard, *An Ice Age Caused by the Genesis Flood*.
[10] L. Vardiman, *Climates before and after the Genesis Flood: numerical models and their implications*, Institute for Creation Research, El Cajon, California, 2001.

mechanisms for the Ice Age wane, the ice sheets will reach a maximum and then begin to melt. So, an estimate of the time for the Ice Age can be worked out based on the available moisture for snow and the cooling time of the ocean (the primary mechanism) in a cool post-Flood climate.

I used budget equations for the cooling of the ocean and atmosphere, which are simply based on heat inputs minus heat outputs—the difference causing the change in temperatures. Since there is no way to be precise, I used minimums and maximums for the variables in the equations in order to bracket the time. The best estimate is about 500 years after the Flood to reach glacial maximum with an average ice and snow depth of about 2,300 feet (700 m) in the Northern Hemisphere and 4,000 feet (1,220 m) on Antarctica.[11]

Once the conditions for the Ice Age ended, those ice sheets in unfavorable areas melted rapidly. Antarctica and Greenland, possessing a favorable latitude and altitude, would continue to grow during deglaciation and afterward. To calculate the melting rate for the ice sheets over North America and Eurasia, I used the energy balance over a snow cover, which gives a faster rate than the uniformitarians propose based on their models.

An energy balance equation is a straightforward and more physical method of calculating the melt rate. Using maximum and minimum values for the variable in the melt equation, I obtained a best estimate of the average melt rate along the periphery (a 400-mile [645-km] long strip) of the ice sheet in North America at about 33 feet/year (10 m/year). Such a melting rate compares favorably with current melt rates for the melting zones of Alaskan, Icelandic, and Norwegian glaciers today. At this rate, the periphery of the ice sheets melts in less than 100 years. Interior areas of ice sheets would melt more slowly, but the ice would be gone in about 200 years. The ice sheets melt so fast, catastrophic flooding would be expected, such as with the bursting of glacial Lake Missoula described later in this chapter.

Therefore, the total length of time for a post-Flood Ice Age is about 700 years. It was indeed a rapid Ice Age. This is an example of bringing back the Flood into earth history. As a result, processes that seem too slow at today's rates were much faster in the past. The Flood was never disproved; it was *arbitrarily* rejected in the 1700s and 1800s by secular intellectuals in favor of slow processes over millions of years.

[11] Oard, *An Ice Age Caused by the Genesis Flood.*

How Many Ice Ages?

Still, there is the claim of many ice ages. Most formerly glaciated areas show evidence for only one ice age, and a substantial amount of information indicates only one ice age.[12] The idea of multiple ice ages is essentially a *uniformitarian assumption*. Today this idea is strongly based on oxygen isotope ratios from seafloor sediments. The paleothermometers developed from these data assume highly questionable statistical comparisons between peaks and valleys in temperature, which are claimed to correspond to orbital changes in the heating of the earth. In a provocative paper concluding that only one ice sheet covered southern and central Alberta late in the uniformitarian timescale, Robert Young and others stated: "Glacial reconstructions commonly assume a multiple-glaciation hypothesis in all areas that contain a till cover."[13]

Areas that appear to have evidence of more than one ice age can be reinterpreted to be the deposits from one ice sheet that advanced and retreated over a short period. The more modern understanding of glacial activity indicates that ice sheets are very dynamic. We do not need 100,000 years for each ice age or 2.5 million years for multiple ice ages.

One of the key assumptions in the multiple glaciation hypothesis is the astronomical model of ice ages. This mechanism is based on cyclical past changes in the geometry of the earth's orbit. Uniformitarian scientists believe that a decrease in solar radiation at about 60° N in summer, resulting from orbital changes, causes repeating ice ages, either every 100,000 years or every 40,000 years. By matching wiggles in variables taken from deep-sea cores, uniformitarian scientists believe they have proven the astronomical mechanism of multiple ice ages.[14] There are many problems with this model and relating deep-sea cores to it; mainly, the decrease in sunshine is too small.[15] Didier Paillard stated,

> Nevertheless, several problems in classical astronomical theory of paleoclimate have indeed been identified: (1) The main cyclicity in the paleoclimate record is close to 100,000 years, but there is [*sic*] no significant orbitally induced changes in the radiative [sunshine] forcing of the Earth in this frequency range (the "100-kyr Problem").[16]

---

[12] Ibid., 135–166.

[13] R.R. Young et. al., A single, late Wisconsin, Laurentide glaciation, Edmonton area and southwestern Alberta, *Geology* 22:683–686, 1994.

[14] J.D. Hays, J. Imbrie, and N.J. Shackleton, Variations in the earth's orbit: pacemaker of the ice ages, *Science* 194:1121–1132, 1976.

[15] Oard, *The Frozen Record,* 111–122.

[16] Paillard, Glacial cycles: toward a new paradigm, 325.

Although the main cycle in the astronomical model is 100,000 years, the change in sunshine at high northern latitudes is insignificant for such a dramatic change as an ice age.

Is the Ice Age Biblical?

Since the Flood offers a viable explanation for the Ice Age, one could expect that the Ice Age would be mentioned in the Bible. It is possible that the book of Job, written about 500 years or so after the Flood, may include a reference to the Ice Age in Job 38:29–30, which says, "From whose womb comes the ice? And the frost of heaven, who gives it birth? The waters harden like stone, and the surface of the deep is frozen." However, Job could have observed frost and lake ice during winter in Palestine, especially if temperatures were colder because of the Ice Age. The reason the Ice Age is not directly discussed in the Bible is probably because the Scandinavian ice sheet and mountain ice caps were farther north than the region where the Bible was written. Only an increase in the snow coverage of Mt. Hermon and possibly more frequent snowfalls on the high areas of the Middle East would have been evident to those living in Palestine.

How Are "Ancient Ice Ages" Explained?

The evidence for "ancient ice ages" is found in the hard rocks; these deposits are not on the surface like the deposits from the post-Flood Ice Age. There are substantial difficulties in interpreting these rocks as from ancient ice ages.[17] An alternative mechanism can easily explain these deposits within a biblical framework. This mechanism is gigantic submarine landsides that occurred during the Genesis Flood.

The Mystery of the Woolly Mammoths

Millions of woolly mammoth bones, tusks, and a few carcasses have been found frozen in the surface sediments of Siberia, Alaska, and the Yukon Territory of Canada—a major mystery of uniformitarian paleoclimate. The woolly mammoths were part of a Northern Hemisphere community of animals that lived and died during the post-Flood Ice Age.[18] Woolly

---

[17] M.J. Oard, *Ancient Ice Ages or Gigantic Submarine Landslides?* Creation Research Society Monograph No. 6, Chino Valley, Arizona, 1997.
[18] M.J. Oard, *Frozen In Time: The Woolly Mammoths, the Ice Age, and the Bible*, Master Books, Green Forest, Arkansas, 2004.

Figure 9. Large dust drift to the top of a house during the dust bowl era in the Midwest.

mammoths probably died after the Flood because there are thousands of carcasses scattered across Alaska and Siberia resting above Flood deposits. And there must have been sufficient time for the mammoths to have repopulated these regions after the Flood. The post-Flood Ice Age provides an explanation for the mystery of the woolly mammoths, as well as many other Ice Age mysteries.

The mammoths spread into these northern areas during early and middle Ice Age time because summers were cooler and winters warmer. The areas were unglaciated (just the mountains glaciated) and a rich grassland. However, late in the Ice Age, winter temperatures turned colder and the climate drier with strong wind storms. The mammoths died by the millions and were buried by dust, which later froze, preserving the mammoths. Severe dust storms that produce tall dust drifts (Figure 9) can also explain a number of the secondary mysteries, such as some carcasses that show evidence of suffocation in a generally standing position, and how they become entombed into rock-hard permafrost (for a more complete treatment of this subject, please see my book, *Frozen in Time*).

Is Glacial Lake Missoula Related to the Ice Age?

At the peak of the Ice Age, a finger of the ice sheet in western Canada and the northwest United States filled up the valleys of northern Idaho. A huge lake 2,000 feet (610 m) deep was formed in the valleys of western Montana. This was glacial Lake Missoula (Figure 10). In the course of time, the lake burst and emptied in a few days, causing an immense flood several hundred feet deep that

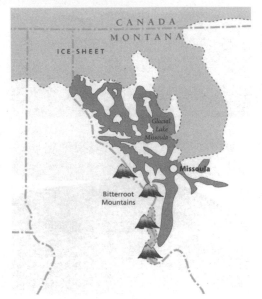

Figure 10. Map of ice sheet and glacial Lake Missoula (drawn by Mark Wolfe)

carved out canyons and produced many flood features from eastern Washington into northwest Oregon (Figure 11).

This flood can help us understand the global Flood. Interestingly, the Lake Missoula flood was rejected for 40 years despite tremendous evidence because of the anti-biblical bias in historical science.[19]

Now this flood is not only accepted, but uniformitarian scientists now believe many more of them occurred. They postulate 40 to 100 at the peak of their last ice age, with perhaps hundreds more from previous ice ages. However, the evidence

Figure 11. The Potholes, remnants of a 400-foot (120 m) high waterfall. The lakes at the bottom are remnant plunge pools.

---

[19] M.J. Oard, *The Missoula Flood Controversy and the Genesis Flood*, Creation Research Society Monograph No. 13, Chino Valley, AZ, 2004.

is substantial that there was only one gigantic Lake Missoula flood, with possibly several minor floods afterward.[20]

What about Ice Cores?

Uniformitarian scientists claim to be able to count annual layers in the Greenland ice sheet to determine its age, in the same way people can count tree rings. In doing so, they arrive at 110,000 years near the bottom of the Greenland ice sheet. Similar claims for a much greater age are made for the Antarctica ice sheet. These claims are equivocal and are essentially based on the uniformitarian belief that the ice sheets are millions of years old. The data from ice cores can be better explained within the post-Flood Ice Age model, which dramatically reduces the calculated age to well within the biblical limit.[21]

Conclusion

Although a major mystery of uniformitarian history, the Ice Age is readily explained by the climatic consequences of the Genesis Flood—it was a short Ice Age of about 700 years, and there was only one Ice Age.[22] We do not need the hundred thousand years for one ice age, or the few million years for multiple ice ages, as claimed by uniformitarian scientists.

Even their claim of ancient ice ages in the hard rocks can be accounted for by gigantic submarine landslides during the Flood. The post-Flood rapid Ice Age can also account for a number of major mysteries and other interesting phenomena that occurred during the Ice Age, such as the Lake Missoula flood and the life and death of the woolly mammoths in Siberia and elsewhere. When we stick to the Genesis account of the Flood and the short scriptural timescale, major secular/uniformitarian mysteries are readily explained.[23]

---

[20] Ibid.

[21] L. Vardiman, *Ice cores and the Age of the Earth*, Institute for Creation Research, El Cajon, California, 1993; Oard, *The Frozen Record*.

[22] Oard, *An Ice Age Caused by the Genesis Flood*; Oard, *Ancient Ice Ages or Gigantic Submarine Landslides?* M.J. Oard and B. Oard, *Life in the Great Ice Age*, Master Books, Green Forest, Arkansas, 1993.

[23] For more on the Ice Age, see www.answersingenesis.org/go/ice-age.

17

Are There Really
Different Races?

KEN HAM

What if a Chinese person were to marry a Polynesian, or an African with black skin were to marry a Japanese, or a person from India were to marry a person from America with white skin—would these marriages be in accord with biblical principles?

A significant number of Christians would claim that such "interracial" marriages directly violate God's principles in the Bible and should not be allowed.

Does the Word of God really condemn the marriages mentioned above? Is there ultimately any such thing as interracial marriage?

To answer these questions, we must first understand what the Bible and science teach about "race."

What Constitutes a "Race"?

In the 1800s, before Darwinian evolution was popularized, most people, when talking about "races," would be referring to such groups as the "English race," "Irish race," and so on. However, this all changed in 1859 when Charles Darwin published his book *On the Origin of Species by Means*

of Natural Selection or the Preservation of Favoured Races in the Struggle for Life.

Darwinian evolution was (and still is[1]) inherently a racist philosophy, teaching that different groups or "races" of people evolved at different times and rates, so some groups are more like their apelike ancestors than others. Leading evolutionist Stephen Jay Gould claimed, "Biological arguments for racism may have been common before 1859, but they increased by orders of magnitude following the acceptance of evolutionary theory."[2]

The Australian Aborigines, for instance, were considered the missing links between the apelike ancestor and the rest of mankind.[3] This resulted in terrible prejudices and injustices towards the Australian Aborigines.[4]

Ernst Haeckel, famous for popularizing the now-discredited idea that "ontogeny recapitulates phylogeny,"[5] stated:

At the lowest stage of human mental development are the Australians, some tribes of the Polynesians, and the Bushmen, Hottentots, and some of the Negro tribes. Nothing, however, is perhaps more remarkable in this respect, than that some of the wildest tribes in southern Asia and eastern Africa have no trace whatever of the first foundations of all human civilization, of family life, and marriage. They live together in herds, like apes.[6]

Racist attitudes fueled by evolutionary thinking were largely responsible for an African pygmy being displayed, along with an orangutan, in a cage in the Bronx zoo.[7] Indeed, Congo pygmies were once thought to be "small ape-like, elfish creatures" that "exhibit many ape-like features in their bodies."[8]

---

[1] J.P. Rushton, professor of psychology at the University of Western Ontario, Lond, Ontario, Canada, Race, Evolution and Behavior, www.harbornet.com/folks/theedrich/JP_Rushton/Race.htm.

[2] S.J. Gould, *Ontogeny and Phylogeny*, Belknap-Harvard Press, Cambridge, Massachusetts, 1977, 127–128.

[3] Missing links with mankind in early dawn of history, *New York Tribune*, p. 11, February 10, 1924.

[4] D. Monaghan, The body-snatchers, *The Bulletin*, November 12, 1991, pp. 30–38; Blacks slain for science's white superiority theory, *The Daily Telegraph Mirror*, April 26, 1994.

[5] For more information on the fallacious nature of this idea, see www.answersingenesis.org/go/embryonic.

[6] E. Haeckel, *The History of Creation*, 1876, 363–363.

[7] J. Bergman, Ota Benga: the man who was put on display in the zoo! *Creation* 16(1):48–50, 1993.

[8] A.H.J. Keane, Anthropological curiosities — the pygmies of the world, *Scientific American Supplement* 64, no. 1650 (August 17, 1907): 99.

As a result of Darwinian evolution, many people started thinking in terms of the different people groups around the world representing different "races," but within the context of evolutionary philosophy. This has resulted in many people today, consciously or unconsciously, having ingrained prejudices against certain other groups of people.[9]

However, *all* human beings in the world today are classified as *Homo sapiens sapiens*. Scientists today admit that, biologically, there really is only one race of humans. For instance, a scientist at the Advancement of Science Convention in Atlanta stated, "Race is a social construct derived mainly from perceptions conditioned by events of recorded history, and it has no basic biological reality." This person went on to say, "Curiously enough, the idea comes very close to being of American manufacture."[10]

Reporting on research conducted on the concept of race, ABC News stated, "More and more scientists find that the differences that set us apart are cultural, not racial. Some even say that the word *race* should be abandoned because it's meaningless." The article went on to say that "we accept the idea of race because it's a convenient way of putting people into broad categories, frequently to suppress them—the most hideous example was provided by Hitler's Germany. And racial prejudice remains common throughout the world."[11]

In an article in the *Journal of Counseling and Development*,[12] researchers argued that the term "race" is basically so meaningless that it should be discarded.

More recently, those working on mapping the human genome announced "that they had put together a draft of the entire sequence of the

[9] This is not to say that *evolution* is the cause of racism. *Sin* is the cause of racism. However, Darwinian evolution fueled a particular form of racism.

[10] R.L. Hotz, Race has no basis in biology, researchers say, *Cincinnati Enquirer*, p. A3, February 20, 1997.

[11] We're all the same, ABC News, September 10, 1998, www.abcnews.com/sections/science/DyeHard/dye72.html.

[12] S.C. Cameron and S.M. Wycoff, The destructive nature of the term race: growing beyond a false paradigm, *Journal of Counseling & Development*, 76:277–285, 1998.

human genome, and the researchers had unanimously declared, there is only one race—the human race."[13]

Personally, because of the influences of Darwinian evolution and the resulting prejudices, I believe everyone (and especially Christians) should abandon the term "race(s)." We could refer instead to the different "people groups" around the world.

The Bible and "Race"

The Bible does not even use the word race in reference to people,[14] but it

ONE BLOOD
Acts 17:26
Adam & Eve
1 Corinthians 15:45
Genesis 3:20

Sons & Daughters
Genesis 5:4

Noah & Sons
Genesis 9:17-19

People at Tower of Babel
Genesis 11:8-9

Different People Groups/Cultures

does describe all human beings as being of "one blood" (Acts 17:26). This of course emphasizes that we are all related, as all humans are descendants of the first man, Adam (1 Corinthians 15:45),[15] who was created in the image of God (Genesis 1:26–27).[16] The Last Adam, Jesus Christ (1 Corinthians 15:45) also became a descendant of Adam. Any descendant of Adam can be saved because our mutual relative by blood (Jesus Christ) died and rose again. This is why the gospel can (and should) be preached to all tribes and nations.

CAN THE BIBLE BE USED TO JUSTIFY RACIST ATTITUDES?

The inevitable question arises, "If the Bible teaches all humans are the same, where was the church during the eras of slavery and segregation? Doesn't the Bible actually condone the enslavement of a human being by another?"

---

[13] N. Angier, Do races differ? Not really, DNA shows, New York Times web, Aug. 22, 2000.

[14] In the original, Ezra 9:2 refers to "seed," Romans 9:3 to "kinsmen according to the flesh."

[15] For more on this teaching, see chapter 6, Cain's Wife—Who Was She?

[16] Contrary to popular belief, mankind does not share an apelike ancestor with other primates. To find out the truth behind the alleged apemen, visit www.answersingenesis.org/go/anthropology.

Both the Old and New Testaments of the Bible mention slaves and slavery. As with all other biblical passages, these must be understood in their grammatical-historical context.

Dr. Walter Kaiser, former president of Gordon-Conwell Theological Seminary and Old Testament scholar, states:

> The laws concerning slavery in the Old Testament appear to function to moderate a practice that worked as a means of loaning money for Jewish people to one another or for handling the problem of the prisoners of war. Nowhere was the institution of slavery as such condemned; but then, neither did it have anything like the connotations it grew to have during the days of those who traded human life as if it were a mere commodity for sale. ... In all cases the institution was closely watched and divine judgment was declared by the prophets and others for all abuses they spotted.[17]

Job recognized that all were equal before God, and all should be treated as image-bearers of the Creator.

> If I have despised the cause of my male or female servant when they complained against me, what then shall I do when God rises up? When He punishes, how shall I answer Him? Did not He who made me in the womb make them? Did not the same One fashion us in the womb? (Job 31:13–15).

In commenting on Paul's remarks to the slaves in his epistles, Peter H. Davids writes:

> The church never adopted a rule that converts had to give up their slaves. Christians were not under law but under grace. Yet we read in the literature of the second century and later of many masters who upon their conversion freed their slaves. The reality stands that it is difficult to call a person a slave during the week and treat them like a brother or sister in the church. Sooner or later the implications of the kingdom they experienced in church seeped into the behavior of the masters during the week. Paul did in the end create a revolution, not one from without, but one from within, in which a changed heart produced changed behavior and through that in the end brought about social change. This change happened wherever the kingdom of God was expressed through the church, so the

---

[17] W.C. Kaiser, Jr. et al., *Hard Sayings of the Bible*, InterVarsity Press, Downers Grove, Illinois, 1996, 150.

world could see that faith in Christ really was a transformation of the whole person.[18]

Those consistently living out their Christian faith realize that the forced enslavement of another human being goes against the biblical teaching that all humans were created in the image of God and are of equal standing before Him (Galatians 3:28; Colossians 3:11). Indeed, the most ardent abolitionists during the past centuries were Bible-believing Christians. John Wesley, Granville Sharp, William Wilberforce, Jonathan Edwards, Jr., and Thomas Clarkson all preached against the evils of slavery and worked to bring about the abolition of the slave trade in England and North America. Harriet Beecher Stowe conveyed this message in her famous novel *Uncle Tom's Cabin*. And of course, who can forget the change in the most famous of slave traders? John Newton, writer of "Amazing Grace," eventually became an abolitionist after his conversion to Christianity, when he embraced the truth of Scripture.

"Racial" Differences

But some people think there must be different races of people because there appear to be major differences between various groups, such as skin color and eye shape.

The truth, though, is that these so-called "racial characteristics" are only minor variations among people groups. If one were to take any two people anywhere in the world, scientists have found that the basic genetic differences between these two people would typically be around 0.2 percent—even if they came from the same people group.[19] But these so-called "racial" characteristics that people think are major differences (skin color, eye shape, etc.) "account for only 0.012 percent of human biological variation."[20]

Dr. Harold Page Freeman, chief executive, president, and director of surgery at North General Hospital in Manhattan, reiterates, "If you ask what percentage of your genes is reflected in your external appearance, the basis by which we talk about race, the answer seems to be in the range of 0.01 percent."[21]

In other words, the so-called "racial" differences are absolutely trivial— overall, there is more variation *within* any group than there is *between* one

---

[18] Ref. 17, 644.
[19] J.C. Gutin, End of the rainbow, *Discover*, pp. 72–73, November 1994.
[20] Ref. 12.
[21] Ref. 13.

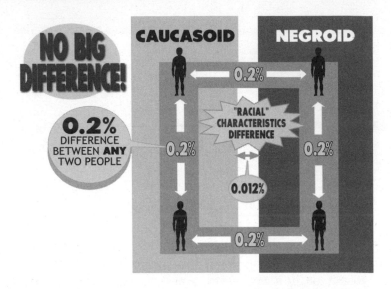

group and another. If a white person is looking for a tissue match for an organ transplant, for instance, the best match may come from a black person, and vice versa. ABC News claims, "What the facts show is that there are differences among us, but they stem from culture, not race."[22]

The only reason many people think these differences are major is because they've been brought up in a culture that has taught them to see the differences this way. Dr. Douglas C. Wallace, professor of molecular genetics at Emory University School of Medicine in Atlanta, stated, "The criteria that people use for race are based entirely on external features that we are programmed to recognize."[23]

If the Bible teaches and science confirms that all are of the same human race and all are related as descendants of Adam, then why are there such seemingly great differences between us (for example, in skin color)? The answer, again, comes with a biblically informed understanding of science.

Skin "Color"

Jesus loves the little children, all the children of the world. Red and yellow, black and white, they are precious in His sight.

When Jesus said, "Let the little children come to Me, and do not forbid them; for of such is the kingdom of heaven" (Matthew 19:14), He did not

---

[22] Ref. 11.
[23] Ibid.

distinguish between skin colors. In fact, scientists have discovered that there is one major pigment, called melanin, that produces our skin color. There are two main forms of melanin: eumelanin (brown to black) and pheomelanin (red to yellow). These combine to give us the particular shade of skin that we have.[24]

Melanin is produced by melanocytes, which are cells in the bottom layer of the epidermis. No matter what our shade of skin, we all have approximately the same concentration of melanocytes in our bodies. Melanocytes insert melanin into melanosomes, which transfer the melanin into other skin cells, which are cabaple of dividing (stem cells), primarily in the lowest layer of the epidermis. According to one expert,

> The melanosomes (tiny melanin-packaging units) are slightly larger and more numerous per cell in dark-skinned than light skinned people. They also do no degrade as readily, and disperse into adjacent skin cells to a higher degree.[25]

In the stem cells, the pigment serves its function as it forms a little dark umbrella over each nucleus. The melanin protects the epidermal cells from being damaged by sunlight. In people with lighter shades of skin, much of the pigment is lost after these cells divide and their daughter cells move up in the epidermis to form the surface dead layer—the stratum corneum.

Geneticists have found that four to six genes, each with

DIFFERENT COLORS or SAME COLOR—DIFFERENT SHADES?

---

[24] Of course, melanin is not the only factor that determines skin shade: blood vessels close to the skin can produce a reddish tinge, while extra layers of adipose tissue (fat) in the skin yield a yellowish tinge. Exposure to the sun can cause increased melanin production, thus darkening skin, but only to a certain point. Other pigments also affect skin shade but generally have very little bearing on how light or dark the skin will be. The major provider of skin color is melanin.

[25] Ackerman, *Histopathologic Diagnosis of Skin Diseases*, Lea & Febiger, Philadelphia, Pennsylvania, 1978, 44; Lever and Schamberg-Lever, *Histopathology of the Skin*, 7th Ed., J.B. Lippincott, Philadelphia, 1990, 18–20.

multiple alleles (or variations), control the amount and type of melanin produced. Because of this, a wide variety of skin shades exist. In fact, it is quite easy for one couple to produce a wide range of skin shades in just one generation, as will be shown below.

Inheritance

DNA (deoxyribonucleic acid) is the molecule of heredity that is passed from parents to child. In humans, the child inherits 23 chromosomes from each parent (the father donates 23 through his sperm, while the mother donates 23 through her egg). At the moment of conception, these chromosomes unite to form a unique combination of DNA and control much of what makes the child an individual. Each chromosome pair contains hundreds of genes, which regulate the physical development of the child. Note that no new genetic information is generated at conception, but a new *combination* of already-existing genetic information is formed.

To illustrate the basic genetic principles involved in determining skin shade, we'll use a simplified explanation,[26] with just two genes controlling the production of melanin. Let's say that the A and B versions of the genes code for a lot of melanin, while the a and b versions code for a small amount of melanin.

If the father's sperm carried the AB version and the mother's ovum carried the AB, the child would be AABB, with a lot of melanin, and thus very dark skin. Should both parents carry the ab version, the child would be aabb, with very little melanin, and thus very light skin. If the father carries AB (very dark skin) and the mother carries ab (very light skin), the child will be AaBb, with a middle brown

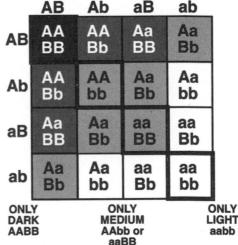

26 The actual genetics involved are much more complicated than this simplified explanation. There are 4 to 6 genes with multiples alleles (versions) of each gene that operate under incomplete dominance, that is, they work together to produce an individual's particular skin shade. However, simplifying the explanation does not take away from the point being made.

shade of skin. In fact, the majority of the world's population has a middle brown skin shade.

A simple exercise with a Punnet Square shows that if each parent has a middle brown shade of skin (AaBb), the combinations that they could produce result in a wide variety of skin shades in just one generation. Based on the skin colors seen today, we can infer that Adam and Eve most likely would have had a middle brown skin color. Their children, and children's children, could have ranged from very light to very dark.

No one really has red, or yellow, or black skin. We all have the same basic color, just different shades of it. We all share the same pigments—our bodies just have different combinations of them.[27]

Melanin also determines eye color. If the iris of the eye has a larger amount of melanin, it will be brown. If the iris has a little melanin, the eye will be blue. (The blue color in blue eyes results from the way light scatters off of the thin layer of brown-colored melanin.)

Hair color is also influenced by the production of melanin. Brown to black hair results from a greater production of melanin, while lighter hair results from less melanin. Those with red hair have a mutation in one gene that causes a greater proportion of the reddish form of melanin (pheomelanin) to be produced.[28]

DNA also controls the basic shape of our eyes. Individuals whose DNA codes for an extra layer of adipose tissue around the eyes have almond-shaped eyes (this is common among Asian people groups). All people groups have adipose tissue around the eyes, some simply have more or less.

Origin of People Groups

Those with darker skin tend to live in warmer climates, while those with lighter skin tend to live in colder climates. Why are certain characteristics more prominent in some areas of the world?

We know that Adam and Eve were the first two people. Their descendants filled the earth. However, the world's population was reduced to eight during the Flood of Noah. From these eight individuals have come all the tribes and nations. It is likely that the skin shade of Noah and his family was middle brown. This would enable his sons and their wives to produce a variety of skin shades in just one generation. Because there was a common language and everybody lived in the same general vicinity, barriers that may have prevented

---

[27] Albinism results from a genetic mutation which prevents the usual production of melanin.
[28] For more information, see www.answersingenesis.org/go/red-hair.

their descendants from freely intermarrying weren't as great as they are today. Thus, distinct differences in features and skin color in the population weren't as prevalent as they are today.

In Genesis 11 we read of the rebellion at the Tower of Babel. God judged this rebellion by giving each family group a different language. This made it impossible for the groups to understand each other, and so they split apart, each extended family going its own way, and finding a different place to live. The result was that the people were scattered over the earth.[29]

Because of the new language and geographic barriers, the groups no longer freely mixed with other groups, and the result was a splitting of the gene pool. Different cultures formed, with certain features becoming predominant within each group. The characteristics of each became more and more prominent as new generations of children were born. If we were to travel back in time to Babel, and mix up the people into completely different family groups, then people groups with completely different characteristics might result. For instance, we might find a fair-skinned group with tight, curly dark hair that has blue, almond-shaped eyes. Or a group with very dark skin, blue eyes, and straight brown hair.[30]

Some of these (skin color, eye shape, and so on) became general characteristics of each particular people group through various selection pressures (environmental, sexual, etc.) and/or mutation.[31] For example, because of the protective factor of melanin, those with darker skin would have been more likely to survive in areas where sunlight is more intense (warmer, tropical areas near the equator), as they are less likely to suffer from diseases such as skin cancer. Those with lighter skin lack the melanin needed to protect them from the harmful UV rays, and so may have been more likely to die before they were able to reproduce. UVA radiation also destroys the B vitamin folate, which is necessary for DNA synthesis in cell division. Low levels of folate in pregnant women can lead to defects in the developing baby. Again, because of this, lighter-skinned individuals may be selected against in areas of intense sunlight.

---

[29] As they went, the family groups took with them the knowledge that had been passed to them about the creation and Flood events. Although these accounts have been changed over time, they reflect the true account found in the Bible. For more information, see www.answersingenesis.org/go/legends.

[30] This assumes that each trait is independently inherited, which may not always be the case. Although there are many instances in which a certain trait shows up in a person of a different ethnic group (e.g., almond-shaped eyes in a woman with very dark skin, or blue eyes in a man with tightly curled brown hair and tan skin).

[31] For more on how selection and mutations operate, see chapter 22 in this book.

On the flip side, melanin works as a natural sunblock, limiting the sunlight's ability to stimulate the liver to produce vitamin D, which helps the body absorb calcium and build strong bones. Since those with darker skin need more sunlight to produce vitamin D, they may not have been as able to survive as well in areas of less sunlight (northern, colder regions) as their lighter-skinned family members, who don't need as much sunlight to produce adequate amounts of vitamin D. Those lacking vitamin D are more likely to develop diseases such as rickets (which is associated with a calcium deficiency), which can cause slowed growth and bone fractures. It is known that when those with darker skin lived in England during the Industrial Revolution, they were quick to develop rickets because of the general lack of sunlight.[32]

Of course, these are generalities. Exceptions occur, such as in the case of the darker-skinned Inuit tribes living in cold northern regions. However, their diet consists of fish, the oil of which is a ready source of vitamin D, which could account for their survival in this area.

Real science in the present fits with the biblical view that all people are rather closely related—there is only one race biologically. Therefore, to return to our original question, there is in essence no such thing as interracial marriage. So we are left with this—is there anything in the Bible that speaks clearly against men and women from different people groups marrying?

The Dispersion at Babel

Note that the context of Genesis 11 makes it clear that the reason for God's scattering the people over the earth was that they had united in rebellion against Him. Some Christians point to this event in an attempt to provide a basis for their arguments against so-called interracial marriage. They believe that this passage implies that God is declaring that people from different people groups can't marry so that the nations are kept apart. However, there is no such indication in this passage that what is called "interracial marriage" is condemned. Besides, there has been so much mixing of people groups over the years, that it would be impossible for every human being today to trace their lineage back to know for certain which group(s) they are descended from.

We need to understand that the sovereign creator God is in charge of the nations of this world. Paul makes this very clear in Acts 17:26. Some people erroneously claim this verse to mean that people from different nations shouldn't marry. However, this passage has nothing to do with marriage. As

---

[32] en.wikipedia.org/wiki/Melanin.

John Gill makes clear in his classic commentary, the context is that God is in charge of all things—where, how, and for how long any person, tribe, or nation will live, prosper, and perish.[33]

In all of this, God is working to redeem for Himself a people who are one in Christ. The Bible makes clear in Galatians 3:28, Colossians 3:11, and Romans 10:12–13 that in regard to salvation, there is no distinction between male or female or Jew or Greek. In Christ, any separation between people is broken down. As Christians, we are one in Christ and thus have a common purpose—to live for Him who made us. This oneness in Christ is vitally important to understanding marriage.

Purpose of Marriage

Malachi 2:15 informs us that an important purpose of marriage is to produce godly offspring—progeny that are trained in the ways of the Lord. Jesus (in Matthew 19) and Paul (in Ephesians 5) make it clear that when a man and woman marry, they become one flesh (because they were one flesh historically—Eve was made from Adam). Also, the man and woman must be one spiritually so they can fulfill the command to produce godly offspring.

This is why Paul states in 2 Corinthians 6:14, "Do not be unequally yoked together with unbelievers. For what fellowship has righteousness with lawlessness? And what communion has light with darkness?"

According to the Bible then, which of the following marriages in the picture on the right does God counsel against entering into?

The answer is obvious—number 3. According to the Bible, the priority in marriage is that a Christian should marry only a Christian.

---

[33] See note on Acts 17:26, in John Gill, D.D., *An exposition of the Old and New Testament*, London: printed for Mathews and Leigh, 18 Strand, by W. Clowes, Northumberland-Court, 1809. Edited, revised, and updated by Larry Pierce, 1994–1995 for Online Bible CD-ROM.

Sadly, there are some Christian homes where the parents are more concerned about their children not marrying someone from another "race" than whether or not they are marrying a Christian. When Christians marry non-Christians, it negates the spiritual (not the physical) oneness in marriage, resulting in negative consequences for the couple and their children.[34]

Roles in Marriage[35]

Of course, every couple needs to understand and embrace the biblical roles prescribed for each family member. Throughout the Scriptures our special roles and responsibilities are revealed. Consider these piercing passages directed to fathers:

> The father shall make known Your truth to the children (Isaiah 38:19).

> Fathers, do not provoke your children to wrath, but bring them up in the training and admonition of the Lord (Ephesians 6:4).

> For I have known him, in order that he may command his children and his household after him, that they keep the way of the LORD, to do righteousness and justice, that the LORD may bring to Abraham what He has spoken to him (Genesis 18:19).

These are just a few of the many verses that mention *fathers* in regard to training children. Additionally, the writer of Psalm 78 continually admonishes fathers to teach their children so they'll not forget to teach their children, so that they might not forget what God has done and keep His commandments. This includes building within their children a proper biblical worldview and providing them with answers to the questions the world asks about God and the Bible (as this book does). It also includes shepherding and loving his wife as Christ loved the church.

Of course, just as God made the role of the man clear, He has also made His intentions known regarding the role of a godly wife. In the beginning, God fashioned a woman to complete what was lacking in Adam, that she might

---

[34] It is true that in some exceptional instances when a Christian has married a non-Christian, the non-Christian spouse, by the grace of God, has become a Christian. This is a praise point but it does not negate the fact that Scripture indicates that it should not have been entered into in the first place. This does not mean that the marriage is not actually valid, nor does it dilute the responsibilities of the marital union—see also 1 Corinthians 7:12–14, where the context is of one spouse becoming a Christian after marriage.

[35] For more on this topic, see *Raising Godly Children in an Ungodly World* by K. Ham and S. Ham, Green Forest, Arkansas, Master Books, 2008.

become his helper, that the two of them would truly become one (Genesis 2:15–25). In other Bible passages the woman is encouraged to be a woman of character, integrity, and action (e.g., Proverbs 31:10–31). Certainly mothers should also be involved in teaching their children spiritual truths.

These roles are true for couples in every tribe and nation.

Rahab and Ruth

The examples of Rahab and Ruth help us understand how God views the issue of marriage between those who are from different people groups but trust in the true God.

Rahab was a Canaanite. These Canaanites had an ungodly culture and were descendants of Canaan, the son of Ham. Remember, Canaan was cursed because of his obvious rebellious nature. Sadly, many people state that Ham was cursed—but this is not true.[36] Some have even said that this (non-existent) curse of Ham resulted in the black "races."[37] This is absurd and is the type of false teaching that has reinforced and justified prejudices against people with dark skin.

In the genealogy in Matthew 1, it is traditionally understood that the same Rahab is listed here as being in the line leading to Christ. Thus Rahab, a descendant of Ham, must have married an Israelite (descended from Shem). Since this was clearly a union approved by God, it underlines the fact that the particular "people group" she came from was irrelevant—what mattered was that she trusted in the true God of the Israelites.

The same can be said of Ruth, who as a Moabitess also married an Israelite and is also listed in the genealogy in Matthew 1 that leads to Christ. Prior to her marriage, she had expressed faith in the true God (Ruth 1:16).

---

[36] See Genesis 9:18–27. Canaan, the youngest of Ham's sons, received Noah's curse. Why? The descendants of Canaan were some of the wickedest people on earth. For example, the people of Sodom and Gomorrah were judged for their sexual immorality and rebellion. It may be that Ham's actions toward his father (Genesis 9:22) had sexual connotations, and Noah saw this same sin problem in Canaan and understood that Canaan's descendants would also act in these sinful ways. (The Bible clearly teaches that the unconfessed sin of one generation is often greater in the next generation.) The curse on Canaan has nothing to do with skin color but rather serves as a warning to fathers to train their children in the nurture and admonition of the Lord. We need to deal with our own sin problems and train our children to deal with theirs.

[37] For example: "We know the circumstances under which the posterity of Cain (and later of Ham) were cursed with what we call Negroid racial characteristics" (Bruce McConkie, Apostle of the Mormon Council of 12, *Mormon Doctrine*, p. 554, 1958); "The curse which Noah pronounced upon Canaan was the origin of the black race" (The Golden Age, *The Watchtower* [now called *Awake!*], p. 702, July 24, 1929).

When Rahab and Ruth became children of God, there was no longer any barrier to Israelites marrying them, even though they were from different people groups.

Real Biblical "Interracial" Marriage

If one wants to use the term "interracial," then the real interracial marriage that God says we should not enter into is when a child of the Last Adam (one who is a new creation in Christ—a Christian) marries one who is an unconverted child of the First Adam (one who is dead in trespasses and sin— a non-Christian).[38]

Cross-Cultural Problems

Because many people groups have been separated since the Tower of Babel, they have developed many cultural differences. If two people from very different cultures marry, they can have a number of communication problems, even if both are Christians. Expectations regarding relationships with members of the extended family, for example, can also differ. Even people from different English-speaking countries can have communication problems because words may have different meanings. Counselors should go through this in detail, anticipating the problems and giving specific examples, as some marriages have failed because of such cultural differences. However, such problems have nothing to do with genetics or "race."

Conclusion

1. There is no biblical justification for claiming that people from different so-called races (best described as people groups) should not marry.

2. The biblical basis for marriage makes it clear that a Christian should marry only a Christian.

When Christians legalistically impose nonbiblical ideas, such as no interracial marriage onto their culture, they are helping to perpetuate prejudices that have often arisen from evolutionary influences. If we are really honest, in countries like America, the main reason for Christians being against interracial marriage is, in most instances, really because of skin color.

---

[38] Examples of such "mixed marriages" and their negative consequences can be seen in Nehemiah 9 and 10, and Numbers 25.

The church could greatly relieve the tensions over racism (particularly in countries like America), if only the leaders would teach biblical truths about our shared ancestry: all people are descended from one man and woman; all people are equal before God; all are sinners in need of salvation; all need to build their thinking on God's Word and judge all their cultural aspects accordingly; all need to be one in Christ and put an end to their rebellion against their Creator.

Christians must think about marriage as God thinks about each one of us. When the prophet Samuel went to anoint the next king of Israel, he thought the oldest of Jesse's sons was the obvious choice due to his outward appearance. However, we read in 1 Samuel 16:7, "But the LORD said to Samuel, 'Do not look at his appearance or at his physical stature, because I have refused him. For the LORD does not see as man sees; for man looks at the outward appearance, but the LORD looks at the heart.'" God doesn't look at our outward biological appearance; He looks on our inward spiritual state. And when considering marriage, couples should look on the inside spiritual condition of themselves and each other because it is true that what's on the inside, spiritually, is what really matters.

18

Are ETs & UFOs Real?

JASON LISLE

Are there extraterrestrial life forms out there? The question of life on other planets is a hot topic in our culture today. Science fiction movies and television shows often depict strange creatures from far-away planets. But these ideas are not limited merely to science fiction programming. Many secular scientists believe that one day we will actually discover life on other planets. There are even projects like the Search for Extra-Terrestrial Intelligence (SETI) that scan the heavens with powerful radio telescopes listening for signals from intelligent aliens. Many Christians have bought into the idea of extraterrestrial alien life. But is this idea really biblical? The Christian should constantly examine ideas in light of Scripture and take "every thought into captivity to the obedience of Christ" (2 Corinthians 10:5).

CREATIONWISE

IT'S MIND BOGGLING TO THINK OF THE VASTNESS OF CREATION! THE BIBLE IS ONLY ONE LITTLE BOOK. JUST THINK OF ALL THE INFORMATION GOD HASN'T GIVEN TO US!

YES, BUT WHAT HAVE YOU DONE WITH THE INFORMATION GOD **HAS** GIVEN TO US?

© AiG 2003

The Evolution Connection

The idea of extraterrestrial life stems largely from a belief in evolution. Recall that in the evolutionary view, the earth is "just another planet"—one where the conditions just happened to be right for life to form and evolve. If there are countless billions of other planets in our galaxy, then surely at least a handful of these worlds have also had the right conditions. Extraterrestrial life is almost inevitable in an evolutionary worldview.

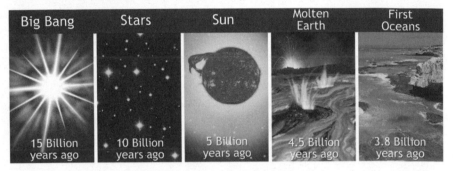

Big Bang	Stars	Sun	Molten Earth	First Oceans
15 Billion years ago	10 Billion years ago	5 Billion years ago	4.5 Billion years ago	3.8 Billion years ago

However, the notion of alien life does not square well with Scripture. The earth is unique. God designed the earth for life (Isaiah 45:18). The other planets have an entirely different purpose than does the earth, and thus they are designed differently. In Genesis 1 we read that God created plants on the earth on Day 3, birds to fly in the atmosphere and marine life to swim in the ocean on Day 5, and animals to inhabit the land on Day 6. Human beings were also made on Day 6 and were given dominion over the animals. But where does the Bible discuss the creation of life on the "lights in the expanse of the heavens"? There is no such description because the lights in the expanse were not designed to accommodate life. God gave care of the earth to man, but the heavens are the Lord's (Psalm 115:16). From a biblical perspective, extraterrestrial life does not seem reasonable.

Water covered Earth	Dry land and plants	Sun, moon, and stars	Sea and flying creatures	Land animals and Man
Day 1-2	Day 3	Day 4	Day 5	Day 6

Problems are multiplied when we consider the possibility of *intelligent* alien life. Science fiction programming abounds with races of people who evolved on other worlds. We see examples of Vulcans and Klingons—pseudo-humans similar to us in most respects but different in others. As a plot device, these races allow the exploration of the human condition from the perspective of an outsider. Although very entertaining, such alien races are theologically problematic. Intelligent alien beings cannot be redeemed. God's plan of redemption is for human beings: those descended from Adam. Let us examine the conflict between the salvation message and the notion of alien life.

The Redemption of Mankind

The Bible teaches that the first man, Adam, rebelled against God (Genesis 3). As a result, sin and death entered the world (Romans 5:12). We are all descended from Adam and Eve (Genesis 3:20) and have inherited from them a sin nature (Romans 6:6, 20). This is a problem: sin is a barrier that prevents man from being right with God (Isaiah 59:2). But God loves us despite our sin and provided a plan of redemption—a way to be reconciled with God.

After Adam and Eve sinned, God made coats of skins to cover them (Genesis 3:21). He therefore had to kill at least one animal. This literal action is symbolic of our salvation; an innocent Lamb (Christ—the Lamb of God) would be sacrificed to provide a covering for sin (John 1:29). In the Old Testament, people would sacrifice animals to the Lord as a reminder of their sin (Hebrews 10:3) and as a symbol of the One to come, the Lord Jesus, who would actually pay the penalty for sin.

The animal sacrifices did not actually pay the penalty for sin (Hebrews 10:4, 11). Animals are not related to us; their shed blood cannot count for ours. But the blood of Christ can. Christ is a blood relative of ours since He is descended from Adam as are we; all human beings are of "one blood" (Acts 17:26). Furthermore, since Christ is also God, His life is of infinite value, and thus His death can pay for all the sins of all people. That is why only the Lord Himself could be our Savior (Isaiah 45:21). Therefore, Christ died once for all (Hebrews 10:10).

The Redemption of ET?

When we consider how the salvation plan might apply to any hypothetical extraterrestrial (but otherwise human-like) beings, we are presented with a problem. If there were Vulcans or Klingons out there, how would they be saved? They are not blood relatives of Jesus, and so Christ's shed blood cannot pay for their sin. One might at first suppose that Christ also visited their world, lived there, and died there as well, but this is antibiblical. Christ died *once* for *all* (1 Peter 3:18; Hebrews 9:27–28, 10:10). Jesus is now and forever both God and man; but He is *not* an alien.

One might suppose that alien beings have never sinned, in which case they would not need to be redeemed. But then another problem emerges: they suffer the effects of sin, despite having never sinned. Adam's sin has affected all of creation—not just mankind. Romans 8:20–22 makes it clear that the entirety of creation suffers under the bondage of corruption. These kinds of issues highlight the problem of attempting to incorporate an antibiblical notion into the Christian worldview.

Extraterrestrial life is an evolutionary concept; it does not comport with the biblical teachings of the uniqueness of the earth and the distinct spiritual position of human beings. Of all the worlds in the universe, it was the earth that God Himself visited, taking on the additional nature of a human being, dying on a cross, and rising from the dead in order to redeem all who would trust in Him. The biblical worldview sharply contrasts with the secular worldview when it comes to alien life. So, which worldview does the scientific evidence support? Do modern observations support the secular notion that the universe is teeming with life, or the biblical notion that earth is unique?

Where Is Everybody?

So far, no one has discovered life on other planets or detected any radio signals from intelligent aliens. This is certainly what a biblical creationist would expect. Secular astronomers continue to search for life on other worlds, but they have found only rocks and inanimate matter. Their radio searches are met with silence. The real world is the biblical world—a universe designed by God with the earth at the spiritual focal point, not an evolutionary universe teeming with life.

When it comes to extraterrestrial life, science is diametrically opposed to the evolutionary mentality. We currently have *no* evidence of alien life forms. This problem is not lost on the secular scientists. It has been said that the atomic scientist Enrico Fermi was once discussing the topic of extraterrestrial life when he asked the profound question, "Where is everybody?" Since there are quite possibly multiple billions of planets in our galaxy, and since in the secular view these are all accidents, it is almost inevitable that some of these had the right conditions for life to evolve. And if some of these worlds are billions of years older than ours, then at least some of them would have evolved intelligent life eons ago. The universe should therefore have countless numbers of technologically superior civilizations, any one of which could have colonized our galaxy ages ago. Yet, we find no evidence of these civilizations. Where is everybody? This problem has become known as the "Fermi paradox."

This paradox for evolution is a *feature* of creation. We have seen that the earth is designed for life. With its oceans of liquid water, a protective

atmosphere containing abundant free oxygen, and a distance from the sun that is just right for life, earth was certainly designed by God to be inhabited. But the other planets of the universe were not. From the sulfuric acid clouds of Venus to the frozen wasteland of Pluto, the other worlds of our solar system are beautiful and diverse, but they are not designed for life.

What about UFOs?

Sometimes after I speak on the topic of extraterrestrial life, someone will ask me about UFOs. A UFO (unidentified flying object) is just that—an object seen in the sky that is unidentified to the person seeing it. People often want me to explain a sighting of some unknown flying object which they or often a friend have claimed to see. (Sometimes the implication is that if I can't explain it, it somehow proves that it must be an alien spacecraft; but such reasoning is completely vacuous.[1]) These kinds of questions are unreasonable. It is one thing to be asked to interpret evidence that we have, but it is unrealistic to ask someone to interpret undocumented second- or third-hand stories with no actual evidence available for inspection.

There is no doubt that some people sincerely have seen things in the sky that they do not understand. This is hardly surprising since there are lots of things "up there," which can be misunderstood by people not familiar with them. These include Venus, satellites, the international space station, the space shuttle, rockets, Iridium flares, manmade aircraft, internal reflections, meteors, balloons, fireflies, aurorae, birds, ball lightning, lenticular clouds, parhelia, etc. However, a person unfamiliar with these would see a UFO, since the object is "unidentified" to him or her. It is how people interpret what they see that can be questionable.

Remember that we always interpret evidence in light of our worldview. It is therefore crucial to have a correct, biblical worldview. The fallacious worldview of atheism/naturalism may lead someone to draw erroneous conclusions about what they see. From a biblical worldview, we expect to occasionally see things that are not easily explained, since our minds are finite. But UFOs are not alien spacecraft, and of course, there is no tangible evidence to support such a notion.

---

[1] The argument is that alien spacecraft could not be explained by a natural phenomenon. Therefore, it is suggested that witnessing something that cannot be explained naturally must prove the existence of alien spacecraft. This is a logical fallacy called "affirming the consequent." It's equivalent to saying, "All white dwarf stars are white. Fred is white; therefore Fred is a white dwarf star."

Why the Hype?

In the 1990s the television series *The X-files* entertained millions of fans with stories of aliens, government conspiracies, and one dedicated FBI agent's relentless search for truth. The show's motto, "The truth is out there," is a well-known phrase for sci-fi fans. But why is there such hype surrounding the notion of extraterrestrial life? Why is science fiction programming so popular? Why does SETI spend millions of dollars searching for life in outer space?

The discovery of intelligent extraterrestrial life would certainly be seen as a vindication of evolution; it is an expectation from a naturalistic worldview. But the desire to meet aliens, especially intelligent, technologically advanced ones, seems much more deeply felt than merely to vindicate evolutionary predictions. What is the *real* issue? I've heard a number of different answers from secular astronomers.

In some cases a belief in ETs may stem from a feeling of cosmic loneliness: "If there are aliens, then we would not be alone in the universe." In many cases it comes from an academic desire to learn the mysteries of the universe; a highly developed alien race might have advanced knowledge to pass on to us. Perhaps such knowledge is not merely academic; the hypothetical aliens may know the answers to fundamental questions of existence: "Why am I here? What is the meaning of life?" and so on. An advanced alien race might have medical knowledge far exceeding our own—knowledge which could be used to cure our diseases. Perhaps their medical technology would be so far advanced that they even hold the secret of life and death; with such incredible medical knowledge, perhaps human beings would no longer have to die—*ever*.

In a way, a belief in extraterrestrial life has become a secular replacement for God. God is the one who can heal every disease. God is the one in whom all the treasures of wisdom and knowledge are deposited (Colossians 2:3). God is the one who can answer the fundamental questions of our existence. God alone possesses the gift of eternal life (John 17:3). It is not surprising that the unbelieving scientist would feel a sense of cosmic loneliness, having rejected his Creator. But, we are not alone in the universe; there is God. God created us for fellowship with Him; thus we have an innate need for Him and for purpose. Although human beings have rejected God, in Adam and by our sins as well, our need for fellowship with Him remains.

When I think of the majority of intelligent scientists who have studied God's magnificent creation but have nonetheless rejected Him and have instead chosen to believe in aliens and millions of years of evolution, I am reminded of Romans 1:18–25. God's invisible qualities—His eternal power and divine nature—are clearly revealed in the natural world so that there is no excuse for rejecting God or suppressing the truth about Him. The thinking of man apart from God is nothing more than futile speculations. Exchanging the truth of God, such as creation, for a lie, such as evolution, and turning to a mere creature such as hypothetical aliens for answers is strikingly similar to what is recorded in Romans 1:25.

But when we start from the Bible, the evidence makes sense. The universe is consistent with the biblical teaching that the earth is a special creation. The magnificent beauty and size of a universe, which is apparently devoid of life except for one little world where life abounds, is exactly what we would expect from a biblical worldview. The truth is not "out there;" the truth is *in there*—in the Bible! The Lord Jesus is the truth (John 14:6). So when we base our thinking on what God has said in His Word, we find that the universe makes sense.

19

Does Distant Starlight Prove the Universe Is Old?

JASON LISLE

Critics of biblical creation sometimes use distant starlight as an argument against a young universe. The argument goes something like this: (1) there are galaxies that are so far away, it would take light from their stars billions of years to get from there to here; (2) we can see these galaxies, so their starlight has already arrived here; and (3) the universe must be at least billions of years old—much older than the 6,000 or so years indicated in the Bible.

Many big bang supporters consider this to be an excellent argument against the biblical timescale. But when we examine this argument carefully, we will see that it does not work. The universe is very big and contains galaxies that are very far away, but that does not mean that the universe must be billions of years old.

The distant starlight question has caused some people to question cosmic distances. "Do we really know that galaxies are so far away? Perhaps they are much closer, so the light really doesn't travel very far."[1] However, the techniques that astronomers use to measure cosmic distances are generally logical and scientifically sound. They do not rely on evolutionary assumptions about the past. Moreover, they are a part of *observational* science (as opposed to historical/origins science); they are testable and repeatable in the present. You could repeat the experiment to determine the distance to

---

[1] See the DVD *Astronomy: What Do We Really Know?* by Dr. Jason Lisle for a more complete treatment of these questions, available at www.answersbookstore.com.

a star or galaxy, and you would get approximately the same answer. So we have good reason to believe that space really is very big. In fact, the amazing size of the universe brings glory to God (Psalm 19:1).

Some Christians have proposed that God created the beams of light from distant stars already on their way to the earth. After all, Adam didn't need any time to grow from a baby because he was made as an adult. Likewise, it is argued that the universe was made mature, and so perhaps the light was created in-transit. Of course, the universe was indeed made to function right from the first week, and many aspects of it were indeed created "mature." The only problem with assuming that the light was created in-transit is that we see things happen in space. For example, we see stars change brightness and move. Sometimes we see stars explode. We see these things because their light has reached us.

But if God created the light beams already on their way, then that means none of the events we see in space (beyond a distance of 6,000 light-years) actually happened. It would mean that those exploding stars never exploded or existed; God merely painted pictures of these fictional events. It seems uncharacteristic of God to make illusions like this. God made our eyes to accurately probe the real universe; so we can trust that the events that we see in space really happened. For this reason, most creation scientists believe that light created in-transit is not the best way to respond to the distant starlight argument. Let me suggest that the answer to distant starlight lies in some of the unstated assumptions that secular astronomers make.

The Assumptions of Light Travel-time Arguments

Any attempt to scientifically estimate the age of something will necessarily involve a number of *assumptions*. These can be assumptions about the starting conditions, constancy of rates, contamination of the system, and many others. If even one of these assumptions is wrong, so is the age estimate. Sometimes an incorrect worldview is to blame when people make faulty assumptions. The distant starlight argument involves several assumptions that are questionable—any one of which makes the argument unsound. Let's examine a few of these assumptions.

The Constancy of the Speed of Light

It is usually assumed that the speed of light is constant with time.[2] At today's rate, it takes light (in a vacuum) about one year to cover a distance of 6 trillion miles. But has this always been so? If we incorrectly assume that the rate has always been today's rate, we would end up estimating an age that is much older than the true age. But some people have proposed that light was much quicker in the past. If so, light could traverse the universe in only a fraction of the time it would take today. Some creation scientists believe that this is the answer to the problem of distant starlight in a young universe.

However, the speed of light is not an "arbitrary" parameter. In other words, changing the speed of light would cause other things to change as well, such as the ratio of energy to mass in any system.[3] Some people have argued that the speed of light can never have been much different than it is today because it is so connected to other constants of nature. In other words, life may not be possible if the speed of light were any different.

This is a legitimate concern. The way in which the universal constants are connected is only partially understood. So, the impact of a changing speed of light on the universe and life on earth is not fully known. Some creation scientists are actively researching questions relating to the speed of light. Other creation scientists feel that the assumption of the constancy of the speed of light is probably reasonable and that the solution to distant starlight lies elsewhere.

The Assumption of Rigidity of Time

Many people assume that time flows at the same rate in all conditions. At first, this seems like a very reasonable assumption. But, in fact, this assumption is false. And there are a few different ways in which the nonrigid nature of time could allow distant starlight to reach earth within the biblical timescale.

Albert Einstein discovered that the rate at which time passes is affected by motion and by gravity. For example, when an object moves very fast, close

---

[2] Many people mistakenly think that Einstein's theory of relativity demands that the speed of light has not changed in time. In reality, this is not so. Relativity only requires that two different observers would measure the same velocity for a beam of light, even if they are moving relative to each other.

[3] This follows from the equation $E=mc^2$, in which c is the speed of light and E is the energy associated with a given amount of mass (m).

to the speed of light, its time is slowed down. This is called "time-dilation." So, if we were able to accelerate a clock to nearly the speed of light, that clock would tick very slowly. If we could somehow reach the speed of light, the clock would stop completely. This isn't a problem with the clock; the effect would happen regardless of the clock's particular construction because it is time itself that is slowed. Likewise, gravity slows the passage of time. A clock at sea-level would tick slower than one on a mountain, since the clock at sea-level is closer to the source of gravity.

It seems hard to believe that velocity or gravity would affect the passage of time since our everyday experience cannot detect this. After all, when we are traveling in a vehicle, time appears to flow at the same rate as when we are standing still. But that's because we move so slowly compared to the speed of light, and the earth's gravity is so weak that the effects of time-dilation are correspondingly tiny. However, the effects of time-dilation have been measured with atomic clocks.

Since time can flow at different rates from different points of view, events that would take a long time as measured by one person will take very little time as measured by another person. This also applies to distant starlight. Light that would take billions of years to reach earth (as measured by clocks in deep space) could reach earth in only thousands of years as measured by clocks on earth. This would happen naturally if the earth is in a *gravitational well*, which we will discuss below.

Many secular astronomers assume that the universe is infinitely big and has an infinite number of galaxies. This has never been proven, nor is there evidence that would lead us naturally to that conclusion. So, it is a leap of "blind" faith on their part. However, if we make a different assumption instead, it leads to a very different conclusion. Suppose that our solar system is located near the center of a finite distribution of galaxies. Although this cannot be proven for certain at present, it is fully consistent with the evidence; so it is a reasonable possibility.

In that case, the earth would be in a *gravitational well*. This term means that it would require energy to pull something away from our position into deeper space. In this gravitational well, we would not "feel" any extra gravity, nonetheless time would flow more slowly on earth (or anywhere in our solar system) than in other places of the universe. This effect is thought to be very small today; however, it may have been much stronger in the past. (If the universe is expanding as most astronomers believe, then physics demands that such effects would have been stronger when the universe was smaller). This being the case, clocks on earth would have ticked much more slowly than clocks in deep space. Thus, light from the most distant galaxies would arrive on earth in only a few thousand years as measured by clocks on earth. This idea is certainly intriguing. And although there are still a number of mathematical details that need to be worked out, the premise certainly is reasonable. Some creation scientists are actively researching this idea.

Assumptions of Synchronization

Another way in which the relativity of time is important concerns the topic of synchronization: how clocks are set so that they read the same time at the same time.[4] Relativity has shown that synchronization is not absolute. In other words, if one person measures two clocks to be synchronized, another person (moving at a different speed) would *not* necessarily measure those two clocks to be synchronized. As with time-dilation, this effect is counter-intuitive because it is too small to measure in most of our everyday experience. Since there is no method by which two clocks (separated by a distance) can be synchronized in an absolute sense, such that all observers would agree regardless of motion, it follows that there is some flexibility in how we choose what constitutes synchronized clocks. The following analogy may be helpful.

Imagine that a plane leaves a certain city at 4:00 p.m. for a two-hour flight. However, when the plane lands, the time is still 4:00. Since the plane arrived at the same time it left, we might call this an instantaneous trip. How is this possible? The answer has to do with time zones. If the plane left Kentucky at 4:00 p.m. local time, it would arrive in Colorado at 4:00 p.m. local time. Of course, an observer on the plane would experience two hours of travel. So, the trip takes two hours as measured by *universal time*. However, as long as the plane is traveling west (and providing it travels fast enough), it will always naturally arrive at the same time it left as measured in *local time*.

There is a cosmic equivalent to local and universal time. Light traveling toward earth is like the plane traveling west; it always remains at the same cosmic local time. Although most astronomers today primarily use cosmic universal time (in which it takes light 100 years to travel 100 light-years), historically cosmic local time has been the standard. And so it may be that the Bible also uses cosmic local time when reporting events.

---

[4] For a discussion on synchrony conventions see W.C. Salmon, The philosophical significance of the one-way speed of light, *Nous* **11**(3):253–292, Symposium on Space and Time, 1977.

Since God created the stars on Day 4, their light would leave the star on Day 4 and reach earth on Day 4 *cosmic local time*. Light from all galaxies would reach earth on Day 4 if we measure it according to cosmic local time. Someone might object that the light itself would experience billions of years (as the passenger on the plane experiences the two hour trip). However, according to Einstein's relativity, light does not experience the passage of time, so the trip would be instantaneous. Now, this idea may or may not be the reason that distant starlight is able to reach earth within the biblical timescale, but so far no one has been able to prove that the Bible does *not* use cosmic local time. So, it is an intriguing possibility.[5]

The Assumption of Naturalism

One of the most overlooked assumptions in most arguments against the Bible is the assumption of *naturalism*. Naturalism is the belief that nature is "all that there is." Proponents of naturalism *assume* that all phenomena can be explained in terms of natural laws. This is not only a blind assumption, but it is also clearly antibiblical. The Bible makes it clear that God is not bound by natural laws (they are, after all, *His* laws). Of course God can use laws of nature to accomplish His will; and He usually does so. In fact, natural laws could be considered a description of the way in which God normally upholds the universe. But God is supernatural and is capable of acting outside natural law.

This would certainly have been the case during Creation Week. God created the universe supernaturally. He created it from nothing, not from previous material (Hebrews 11:3). Today, we do not see God speaking into existence new stars or new kinds of creatures. This is because God ended His work of creation by the seventh day. Today, God sustains the universe in a different way than how He created it. However, the naturalist erroneously assumes that the universe was created by the same processes by which it operates today. Of course it would be absurd to apply this assumption to most other things. A flashlight, for example, operates by converting electricity into light, but the flashlight was not created by this process.

Since the stars were created during Creation Week and since God made them to give light upon the earth, the way in which distant starlight arrived on earth may have been supernatural. We cannot assume that past acts of God are necessarily understandable in terms of a current scientific mechanism, because

---

[5] See Distant Starlight and Genesis, *TJ* **15**(1):80–85, 2001; available online at www. answersingenesis.org/tj/v15/i1/starlight.asp.

science can only probe the way in which God sustains the universe today. It is irrational to argue that a supernatural act cannot be true on the basis that it cannot be explained by natural processes observed today.

It is perfectly acceptable for us to ask, "Did God use natural processes to get the starlight to earth in the biblical timescale? And if so, what is the mechanism?" But if no natural mechanism is apparent, this cannot be used as evidence against *supernatural* creation. So, the unbeliever is engaged in a subtle form of circular reasoning when he uses the assumption of naturalism to argue that distant starlight disproves the biblical timescale.

Light Travel-Time: a Self-Refuting Argument

Many big bang supporters use the above assumptions to argue that the biblical timescale cannot be correct because of the light travel-time issue. But such an argument is self-refuting. It is fatally flawed because the big bang has a light travel-time problem of its own. In the big bang model, light is required to travel a distance much greater than should be possible within the big bang's own timeframe of about 14 billion years. This serious difficulty for the big bang is called the "horizon problem."[6] The following are the details.

In the big bang model, the universe begins in an infinitely small state called a singularity, which then rapidly expands. According to the big bang model, when the universe is still very small, it would develop different temperatures in different locations (Figure 1A). Let's suppose that point A is hot and point B is cold. Today, the universe has expanded (Figure 1B), and points A and B are now widely separated.

However, the universe has an extremely uniform temperature at great distance—beyond the farthest known galaxies. In other words, points A and B have almost exactly the same temperature today. We know this because we see electromagnetic radiation coming from all directions in space in the form of microwaves. This is called the "cosmic microwave background" (CMB). The frequencies of radiation have a characteristic temperature of 2.7 K (-455°F) and are *extremely* uniform in all directions. The temperature deviates by only one part in 10^5.

The problem is this: How did points A and B come to be the same temperature? They can do this only by exchanging energy. This happens in many systems: consider an ice cube placed in hot coffee. The ice heats up and the coffee cools down by exchanging energy. Likewise, point A can give energy to

---

[6] See www.answersingenesis.org/creation/v25/i4/lighttravel.asp.

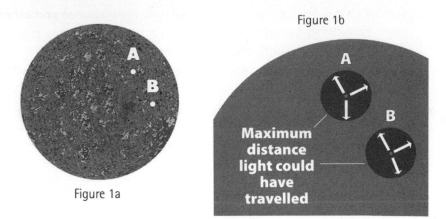

Figure 1b

Figure 1a

Maximum distance light could have travelled

The Horizon Problem

point B in the form of electromagnetic radiation (light), which is the fastest way to transfer energy since nothing can travel faster than light. However, using the big bang supporters' own assumptions, including uniformitarianism and naturalism, there has not been enough time in 14 billion years to get light from A to B; they are too far apart. This is a light travel-time problem—and a very serious one. After all, A and B have almost exactly the same temperature today, and so must have exchanged light multiple times.

Big bang supporters have proposed a number of conjectures which attempt to solve the big bang's light travel-time problem. One of the most popular is called "inflation." In "inflationary" models, the universe has two expansion rates; a normal rate and a fast inflation rate. The universe begins with the normal rate, which is actually quite rapid, but is slow by comparison to the next phase. Then it briefly enters the inflation phase, where the universe expands much more rapidly. At a later time, the universe goes back to the normal rate. This all happens early on, long before stars and galaxies form.

The inflation model allows points A and B to exchange energy (during the first normal expansion) and to then be pushed apart during the inflation phase to the enormous distances at which they are located today. But the inflation model amounts to nothing more than storytelling with no supporting evidence at all. It is merely speculation designed to align the big bang to conflicting observations. Moreover, inflation adds an additional set of problems and difficulties to the big bang model, such as the cause of such inflation and a graceful way to turn it off. An increasing number of secular astrophysicists are rejecting inflation for these reasons and others. Clearly, the horizon problem remains a serious light travel-time problem for the big bang.

The critic may suggest that the big bang is a better explanation of origins than the Bible since biblical creation has a light travel-time problem—distant starlight. But such an argument is not rational since the big bang has a light travel-time problem of its own. If both models have the same problem *in essence*,[7] then that problem cannot be used to support one model over the other. Therefore, distant starlight cannot be used to dismiss the Bible in favor of the big bang.

Conclusions

So, we've seen that the critics of creation must use a number of assumptions in order to use distant starlight as an argument against a young universe. And many of these assumptions are questionable. Do we know that light has always propagated at today's speed? Perhaps this is reasonable, but can we be absolutely certain, particularly during Creation Week when God was acting in a supernatural way? Can we be certain that the Bible is using "cosmic universal time," rather than the more common "cosmic local time" in which light reaches earth instantly?

We know that the rate at which time flows is not rigid. And although secular astronomers are well aware that time is relative, they *assume* that this effect is (and has always been) negligible, but can we be certain that this is so? And since stars were made during Creation Week when God was *supernaturally* creating, how do we know for certain that distant starlight has arrived on earth by entirely *natural* means? Furthermore, when big bang supporters use distant starlight to argue against biblical creation, they are using a self-refuting argument since the big bang has a light travel-time problem of its own. When we consider all of the above, we see that distant starlight has never been a legitimate argument against the biblical timescale of a few thousand years.

As creation scientists research possible solutions to the distant starlight problem, we should also remember the body of evidence that is consistent

---

[7] The details, of course, differ. The big bang does not have a problem with distant starlight as such. But then again, biblical creation does not have a horizon problem. (The cosmic microwave background does not need to start with different temperatures in a creationist cosmogony.) However, both problems are the same in *essence*: how to get light to travel a greater distance than seems possible in the time allowed.

with the youth of the universe. We see rotating spiral galaxies that cannot last multiple billions of years because they would be twisted-up beyond recognition. We see multitudes of hot blue stars, which even secular astronomers would agree cannot last billions of years.[8] In our own solar system we see disintegrating comets and decaying magnetic fields that cannot last billions of years; and there is evidence that other solar systems have these things as well. Of course, such arguments also involve assumptions about the past. That is why, ultimately, the only way to know about the past *for certain* is to have a reliable historic record written by an eyewitness. That is exactly what we have in the Bible.

---

[8] Secular astronomers believe that blue stars must have formed relatively recently. But there are considerable difficulties in star formation scenarios—problems with magnetic fields and angular momentum to name a couple.

20

Did Jesus Say He Created in Six Literal Days?

KEN HAM

A very important question we must ask is, "What was Jesus' view of the days of creation? Did He say that He created in six literal days?"

When confronted with such a question, most Christians would automatically go to the New Testament to read the recorded words of Jesus to see if such a statement occurs.

Now, when we search the New Testament Scriptures, we certainly find many interesting statements Jesus made that relate to this issue. Mark 10:6 says, "But from the beginning of the creation, God 'made them male and female.'" From this passage, we see that Jesus clearly taught that the creation was young, for Adam and Eve existed "from the beginning," not billions of years after the universe and earth came into existence. Jesus made a similar statement in Mark 13:19 indicating that man's sufferings started very near the beginning of creation. The parallel phrases of "from the foundation of the world" and "from the blood of Abel" in Luke 11:50–51 also indicate that Jesus placed Abel very close to the beginning of creation, not billions of years after the beginning. His Jewish listeners would have assumed this meaning in Jesus' words, for the first-century Jewish historian Josephus indicates that the Jews of his day believed that both the first day of creation and Adam's creation were about 5,000 years before Christ.[1]

---

[1] See William Whiston, transl., *The Works of Josephus*, Hendrickson, Peabody, Massachusetts, p. 850, 1987, and Paul James-Griffiths, "Creation days and Orthodox Jewish Tradition," *Creation* 26(2): 53–55, www.answersingenesis.org/creation/v26/i2/tradition.asp.

In John 5:45–47, Jesus says, "Do not think that I shall accuse you to the Father; there is one who accuses you—Moses, in whom you trust. For if you believed Moses, you would believe Me; for he wrote about Me. But if you do not believe his writings, how will you believe My words?" In this passage, Jesus makes it clear that one must believe what Moses wrote. And one of the passages in the writings of Moses in Exodus 20:11 states: "For in six days the LORD made the heavens and the earth, the sea, and all that is in them, and rested the seventh day. Therefore the LORD blessed the Sabbath day and hallowed it." This, of course, is the basis for our seven-day week—six days of work and one day of rest. Obviously, this passage was meant to be taken as speaking of a total of seven literal days based on the Creation Week of six literal days of work and one literal day of rest.

In fact, in Luke 13:14, in his response to Jesus healing a person on the Sabbath, the ruler of the synagogue, who knew the law of Moses, obviously referred to this passage when he said, "There are six days on which men ought to work; therefore come and be healed on them, and not on the Sabbath day." The sabbath day here was considered an ordinary day, and the six days of work were considered ordinary days. This teaching is based on the Law of Moses as recorded in Exodus 20, where we find the Ten Commandments—the six-day Creation Week being the basis for the Fourth Commandment.

We should also note the way Jesus treated as historical fact the accounts in the Old Testament, which religious and atheistic skeptics think are unbelievable mythology. These historical accounts include Adam and Eve as the first married couple (Matthew 19:3–6; Mark 10:3–9), Abel as the first prophet who was killed (Luke 11:50–51), Noah and the Flood (Matthew 24:38–39), Moses and the serpent in the wilderness (John 3:14), Moses and the manna from heaven to feed the Israelites in the wilderness (John 6:32–33, 49), the experiences of Lot and his wife (Luke 17:28–32), the judgment of Sodom and Gomorrah (Matthew 10:15), the miracles of Elijah (Luke 4:25–27), and Jonah and the big fish (Matthew 12:40–41). As New Testament scholar John Wen-

AFTER EDEN by Dan Lietha

I DON'T BELIEVE THE EARTH WAS CREATED IN 6 DAYS LIKE IT SAYS IN GENESIS.

HOW DO YOU KNOW THAT? WERE YOU THERE?

YES! I WAS THERE!

© 2001 AIG

For by Him (Jesus) were all things created, that are in heaven, and that are in earth. Colossians 1:16a

ham has compellingly argued, Jesus did not allegorize these accounts but took them as straightforward history, describing events that actually happened just as the Old Testament describes.[2] Jesus used these accounts to teach His disciples that the events of His death, Resurrection, and Second Coming would likewise certainly happen in time-space reality.

These passages taken together strongly imply that Jesus took Genesis 1 as literal history describing creation in six 24-hour days. But are there any more explicit passages?

I believe there are. However, one has to approach this issue in a slightly different manner. We are not limited to the New Testament when we try to find out if Jesus stated He created in six days; we can also search the Old Testament. After all, Jesus is the Second Person of the Trinity and therefore has always existed.

First, Colossians makes it clear that Jesus Christ, the Son of God, was the one who created all things: "For by Him all things were created that are in heaven and that are on earth, visible and invisible, whether thrones or dominions or principalities or powers. All things were created through Him and for Him. And He is before all things, and in Him all things consist" (Colossians 1:16–17).

We are also told elsewhere in Scripture how Jesus created: "By the word of the LORD the heavens were made, And all the host of them by the breath of His mouth. For He spoke, and it was done; He commanded, and it stood fast" (Psalm 33:6, 9). We see the meaning of this when we consider the miracles of Jesus during His earthly ministry. All the miracles occurred instantly—at His

History of the Cosmos and Man

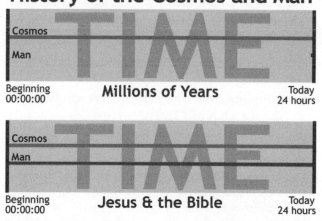

² John Wenham, *Christ and the Bible*, IVPress, Downers Grove, Illinois, pp. 11–37, 1973.

Word. He instantly turned water into wine in His very first miracle, which "revealed His glory" as the Creator (John 2:1–11; John 1:1–3, 14, 18). It was the instant calming of the wind and the waves that convinced His disciples that He was no mere man. So it was with all His miracles (Mark 4:35–41). He did not speak and wait for days, weeks, months, or years for things to happen. He spoke and it was done. So, when He said, "Let there be ..." in Genesis 1, it did not take long ages for things to come into existence.

We also know that Jesus is in fact called the Word: "In the beginning was the Word, and the Word was with God, and the Word was God. He was in the beginning with God. All things were made through Him, and without Him nothing was made that was made" (John 1:1–3).

Jesus, who is the Word, created everything by simply speaking things into existence.

Now, consider Exodus 20:1: "And God spoke all these words, saying ... ." Because Jesus is the Word, this must be a reference to the preincarnate Christ speaking to Moses. As we know, there are a number of appearances of Christ (theophanies) in the Old Testament. John 1:18 states: "No one has seen God at any time. The only begotten Son, who is in the bosom of the Father, He has declared Him." There is no doubt, with rare exception, that the preincarnate Christ did the speaking to Adam, Noah, the patriarchs, Moses, etc. Now, when the Creator God spoke as recorded in Exodus 20:1, what did He (Jesus) say? As we read on, we find this statement: "For in six days the LORD made the heavens and the earth, the sea, and all that is in them, and rested the seventh day" (Exodus 20:11).

Yes, Jesus did explicitly say He created in six days.[3] Not only this, but the one who spoke the words "six days" also wrote them down for Moses: "Then the LORD delivered to me two tablets of stone written with the finger of God, and on them were all the words which the LORD had spoken to you on the mountain from the midst of the fire in the day of the assembly" (Deuteronomy 9:10).

Jesus said clearly that He created in six days. And He even did something He didn't do with most of Scripture—He wrote it down Himself. How clearer and more authoritative can you get than that?

---

[3] Even if someone is convinced that God the Father was the speaker in Exodus 20:11, the Father and Son would never disagree. Jesus said in John 10:30: "I and my Father are one" [neuter—one in the essence of deity, not one in personality]. He also said, "I speak these things as the Father taught me," and "I always do the things that are pleasing to Him" (John 8:28–29).

21

How Did Defense/Attack Structures Come About?

ANDY MCINTOSH & BODIE HODGE

The Relevance of the Issue of DAS (Defense/Attack Structures)

Many people question the goodness of God when they see "nature, red in tooth and claw,"[1] and therefore, they accuse those who believe in the Bible of not seeing reality in nature's fight for survival, which in the view of the secular scientists substantiates evolution.

In the past, many Bible-believers looked to nature as evidence of God's design in nature and attributed the features animals possessed to kill prey or defend themselves as all part of God's original design.

For example, in 1802 William Paley wrote the now-classic book *Natural Theology: or, Evidences of the Existence and Attributes of the Deity, Collected from the Appearances of Nature*. In this work, Paley makes the argument for the design in nature being attributed to a designer—God—and included features that were "red in tooth and claw" as part of this original design.

Darwin, who read Paley's work, realized that organisms have certain design features that make them fit for the environments in which they live. In other words, they were well designed for what they do—even the ability to cause pain, suffering, and death. However, Darwin later

---

[1] From "In Memoriam" by Alfred Lord Tennyson, 1850.

saw difficulties with Paley's argument concerning design. To Darwin, a creation capable of inflicting pain and death seemed to deny a good and loving Creator God.

Darwin could see that the idea of a benevolent designer did not square with the world that he observed. How could a good God be the author of death and bloodshed? The answer of Darwin and many others was to turn from the God of the Bible to a belief in man's ideas about the past that include millions of years of death and suffering.

A most notable adherent to this view in our present day is David Attenborough. Attenborough is the presenter of many popular nature documentaries produced by the British Broadcasting Corporation. In a similar journey to that of Darwin, he argues strongly for belief in evolution because of the suffering that the natural world exhibits. The quote below is very revealing as to what has moved Attenborough to an evolutionary position.

> When Creationists talk about God creating every individual species as a separate act, they always instance hummingbirds, or orchids, sunflowers and beautiful things. But I tend to think instead of a parasitic worm that is boring through the eye of a boy sitting on the bank of a river in West Africa, [a worm] that's going to make him blind. And [I ask them], "Are you telling me that the God you believe in, who you also say is an all-merciful God, who cares for each one of us individually, are you saying that God created this worm that can live in no other way than in an innocent child's eyeball? Because that doesn't seem to me to coincide with a God who's full of mercy."[2]

Eagles have pointed claws and sharp beaks.

The examples of Darwin and Attenborough show why the issue of defense/attack structures (DAS) is important, and how it is closely

---

[2] From M. Buchanan, Wild, wild life, *Sydney Morning Herald*, The Guide, p. 6, March 24, 2003.

related to the existence of suffering and death in the world around us. Defense/attack structures include anything from claws and flesh-tearing beaks on birds of prey or the claws and teeth of cats, to a wasp's stinger or a poison dart frog's toxin.

What Are Some Defense/Attack Structures?

Examples of defense/attack structures are numerous in the world around us, existing in plants as well as animals. Let's look at a few.

PLANT—VENUS FLYTRAP

A great example in plants is the Venus flytrap. This plant snaps two of its lobes on any unsuspecting fly that ventures inside. The mechanism by which the trap snaps shut involves a complex interaction between elasticity, osmotic pressure in the cellular plant material, and growth. When the plant is open, the lobes are convex (bent outwards), but when it is closed, the lobes are concave (forming a cavity). It is stable in both the open and closed positions, but it changes states to close quickly when triggered.[3]

ARACHNID—SPIDER

A good example of DAS is the spider. Spider webs are renowned for their potential to catch flying insects, such as flies and moths. The sophistication of silk production through special glands that keep the polymer soft right up until it is exuded behind the spider is still not understood.[4] Furthermore, the ability of the spider to make some strands sticky and others not, so that the spider itself only walks on the non-sticky parts is clearly a clever design feature. Not all spiders make webs, but they are all capable of producing silk in several varieties. Though the predatory nature of spiders is universal, the actual prey-catching technique of web-building is not the same for each species.

---

[3] Y. Forterre et. al., How the Venus flytrap snaps, *Nature* **433**(7024): 421–5, 2005, found online at www.nature.com/nature/journal/v433/n7024/abs/nature03185.html; How a Venus flytrap snaps up its victims, *New Scientist*, January 29, 2005, found online at www. newscientist.com/channel/life/mg18524845.900.

[4] G. De Luca and A.D. Rey, Biomimetics of spider silk spinning process, pp. 127–136, Design and Nature III: Comparing Design in Nature with Science and Engineering, Vol. 87 of *WIT Transactions on Ecology and the Environment*, C.A. Brebbia, ed., WIT Press, 2006; See also en.wikipedia.org/wiki/Spider_silk.

INSECT—BOMBARDIER BEETLE

Another example in the insect world, and probably the most extraordinary, is the bombardier beetle. This insect possesses a sophisticated defense apparatus, which involves shooting a hot (212°F/100°C) noxious mixture of chemicals out of a special swivel nozzle in its backside, into the face of predators such as rodents, birds, frogs, or other insects.

ANIMALS—CATS AND REPTILES

Of the numerous examples of DAS in the animal world, the meat-eating lion, tiger, and other large cats (cheetah, lynx, etc.) would be the most obvious. It should be noted though that these creatures are not solely dependent on a carnivorous diet because there are known cases of large cats being able to survive on a vegetarian diet when meat has been not available in zoos.[5]

Many animals in the reptile world also give us excellent examples of DAS. Chameleons have the ability to flick their tongues in only fractions of a second to capture their prey. Crocodiles and alligators have powerful jaws, and snakes possess poisonous fangs or deadly coils. The anaconda can kill bulls and tapirs easily with its extremely strong muscles.[6]

Alligator teeth are long and sharp.

These are but a few of the DAS found around the world. If you check the plants and animals in your area, you can probably spot some of these and other defense/attack structures.

Why, Biblically, Is the World Like This?

The biblical response to DAS is that the theology of Darwin and Attenborough has made a major assumption—the world is now what it always

---

[5] B. Hodge, Unexpectedly vegetarian animals—what does it mean? www.answersingenesis.org/articles/2009/06/02vegetarian-animals.

[6] H. Mayell, Anaconda expert wades barefoot in Venezuela's swamps, National Geographic News, March 13, 2003; found online at news.nationalgeographic.com/news/2002/04/0430_020503_anacondaman.html.

has been. The Bible, as early as Genesis 3, makes it clear that this is not the case.

The world (and indeed the universe) was originally perfect. Six times in Genesis 1 it states that what God had made was "good" and the seventh time that "God saw everything that He had made, and indeed it was very good" (Genesis 1:31). A perfect God would make nothing less. In fact, Moses, who also penned Genesis, declared in Deuteronomy 32:4 that all of God's works are perfect. The original creation was perfect, but we can see by looking at the world around us that there has been a drastic change. The change was a result of the Fall of man—an event which fundamentally altered the world.

The original world had no parasites boring into children's eyes or any other part of nature being "red in tooth and claw." The death and suffering in the past and in the present is a result of man's sin and rebellion against God. When the first man Adam disobeyed his Creator, all of creation was cursed, bringing disease, sickness, pain, suffering, and death into the world.

When God spoke to Adam, He said, "Because you have heeded the voice of your wife, and have eaten from the tree of which I commanded you, saying, 'You shall not eat of it': cursed is the ground for your sake; in toil you shall eat of it all the days of your life. Both thorns and thistles it shall bring forth for you, and you shall eat the herb of the field. In the sweat of your face you shall eat bread till you return to the ground, for out of it you were taken; for dust you are, and to dust you shall return" (Genesis 3:17–19).

God also told Eve, "I will greatly multiply your sorrow and your conception; in pain you shall bring forth children; your desire shall be for your husband, and he shall rule over you" (Genesis 3:16).

And earlier still, the Bible records what God spoke to the serpent: "So the LORD God said to the serpent: 'Because you have done this, you are cursed more than all cattle, and more than every beast of the field; on your belly you shall go, and you shall eat dust all the days of your life'" (Genesis 3:14). So in essence there were several changes at the Fall.

This is not just an Old Testament doctrine. The New Testament picks up on the inseparable connection between the world's state and man's condition. In Romans 8:22–23, Paul states, "For we know that the whole creation groans and labors with birth pangs together until now. Not only that, but we also who have the firstfruits of the Spirit, even we ourselves groan within ourselves, eagerly waiting for the adoption, the redemption of our body."

While the world has been cursed because of man's rebellion in Adam, there is coming a day—a day for the "redemption of our body" (Romans

Verse	Some of the known effects	Said to
Genesis 3:14	1. Serpent cursed more than other animals—specifically mentions crawling on its belly and eating dust. 2. Other animals are cursed; to what extent, we aren't told.	Serpent
Genesis 3:16	1. Increased pain and sorrow in childbearing and raising children. 2. Their desire will be for their husbands.	Woman/Eve
Genesis 3:17–19	1. Ground is cursed—specifically mentions thorns and thistles and the pain and sorrow associated with working the ground. We aren't told the other effects of the Curse. 2. Death—mankind would return to dust.	Man/Adam

8:23)—when at the resurrection of God's people, the world will also be liberated from the Curse. In Romans 8, Paul makes it clear that the extent of this Curse encompasses the whole creation.

When we look at defense/attack structures in the animal or plant kingdom, we must look at them in the context of a truly biblical theology. Let's review the clear teachings from Scripture.

1. Man and animals were originally created as vegetarian (Genesis 1:29–30). Throughout Genesis 1 the Lord states repeatedly that the created order was "good" and then in Genesis 1:31, "very good." Thus, "nature, red in tooth and claw" was not part of God's original creation.

2. In verse 30, God explicitly states, "Also, to every beast of the earth, to every bird of the air, and to everything that creeps on the earth, in which there is life, I have given every green herb for food." Literally in the Hebrew, the phrase "in which there is life" is *nephesh chayyah*. This phrase is translated "living soul" and is used in Genesis 1:20–21 and Genesis 2:7 when referring to man and animals. However, this phrase is never used in reference to plants (or invertebrates), thus highlighting the difference between plant life and human and animal life.

3. The Curse in Genesis 3 caused a major change in both animals and plants. The animals were cursed; Genesis 3:14 says, "You are cursed *more than all cattle*, and *more than every beast of the field* [emphasis added]." The plants were also cursed; Genesis 3:17–18 says, "Cursed is the ground for your sake; in toil you shall eat of it all the days of your life. Both thorns and thistles it shall bring forth for you, and you shall eat the herb of the field." (There is evidence that thorns are formed from altered leaves.[7])

4. It was not until after the Flood that God allowed man to eat meat (Genesis 1:29–30, 9:3).

5. Later in Scripture the prophet Isaiah refers to a future time when there will be a reverse of the Curse: "The wolf also shall dwell with the lamb, the leopard shall lie down with the young goat, the calf and the young lion and the fatling together; and a little child shall lead them" (11:6). "The wolf and the lamb shall feed together, the lion shall eat straw like the ox, and dust shall be the serpent's food. They shall not hurt nor destroy in all My holy mountain, says the LORD" (65:25).

6. The book of Revelation speaks of a time when the Curse will be removed (22:3) and there will be no more pain, suffering, or death (21:4).

The Bible provides us with a big picture as we look at defense/attack structures.

Two Major Perspectives to Understand DAS Biblically

Two primary alternatives can easily explain defense/attack structures from a biblical perspective: (1) the present features used in defense and attack were not originally used for that purpose, and (2) the DAS design features were brought in by God *as a result of* the Fall.

The first perspective—that the present features were not originally used for defense/attack purposes—indicates that DAS were used for different functions before the Fall. Another way to clarify this perspective is to say that the design was the same but the function was different.

Let's take sharp teeth as an example. When people see animals with sharp teeth, they most commonly interpret this to mean that the animal is

---

7 S. Carlquist, Ontogeny and comparative anatomy of thorns of Hawaiian Lobeliaceae, *American Journal of Botany*, **49**(4): 413–419, April 1962.

a meat-eater. When scientists find fossils of creatures with sharp teeth, they also interpret this to mean that the animal was a meat-eater. But is this a proper interpretation? Not really. Sharp teeth in animals indicate only one thing—the animal has sharp teeth.

Creatures with sharp teeth do not necessarily use them to rip other animals apart today. For example, the giant panda has very sharp teeth, yet it eats entirely bamboo shoots. Also, the fruit bat, which at first might appear to have teeth consistent with a carnivorous diet, eats primarily fruit. The Bible teaches that animals were created to be vegetarian (Genesis 1:30); so, we must be careful not to merely assume what an animal ate based on its teeth.

Other DAS can also be explained in this way. Claws could have been

T. rex originally ate vegetables.

Bears have sharp teeth, but they eat many vegetarian meals.

used to grip vegetarian foods or branches for climbing. And chameleon tongues could have been used to reach out and grab vegetarian foods, etc. This perspective has the advantage of never having to suggest that God designed a structure or system feature to be harmful to another living creature of His creation.

It is evident that for the silk-producing structure in spiders, it is hard to establish an alternative function for these glands, though spiders have been shown to catch and eat pollen.[8] The evidence seems to point to such structures being designed as they are to effectively catch things like insects. However, we may simply not know the original harmless function of these structures.

Consequently, many have suggested the fact that some creatures have continued to eat plants, which actually indicates that predatory habits came due to altered function. Bears commonly eat vegetarian foods. There have been lions and vultures documented to refuse eating meat.[9]

Even viruses (genetic carriers that infect a host with almost always deleterious results) may have originally been used in a different and beneficial role before the Fall. In a similar manner, harmful bacteria may have had a different and better purpose than their current function.

However, this perspective does have some shortcomings, especially when we apply it to the whole of DAS. One such problem is that of thorns. It can

[8] *Nature Australia* **26**(7):5, Summer 1999–2000.
[9] B. Hodge, Unexpectedly vegetarian animals—what does it mean? www.answersingenesis. org/articles/2009/06/02vegetarian-animals.

be argued that trees, bushes, etc., use thorns solely as a defense mechanism. But the Bible indicates that thorns and thistles came as a result of the Fall (Genesis 3:17–19). So, something indeed changed at the Curse.

Thorns and Thistles

This first perspective avoids God designing DAS in a perfect world for the purpose of harming something that was alive.

The second perspective—DAS design features were brought in by God *as a result of* the Fall—calls for design alterations after the Fall to allow such attack and defense structures. To clarify, this was the result of man's sin, not God's original design, and the consequences of sin still remain. Such "cursed design" is from God's intelligence as a punishment for the man's, the woman's, and the serpent's disobedience. This second perspective would then better explain some things like sharp teeth, claws, the special glands that make the spider silk, etc.

There is some warrant for this view in Scripture since we know that plants have been made such that now some of them have thorns (physically changed form) and that the serpent changed form to crawl on its belly (physically changed form). Since there was a physical change and this was passed along to off-spring, then there had to be genetic alterations. Some of these changes could have been immediate, and others could have been slower in revealing themselves.

Regardless, the genetic blueprint of these systems must have changed such that DAS became evident. Remembering that God knows the future, it is possible that the devices were placed latently in the genetic code of these creatures at creation and were "turned on" at the Fall. Another possibility is that God redesigned the creatures after the Fall to have DAS features in them. Since defense/attack structures are a reminder of a sin-cursed world full of death and suffering, there was more likely a change after the Fall as opposed to these features being simply dormant.

Scripture that gives implied support to this perspective is that after the Fall, man would know pain and hard work and would eventually die (Genesis 3:19). Some biological change is experienced. Pain and sorrow in childbirth are a direct result of the Fall, and the serpent is radically redesigned after his rebellion. So this overall position may be the better of the two, though we wouldn't be dogmatic.

Conclusion

Both biblical perspectives explain the changes that occurred when man sinned and the world fell from a perfect one to an imperfect one, and both positions have merits. But the Bible doesn't specifically say one way or another. In fact, there could be aspects of both perspectives that may have happened. Not all creatures with DAS need to be explained in the same way. For some it may have been that their existing functions adapted, while there seems to be every indication that other mechanisms came in after the Fall.

Regardless, the accusation that a loving and perfect God made the world as we see it today ignores the Bible's teachings about the results of the Curse. A proper understanding of why there are defense/attack structures in the world today should be a reminder that the world is sin-cursed and that we are all sinners in need of a Savior.

After the Fall, God acted justly. He did what was right. But during the curses in Genesis 3, God did something that only a loving God would do— He gave the first prophecy of redemption. He promised a Savior. Genesis 3:15 says, "And I will put enmity between you and the woman, and between your seed and her Seed; He shall bruise your head, and you shall bruise His heel."

The One who would crush the head of the serpent would be born of a virgin, the seed of a woman. This is the first of many prophecies of Jesus Christ coming as the seed of a woman—a virgin birth. It was truly a loving and gracious God who came to earth in the form of a man and died for us and paid the penalty of our sins on the Cross.

DAS should remind us that when God says something, it will come to pass. When one receives Christ as their Savior, they will one day enjoy eternal life in a world that no longer has any curse or death or suffering or pain (Revelation 21:4, 22:3).

> For God so loved the world that He gave His only begotten Son, that whoever believes in Him should not perish but have everlasting life. For God did not send His Son into the world to condemn the world, but that the world through Him might be saved. He who believes in Him is not condemned; but he who does not believe is condemned already, because he has not believed in the name of the only begotten Son of God (John 3:16–18).

22

Is Natural Selection the Same Thing as Evolution?

GEORGIA PURDOM

Let's listen in on a hypothetical conversation between a biblical creationist (C) and an evolutionist (E) as they discuss some recent scientific news headlines:

E: Have you heard about the research findings regarding mouse evolution?

C: Are you referring to the finding of coat color change in beach mice?

E: Yes, isn't it a wonderful example of evolution in action?

C: No, I think it's a good example of natural selection in action, which is merely selecting information that already exists.

E: Well, what about antibiotic resistance in bacteria? Don't you think that's a good example of evolution occurring right before our eyes?

C: No, you seem to be confusing the terms "evolution" and "natural selection."

E: But natural selection is the primary mechanism that drives evolution.

C: Natural selection doesn't drive molecules-to-man evolution; you are giving natural selection a power that it does not have—one that can supposedly add new information to the genome, as molecules-to-man evolution requires. But natural selection simply can't do that because it works with information that already exists.

Natural selection is an observable process that is often purported to be the underlying mechanism of unobservable molecules-to-man evolution. The concepts are indeed different, though some mistakenly interchange the two. So let's take a closer look. There are two major questions to answer:

1. How do biblical creationists rightly view the observable phenomenon of natural selection?

2. Could this process cause the increase in genetic information necessary for molecules-to-man evolution?

What Is Natural Selection?

Below are some definitions evolutionists use to define "natural selection." The problem biblical creationists have with these definitions lies mostly in their misapplication, as noted by the bolded phrases.

Evolutionary change based on the differential reproductive success of individuals within a species.[1]

The process by which genetic traits are passed on to each successive generation. Over time, natural selection helps species become better adapted to their environment. Also known as "survival of the fittest," **natural selection is the driving force behind the process of evolution.**[2]

The process in nature by which, according to **Darwin's theory of evolution,** only the organisms best adapted to their environment tend to survive and transmit their genetic characters in increasing numbers to succeeding generations while those less adapted tend to be eliminated (**also see evolution**).[3]

From a creationist perspective natural selection is a process whereby organisms possessing specific characteristics (reflective of their genetic makeup) survive better than others in a given environment or under a given selective pressure (i.e., antibiotic resistance in bacteria). Those with

---

[1] Michael A. Park, *Introducing Anthropology: An Integrated Approach*, 2nd Ed., glossary, highered.mcgraw-hill.com/sites/0072549238/student_view0/glossary.html, 2002.

[2] National Geographic's strange days on planet earth, glossary, www.pbs.org/strangedays/glossary/N.html.

[3] Dinosaurs—glossary of terms, www.internal.schools.net.au/edu/lesson_ideas/dinosaurs/glossary.html.

certain characteristics live, and those without them diminish in number or die.

The problem for evolutionists is that natural selection is nondirectional—should the environment change or the selective pressure be removed, those organisms with previously selected for characteristics are typically less able to deal with the changes and may be selected against because their genetic information has decreased—more on this later. Evolution of the molecules-to-man variety, requires directional change. Thus, the term "evolution" cannot be rightly used in the context of describing what natural selection can accomplish.

What Is Evolution?

This term has many definitions just as "natural selection" does. Much of the term's definition depends on the context in which the word "evolution" is used. Below are some recent notable definitions of evolution (note the bold phrases).

> Unfolding in time of a predictable or prepackaged sequence in an inherently **progressive,** or at least **directional manner.**[4]

> The theory that all life forms are **descended** from **one or several common ancestors** that were present on early earth, **three to four billion years** ago.[5]

> The "Big Idea" [referring to evolution] is that living things (species) are related to one another through **common ancestry** from earlier forms that differed from them. Darwin called this **"descent with modification,"** and it is still the best definition of evolution we can use, **especially with members of the general public and with young learners.**[6]

All of these definitions give the same basic idea that evolution is *directional* in producing all the life forms on earth today from one or several ancestral life forms billions of years ago. The last definition is especially intriguing because it indicates that an ambiguous definition of evolution should be used with the public and with children. Most creationists would

---

[4] S.J. Gould, What does the dreaded "E" word *mean*, anyway? *Natural History* **109**(1): 28–44, 2000.

[5] D. O'Leary, *By Design or by Chance?* Castle Quay, Kitchener, Ontario, Canada, 7, 2004.

[6] Eugenie C. Scott, Creation or evolution? www.ncseweb.org/resources/articles/6261_creation_or_evolution__1_9_2001.asp.

agree partially with the idea of "descent with modification" in that species we have today look different from the original kinds that God created (i.e., the great variety of dogs we have now compared to the original created dog kind). The advantage with using such a broad definition for evolution is that it can include any and all supporting models of evolution (such as traditional Darwinism, neo-Darwinism, punctuated equilibrium, etc.) and can spark the least amount of controversy in the public eye.

Historical Background on the Discovery of Natural Selection

Many people give credit to Charles Darwin for formulating the theory of natural selection as described in his book *On the Origin of Species*. Few realize that Darwin only popularized the idea and actually borrowed it from several other people, especially a creationist by the name of Edward Blyth. Blyth published several articles describing the process of natural selection in *Magazine of Natural History* between 1835 and 1837—a full 22 years before Darwin published his book. It is also known that Darwin had copies of these magazines and that parts of *On The Origin of Species* are nearly verbatim from Blyth's articles.[7]

Blyth, however, differed from Darwin in his starting assumptions. Blyth believed in God as the Creator, rather than the blind forces of nature. He believed that God created original kinds, that all modern species descended from those kinds, and that natural selection acted by conserving rather than originating. Blyth also believed that man was a separate creation from animals. This is especially important since humans are made in the image of God, an attribute that cannot be applied to animals (Genesis 1:27). Blyth seemed to view natural selection as a mechanism designed directly or indirectly by God to allow His creation to survive in a post-Fall, post-Flood world. This is very different from Darwin's view. Darwin wrote, "What a book a devil's chaplain might write

Edward Blyth

---

[7] J. Foard, The Darwin papers, "Edward Blyth and natural selection," www.thedarwinpapers. com.

on the clumsy, wasteful, blundering low and horridly cruel works of nature."[8]

Is Natural Selection Biblical?

It is important to see natural selection as a mechanism that God used to allow organisms to deal with their changing environments in a sin-cursed world—especially after the Flood. God foreknew that the Fall and the Flood were going to happen, and so He designed organisms with a great amount of genetic diversity that could be selected for or against, resulting in certain characteristics depending on the circumstances. Whether this information was initially part of the original design during Creation Week before the Fall or was added, in part, at the Fall (as a part of the punishment of man and the world by God),[9] we can't be certain. Regardless, the great variety of information in the original created kinds can only be attributed to an intelligence—God.

In addition, natural selection works to preserve the genetic viability of the original created kinds by removing from the population those with severely deleterious/lethal characteristics. Natural selection, acting on genetic information, is the primary mechanism that explains how organisms could have survived after the Fall and Flood when the world changed drastically from God's original creation.

Let me take a moment to clarify an important theological point so there is no confusion. Death entered the world as the result of sin. Death, therefore, is in the world as a punishment for man's disobedience to God, and it should remind us that the world is sin-cursed and needs a Savior. Death is not a good thing but is called an enemy (1 Corinthians 15:26).

But recall that God, in His infinite wisdom, can make good come out of anything, and death is no exception. God is able to make good come out of even death itself. Natural selection, though fueled by death, helps the population by getting rid of genetic defects, etc. In the same way, without death Christ wouldn't have conquered it and been glorified in His Resurrection.

So what can natural selection accomplish and not accomplish? The table on the next page displays some of the main points.

---

[8] Letter from Charles Darwin to Joseph Hooker, Darwin Archives, Cambridge University, July 13, 1856.
[9] See chapter 21 in this book.

Natural Selection Can	Natural Selection Cannot
1. Decrease genetic information.	1. Increase or provide new genetic information.
2. Allow organisms to survive better in a given environment.	2. Allow organisms to evolve from molecules to man.
3. Act as a "selector."	3. Act as an "originator."
4. Support creation's "orchard" of life.	4. Support evolutionary "tree" of life.

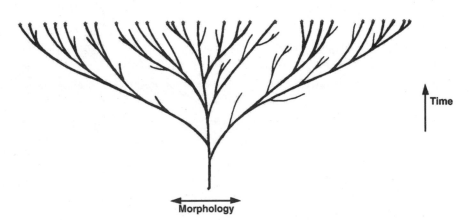

The evolutionary tree, which postulates that all today's species are descended from one common ancestor (which itself evolved from nonliving chemicals).

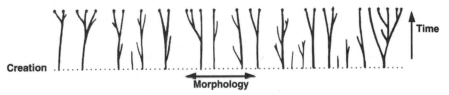

The creationist orchard,[10] which shows that diversity has occurred within the original Genesis kinds over time.[11]

---

10 Dr. Kurt Wise developed the "orchard" analogy in the early 90s.
11 Creationists often refer to each kind as a *baramin*, from Hebrew bara = create and min = kind.

Natural Selection and Dogs

Let's illustrate the possibilities and limitations of natural selection using the example of varying fur length of dogs (designed variation).

There are many different dog species—some with long fur and some with short fur. The original dog kind, most likely resembling today's wolf, had several variants of the gene for fur length. L will be the variant of the gene representing long fur, and S will be the variant of the gene representing short fur.

The original dog kind most likely would have been a mixture of the genes specifying fur length, including both L and S. Because of this makeup, they also most likely had the characteristic of medium fur length. When the original kind (LS dogs) mated, their genetic variability could be seen in their offspring in three ways—LL for long fur, LS for medium fur, and SS for short fur.

If two long-fur dogs then mated, the only possible outcome for the offspring is LL, long fur. As can be seen in the example below, the long-fur dogs have lost the S gene variant and are thus not capable of producing dogs with short fur or medium fur. This loss may be an advantage if these long-fur dogs live in an area with cold temperatures. The long-fur dogs would then be naturally selected for, as they would survive better in the given environment. Eventually, the majority of this area's dog population would have long fur.

However, the loss of the S variant could be a disadvantage to the long-fur dogs if the climate became warmer or if the dogs moved to a warmer climate. Because of their decreased genetic variety (no S gene), they would be unable to produce dogs with short fur, which would be needed to survive better in a warm environment. In this situation, the long-fur dogs would be naturally selected against and die.

When the two dogs representing the dog kind came off Noah's Ark and began spreading across the globe, we can see how the variation favored some animals and not others.

Using the points from the table for what natural selection can accomplish (seen on previous page), it can be seen that:

1. Through natural selection, genetic information (variety) was lost.

2. The long-fur dogs survive better in a cold environment; they are less able to survive in a warm environment and vice versa.

3. A particular characteristic in the dog population was selected for.

4. Dogs are still dogs since the variation is within the boundaries of "kind."

Natural selection of designed variation within the dog kind is not an example of evolution because it does not lead to the formation of a different kind of animal such as a horse, bear, or human. Instead, it is evidence of God's grace in supplying for His creation in the altered environments of a post-Fall, post-Flood world.

Natural Selection and Bacteria

Another example of natural selection is that of antibiotic resistance in bacteria. Such natural selection is commonly portrayed as evolution in action, but in this case, natural selection works in conjunction with mutation rather than designed variation.

Antibiotics are natural products produced by fungi and bacteria, and the antibiotics we use today are typically derivatives of those. Because of this relationship, it is not surprising that some bacteria would have resistance to certain antibiotics; they must do so to be competitive in their environment. In fact, if you took a sample of soil from outside your home, you would find antibiotic-resistant bacteria.

A bacterium can gain resistance through two primary ways:

1. By losing genetic information, and

2. By using a design feature built in to swap DNA—a bacterium gains resistance from another bacterium that has resistance.

Let's take a look at the first. Antibiotics usually bind a protein in the bacterium and prevent it from functioning properly, killing the bacteria. Antibiotic-resistant bacteria have a mutation in the DNA which codes for that protein. The antibiotic then cannot bind to the protein produced from the mutated DNA, and thus the bacteria live. Although the bacteria can survive well in an environment with antibiotics, it has come at a cost. If the antibiotic-resistant bacteria are grown with the nonmutant bacteria in an environment without antibiotics, the nonmutant bacteria will live and the mutant bacteria will die. This is because the mutant bacteria produce a mutant protein that does not allow them to compete with other bacteria for necessary nutrients.

Let's clarify this some by looking at the bacteria *Helicobacter pylori*. Antibiotic-resistant *H. pylori* have a mutation that results in the loss of information to produce an enzyme. This enzyme normally converts an antibiotic to a poison, which causes death. But when the antibiotics are applied to the mutant *H. pylori*, these bacteria can live while the normal bacteria are killed. So by natural selection the ones that lost information survive and pass this trait along to their offspring.

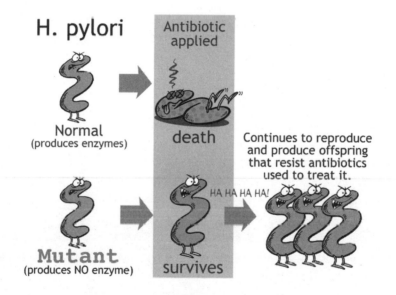

Now let's take a look at the second method. A bacterium can get antibiotic resistance by gaining the aforementioned mutated DNA from another bacterium. Unlike you and me, bacteria can swap DNA. It is important to note that this is still not considered a gain of genetic information since the information already exists and that while the mutated DNA may be new to a particular bacterium, it is not new overall.

Using the points from the table for what natural selection can accomplish, it can be seen that:

1. Through mutation, genetic information was lost.

2. The antibiotic resistant bacteria *only* survive well in an environment with antibiotics; they are less able to survive in the wild. (It is important to keep in mind that the gain of antibiotic resistance is not an example of a beneficial mutation but rather a beneficial outcome of a mutation in a given environment. These types of mutations are rare in other organisms as offspring are more limited in number, therefore, there is a greater need to preserve genetic integrity.)

3. A particular mutation in a bacterial population was selected for.

4. *H. pylori* is still *H. pylori*. No evolution has taken place to change it into something else—it's still the same bacteria with some variation.

Antibiotic resistance in bacteria, rather than being an example of evolution in action, is another example of natural selection seen properly from a biblical/creationist perspective.

Speciation—A Possible Outcome of Natural Selection

A species can be defined as a population of organisms produced by a parent population that has changed so significantly that it can no longer interbreed with the parent population. Using the example of dogs, it is possible that long-fur dogs might change sufficiently (other changes besides fur might also be selected for living in cold environments) to the point that they can no longer mate with short-fur or medium-fur dogs.

Although evolutionists claim that speciation takes long periods of time (millions of years), they are often amazed at how fast species can be observed to form today. Speciation has been observed to

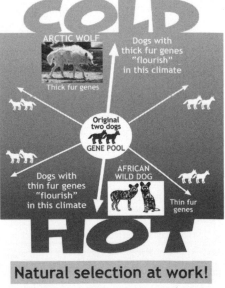

Natural selection at work!

occur in as little as a few years as seen in guppies, lizards, fruit flies, mosquitoes, finches, and mice. This observation does not come as a surprise to creationists as all species alive in the past and today would have had to be produced in fewer than 6,000 years from the original created kinds. In fact, such processes (and perhaps other genetic factors) would have occurred rapidly after the Flood, producing variation within each kind. Such effects are largely responsible for generating the tremendous diversity seen in the living world.[12]

Speciation has never been observed to form an organism of a different kind, such as a dog species producing a cat. Speciation works *only* within a kind. Evolution requires natural selection and speciation to give rise to new kinds from a former kind (e.g., dinosaurs evolving into birds). Speciation, however, leads to a loss of information, not the gain of information required by evolution. Thus, speciation as a possible outcome of natural selection cannot be used as a mechanism for molecules-to-man evolution.

Conclusion

When discussing natural selection as a possible mechanism for evolution, it is important to define terms. Evolutionists and biblical creationists view

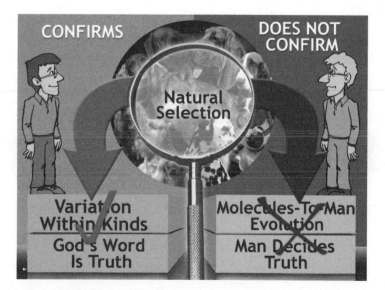

---

[12] G. Purdom, "Evolution" of finch beaks—again, www.answersingenesis.org/articles/aid/v1/n1/evolution-finch-beaks-again.

these terms differently, but it comes down to how we interpret the evidence in light of our foundation. Do we view natural selection using God's Word as our foundation, or do we use man's truth as our foundation?

The creationist view of natural selection is supported biblically and scientifically. Natural selection is a God-ordained process that allows organisms to survive in a post-Fall, post-Flood world. It is an observable reality that occurs in the present and takes advantage of the variations within the kinds and works to preserve the genetic viability of the kinds.

Simply put, the changes that are observed today show variation within the created kind—a horizontal change. For a molecules-to-man evolutionary model, there must be a change from one kind into another—a vertical change. This is simply not observed. We have never seen a bacterium like *H. pylori* give rise to something like a dog. Instead, we simply observe variations within each created kind.

Evolution requires an increase in information that results in a directional movement from molecules to man. Natural selection cannot be a mechanism for evolution because it results in a decrease in information and is not directional. Speciation may occur as a result of natural selection, but it only occurs within a kind. Therefore, it is also not a mechanism for evolution but rather supports the biblical model.

Natural selection cannot be the driving force for molecules-to-man evolution when it does not have that power, nor should it be confused with molecules-to-man evolution. It is an observable phenomenon that preserves genetic viability and allows limited variation within a kind—nothing more, nothing less. It is a great confirmation of the Bible's history.

23

Hasn't Evolution Been Proven True?

A. J. MONTY WHITE

Anyone who has read Genesis 1–11 realizes that the modern teachings of molecules-to-man evolution are at odds with what God says. So what is the response to evolution from a biblical and scientific perspective? Let's take a closer look.

Evolutionists often say that *evolution* simply means "change." However, in reality it means a certain kind of change. The word is now accepted to mean the change of nonliving chemicals into simple life-forms into more complex life-forms and finally into humans—what might be called *from-goo-to-you-via-the-zoo*. We are informed that this change occurred over millions of years, and the dominant mechanism that is supposed to have driven it is natural selection coupled with mutations.

Furthermore, the word *evolution* has also been applied to nonliving things. Almost everything is said to have evolved—the solar system, stars, the universe, as well as social and legal systems. Everything is said to be the product of evolution. However, the three major forms of evolution are

1. Stellar evolution

2. Chemical evolution

3. Biological evolution.

The story of evolution leaves no room for a supernatural Creator. Evolutionary processes are supposed to be purely naturalistic. This means that even the need for a supernatural Creator disappears because it is argued that the natural world can create new and better or more complex creatures by itself. The implication of this is very revealing: evolution means "no God" and if there is no God, then there are no rules—no commandments, no God-given rules which we must obey. We can therefore live our lives as we please, for according to evolutionary philosophy, there is no God to whom we have to give an account. No wonder molecules-to-man evolution is attractive to so many, for it allows them to live as they please. This is called relative morality.

Does the Bible Teach Evolution?

The simple answer to this question is "No." In Genesis 1 we read the account of the creation (not the evolution) of everything—the universe, the sun, moon, and stars, the planet earth with all its varied plant and animal kinds, including the pinnacle of God's creation—humans. Nowhere in this account do we read about molecules-to-man evolution. Furthermore, there was no time for evolution, for God supernaturally created everything in six literal days (Exodus 20:11, 31:17).

There are those who argue that Genesis 1 is a simplified account of evolution. But such a hypothesis does not stand up to scrutiny. A quick look at the order of the events in Genesis 1 and in evolution shows this (see chart below[1]). The order of events is quite different and the Genesis account of creation bears no relation to the evolutionary account of origins.

Evolution	Genesis
Sun before earth	Earth before sun
Dry land before sea	Sea before dry land
Atmosphere before sea	Sea before atmosphere
Sun before light on earth	Light on earth before sun
Stars before earth	Earth before stars
Earth at same time as planets	Earth before other planets
Sea creatures before land plants	Land plants before sea creatures
Earthworms before starfish	Starfish before earthworms

---

[1] T. Mortenson, Evolution vs. creation: the order of events matters! www.answersingenesis. org/docs2006/0404order.asp

Land animals before trees	Trees before land animals
Death before man	Man before death
Thorns and thistles before man	Man before thorns and thistles
TB pathogens & cancer before man (dinosaurs had TB and cancer)	Man before TB pathogens and cancer
Reptiles before birds	Birds before reptiles
Land mammals before whales	Whales before land animals
Land mammals before bats	Bats before land animals
Dinosaurs before birds	Birds before dinosaurs
Insects before flowering plants	Flowering plants before insects
Sun before plants	Plants before sun
Dinosaurs before dolphins	Dolphins before dinosaurs
Land reptiles before pterosaurs	Pterosaurs before land reptiles

In spite of this, some argue that there is a major difference between "make" and "create" (the Hebrew words are *asah* and *bara*, respectively). They argue that God *created* some things—for example, the heaven and the earth as recorded in Genesis 1:1 and the marine and flying creatures as recorded in Genesis 1:21. They then argue that God *made* other things, perhaps by evolution from pre-existing materials—for example, the sun, moon, and stars as recorded in Genesis 1:16, and the beasts and cattle as recorded in Genesis 1:25. Though these words have slightly different nuances of meaning, they are often used interchangeably, as seen clearly where *asah* (to make) and *bara* (to create) are used in reference to the same act (the creation of man, Genesis 1:26–27). Nothing in Genesis 1 leads to the conclusion that God used evolutionary processes to produce His creation.

There is a further problem with believing that the Genesis account of creation should be interpreted as an evolutionary account. One of the things that drives evolution is *death*. Yet the Bible teaches quite clearly that death was introduced into the perfect world as a result of Adam's sin. Neither human nor animal death existed until this event—both humans and animals were originally vegetarian (Genesis 1:29–30 shows that plants are not living creatures, as land and sea creatures, birds, and people are). The original world that God created was death-free, and so evolution could not have occurred before humans were created.

Stellar Evolution: The Big Bang

The big bang is the most prominent naturalistic view of the origin of the universe in the same way that Neo-Darwinian evolution is the naturalistic view of living systems. The difference between what the Bible teaches about the origin of the universe and what the evolutionists teach can be summed up as follows: the Bible teaches that "in the beginning God created" and the evolutionists teach, in essence, that "in the beginning nothing became something and exploded."

According to the big bang, our universe is supposed to have suddenly popped into existence and rapidly expanded and given rise to the countless billions of galaxies with their countless billions of stars.

In support of the idea that nothing can give rise to the universe, cosmologists argue that quantum mechanics predicts that a vacuum can, under some circumstances, give rise to matter. But the problem with this line of reasoning is that a vacuum is *not* nothing; it is something—it is a vacuum that can be made to appear or disappear, as in the case of the Torricellian vacuum, which

is found at the sealed end of a mercury barometer. All logic predicts that if you have nothing, nothing will happen. It is against all known logic and all laws of science to believe that the universe is the product of nothing. This concept is similar to hoping that an empty bank account will suddenly give rise to billions of dollars all on its own.

However, if we accept that the universe and everything in it came from nothing (and also from *nowhere*) then we have to follow this to its logical conclusion. This means that not only is all the physical material of the universe the product of nothing, but also other things. For example, we are forced to accept that nothing (which has no mind, no morals, and no conscience) created reason and logic; understanding and comprehension; complex ethical codes and legal systems; a sense of right and wrong; art, music, drama, comedy, literature, and dance; and belief systems that include God. These are just a few of the philosophical implications of the big bang hypothesis.

Chemical Evolution: The Origin of Life

It is commonly believed (because it is taught in our schools and colleges) that laboratory experiments have proved conclusively that living organisms evolved from nonliving chemicals. Many people believe that life has been created in the laboratory by scientists who study chemical evolution.

The famous experiment conducted by Stanley Miller in 1953 is often quoted as proof of this. Yet the results of such experiments show nothing of the sort. These experiments, designed as they are by intelligent humans, show that under certain conditions, certain organic compounds can be formed from inorganic compounds.

In fact, what the *intelligent* scientists are actually saying is, "If I can just synthesize life in the laboratory, then I will have proven that no *intelligence* was necessary to form life in the beginning." Their experiments are simply trying to prove the opposite—that an intelligence is required to create life.

If we look carefully at Miller's experiment, we will see that what he did fails to address the evolution of life. He took a mixture of gases (ammonia, hydrogen, methane, and water vapor) and he passed an electric current through them. He did this in order to reproduce the effect of lightning passing through a mixture of gases that he thought might have composed the earth's atmosphere millions of years ago. As a result, he produced a mixture of amino acids. Because amino acids are the building blocks of proteins and proteins are considered to be the building blocks of living systems, Miller's experiment was hailed as proof that life had evolved by chance on the earth millions of years ago.

There are a number of objections to such a conclusion.

1. There is no proof that the earth ever had an atmosphere composed of the gases used by Miller in his experiment.

2. The next problem is that in Miller's experiment he was careful to make sure there was no oxygen present. If oxygen was present, then the amino acids would not form. However, if oxygen was absent from the earth, then there would be no ozone layer, and if there was no ozone layer the ultraviolet radiation would penetrate the atmosphere and would destroy the amino acids as soon as they were formed. So the dilemma facing the evolutionist can be summed up this way: amino acids would not form in an atmosphere *with* oxygen and amino acids would be destroyed in an atmosphere *without* oxygen.

3. The next problem concerns the so-called handedness of the amino acids. Because of the way that carbon atoms join up with other atoms, amino acids exist in two forms—the right-handed form and the left-handed form. Just as your right hand and left hand are identical in all respects except for their handedness, so the two forms of amino acids are identical except for their handedness. In all living systems only left-handed amino acids are found. Yet Miller's experiment produced a mixture of right-handed and left-handed amino acids in identical proportions. As only the left-handed ones are used in living systems, this mixture is useless for the evolution of living systems.

4. Another major problem for the chemical evolutionist is the origin of the information that is found in living systems. There are various claims about the amount of information that is found in the human genome, but it can be conservatively estimated as being equivalent to a few thousand books, each several hundred pages long. Where did this information come from? Chance does not generate information. This observation caused the late Professor Sir Fred Hoyle and his colleague, Professor Chandra Wickramasinghe of Cardiff University, to conclude that the evolutionist is asking us to believe that a tornado can pass through a junk yard and assemble a jumbo jet.

The problems outlined above show that, far from creating life in the laboratory, the chemical evolutionists have not shown that living systems arose by chance from nonliving chemicals. Furthermore, the vast amount of information contained in the nucleus of a living cell shows that living systems could not have evolved from nonliving chemicals. The only explanation for the existence of living systems is that they must have been created.

Biological Evolution: Common Descent?

Comparative anatomy is the name given to the science that deals with the structure of animals. Comparing the anatomy of one kind of animal with another is supposed to prove descent from a common ancestor. This is often put forward as strong evidence for evolution. However, the science of comparative anatomy can just as easily be used as evidence of creation, as we shall see.

The bones of a horse are different from our bones, but there is such a similarity that if we are familiar with the human skeleton, we could easily identify and name the bones of a horse. We could do the same if we studied the skeleton of a salamander, a crocodile, a bird, or a bat. However, not only are the bones similar, but so also are other anatomical structures, such as muscles, the heart, the liver, the kidneys, the eyes, the lungs, the digestive tract, and so on. This is interpreted by the evolutionists as proof that these various animals are all descended from a common ancestor.

One of the classic examples that is often used in biology textbooks to illustrate comparative anatomy is the forelimbs of amphibians, reptiles, humans, birds, bats, and quadrupeds. In the illustration, it can be seen that all the forelimbs of these six different types of creatures have an upper arm bone (the humerus) and two lower arm bones (the radius and the ulna), although in the case of the bat there is only one bone, called the radio-ulna.

Evolutionists teach that these structures are said to be homologous when they are similar in structure and origin, but not necessarily in function. But notice how subtly the notion of origins is introduced into the definition. The bat's wing is considered to be homologous to the forelimb of a salamander because it is similar in structure and believed to have the same origin. However, it is not considered to be homologous to the wing of an insect because, even though it has the same function, it is not considered to have the same origin. However, the fact that the two structures are similar does not necessarily mean that they are derived from a common ancestor.

We have to realize that the entire line of reasoning by evolutionists is based upon a single assumption: that the degree of similarity between organisms indicates the degree of supposed relationship of the said organisms. In other words, it is argued that if animals look alike, then they must be closely related (from an evolutionary point of view), and if they do not look very much alike, then they are more distantly related. But this is just an assumption.

The presence of homologous structures can actually be interpreted as evidence for a common designer. Contrary to the oversimplified claim in this figure, the forelimbs of vertebrates do not form in the same way. Specifically, in frogs the phalanges form as buds that grow outward and in humans they form from a ridge that develops furrows inward. The fact that the bones can be correlated does not mean that they are evidence of a single common ancestor.[2]

Figure 9 Homologous structures   **Holt 286**

The forelimbs of vertebrates contain the same kinds of bones, which form in the same way during embryological development.

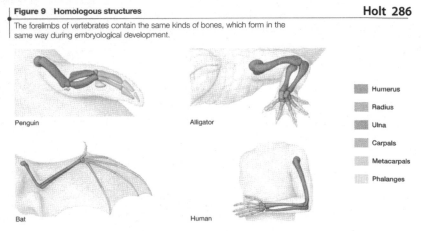

Penguin

Alligator

Bat

Human

Humerus

Radius

Ulna

Carpals

Metacarpals

Phalanges

In fact, there is another logical reason why things look alike—creation by an intelligent designer using a common blueprint. This is the reason that Toyota and Ford motor vehicles look so much alike. They are built to a common plan—you only have to look at them to realize this. However, the problem with the living world is that in many cases either explanation (i.e., evolution or creation) appears to be logical and it is often impossible for us to tell which is the more reasonable explanation. This is why it is important for us to understand which worldview we are using to interpret the evidence.

---

2 R. Patterson, *Evolution Exposed: Biology*, Answers in Genesis, Petersburg, Kentucky, 2009, 72

There is, however, one discovery that appears to make the evolutionary view of descent from a common ancestor look illogical and flawed. This discovery is that structures that appear homologous often develop under the control of genes that are *not* homologous. If the structures evolved from the same source, you would expect the same genes to make the structures. The fact that these structures are similar (or homologous) is apparent, but the reason is not because of Darwinian evolution. It is more logical and reasonable to believe in a common Creator rather than a common ancestor.

Many evolutionists readily admit that they have failed to find evidence of the evolution of large structures such as bones and muscles, so instead they argue that they have found homology among the complex organic molecules that are found in living systems. One of these is hemoglobin, the protein that carries oxygen in red blood cells. Although this protein is found in nearly all vertebrates, it is also found in some invertebrates (worms, starfish, clams, and insects) and also in some bacteria. Yet there is no evidence of the evolution of this chemical—in all cases, the same kind of molecule is complete and fully functional. If evolution has occurred, it should be possible to map out how hemoglobin evolved, but this cannot be done. To the creationist, however, hemoglobin crops up complete and fully functional wherever the Creator deems it fitting in His plan.

Missing Links

Our English word *fossil* is from the Latin *fossilis,* which means "something dug up." The present-day meaning of the word fossil is a relic or trace of past life preserved in the rocks. This can be a preserved hard part of the plant or animal, such as a stem or a leaf or a shell or a bone or a tooth; it can also be a soft part such as skin or even excrement (called coprolites), or it can be a trace made by the creature when it was alive, such as a footprint. All the fossils that are found in all the sedimentary rocks are regarded together as the fossil record.

Charles Darwin proposed the gradual evolution of life forms over a long period of time. If this has happened, you would expect to find this gradual evolution of one kind of life form into another kind to be recorded in the fossil record. However, this evolutionary account of one kind of life form changing into another kind is *not* recorded in the fossils. There are many instances where variations within a kind are found (for example, different varieties of elephant or dinosaur) but there are no examples of in-between kinds. Both evolutionists and creationists agree that the intermediate transitional forms expected on the basis of slow gradual change of one kind of creature into another kind is not found fossilized in the sedimentary rocks. In other words, the transitional forms are missing—hence the term "missing links."

Charles Darwin himself realized that his theory was not supported by the fossil record, for he wrote in his *Origin of Species*:

> The number of intermediate varieties which have formerly existed on earth must be truly enormous. Why then is not every geological forma-tion and every stratum full of such intermediate links? Geology assur-edly does not reveal any such finely graduated organic chain: and this, perhaps, is the most obvious and gravest objection which can be urged against my theory.[3]

When Charles Darwin penned these words, he attributed this absence of transitional forms to what he called the "extreme imperfection" of the fossil record. Since that time, however, literally millions of fossils have been found, but still the transitional forms are absent. The fossil record does not show the continuous development of one kind of creature into another, but it shows different kinds of creatures that are fully functional with no ancestors or de-scendants which are different kinds of creatures.

It cannot be overemphasized that there are many places in the fossil record where it is expected that plenty of intermediate forms should be found—yet they are not there. All the evolutionists ever point to is a handful of highly de-batable transitional forms (e.g., horses), whereas they should be able to show us thousands of incontestable examples. This is very noticeable when looking at the fossil record of some of the more peculiar kinds of animals such as the *cetacean* (whales, dolphins, and porpoises), the *sirenia* (manatees, dugongs, and sea cows), the *pinnipedia* (sea lions, seals, and walruses), kangaroos, bats, dragonflies, and spiders. Their supposed evolutionary origins and descent are represented by missing links and speculations rather than factual evidence.

Even alleged transitional forms in supposed human evolution fall short. In fact, most so-called missing links fall into three categories: extinct ape, living ape, or human. The following chart gives some of the most common scientific names and their classifications.

---

[3] C. Darwin, *The Origin of Species*, Penguin Books, London, 1968, 291.

Name	What is it?*
Australopithecus afarensis, such as "Lucy"	Extinct ape
Australopithecus africanus	Extinct ape
Australopithecus boisei	Extinct ape
Australopithecus robustus	Extinct ape
Pan troglodytes and *Pan paniscus* (chimpanzee)	Living ape
Gorilla gorilla and *Gorilla beringei* (gorilla)	Living ape
Pongo pygmaeus and *Pongo abelii* (orangutan)	Living ape
Ramapithecus	Extinct ape (extinct orangutan)
Homo habilis	Junk category mixing some human and some ape fossils
Homo floresiensis	Human (dwarf, pygmy)
Homo ergaster	Human
Homo erectus, such as "Peking man" and "Java man"	Human**
Homo neanderthalensis (Neanderthals)	Human
Homo heidelbergensis	Human
Homo sapiens (modern & archaic)	Human

* An accurate classification of these kinds of fossils depends on an accurate starting point. Some fossils have been misclassified. The ones labeled as humans (*Homo heidelbergensis, Homo erectus,* etc.), indeed show variation, but they are still human. This is also true of the different ape kinds. Variation, not evolution, is what we would expect from the clear teachings of the Bible.

** For the most part these two classifications are anatomically human. However, a number of finds that are not human but rather apelike have been included as part of the *Homo erectus* category, due to evolutionary beliefs. These apelike finds should be reclassified.[4]

It is obvious that the evolutionists have "faith" in the original existence of the missing transitional forms.

---

[4] For more on supposed human evolution, see chapter 8, "Did humans really evolve from apelike creatures?" in K. Ham et al., *The New Answers Book 2*, Master Books, Green Forest, Arkansas, 2008.

Evolution of New Kinds?

Charles Darwin visited the Galapagos Islands and brought back samples of the different finches that lived on the different islands. He observed that they had different shaped beaks, which appeared to suit the type of food that the finches ate. From this observation, Darwin concluded that a pair or flock of finches had flown to these islands at some time in the past and that the different beaks on the finches had evolved via natural selection, depending on what island they lived on and consequently what they fed on. From these types of simple observations and conclusions, Darwin developed not only the idea of the evolution of species but also the idea of chemicals-to-chemist evolution!

But let us consider exactly what Darwin actually observed—finches living on different islands feeding on different types of food having different beaks. What did he propose? That these finches had descended from a pair or flock of finches. In other words, he proposed that finches begat finches—that is, they reproduced after their own kind. This is exactly what the Bible teaches in Genesis 1.

It cannot be overemphasized that no one has ever seen one kind of plant or animal changing into another different kind. Darwin did not observe this, even though he proposed that it does happen. There are literally thousands of plant and animal kinds on the earth today, and these verify what the Bible indicates in Genesis 1 about plants and animals reproducing after their own kind.

Plants and animals reproducing after their own kind is what we observe, and it is what Charles Darwin observed in finches on the Galapagos Islands. For example, we see different varieties of *Brassica*—kale, cabbage, cauliflower are all varieties of the wild common mustard *Brassica oleracea*. Furthermore, another perfect example of a kind is the hundreds of different varieties of dogs, including spaniels, terriers, bulldogs, Chihuahuas, Great Danes, German shepherds, Irish wolfhounds, and greyhounds, which are all capable of interbreeding, together with wolves, jackals, dingoes, and coyotes. All are descended from the two representatives of the dog kind that came off Noah's Ark.

Conclusion

We have seen that the Bible does not teach evolution. There is no demonstrable evidence for the big bang, and chemical evolution has failed miserably in spite of evolutionists' attempts to create living systems in the laboratory. Similarities in the structure found in living systems can be interpreted better as evidence for a common design rather than a common ancestry. In spite of billions of fossils being found, there are no unquestionable fossils that show a transition between any of the major life forms.

Natural selection (done in the wild) and artificial selection (as done by breeders) produce enormous varieties *within* the different kinds of plants and animals. It has proved an impossible feat, however, to change one kind of creature into a different kind of plant or animal. The so-called "kind barrier" has never been crossed. Such evolution has never been observed. This has been pointed out by none other than evolutionary Professor Richard Dawkins, who confidently asserted in an interview that evolution has been observed but then added, "It's just that it hasn't been observed while it's happening."[5]

---

[5] www.pbs.org/now/transcript/transcript349_full.html#dawkins.

24

Did Dinosaurs Turn into Birds?

DAVID MENTON

Introduction

According to many evolutionists today, dinosaurs are really not extinct but rather are feeding at our bird feeders even as we speak. For many evolutionists, it would seem, birds simply *are* dinosaurs. With this sort of bias, it is quite easy for evolutionists to find supposed evidence to support the notion that birds evolved from dinosaurs.

But what does the Bible tell us about the origin of birds, and just how good is the scientific evidence that some dinosaurs evolved into birds?

What Does the Bible Say about the Origin of Birds?

BIRDS WERE CREATED ON DAY 5 AND DINOSAURS ON DAY 6.

In the first chapter of Genesis, verse 21, we read that on Day 5 of creation, God created "every winged fowl after its kind." This includes birds that flew above the earth (Genesis 1:20). Man and land animals were created on Day 6 of the Creation Week (Genesis 1:24–31). Were there land birds that didn't fly originally? I would leave open the possibility, but a discussion of this is beyond the scope of this chapter. Most ornithologists say that these birds are *secondarily* flightless (i.e., they lost the ability to fly). This would be due to variance within kind or to mutational losses since creation. So, the best possibility is that bird were created on Day 5 as flyers, and some have lost this ability, but I wouldn't be dogmatic.

The extinct aquatic reptiles, such as the plesiosaurs, and the extinct flying reptiles, such as the pterodactyls, are not classified as dinosaurs, and most evolutionists do not believe that they evolved into birds. Thus, for the Bible-believing Christian, both the fact of creation and the order of creation affirm that birds and dinosaurs originated separately.

BIRDS ARE OF MANY DIFFERENT "KINDS."

Genesis 1:21 says that God created every winged bird after its "kind." The following verse says they were to multiply, or reproduce; so the logical connection is that birds of the same kind can reproduce. The Hebrew word for "kind" in Genesis refers to any group of animals capable of interbreeding and reproducing according to their type. For example, all dogs and dog-like animals, such as wolves and coyotes, are capable of interbreeding and thus would represent one "kind," even though some are classified today as different species.

This does not mean, however, that all birds represent a single created kind and thus share a common ancestry. The Bible tells us that there are many different bird kinds (plural). The Levitical dietary laws (Leviticus 11:13–19), for example, list many different bird kinds as being unclean. This gives further biblical support for multiple created bird kinds.

What Do Evolutionists Claim about the Origin of Birds?

Evolutionists have long speculated that birds evolved from reptiles. At one time or another, virtually every living and extinct class of reptiles has been proposed as the ancestor of birds. The famous Darwinian apologist Thomas Huxley was the first to speculate (in the mid 1800s) that birds evolved from dinosaurs.

While this notion has gone in and out of favor over the years, it is currently a popular view among evolutionists. Indeed, the origin of birds from dinosaurs is touted as irrefutable dogma in our schools, biology textbooks, and the popular media.

While evolutionists now agree that birds are related in some way to dinosaurs, they are divided over whether birds evolved from some early shared ancestor of the dinosaurs within the archosauria (which includes alligators, pterosaurs, plesiosaurs, ichthyosaurs, and thecodonts) or directly from advanced theropod dinosaurs (bipedal meat-eating dinosaurs, such as the well-known *Tyrannosaurus rex*). The latter view has gained in popularity since 1970, when

John Ostrom discovered a rather "bird-like" early Cretaceous theropod dinosaur called *Deinonychus*.

An adult *Deinonychus* measured about 12 feet (3.5 m) long, weighed over 150 pounds (68 kg), and was about 5 feet (1.5 m) tall standing on its two hind legs. Like other theropods (which means "beast foot"), *Deinonychus* had forelimbs much smaller than its hind limbs, with hands bearing three fingers and feet bearing three toes. The most distinctive feature of *Deinonychus* (which means "terrible claw") is a large curved talon on its middle toe.

One of the main reasons that *Deinonychus* and other similar theropod dinosaurs (called dromaeosaurs) seemed to be plausible ancestors to birds is that, like birds, these creatures walked solely on their hind legs and have only three digits on their hands. But as we shall see, there are many problems with transforming any dinosaur, and particularly a theropod, into a bird.

Problems with Dinosaurs Evolving into Birds

WARM-BLOODED VS. COLD-BLOODED

Seemingly forgotten in all the claims that birds are essentially dinosaurs (or at least that they evolved from dinosaurs) is the fact that dinosaurs are reptiles. There are many differences between birds and reptiles, including the fact that (with precious few exceptions) living reptiles are cold-blooded creatures, while birds and mammals are warm-blooded. Indeed, even compared to most mammals, birds have exceptionally *high* body temperatures resulting from a high metabolic rate.

The difference between cold- and warm-blooded animals isn't simply in the relative temperature of the blood but rather in their ability to maintain a constant body core temperature. Thus, warm-blooded animals such as birds and mammals have internal physiological mechanisms to maintain an essentially constant body temperature; they are more properly called "endothermic." In contrast, reptiles have a varying body temperature influenced by their surrounding environment and are called "ectothermic." An ectothermic animal can adjust its body temperature behaviorally (e.g., moving between shade and sun), even achieving higher body temperature than a so-called warm-blooded animal, but this is done by outside factors.

In an effort to make the evolution of dinosaurs into birds seem more plausible, some evolutionists have argued that dinosaurs were also endothermic,[1] but there is no clear evidence for this.[2]

One of the lines of evidence for endothermic dinosaurs is based on the microscopic structure of dinosaur bones. Fossil dinosaur bones have been found containing special microscopic structures called osteons (or Haversian systems). Osteons are complex concentric layers of bone surrounding blood vessels in areas where the bone is dense. This arrangement is assumed by some to be unique to endothermic animals and thus evidence that dinosaurs are endothermic, but such is not the case. Larger vertebrates (whether reptiles, birds, or mammals) may also have this type of bone. Even tuna fish have osteonal bone in their vertebral arches.

Another argument for endothermy in dinosaurs is based on the eggs and assumed brood behavior of dinosaurs, but this speculation too has been challenged.[3] There is in fact no theropod brooding behavior not known to occur in crocodiles and other cold-blooded living reptiles.

Alan Feduccia, an expert on birds and their evolution, has concluded that "there has never been, nor is there now, any evidence that dinosaurs were endothermic."[4] Feduccia says that despite the lack of evidence "many authors have tried to make specimens conform to the hot-blooded theropod dogma."

"BIRD-HIPPED" VS. "LIZARD-HIPPED" DINOSAURS

All dinosaurs are divided into two major groups based on the structure of their hips (pelvic bones): the lizard-hipped dinosaurs (saurischians) and the bird-hipped dinosaurs (ornithiscians). The main difference between the two hip structures is that the pubic bone of the bird-hipped dinosaurs is directed toward the rear (as it is in birds) rather entirely to the front (as it is in mammals and reptiles).

But in most other respects, the bird-hipped dinosaurs, including such huge quadrupedal sauropods as *Brachiosaurus* and *Diplodocus*, are even less

---

[1] R.T. Bakker, Dinosaur renaissance, *Scientific American* **232**:58–78, 1975.

[2] A. Feduccia, Dinosaurs as reptiles, *Evolution* **27**:166–169,1973; A. Feduccia, *The Origin and Evolution of Birds*, 2nd Ed., Yale University Press, New Haven, Connecticut, 1999.

[3] N.R. Geist and T.D. Jones, Juvenile skeletal structure and the reproduction habits of dinosaurs, *Science* **272**:712–714,1996.

[4] A. Feduccia, T. Lingham-Soliar, and J.R. Hinchliffe, Do feathered dinosaurs exist? Testing the hypothesis on neontological and paleontological evidence, *Journal of Morphology* **266**:125–166, 2005.

bird-like than the lizard-hipped, bipedal dinosaurs such as the theropods. This point is rarely emphasized in popular accounts of dinosaur/bird evolution.

THE THREE-FINGERED HAND

One of the main lines of evidence sighted by evolutionists for the evolution of birds from theropod dinosaurs is the three-fingered "hand" found in both birds and theropods. The problem is that recent studies have shown that there is a digital mismatch between birds and theropods.

Most terrestrial vertebrates have an embryological development based on the five-fingered hand. In the case of birds and theropod dinosaurs, two of the five fingers are lost (or greatly reduced) and three are retained during development of the embryo. If birds evolved from theropods, one would expect the same three fingers to be retained in both birds and theropod dinosaurs, but such is not the case. Evidence shows that the fingers retained in theropod dinosaurs are fingers 1, 2, and 3 (the "thumb" is finger 1) while the fingers retained in birds are 2, 3, and 4.[5]

AVIAN VS. REPTILIAN LUNG

One of the most distinctive features of birds is their lungs. Bird lungs are small in size and nearly rigid, but they are, nevertheless, highly efficient to meet the high metabolic needs of flight. Bird respiration involves a unique "flow-through ventilation" into a set of nine interconnecting flexible air sacs sandwiched between muscles and under the skin. The air sacs contain few blood vessels and do not take part in oxygen exchange, but rather function like bellows to move air through the lungs.

The air sacs permit a unidirectional flow of air through the lungs resulting in higher oxygen content than is possible with the bidirectional air flow through the lungs of reptiles and mammals. The air flow moves through the same tubes at different times both into and out of the lungs of reptiles and mammals, and this results in a mixture of oxygen-rich air with oxygen-depleted air (air that has been in the lungs for awhile). The unidirectional flow

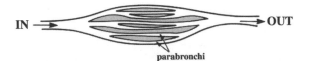

IN → OUT

parabronchi

---

[5] Feduccia et al., 2005.

through bird lungs not only permits more oxygen to diffuse into the blood but also keeps the volume of air in the lungs nearly constant, a requirement for maintaining a level flight path.

If theropod dinosaurs are the ancestors of birds, one might expect to find evidence of an avian-type lung in such dinosaurs. While fossils generally do not preserve soft tissue such as lungs, a very fine theropod dinosaur fossil (*Sinosauropteryx*) has been found in which the outline of the visceral cavity has been well preserved. The evidence clearly indicates that this theropod had a lung and respiratory mechanics similar to that of a crocodile—not a bird.[6] Specifically, there was evidence of a diaphragm-like muscle separating the lung from the liver, much as you see in modern crocodiles (birds lack a diaphragm). These observations suggest that this theropod was similar to an ectothermic reptile, not an endothermic bird.

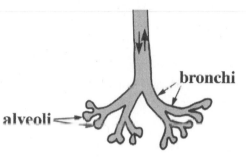

Origin of Feathers

DO FEATHERED DINOSAURS EXIST?

Feathers have long been considered to be unique to birds. Certainly all living birds have feathers of some kind, while no living creature other than birds has been found to have a cutaneous appendage even remotely similar to a feather. Since most evolutionists are certain that birds evolved from dinosaurs (or at least are closely related to them), there has been an intense effort to find dinosaur fossils that show some suggestion of feathers or "protofeathers." With such observer bias, one must be skeptical of recent widely publicized reports of feathered dinosaurs.

Dinosaurs are reptiles, and so it is not surprising that fossil evidence has shown them to have a scaly skin typical of reptiles. For example, a recently discovered well-preserved specimen of *Compsognathus* (a small theropod dinosaur of the type believed to be most closely related to birds) showed unmistakable evidence of scales but alas—no feathers.[7]

---

[6] J.A. Ruben, T.D. Jones, N.R. Geist, and W.J. Hillenius, Lung structure and ventilation in theropod dinosaurs and early birds, *Science* **278**:1267–1270, 1997.
[7] U.B. Gohlich and L.M. Chiappe, A new carnivorous dinosaur from the late Jurassic Solnhofen archipelago, *Nature* **440**:329–332, 2006.

Still, there have been many claims of feathered dinosaurs, particularly from fossils found in Liaoning province in northeastern China.[8] The earliest feathered dinosaur from this source is the very unbird-like dinosaur *Sinosauropteryx,* which lacks any evidence of structures that could be shown to be feather-like.[9]

Structures described as "protofeathers" in the dinosaur fossils *Sinosauropteryx* and *Sinithosaurus* are filamentous and sometimes have interlaced structures bearing no obvious resemblance to feathers. It now appears likely that these filaments (often referred to as "dino-fuzz") are actually connective tissue fibers (collagen) found in the deep dermal layer of the skin. Feduccia laments that "the major and most worrying problem of the feathered dinosaur hypothesis is that the integumental structures have been homologized with avian feathers on the basis of anatomically and paleontologically unsound and misleading information."[10]

Complicating matters even further is the fact that true birds have been found among the Liaoning province fossils in the same layers as their presumed dinosaur ancestors. The obvious bird fossil *Confuciusornis sanctus,* for example, has long slender tail feathers resembling those of a modern scissor-tail flycatcher. Two taxa (*Caudipteryx* and *Protarchaeopteryx*) that were thought to be dinosaurs with true feathers are now generally conceded to be flightless birds.[11]

Thus far, the only obvious dinosaur fossil with obvious feathers that was "found" is *Archaeoraptor liaoningensis.* This so-called definitive feathered dinosaur was reported with much fanfare in the November 1999 issue of *National Geographic* but has since been shown to be a fraud.

What would it prove if features common to one type of animal were found on another? Nothing. Simply put, God uses various designs with various creatures. Take the platypus, for example—a mosaic. It has several design features that are shared with other animals, and yet it is completely distinct. So if a dinosaur (or mammal) is ever found with feathers, it would call into

---

[8] P.J. Chen, Z.M. Dong, and S.N. Zheng, An exceptionally well-preserved theropod dinosaur from the Yixian formation of China, *Nature* 391:147–152,1998; X. Xu, X.Wang, and X. Wu, A dromaeosaurid dinosaur with a filamentous integument from the Yixian formation of China, *Nature* 401:262–266, 1999; P.J. Currie and P.J. Chen, Anatomy of *Sinosauropteryx prima* from Liaoning, northeastern China, *Can. J. Earth Sci.* 38:1705–1727, 2001.

[9] Feduccia et al., 2005.

[10] Feduccia et al., 2005.

[11] Feduccia et al., 2005.

question our human criteria for classification, not biblical veracity. What's needed to support evolution is *not* an unusual mosaic of complete traits, but a trait in transition, such as a "scale-feather," what creationist biologists would call a "sceather."

FEATHERS AND SCALES ARE DISSIMILAR.

If birds evolved from dinosaurs or any other reptile, then feathers must have evolved from reptilian scales. Evolutionists are so confident that feathers evolved from scales that they often claim that feathers are very similar to scales. The popular Encarta computerized encyclopedia (1997) describes feathers as a "horny outgrowth of skin peculiar to the bird but similar in structure and origin to the scales of fish and reptiles."[12]

In actual fact, feathers are profoundly different from scales in both their structure and growth. Feathers grow individually from tube-like follicles similar to hair follicles. Reptilian scales, on the other hand, are not individual follicular structures but rather comprise a continuous sheet on the surface of the body. Thus, while feathers grow and are shed individually (actually in symmetrically matched pairs!), scales grow and are shed as an entire sheet of skin.

The feather vane is made up of hundreds of barbs, each bearing hundreds of barbules interlocked with tiny hinged hooklets. This incredibly complex structure bears not the slightest resemblance to the relatively simple reptilian scale. Still, evolutionists continue to publish imaginative scenarios of how long-fringed reptile scales evolved by chance into feathers, but evidence of "sceathers" eludes them.

---

[12] Encarta 98 Encyclopedia. 1993–1997.

Archaeopteryx, a True Bird, Is Older than the "Feathered" Dinosaurs.

One of the biggest dilemmas for those who want to believe that dinosaurs evolved into birds is that the so-called feathered dinosaurs found thus far are dated to be about 20 million years more recent than *Archaeopteryx*. This is a problem for evolution because *Archaeopteryx* is now generally recognized to be a true bird.[13] Some specimens of this bird are so perfectly fossilized that even the micro-

A reconstruction of *Archaeopteryx* as displayed in a natural history museum in Stolkholm, Sweden

Photo by Bodie Hodge

scopic detail of its feathers is clearly visible. So, having alleged missing links of dinosaurs changing into birds when birds already exist doesn't help the case for evolution.

For many years *Archaeopteryx* has been touted in biology textbooks and museums as the perfect transitional fossil, presumably being precisely intermediate between reptiles and birds. Much has been made over the fact that *Archaeopteryx* had teeth, fingers on its wings, and a long tail—all supposedly proving its reptilian ancestry. While there are no living birds with teeth, other fossilized birds such as *Hesperornis* also had teeth. Some modern birds, such as the ostrich, have fingers on their wings, and the juvenile hoatzin (a South American bird) has well-developed fingers and toes with which it can climb trees.

Origin of Flight

One of the biggest problems for evolutionists is explaining the origin of flight. To make matters worse, evolutionists believe that the flying birds evolved before the nonflying birds, such as penguins.

The theropod type of dinosaur that is believed to have evolved into flying birds is, to say the least, poorly designed for flight. These dinosaurs have small

---

[13] P.J. Currie et al., eds., *Feathered Dragons: Studies on the Transition from Dinosaurs to Birds*, Indiana University Press, Bloomington, Indiana, 2004.

forelimbs that typically can't even reach their mouths. It is not clear what theropods, such as the well-known *T. rex,* did with its tiny front limbs. It is obvious that they didn't walk, feed, or grasp prey with them, and they surely didn't fly with them!

Another problem is that this bipedal type of dinosaur had a long heavy tail to balance the weight of a long neck and large head. Decorating such a creature with feathers would hardly suffice to get it off the ground or be of much benefit in any other way.

Conclusion

Having a true bird appear before alleged feathered dinosaurs, no mechanism to change scales into feathers, no mechanism to change a reptilian lung into an avian lung, and no legitimate dinosaurs found with feathers are all good indications that dinosaurs didn't turn into birds. The evidence is consistent with what the Bible teaches about birds being unique and created after their kinds.

Genesis is clear that God didn't make birds from pre-existing dinosaurs. In fact, dinosaurs (land animals made on Day 6) came *after* winged creatures made on Day 5, according to the Bible. Both biblically and scientifically, chicken eaters around the world can rest easy—they aren't eating mutant dinosaurs.

25

Does Archaeology Support the Bible?

CLIFFORD WILSON

It is a biblical principle that matters of testimony should be established by the mouths of two or three witnesses. According to Hebrew law, no person could be found guilty of an offence without properly attested evidence from witnesses, even though this law was put aside at the trial of Jesus.

When it comes to the Word of God, a similar principle is demonstrated from the modern science of archaeology. We are told in Psalm 85:11, "Truth shall spring out of the earth," and in Psalm 119:89, "Forever, O Lord, Your word is settled in heaven." God's Word is sure. It outlasts human generations, and in His own time God vindicates its truth. This puts God's Word in a unique category: it is the "other side" of the two-way communication pattern between God and man. Man's speech distinguishes him uniquely from all the animals, and God's written Word distinguishes His special communication to man as immeasurably superior to all other supposed revelations.

According to that biblical principle of "two or three witnesses," we shall now select evidences that support the truth and accuracy of God's Word. In every area, the evidence has been forthcoming: God has vindicated His Word, and His Book is a genuine writing, with prophecies and revelation that must be taken seriously. His Book is unique because it is His Book.

Those inspired men of old wrote down God's message, applicable to themselves in their own times, and also applicable to men and women across the centuries, right down to the present century. The Bible is the "other side" of the Christian's study of the miracle of language. It is God's chosen way of revealing His thoughts—the deep things which are unsearchable except by the revelation of the Holy Spirit.

In the following outline we suggest certain divisions of the Word of God. Then we list three significant evidences from archaeology to confirm that the witness is sufficient to cause the case to be accepted for each section—God's Word is indeed Truth.

Major Evidences Regarding Genesis 1–11

Genesis 1–11 is the "seed-plot of the Bible," an introduction to Abraham and great doctrines, such as God the Creator, Friend, Revealer, Judge, Redeemer, Restorer, and Sustainer. It is actual history, and it is a summary of beginnings.

1. Enuma Elish—This is the Babylonian Creation Record. We also have the Ebla Creation Tablet. The Bible record is clearly superior to this as the Enuma Elish has creation from pre-existing matter, which really isn't creation at all. The Bible is the true account of this historical event.

One of the Babylonian Creation Tablets, Enuma Elish

2. The Epic of Gilgamesh includes the Babylonian Flood Story. Again, the biblical record is greatly superior. As Nozomi Osanai wrote in her master's thesis on a comparison between Noah's Flood and the Gilgamish Epic, "According to the specifics, scientific reliability, internal consistency, the correspondence to the secular records, and the existence of common elements among the flood traditions around the world, the Genesis account seems to be more acceptable as an accurate historical record."[1]

Part of the Gilgamesh Epic

---

[1] N. Osanai, A comparative study of the flood accounts in the Gilgamesh Epic and Genesis, www.answersingenesis.org/go/gilgamesh.

3. Long-living Kings at Kish (Sumer)—These kings supposedly lived from 10,000 to 64,000 years ago. The Bible's record is conservative and is the true account, while the Babylonian and other traditions have been embellished over time. It was later realized that the Babylonians had two bases for arithmetic calculations, based on either tens or sixties. When the records were retranslated using the system of tens rather than sixties, they came to a total within 200 years of the biblical record.

Major Evidences Regarding Genesis 11–36

This section contains Patriarchal records, with special reference to Abraham, the father of the Hebrews.

1. Abraham's home city of Ur was excavated by Sir Leonard Woolley, with surprising evidence of near-luxury.[2]

2. The customs of Patriarchal times, as described in the Bible, are endorsed by archaeological finds at such places as Ur, Mari, Boghazkoi, and Nineveh. These were written records from that day—not just put down in writing many centuries later. They bear the marks of eyewitness reporting.

Ur Nammu, the King of Ur who claimed to build a famous tower

Thus, Abraham's relationship with Hagar is seen in a different light by understanding that the woman who could not personally bear a child for her husband should provide him with one of her maidservants. In the Bible record we are told that it was Sarah who made the approach to Abraham, and her maid Hagar was a willing accomplice in having Abraham's child. Thus, she gained economic security and personal prestige. We stress it was not Abraham who made the first approach to Hagar, but Abraham's wife Sarah did in keeping with the customs of the day.

---

[2] There was another Ur to the north, mentioned in the Ebla Tablets. The same name was often used for another city. Woolley's "Ur" in the south was Abraham's city.

The records of the five kings who fought against four kings (Genesis 14) are interesting, in that the names of the people concerned fit the known words and names of the times.

3. Abraham's negotiations with the Hittites (Genesis 23) are accurate and follow the known forms of such Hittite transactions. Neo-Hittites came later, but there were distinct language relationships. The Bible was right in calling the earlier people "sons of Hatti" or "Hittites."

Interestingly, the Hittite word for *retainers*, which means "servants trained in a man's own household" is *hanakim* (Genesis 14:14). This term is used only here in the Bible. Execration texts of the Egyptians (found on fragments of ceramic pots, which seem to have been used in ritual magic cursing of surrounding peoples) gives us the meaning of this term, and it is correctly used in the Bible record in Genesis 14.

Major Evidences Regarding Genesis 37–50

This section tells us the history of Joseph, the son of Jacob and great-grandson of Abraham. His brothers sell him to the Ishmaelites who sell him to an Egyptian eunuch. Joseph becomes successful in Egypt and helps to settle all of Israel there.

1. Known Egyptian titles such as "captain of the guard" (Genesis 39:1), "overseer" (39:4), "chief of the butlers" and "chief of the bakers" (40:2), "father to the Pharaoh" (actually "father to the gods," which to Joseph was blasphemous because he could not accept Pharaoh as a manifestation of Ra the sun god; Joseph Hebraized the title, so that he did not dishonor the Lord), "Lord of Pharaoh's House" (the palace), and "Ruler of all Egypt" (Genesis 45:8) attest to the historicity of this account.

2. Joseph's installation as vizier (chief minister) is very similar to other recorded ceremonies. His new name was Zaphnath-Paaneah, meaning "head of the sacred college" (Genesis 41:41–45). Other Egyptian phrases and other local color are also plentiful throughout the record (e.g., embalming and burial practices [Genesis 50]).

3. The Dead Sea Scrolls make the number of the people of Jacob 75, not 70, in Genesis 46:27, not 70, thus correcting a scribal error and showing that Stephen's figure was right (Acts 7:14).[3]

Major Evidences Regarding Exodus to Deuteronomy

These are the other four books of the Pentateuch, written by Moses, and probably at times in consultation with Aaron, the chief priest, and Joshua, the military leader.

1. The Law of Moses was written by a man raised in the courts of pharaoh, and it was greatly superior to other law codes, such as those of the Babylonian king Hammurabi, and the Eshnunna code that was found near modern Baghdad.

2. The covenant forms of the writings of Moses follow the same format as those of the Hittites, as endorsed by Professor George Mendenhall. The law code is a unity, dating to about 1500 BC (the time of Moses). These

The Eshnunna Law Code dating to c.1900 BC

writings come from one source only, and there is no one to fit this requirement at this time except Moses. Ethical concepts of the Law were not too early for Moses, despite earlier hyper-criticism. (Ebla tablets from Syria pre-date Moses and, for example, include penalties against rape.)

At this point it is relevant to comment on two world-famous archaeologists with whom I had the privilege of working as an area supervisor with the American Schools of Oriental Research at the excavation of Gezer in Israel many years ago. Each of them (at two separate excavations) gave wonderful lectures to 140 American college students.

---

[3] This may not be correcting a scribal error since the 70 figure is referring to the number of Jacob's descendants previously listed in Genesis 46. Thus, it could be excluding Jacob and his two wives and two concubines, which give the number 75 of which Stephen spoke. See Eric Lyons, *Jacob's Journey to Egypt*, Apologetics Press website, http://www.apologeticspress.org/articles/619, 2003.

At the time of his lecture, Professor Nelson Glueck stated, "I have excavated for thirty years with a Bible in one hand and a trowel in the other, and in matters of historical perspective I have never found the Bible to be in error." Being a world-class Jewish scholar, Professor Glueck would have meant the Old Testament when he referred to the Bible, but it is also true that at least on one occasion, to my knowledge, he defended the accuracy of the New Testament writings as well.

The other lecture was given by Professor George Ernest Wright of Harvard University. He spoke on the validity of the writings of Moses, especially the covenant documents in the Pentateuch. He stated that the research of Professor George Mendenhall had led to the conclusion—with which he agreed—that the covenant documents of Moses were a unity and must be dated to approximately 1500 BC.

In further conversation after the lecture, Professor Wright told me that he had lectured for 30 years to graduate students—especially at Harvard—and he had told them that they could forget Moses in the Pentateuch. He now acknowledged that for thirty years he had been wrong, and that Moses really had been personally involved in the actual writing of the Pentateuch.

3. The ten plagues or judgments against the *leading gods* of Egypt (Exodus 12:12) are seen as real judgments, with a leading god of Egypt selected for judgment with each of the plagues.

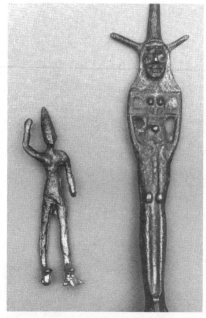

Canaanite deities, Baal and Asherah

Major Evidences Regarding Joshua to Saul

This section includes the conquest, the judges, and the early kingdom.

1. Deities such as Baal, Asherah, and Dagan are properly identified in association with the right people.

2. City-states are also identified (e.g., Hazor as "the head of those kingdoms" [Joshua 11:10]. The excavation of Hazor corroborated its great size).

3. Saul's head and armor were put into two temples at Beth-Shan. Both

Philistine and Canaanite temples were found. The Bible record was endorsed when such an endorsement seemed unlikely (1 Samuel 31:9–10 and 1 Chronicles 10:10).

Major Evidences Regarding David to Solomon

At this time the Kingdom of Israel is established.

1. David's elegy at Saul's death is an accurate reflection of the literary style of his times. Excavations at Ras Shamra (the ancient Ugarit in Syria) clarified various expressions, such as "upsurgings of the deep" instead of "fields of offerings" as in 2 Samuel 1:21.

2. Following the discovery of the Ugaritic library, it has become clear that the Psalms of David should be dated to his times and not to the Maccabean period, 800 years later, as critics claimed. The renowned scholar William Foxwell Albright wrote, "To suggest that the Psalms of David should be dated to the Maccabean period is absurd."[4]

3. Solomonic cities such as Hazor, Megiddo, and Gezer (1 Kings 9:15) have been excavated. Solomon even used similar blueprints for some duplicated buildings.

Major Evidences Regarding the Assyrian Period

This was the time of "The Reign of Terror," not long after Solomon's death.

The entrance to the Solomonic city of Gezer

---

[4] W.F. Albright, *History, Archaeology, and Christian Humanism*, McGraw-Hill, New York, 1964, 35.

1. Isaiah 20:1 was challenged by critics because they knew of no king named Sargon in lists of Assyrian kings. Now Sargon's palace has been recovered at Khorsabad, including a wall inscription and a library record endorsing the battle against the Philistine city of Ashdod (mentioned in Isaiah 20:1).

2. Assyrian titles such as *tartan* (commander-in-chief), and several others, are used casually yet confidently by Bible writers.

King Sargon of Assyria, mentioned at Isaiah 20:1

Other Assyrian titles such as *rabmag, rabshakeh,* and *tipsarru* were also used by Bible writers. As the Assyrians disappeared from history after the Battle of Carchemish in 605 BC, this retention of "obsolete" words is a strong pointer to the eyewitness nature of the records. Thus it points also to the genuineness of the prophecies because the same men who wrote the historical facts also wrote prophecies.

3. The death of Sennacherib is recorded at Isaiah 37:38 and 2 Kings 19:37 and is confirmed in the records of Sennacherib's son, Esarhaddon. It was later added to by Esarhaddon's son Ashurbani-pal.

Part of a pathway excavated by Dr. Clifford Wilson between Sennacherib's palace and the temple where his sons killed him

Various details about Nineveh and the account of Jonah point to the Bible's historicity. The symbol of Nineveh was a pregnant woman with a fish in her womb.

Adad-Nirari III, who might have been the king of Jonah's time, introduced remarkable reforms—possibly after the message of the prophet

Jonah. Adad-Nirari's palace was virtually alongside the later construction of what is known as "Nebi Yunis" ("the prophet Jonah"). That structure is the supposed site of the tomb of Jonah, and although that is unlikely, the honoring of Jonah is very interesting.

Major Evidences Regarding the Babylonians and Nebuchadnezzar

Nebuchadnezzar sacked Jerusalem and took Judah into captivity.

1. Daniel knew that Nebuchadnezzar was responsible for the splendor of Babylon (Daniel 4:30). This was unknown to modern historians until it was confirmed by the German professor Koldewey, who excavated Babylon approximately 100 years ago.

2. We now know from the Babylonian Chronicle that the date of Nebuchadnezzar's capture of Jerusalem was the night of March 15/16, 597 BC. We also know that Belshazzar really was the king of Babylon at this time because his father Nabonidus, who was undertaking archaeological research, was away from Babylon for about 10 years. He appointed his son Belshazzar as co-regent during that time.

3. Prophecies against Babylon (e.g., Jeremiah 51 and 52) have been literally fulfilled. Nebuchadnezzar wrote that the walls of Babylon would be a perpetual memorial to his name, but Jeremiah said, "The broad walls of

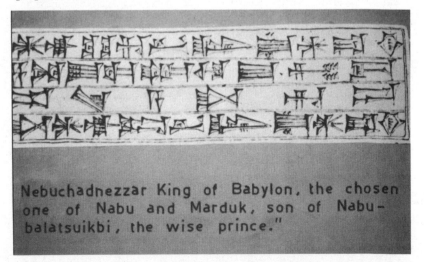

"Nebuchadnezzar King of Babylon, the chosen one of Nabu and Marduk, son of Nabu-balatsuikbi, the wise prince."

Critics said 'There was no such king,' but his palace and library were uncovered

Babylon shall be utterly broken" (Jeremiah 51:58). Jeremiah, inspired by God, has been confirmed.

Major Evidences Regarding Cyrus and the Medes and Persians

The Medes and the Persians took over after the Babylonians.

1. Cyrus became king over the Medes and Persians. We read of Cyrus when his name was recorded prophetically in Isaiah 44:28 and 45:1. He issued the famous Cyrus Decree that allowed captive peoples to return to their own lands (2 Chronicles 36:22–23 and Ezra 1:1–4). The tomb of Cyrus has been found.

2. God was in control of His people's history—even using a Gentile king to bring His purposes to pass. The Cyrus Cylinder (a clay cylinder found in 1879 inscribed in Babylonian cuneiform with an account of Cyrus' conquest of Babylon in 539 BC) confirms that Cyrus had a conquest of Babylon.

The Cyrus Cylinder—Isaiah referred to him prophetically

3. Some Jews remained in Babylon, as shown in the book of Esther. The type of "unchanging" laws of the Medes and Persians shown therein (Esther 1:19) is endorsed from Aramaic documents recovered from Egypt.

Major Evidences Regarding Ezra and Nehemiah

This was the time of the resettlement in the land after the exile in Babylon.

1. Elephantine papyri, the Dead Sea Scrolls, Targums of Job, etc., show that Aramaic was then in use, as Ezra indicates.

2. Sanballat was, as the Bible says, the Governor of Samaria (Nehemiah 4 and 6), though it was claimed by many writers that Sanballat was much later than Nehemiah. Several Sanballats are now known, and recovered letters even refer to Johanan (Nehemiah 12:13). Geshem the Arab (Nehemiah 6) is also known. Despite longstanding criticisms, Ezra and Nehemiah are accurate records of an actual historical situation.

3. The letters about San-ballat (above) clear up a dating point regarding Nehemiah. Nehemiah's time was with Artaxerxes I who ruled from 465 to 423 BC, not Artaxerxes II. This illustrates the preciseness with which Old Testament dating is very often established by modern research.

Part of the restored wall of Nehemiah

Major Evidences Regarding the Dead Sea Scrolls

The Dead Sea Scrolls

1. After approximately 2,000 years of being buried in caves near the Dead Sea, these scrolls came to light again in AD 1947. The Jews were searching for a Messiah or Messiahs—the king-like David, the great High Priest of the people of Israel, the High Priest after the order of Melchizedek, the prophet like Moses, and possibly the pierced Messiah.

    I say "possibly the pierced Messiah" because this refers only to a very small fragment. Also, the future and the imperfect tenses in the Hebrew language are very often the same and can only be determined by the context.

In this case the prophecy could be saying that the expected Messiah will be "pierced" or that "he was pierced." Isaiah 11:4 states, "And with the breath of His lips He shall *slay* the wicked [emphasis added]." And in the NASB, Isaiah 53:5 says, "He was *pierced through* for our transgressions [emphasis added]." Both statements

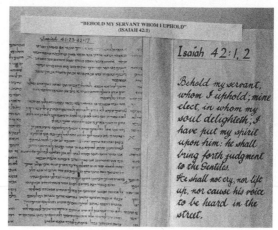

Isaiah 42:1, 2

Behold my servant, whom I uphold; mine elect, in whom my soul delighteth; I have put my spirit upon him: he shall bring forth judgment to the Gentiles. He shall not cry, nor lift up, nor cause his voice to be heard in the street.

Part of the main Scroll of Isaiah recovered alongside the Dead Sea

are relevant, for in fact the Messiah *was* pierced, and in a coming judgment those who have rejected the Messiah *will be* pierced.

2. The Scrolls have provided copies of most of the Old Testament, for fragments of every Old Testament book except Esther have been found in Hebrew, about 1,000 years earlier than previous extant Hebrew copies. (A writing from the book of Esther is found in another scroll.)

3. Considerable light was thrown on New Testament backgrounds and on the Jewish nature of John's Gospel. For example, contrasts such as "light and darkness" are common to John and the "War Scroll," a text that describes the eschatological last battle; and Hebrew was still a living language, not just a priestly language.

The Dead Sea Scroll of Isaiah also shows an old form of the Hebrew letter "tau," which looks like an "X" in the margin of the scroll. It occurs 11 times, at Isaiah 32:1, 42:1, 42:5, 42:19, 44:28, 49:5–7, 55:3–4, 56:1–2, 56:3, 58:13, and 66:5. As already stated, both the records of the Assyrians and the Dead Sea Scrolls (with a near-complete copy of Isaiah) were totally hidden from human eyes for about 2,000 years. Most of the content of these two sources overlapped and thus confirmed the evidence for the genuineness of the prophecies of Isaiah.

An important point about the finding of these scrolls is that they relate to the uncovering of the Assyrian palaces from the 1840s onwards. Isaiah gives a number of historical facts relating to the Assyrians that remarkably confirm the accuracy of Isaiah.

Possibly, the finding of the Dead Sea Scrolls is one of the most wonderful facts regarding the relevance of biblical archaeology and the Bible.[4]

Major Evidences Regarding the Person of Our Lord Jesus

Events surrounding the words and actions of Jesus have been authenticated by archaeological discoveries.

1. Problems about the census at the time of our Lord's birth have been resolved by the findings of important papyrus documents. These documents were found in Egypt inside sacred, embalmed crocodiles. The documents were the Jewish priestly writings that were written immediately before, during, and just after New Testament times.

The excavators Granfell and Hunt reported that their evidence showed that this was the first census (poll tax—enrollment) that took place in the time of Quirinius. (Another inscription has shown that Quirinius was in Syria twice—first as a military leader at a time of civil unrest, and later as Governor of Syria.) The census was probably delayed in Palestine because of that civil unrest.

Part of an inscription about enrolling for the poll tax

2. Those papyrus findings have thrown much light on the words our Lord used. It is indeed true that He spoke the language of His time on earth (Mark 12:37).

3. Pilate is now better known because of a recovered inscription at Caesarea. The John Rylands papyrus (AD 125) records part of the trial before Pilate, fragments of which are recorded in John 18:31–33, 37–38.

---

[4] Many other points of interest from the Dead Sea Scrolls are outlined in the book *The Stones Still Shout* by Clifford Wilson.

Both sides of the Rylands Papyrus

Major Evidences Regarding the New Testament, the Early Church, and the Early Years of Christianity

The documents of the New Testament have been validated as accurate historical documents.

1. The papyrii from those Egyptian "talking crocodiles" have demonstrated that the New Testament documents are remarkable records of the times claimed for them in the language of "everyday" people. Those everyday expressions from Paul's time have also thrown much light on Paul's writings themselves.

2. The findings of Sir William Ramsay and his successors in Asia Minor reestablished the veracity of Luke the historian and other New Testament writers.

The three Bible writings most attacked by critics were the Moses' Pentateuch, Ezra/Nehemiah, and Luke. Every one of these has been remarkably confirmed as being accurate and reliable by the research of credible scholars.

3. A flood of evidence shows the continuity between the New Testament documents (e.g., the Rylands Papyrus with parts of John 18:31–33 on one side and 37–38 on the other) and the abundant evidence from the secular Roman writers and the early church fathers.

Does Archaeology Prove the Bible?

Even when excavators are digging to uncover a past time period dealt with in the Bible, it is by no means sure that direct biblical history will be unearthed. Such findings are hoped for, not only by Bible students, but by disinterested archaeologists as well, because they know that they must take Bible records seriously. A link with Bible history is an excellent dating point, always desirable but not possible or achieved. These findings are excellent *confirmations* of God's Word, as opposed to "proving the Bible."

Archaeologists are scholars, usually academics with interest in the Bible as an occasional source book. A substantial number of scholarly archaeologists are committed Christians, but they are a minority. Many people believe that all archaeologists set out to verify biblical history, but that is not the case. Many excavators have virtually no interest in the Bible, but there are notable exceptions.

Superiority Despite Attacks by Critics

We have already said that we do not use the statement: "Archaeology proves the Bible." In fact, such a claim would be putting archaeology above the Bible. What happens when seemingly assured results of archaeology are shown to be wrong after all? Very often archaeology does endorse particular Bible events. And some would say that in this way it "proves the Bible." But such a statement should be taken with reservation because archaeology is the support, not the main foundation.

Thousands of facts in the Bible are not capable of verification because the evidence has long since been lost. However, it is remarkable that where confirmation is possible and has come to light, the Bible survives careful investigation in ways that are unique in all literature. Its superiority to attack, its capacity to withstand criticism, and its amazing facility to be proved right are all staggering by any standards of scholarship. Seemingly assured results "disproving" the Bible have a habit of backfiring.

Over and over again the Bible has been vindicated from Genesis to Revelation. The superiority of Genesis 1–11 has been established, and the patriarchal backgrounds have been endorsed. The writings of Moses *do* date to his time, and the record of the conquest of Canaan under Joshua has many indications of eyewitness recording.

David's Psalms were clearly products of his time, and records about Solomon should no longer be written off as "legendary." Solomon was a literary giant, a commercial magnate, and a powerful ruler—under God. God alone gave Israel their "golden age."

The Assyrian period has given dramatic confirmation to biblical records, with excavations of palace after palace over the last 150 years. Such excavations constantly add to our understanding of the background to Old Testament kings, prophets, peoples, and incidents.

The exile in Babylon is endorsed at various points, and the Cyrus Decree makes it clear that captured people could return to their own lands and worship according to their own beliefs. Ezra and Nehemiah are accurate reflections of that post-exilic period.

Likewise, the New Testament documents have been consistently demonstrated as factual, eyewitness records. Kings, rulers, and officials are named unerringly; titles are used casually but with remarkable accuracy; geographic boundaries are highlighted; and customs are correctly touched on.

It is indeed true that "truth shall spring out of the earth" (Psalm 85:11).

Archaeology as It Relates to the Biblical Record

Our understanding of essential biblical doctrine has never changed because of archaeological findings. It should be acknowledged, however, that at times it has been necessary to look again to see just what the Bible is actually saying. There have been times when new light has been thrown on words used in Scripture in both Old and New Testaments.

We have seen that the titles of officials of Israel's neighbors are now better understood and that many words are better understood because of the records in clay, on papyrus, and on stone.

The Old Testament is an ancient book, not a modern record, and its style is that of the East and not the West. At times it must be interpreted, based on its context, in the symbolic and figurative style of the Jews of ancient times, and not according to the "scientific precision" of our modern materialistic age.

Sometimes the Bible uses "the language of phenomena"—as when it refers to the sun rising. Scientifically speaking, the earth is what "rises." However, though the Bible is not a science textbook, it is yet wonderfully true that where the Bible touches on science it is astonishingly accurate.

The more this new science of archaeology touches the records of the Bible, the more we are convinced that it is a unique record. At many points it is greatly superior to other writings left by neighboring people.

We have not said, "Archaeology proves the Bible," and we do not suggest it. To do so would be quite wrong, even though such a statement is often made by those introducing a lecturer on biblical archaeology. The Bible itself is the absolute; archaeology is not. If archaeology could prove the Bible, archaeology would be greater than the Bible, but it is not. The Bible comes with the authority of almighty God. It is His Word, and He is greater than all else.

Nevertheless, archaeology has done a great deal to restore confidence in the Bible as the revealed Word of God. It has thrown a great deal of light on previously obscure passages and has helped us to understand customs, culture, and background in many ways that seemed most unlikely to our fathers in a previous generation. Archaeology is highly relevant for understanding the Bible today.

The Value of Archaeology for the Bible Student

Archaeology has done a great deal to cause many scholars to take the Bible much more seriously. It has touched the history and culture of Israel and her neighbors at many points and has often surprised researchers by the implicit accuracy of its statements.

If it can be shown (as it can) that the Bible writers lived and gave their message against the backgrounds claimed for them, it becomes clear that their amazing prophetic messages are also genuine, written long before the events they prophesied. Consider five important ways in which archaeology has been of great value for Bible students.

1. Archaeology confirms Bible history, and it often shows that Bible people and incidents are correctly referred to.

One example is that of Sargon, a king named in Isaiah 20:1. Critics at one time said that there was no such king. But then his palace was found at Khorsabad, and there was a description of the very battle referred to by Isaiah. Another illustration is the death of the Assyrian King Sennacherib. His death is recorded in Isaiah 37 and also in the annals of Sennacherib's son Esarhaddon, whom Isaiah says succeeded Sennacherib.

2. Archaeology gives local color, indicating that the background is authentic.

Laws and customs, gods, and religious practices are shown to be associated with times and places mentioned in the Bible. Rachel's stealing her father's clay gods illustrates the correct understanding of customs: she and Leah asked, "Is there yet any portion or inheritance for us in our father's house?" (Genesis 31:14). She knew the teraphim (clay gods) were associated with title deeds, which was a custom of that time.

3.   Archaeology provides additional facts.

Archaeological facts help the Bible student understand times and circumstances better than would otherwise be possible. Bible writers tell us the names of such Assyrian kings as Sennacherib and Esarhaddon, and we now know a great deal more about these rulers from records recovered in their palaces and libraries.

4.   Archaeology has proved of tremendous value in Bible translations.

The meanings of words and phrases are often illuminated when found in other contexts. 2 Kings 18:17, for example, correctly uses three Assyrian army titles. Those terms are *tartan* (commander-in-chief), *rabshakeh* (chief of the princes), and *rabsaris* (chief eunuch). The meanings of these words were unknown at the time of the production of the King James Version of the Bible in 1611.

Only when Assyrian palaces were excavated was a great deal of light thrown onto their meanings. The fact that these titles are correctly used in the Old Testament is another strong argument for eyewitness recording. People do not know the titles of their enemy without some form of contact.

5.   Archaeology has demonstrated the accuracy of many Bible prophecies.

The prophecies against Nineveh, Babylon, and Tyre in Isaiah are typical examples, as are the early records of creation in the Bible. It is also highly important that Isaiah and others so accurately pointed to the coming Messiah. At many points their history has been vindicated, and so have their prophecies about Jesus.

This spiritual application is surely one of the most important aspects of biblical archaeology, reminding us that "holy men of God spoke as they were moved by the Holy Spirit" (2 Peter 1:21).

Archaeology has done much to demonstrate that "the Bible was right after all." Its early records of creation, Eden, the Flood, long-living men, and the dispersal of the nations are not mere legends after all. Other tablets recording the same events have been recovered, but they are often distorted and corrupted.

The Bible record is immensely superior, and quite credible. Those early Bible records can no longer be written off as myth or legend.

"For ever, O Lord, Your word is settled in heaven" (Psalm 119:89).

A Memory Aid Showing the Relevance of Archaeology to the Bible

S   Superiority—Creation, Flood, Tower of Babel, Laws of Moses, Psalms of David, genuine prophets of Israel, the teachings of Jesus.

C   Customs—Rachel stealing clay gods; Joseph's story; religious practices; ruthlessness of Assyrians; unchangeable laws of Medes and Persians; enrolling for census when Jesus was born.

A   Additional information—Moabite Stone; Jehu and the Black Obelisk of Shalmaneser; the assassination of Assyrian King Sennacherib; Belshazzar as co-regent with his father Nabonidus; new light on New Testament backgrounds from the Dead Sea Scrolls and other manuscripts and inscriptions.

L   Language and Languages—Hebrew, Aramaic, and Greek. Others are touched in passing, including Egyptian, Canaanite, Philistine, Babylonian, Persian, Latin, and Assyrian.

P   Prophecy—about Bible lands and people, as well as the Lord Jesus Christ. The local color and the integrity of prophecies demonstrate the uniqueness of the Bible.

S   Specific Incidents and People— Sargon's victory against Ashdod (Isaiah 20:1); the death of Sennacherib (Isaiah 37); Nebuchadnezzar the King of Babylon who campaigned against Jerusalem and Judah; various rulers (such as the Herods) correctly identified (the Gospels and Acts); the census in the time of Caesar Augustus.

Many people have commented that they do not have the knowledge to talk about archaeology and the Bible; this acrostic SCALPS should help.[6]

First Peter 3:15 urges us to "always be ready to give a defense to everyone who asks you a reason for the hope that is in you, with meekness and fear."

That's a command to Christians!

---

[6] This acrostic may be photocopied and enlarged.

26

Why Does God's Creation Include Death & Suffering?

TOMMY MITCHELL

Why do bad things happen? Through the ages, human beings have sought to reconcile their understanding of an all-powerful, loving God with the seemingly endless suffering around them.

One prominent example of this struggle is the media mogul Ted Turner. Having lost his faith after his sister died of a painful disease, Turner claimed, "I was taught that God was love and God was powerful, and I couldn't understand how someone so innocent should be made or allowed to suffer so."[1]

Is God responsible for human suffering? Is God cruel, capricious, and vindictive, or is He too weak to prevent suffering? If God truly is sovereign, how can He let someone He loves suffer?

A World of Misery and Death

Each day brings new tragedy. A small child is diagnosed with leukemia and undergoes extensive medical treatment only to die in his mother's arms. A newlywed couple is killed by a drunk driver as they leave for their honeymoon. A faithful missionary family is attacked

---

[1] Associated Press, Ted Turner was suicidal after breakup, www.nytimes.com/aponline/arts/ AP-People-Turner.html, April 16, 2001.

and killed by the very people they were ministering to. Thousands are killed in a terrorist attack. Hundreds drown in a tsunami, while scores of others are buried in an earthquake.

How are these things possible if God really loves and cares for us? Is He a God of suffering?

Man's usual response to tragedy is to blame God, as Charles Darwin did after the death of his beloved daughter Annie.

"Annie's cruel death destroyed Charles's tatters of beliefs in a moral, just universe. Later he would say that this period chimed the final death-knell for his Christianity ... . Charles now took his stand as an unbeliever."[2]

Is this the proper response? A correct view of history, found in the Bible, provides the answer.

Was God's Creation Really "Very Good"?

In the beginning, about 6,000 years ago, God created the universe and everything in it in six actual days. At the end of His creative acts on the sixth day, God "saw everything that He had made, and indeed it was very good" (Genesis 1:31).

---

[2] A. Desmond and J. Moore, *Darwin: The Life of a Tormented Evolutionist*, W.W. Norton & Company, New York, 1991, 387.

To have been very good, God's creation must have been without blemish, defect, disease, suffering, or death. There was no "survival of the fittest." Animals did not prey on each other, and the first two humans, Adam and Eve, did not kill animals for food. The original creation was a beautiful place, full of life and joy in the presence of the Creator.

Both humans and animals were vegetarians at the time of creation. In Genesis 1:29–30 the Lord said, "See, I have given you every herb that yields seed which is on the face of all the earth, and every tree whose fruit yields seed; to you it shall be for food. Also, to every beast of the earth, to every bird of the air, and to everything that creeps on the earth, in which there is life, I have given every green herb for food."

This passage shows clearly that in God's very good creation, animals did not eat each other (and thus, there was no animal death), as God gave Adam, Eve, and the animals only plants to eat. (It was not until after the worldwide Flood of Noah's Day—1,600 years later—that man was allowed to eat meat, according to Genesis 9:3.)

Because eating a plant can kill it, some people claim that death was part of the original creation. The Bible makes a distinction, though, between plants and animals. This distinction is expressed in the Hebrew word *nephesh*, which describes an aspect of life attributed only to animals and humans. *Nephesh* can be translated "breathing creature" or

"living creature" (see Genesis 1:20–21, 24). Plants do not possess this *nephesh* quality and so cannot die in the scriptural sense.

The original creation was very good. According to Moses in Deuteronomy 32:4, "His work is perfect." Obviously, things are not like this any longer.

Why Do We Die Now?

If there was no animal or human death when God finished His creation and pronounced it very good, why do we die now? We see death all around us today. Something must have happened to change creation—that something was sin.

God placed Adam and Eve in a perfect paradise. As their Creator, He had authority over them. In His authority, God gave Adam a rule: "But of the tree of the knowledge of good and evil you shall not eat, for in the day that you eat of it you shall surely die" (Genesis 2:17).

Sometime after God declared His completed creation "very good" at the end of the sixth day, one of God's angels, Lucifer, led a rebellion against their Creator.[3] Lucifer then took on the form of a serpent and tempted Eve to eat the fruit God had forbidden. Both Adam and Eve ate it. Their actions resulted in the punishment that God had warned them about. God is holy and cannot tolerate sin in His presence. The just Creator righteously kept His promise that punishment would follow their disobedience. With the rebellious actions of one man, death entered God's creation.

---

[3] The Bible is not clear when Lucifer rebelled or when Adam and Eve sinned. However, we can surmise that it was not too long after God put Adam and Eve in the Garden of Eden, as He told them to be fruitful and multiply, and they obviously had not had an opportunity to conceive a child before they rebelled.

Ashamed and afraid, Adam and Eve tried to escape the consequences of their sin by making coverings of fig leaves. But by themselves, they could not cover what they had done. They needed something else to

provide a covering. According to the writer of Hebrews, "Without shedding of blood, there is no remission [of sin]" (9:22). A blood sacrifice was necessary to cover their guilt before God.

To illustrate the horrible consequences of sin, God killed an animal and made coats of skin (depicted at left) to cover Adam and Eve. We are not told what type of animal was killed, but perhaps it was something like a lamb to symbolize Jesus Christ, the Lamb of God, who would shed His own blood to take away our sins.

Genesis 3 also reveals that the ground was cursed. Thorns and thistles were now part of the world. Animals were cursed, the serpent more than the rest. The world was no longer perfect but sin-cursed. Suffering and death now abounded in that once-perfect creation.

What Does All This Have to Do with Me?

If it was Adam's decision to disobey God that brought sin into the world, why do we all have to suffer punishment?

After Adam and Eve sinned and were banished from the Garden of Eden (Genesis 3:20–24), they began to have children. Each child inherited Adam's sinful nature, and each child rebelled against his or her Creator. Every human is a descendant of Adam and Eve, born with the same problem: a sinful nature.

If we are honest with ourselves, we will realize that Adam is a fair representative for all of us. If a perfect person in a perfect place decided to disobey God's rules, none of us would have done better. The Apostle Paul writes, "Therefore, just as through one man sin entered the world,

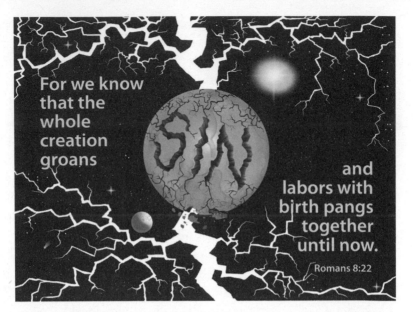

For we know that the whole creation groans and labors with birth pangs together until now.

Romans 8:22

and death through sin, and thus death spread to all men, because all sinned" (Romans 5:12).

As children of Adam, we all inherit Adam's sin nature. We have all, at some point, disobeyed a command from the Creator, so we all deserve to die and suffer eternal punishment in hell. We must understand that not one of us is innocent before God. Romans 3:23 says, "For all have sinned and fall short of the glory of God." Not one of us is worthy to stand before the Creator of the universe because we would each bring a sinful, rebellious nature into His presence.

In the beginning, God sustained His creation in its perfect state. The account of the Israelites wandering in the wilderness provides a glimpse of how things might have been in the original creation. The garments of the Israelites did not wear out, nor did their feet swell for the forty years they camped in the desert (Deuteronomy 8:4). God is omnipotent and perfectly capable of sustaining and protecting His creation.

When Adam sinned, however, the Lord cursed the universe. In essence there was a change, and along with that change God began to uphold the creation in a cursed state. Suffering and death entered into His creation. The whole universe now suffers from the effects of sin (Romans 8:22).

The sad things (e.g., the death of a loved one, tsunamis that kill thousands, hurricanes that leave many dead or homeless, etc.) that happen around us and to us are reminders that sin has consequences and that the world needs a Savior.

God took pleasure in all of His creation (Revelation 4:11), but He loved people most of all. He uses the deterioration of the created universe to show us the consequences of our sin. If we did not experience the consequences of our rebellion against the Creator, we would never understand that we need salvation from our sin, and we would never receive His offer of mercy for our sin.

Most people easily recognize that there is a problem in the world. We need to realize that there is One who has overcome this problem of death and suffering—Jesus Christ.

Is There Any Hope?

Sadly, the consequences for our sin are much worse than life in a cursed universe. In addition to living our lives in a sin-filled creation, we must all die physically and then face a punishment much more horrible than anything we have ever known: the second death. The Apostle John tells of a lake of fire called the "second death" that awaits all those whose names are not written in the book of life (Revelation 20:14–15). This second death is the final punishment for our sin.

Even though we rebelled against Him and brought punishment on ourselves, God loves His children and does not want them to spend eternity in hell. Our merciful Creator has provided a way to be reconciled to Him and to escape the terrible eternal punishment for our sin. This way of escape is through the death and resurrection of Jesus Christ.

Jesus Christ, who is God, came to earth as a man, lived a sinless life, and then died to pay the penalty for sin. The Apostle Paul tells us that "as through one man's offense judgment came to all men, resulting in condemnation, even so through one Man's righteous act the free gift came to all men, resulting in justification of life" (Romans 5:18).

God is righteous and justly sentenced man to death, so we received the punishment we deserve. However, God exercised grace because of His love for us and took that punishment upon Himself as the payment for our sin.

Take heart! Christ did not remain in the grave. He showed that He has power over death by rising on the third day after He was buried. Because Christ clearly demonstrated His power over death, those who believe in Him can know that they too will live, and death will have no sting. In fact, the Bible says,

> So when this corruptible has put on incorruption, and this mortal has put on immortality, then shall be brought to pass the saying that is written: "Death is swallowed up in victory. O Death, where is your sting? O Hades, where is your victory?" (1 Corinthians 15:54–55).

In Christ, those who have received the free gift of eternal life can look forward to spending eternity with Him in a perfect, pain-free place (Revelation 21:4). As the Apostle Paul wrote,

> For by grace you have been saved through faith, and that not of yourselves; it is the gift of God, not of works, lest anyone should boast (Ephesians 2:8–9).

Some may suggest that if God really loved us, He would put us in a perfect place where nothing painful can touch us. However, He already did that once, and Adam rebelled. Given the same opportunity, each one of us would do the same thing. God demonstrated His love by dying for the world and rising again. All who receive the free gift of eternal life will spend eternity with Him.

Compared to eternity, the time we spend here in a cursed world is insignificant. God will complete His demonstration of love by placing those who receive His salvation in a perfect place forever.

The Restoration of All Things

The Bible describes death as the last enemy that will be destroyed (1 Corinthians 15:26). Revelation 21:4 says that "God will wipe away every tear from their eyes; there shall be no more death, nor sorrow, nor crying. There shall be no more pain, for the former things have passed away." Those who have received salvation look forward to the time when the Lord will revoke the Curse and restore the universe to a perfect state like the one it had before man sinned (Revelation 22:3).

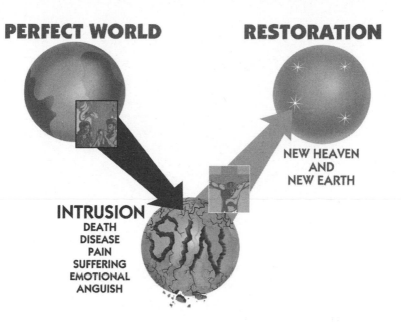

PERFECT WORLD

RESTORATION

NEW HEAVEN
AND
NEW EARTH

INTRUSION
DEATH
DISEASE
PAIN
SUFFERING
EMOTIONAL
ANGUISH

The Lord not only loves His children enough to die for their sin, He also promises to fix the ruined world by creating a new heavens and new earth (Revelation 21:1). And just as the first Adam brought death into the world, Christ, as the "last Adam," brings renewed life into the world.

As Paul wrote,

And so it is written, "The first man Adam became a living being." The last Adam became a life-giving spirit (1 Corinthians 15:45).

The Alternate View of History

Those who reject the Creator must explain how the world came into existence without God.

Evolutionists and most other "long agers" believe that 13–14 billion years ago, a big bang caused the universe to begin from nothing. Galaxies, stars, and planets formed as matter—scattered across the universe—cooled and coalesced. About five billion years ago, the earth itself began to form. The earth, it is claimed, cooled for a billion years or so, water formed on the surface, and in this primordial ocean, molecules somehow arranged themselves together to form the simplest one-celled life forms.

Due to environmental stresses and other forces, directionless mutations, say evolutionists, led to survival advantages for certain organisms. These organisms gradually changed into progressively more complex organisms. The strongest organisms were able to survive and reproduce, and the weaker organisms died off or were killed by the stronger creatures.

This merciless process eventually produced ape-like creatures who evolved into man himself. Thus humans are the ultimate product (so far!) of millions of years of death and suffering.

This naturalistic view of the universe uses the fossil record as proof for the belief that creatures became more advanced over millions of years. This view teaches that the fossil record is a record of millions of years of disease, struggle, and death. The late famous evolutionist Carl Sagan declared that "the secrets of evolution are time and death."[4]

Evolution requires millions of years of struggle and death.

Does This Really Matter?

The Bible says that death came as the result of man's sin. Evolution says that death has always been a part of nature. Can both be true? Obviously not.

---

[4] C. Sagan, *Cosmos Part 2: One Voice in the Cosmic Fugue,* produced by Public Broadcasting Service, Los Angeles, with affiliate station KCET-TV. First aired in 1980 on PBS stations throughout the US.

If the fossil record represents millions of years of earth history, there must have been millions of years of death, struggle, and disease before man appeared, contrary to what Genesis teaches.

"Theistic evolution" is an idea that attempts to merge the Genesis account and the concept of millions of years of evolution. Theistic evolution postulates millions of years of death before God stepped into the process, at some point, and created the Garden of Eden. As

illustrated below, theistic evolution requires God to call millions of years of death and suffering "very good."

On the other hand, if the fossil record is the product of a catastrophic global Flood in which vast numbers of organisms were suddenly buried

The incorrect view:

The correct view:

in chemical-rich water and sediment, the need to postulate millions of years of history goes away. God's account of a perfect world ruined by sin and destroyed by a watery judgment (Genesis 6–9) is consistent with the fossil evidence in the world.

God's promise of future restoration, "the restitution of all things" (Acts 3:21), would be nonsensical if evolution really happened. Only an original creation free from death makes God's promise of restoration logical. A perfect creation cannot be the promised future restoration if no perfect creation existed in the past.

Where Do Caring and Mercy Come From?

While many evolutionists cry out that a loving God is inconsistent with this world of cruelty we inhabit, they conveniently overlook other things. For example, how does evolution explain mercy, charity, and caring? If evolution is true, the driving force of nature is "survival of the fittest." Those less able to compete are destined to die. Any attempt to rescue these "less competitive" people would be to work against the most fundamental force of nature. The existence of doctors, hospitals, charitable organizations, and even a police force is contrary to raw evolutionary forces.

The evolutionist has no basis for moral judgments. If man is just the result of millions of years of evolution, our behavior is based on random chemical reactions. There is no ultimate moral code. All morality is relative. So if a person needs money, why is it wrong to rob someone? According to evolution, the stronger person should succeed. Might makes right. So in the evolutionary view, such violence is a natural, and necessary, part of the world.

Those who have a worldview based on the Bible have a consistent basis for acts of kindness, charity, or caring. We are commanded in Scripture to love our neighbors as ourselves, to perform acts of mercy, and to care for the widows and orphans. If we take evolution to its logical conclusion, we will conclude that these widows and orphans should die because they are a drain on the resources of nature.

Only Bible-believers ultimately offer the world a basis to make moral judgments. Those who reject the Bible have no basis for morality.

What about Individual Suffering?

In John 9 Jesus addressed the issue of personal suffering. When His disciples assumed that a man's blindness was the result of the man's sin, Jesus answered, "Neither this man nor his parents sinned, but that the works of God should be revealed in him" (John 9:3). Jesus did not consider the man's suffering to be wasted or capricious, because God would be glorified in the man's life.

The book of Job tells the history of a righteous man who pleased God but nevertheless suffered the loss of his wealth, his ten children, and his health. His friends were sure his sufferings represented judgment for some secret sins, but God denied this accusation. Many people have taken comfort simply in knowing that their personal tragedies did not necessarily represent personal judgments.

Jesus demonstrated that His love for us is not incompatible with personal suffering when Lazarus was sick and about to die. "When Jesus heard that, He said, 'This sickness is not unto death, but for the glory of God, that the Son of God may be glorified through it.' Now Jesus loved Martha and her sister and Lazarus" (John 11:4–5).

Jesus clearly loved Lazarus and his grieving family, but He was able to see a purpose to suffering that they could not see. Christ clearly revealed to them that He had power over death (by raising Lazarus from the dead), even prior to His crucifixion and resurrection.

Jesus commented on the purpose of tragedy after the tower of Siloam collapsed, killing eighteen people. "Or those eighteen on whom the tower in Siloam fell and killed them, do you think that they were worse sinners than all other men who dwelt in Jerusalem? I tell you, no; but unless you repent you will all likewise perish" (Luke 13:4–5).

These examples show that it is not necessarily an individual's sin that leads to suffering, but sin in general already has. God may use suffering as a reminder that sin has consequences—and perhaps for other purposes we do not fully investigate in this chapter. But the presence of suffering does not mean God does not love us. Quite the opposite—Christ came and suffered with us and took that punishment when He didn't have to.

In times of suffering, Christians honor the Lord by trusting Him and knowing that He loves them and has a purpose for their lives. The presence of suffering in the world should remind us all that we are sinners in a sin-cursed world and also prompt us to tell others about the salvation available in Christ—after all, that would be the loving thing to do. We can tell people the truth of how they, too, can be saved from this sin-cursed world and live eternally with a perfect and good God.

> For our light affliction, which is but for a moment, is working for us a far more exceeding and eternal weight of glory, while we do not look at the things which are seen, but at the things which are not seen. For the things which are seen are temporary, but the things which are not seen are eternal (2 Corinthians 4:17–18).

27

How Can I Use This Information to Witness?

KEN HAM

In 1959, I turned eight years old. It was a historic year for my home-land of Australia because a famous American evangelist conducted a series of crusades in the large cities of Melbourne and Sydney.

Some commentators claimed this was the closest Australia ever came to revival.[1]

In the years following, Australia has not seen such an influential crusade. Later crusades did not seem to match the apparent results of 1959.

Today, when such crusades are conducted, whether in Australia, America or other countries, statistics indicate that the small percentage of people who do go forward for first-time commitments seem to fall away or are not incorporated into any church.[2]

Why was it that, even though the entire Australian society "buzzed" as a result of these 1959 crusades, there seemed to be no lasting major impact on the culture itself? And why has Australia's culture (and other Western cultures) been continuously declining in regard to Christian morality, despite numerous evangelistic campaigns?

---

[1] S. Piggin, *Evangelical Christianity in Australia: Spirit, Word and World*, Oxford University Press, Melbourne, 1996, 154–171.
[2] R. McCune, *Promise Unfulfilled: The Failed Strategy of Modern Evangelicalism*, Ambassador International, Greenville, South Carolina, 2004, 80–82.

It really comes down to understanding the difference between "Jews" and "Greeks" (using the terms as types).

"Crusades" Conducted by Paul and Peter

In 1 Corinthians 1:23 we read the words of the Apostle Paul, "But we preach Christ crucified, to the *Jews a stumbling block*, and to the *Greeks foolishness*" (emphasis added).

In Acts 2, the Apostle Peter preached a bold message that was primarily directed to Jews (or those familiar with the Jewish religion). The main

thrust of his message concerned the death and resurrection of Christ and the need for salvation.

The Scripture records that 3,000 people responded positively to Peter's message. This was a phenomenally successful "crusade."

Now in Acts 17, when Paul preached a similar message concerning the resurrection of Christ to the Greek philosophers, their response indicated that they thought the message was really foolishness.

Why the Difference in Response?

In Acts 2, Peter was preaching to people (Jews) who, at that time, believed in the God of creation as recorded in the Old Testament. They understood the meaning of sin because they knew about the Fall of the first human couple in Genesis 3. They also had the Law of Moses, so they knew exactly what God expected of them and how they fell short. They were not indoctrinated in the evolutionary ideas that the Greeks had developed. (More about that in a moment.) The Word of God had credibility in their eyes and was considered sacred.

The Jews also understood the need for a sacrifice for sin because, after all, according to Acts 2, they were there on that particular day (the day of Pentecost) to sacrifice animals, as they had always done. However, most of the Jews had rejected Jesus as the Messiah, so Peter challenged them concerning who Jesus was and what He had done on the Cross.

Here, then, is an important observation to note: the Jews had the foundational knowledge of creation and sin to understand the message of salvation. Peter didn't have to convince his audience that God was Creator or that man had sinned. He could concentrate on the message of the Cross.

Peter, you see, didn't have to establish the credibility of God's Word or convince the Jews about creation (as opposed to naturalistic explanations of origins or deal with teaching about supposed millions of years—these were not really issues in the Jewish culture at that time).

Evolution in Ancient Times

Now in Acts 17, Paul was preaching to Greek philosophers. In their culture, they did not have any understanding of the God of creation as the Jews understood. They believed in many gods, and that the gods, like humans, had evolved. The Epicureans, for instance, believed man evolved from the dirt (in fact, they were the atheists of the age).

The Greeks had no understanding of sin or what was necessary to atone for sin. God's Word to the Jews had no credibility in this evolution-based culture. Thus when Paul preached the same basic message Peter gave in Acts 2, the Greeks did not understand—it was "foolishness" to them.

As you read on in Acts 17, it's fascinating to see what Paul tried to do in reaching the Greeks with the gospel. He talked to them about the "unknown God" (referred to on one of the Greek altars) and proceeded to define the true God of creation to them.

Paul also explained that all people were of "one blood" (from one man, Adam), thus laying the foundational history necessary to

understand the meaning of the first man Adam's sin and the need for salvation for all of us as Adam's descendants.[3] He countered their evolutionary beliefs, thus challenging their entire way of thinking in a very foundational way.

Having done this, Paul then again preached the message of Christ and the Resurrection. Although some continued to sneer, others were interested to hear more (their hearts were opened) and some were converted to Christ.

Even though Paul didn't see 3,000 people saved as Peter did, Paul was nonetheless very successful (from a human perspective, knowing it is God who opens people's hearts to the truth, as 1 Corinthians 2:14 teaches).

Think about what he had to do: Paul had to first change "Greeks" into "Jews."

In other words, he had to take pagan, evolutionist Greeks and change their whole way of thinking about life and the universe, and then get them to think like Jews concerning the true foundation of history recorded in Genesis.

No wonder only a few were converted at first. Such a change is a dramatic one. Imagine, for example, trying to change an Aborigine from my homeland into an American in regard to his whole way of thinking? Such a change would be extremely difficult, to say the least.

The Culture Change

Now let's go back to 1959. At that time in Australia's history, it was common for public school students to have prayer (even reciting the Lord's Prayer) at an assembly before the start of the day. In elementary schools, it was also not uncommon for students to

---

[3] To understand what the Bible teaches about the origin of the so-called races around the world, see chapter 17: Are There Really Different "Races"?

be read a section of the Bible or a Bible "story" before they started the day. On the weekends, many children went to Sunday schools. Then through the week, ministers of religion even visited schools and taught students about the Bible.

I suggest to you that generations ago, even in Australia (which did not have a strong Christian heritage that America had), the culture was somewhat like the "Jews." Most people knew the basic concepts of the Christian religion concerning creation, sin, and the message of salvation. So when an evangelist came and preached the message of the Cross, it was sort of like Peter preaching to the Jews in Acts 2. They had the foundational knowledge to understand the message and responded accordingly.

Now, even though much of the Australian society was like the "Jews" in the sense that many people could understand biblical terms—because of the relative familiarity with the Bible "stories"—I believe these "Jews" were already becoming "Greeks" in regard to their thinking about reality. Fifty years ago, Australia's public schools were teaching millions of years and evolutionary ideas. In a low-key way, these schools were subtly undermining the credibility of the Bible's history.

This is one of the reasons that I believe there seems to have been no real lasting Christian impact on the Australian culture, and the culture has progressively become more anti-Christian since then. Underneath it all, Australians still had questions about the validity of the Bible as a whole.

Now today in Australia, saying a prayer during a school assembly or sharing Bible "stories" to start the school day are unheard of. In addition, evolution is also taught as "fact" throughout the education system.

Biblical Illiteracy

The last two generations in Australia have had little or no knowledge of the Bible. By and large they have been thoroughly indoctrinated in an atheistic, evolutionary philosophy. Children don't automatically go to Sunday school or church programs as they used to. Ministers of religion are finding it more and more difficult to conduct programs in schools. And sadly, most church leaders tell their congregations that it's fine to believe in millions of years and/or evolutionary ideas, as long as God is somehow involved.

After years of subtle indoctrination and with an increasing emphasis on rejecting a literal Genesis, Australians basically reject the credibility of the Genesis history, and thus they doubt the reliability of the rest of the Bible.

Whether it's Australia, America, Great Britain or elsewhere, Western societies are no longer made up mainly of "Jews" but are more like the pagan Greeks: increasingly anti-Christian, and holding to a predominantly atheistic, evolutionary secular philosophy.

Indeed, they are probably even worse than Paul's opponents 2,000 years ago. The Greeks at least asked to hear him out; today many secularists try to suppress Christian teachings. In our modern time, there is a remnant of "Jews" who still have an understanding of Christian terminology, but this group is quickly becoming a smaller and smaller minority.

Today's "Greeks" do not have the foundational knowledge to fully understand the gospel. They have been led to believe that the Bible is not a credible book; its history in Genesis (creation in six days and a global Flood) is not seen to be true because so many people have been indoctrinated to believe in millions of years and evolution. Thus when an evangelist today preaches the message of the Cross, like the Greeks in Acts 17, it is foolishness to them.

How Can We Reach Today's "Greeks" Then?

As Paul understood, the "Greeks" need to be turned into "Jews." Their wrong foundation concerning evolution and millions of years

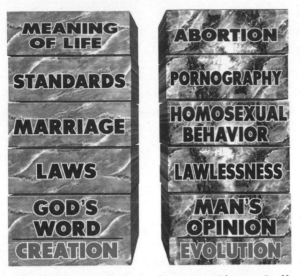

needs to be changed to one of understanding and believing that the Bible's account of creation and the Fall of man is true (i.e., that man is a sinner).

Once they have this different foundation, these "Greeks" can better understand the message of Christ and, we pray, respond accordingly and receive Christ. Sadly, most Christian leaders in recent decades didn't realize this shift. This approach of trying to "turn Greeks into Jews" to make people more open to the gospel message really should have been used even back in 1959 and before.

In the 1900s, the seeds of "Greek" thinking were already infiltrating the minds of people within and without the Christian church. The church by and large was not giving answers in dealing with evolutionary ideas and establishing the credibility of the Bible.

This could have made a real difference in the way people saw the Bible. If they had understood that it wasn't just a book of spiritual and moral issues but a book of history that could really be trusted, then they would have been more likely to trust the gospel based in that history.

When you compare this situation in Australia to the condition of the United States or Great Britain, it is easy to see a similar set of circumstances. Generations ago, their cultures were like the "Jews." The Bible, prayer, creation, etc. were a part of everyday life in public (government-run) schools—so most people were "Jews" in much of their thinking about spiritual matters.

But the seeds of "Greek" thinking were also being laid down subtly through the education system. Even in 1925, public-school students in America were sadly being taught that the Caucasians were the "highest race" and that the earth was millions of years old—by a textbook that also promoted so-called "mercy killing."[4]

Generations in the US (and in other countries) have now come through an education system that is basically devoid of the knowledge of God. In fact, Christianity is often taught *against* or relegated to mere personal belief instead of objective truth about world history. The Bible, prayer, and creation have basically been thrown out of the public education system. Students by and large are taught evolution as fact. The Bible is not a credible book in the eyes of most of these students. They are "Greeks."

If we want to evangelize the once-Christianized Western world today, there needs to be an understanding that the cultures have become Greek-like. The message will not be understood by such people until they can be changed from "Greeks" into "Jews."

The culture today needs the answers from science and the Bible to counter evolutionary and "millions of years" teaching so that the literal history of Genesis 1–11 is established— thus giving credibility to the gospel (in fact, *all* Christian doctrine) that is founded in this history. Indeed, such "creation evangelism" is a part of the beginning of the process of changing "Greeks" into "Jews" so they will better understand the gospel message and respond to it.

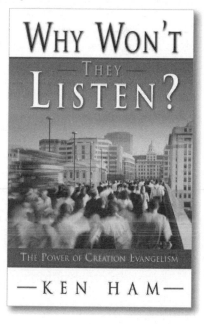

Much more about how to effectively evangelize our secular, "evolutionized" world (including practical advice) can be found in the book *Why Won't They Listen?*[5]

4 G.W. Hunter, *A Civic Biology Presented in Problems*, American Book Company, New York, 1914, 196.
5 K. Ham, *Why Won't They Listen?* Master Books, Green Forest, Arkansas, 2002.

Bonus

How Can We Use Dinosaurs to Spread the Creation Gospel Message?

BUDDY DAVIS

Dinosaurs are some of the most fascinating animals, and children especially are intrigued by them. This is one reason why evolutionists use them, over and over, to teach millions of years and evolution. Christians, however, should use dinosaurs to teach the true history of the universe. When children, young people, and adults are informed about the truth of dinosaurs, they can answer the questions of a skeptical world of and spread the good news of the gospel. When dinosaurs are used to spread the gospel, they become "missionary lizards."

Evidence of Creation

According to evolutionary teaching, dinosaurs roamed the earth millions of years ago and evolved from other types of animals. But what does the Bible say about the origin and history of dinosaurs? From Genesis 1:24–31, we can glean that dinosaurs were created on Day 6, the same day that God made the other land-dwelling, air-breathing animals, along with the first man and woman. Dinosaurs did not evolve from other animals, nor did any other animal evolve from dinosaurs. God created the original kinds of dinosaurs, and they multiplied from there, reproducing according to their kind.

As scientists have studied the fossils of dinosaurs, they have found that dinosaurs can be divided into two main groups: saurischian ("lizard-hipped") and ornithischian ("bird-hipped"). In saurischian dinosaurs, the ischium and pubis bones are forked beneath the ilium. This group of dinosaurs includes the large sauropods, such as *Apatosaurus* and *Diplodocus*. In ornithischian dinosaurs, the pubis and ischium lie side by side underneath the ilium. Ornithischian dinosaurs include *Stegosaurus*, *Triceratops*, and *Hadrosaurus*—the "duck-billed" dinosaur.

These two groups of dinosaurs are still dinosaurs, however, even though they vary in many ways. God created the various dinosaur kinds with great variety. This variety is seen in some of the most popular dinosaurs.

Popular Dinosaurs

Scientists have classified over 300 dinosaur species, but it is reasonable to assume that different sizes, varieties, and sexes of the same kind of dinosaur have ended up with different names. There may have been only 50 or fewer original kinds of dinosaurs that God created on Day 6 of Creation Week.

The following are some of the most well-known and popular dinosaurs with some interesting facts about them.

1) *Stegosaurus*—"Roofed lizard." 30 feet (9 m) long. Weighed 2–4 tons (1.8–3.6 metric tons). Found in North America. Group: Ornithischia.

    It was once believed that the rows of plates on *Stegosaurus*'s back were just for protection. Scientists now believe that they were used as solar panels. The plates were thin and full of blood vessels. They were embedded into the skin and not part of the back and tail bone. The neck, hips, and tail of the *Stegosaurus* were further protected by small boney-like studs. The tail was flexible and armed with at least four horns.

2) *Brachiosaurus*—"Arm lizard." 80 feet (24 m) long. Weighed 50 tons (45 metric tons). Found in America, Europe, and Africa. Group: Saurischia.

   Brachiosaurus stood more than 37 feet (11 m) high, twice the size of a giraffe! Scientists today question whether this giant dinosaur could have been able to raise his neck straight up. *Brachiosaurus* was supported by very long front legs, giving the back a sloping appearance. These giants were among the largest animals to have walked the earth.

3) *Ankylosaurus*—"Fused lizard." 33 feet (10 m) long. Weighed 4 tons (3.6 metric tons). Lived in Asia, North America, Europe, and South America. Group: Ornithischia.

   Ankylosaurus is the most popular of the ankylosaurs. The club on its tail weighed over 100 pounds (45 kg). It was like a knight in armor. Its body was covered with a protective armor with rows of horns; even the eyelids were armored.

4) *Triceratops*—"Three-horned face." 30 feet (9 m) long. Weighed 6 tons (5.4 metric tons). Lived in North America. Group: Ornithischia.

   Triceratops was a short-frilled ceratopsian. It had two brow horns that grew up to 3 feet (1 m) long. The nose horn was much shorter. The frill also had rows of small horn-like bones lining the outside edge. The frill was made of solid bone. *Triceratops* was one of the most massive of all dinosaurs.

5) *Compsognathus*—"Elegant jaw." 3–4 feet (1–1.2 m). Weighed about 5 pounds (2 kg). Found in Western Europe. Group: Saurischia.

   Compsognathus was one of the smallest dinosaurs; its body was the size of a chicken. The skull was delicate, and the jaw appeared fragile. The skull and jaw were armed with small, curved teeth. The slender body supported a long tail used for balance.

6) *Tyrannosaurus rex*—"Tyrant lizard." 40 feet (12 m) long. Weighed 7 tons (6.4 metric tons). Found in North America. Group: Saurischia.

   This is one of the most famous and well-known dinosaurs. *T. rex* had 50 to 60 teeth with some of its jaw teeth over 7 inches (18 cm) long. The teeth were curved, serrated, and very strong. If a tooth was broken, a new one would replace it. His bottom jaw could flex allowing him to swallow huge chunks of food. The skull of one *T. rex* was 5 feet (1.5 m) long, and scientists who have studied CAT scans of the skull believe that the *T. rex*'s sense of smell and hearing was very good.

   T. rex had small arms that were no bigger than a man's arm. They appear to have been well-muscled like a weight-lifter. It is not known exactly how the *T. rex* used them.

7) *Velociraptor*—"Swift hunter." 6.6 feet (2 m) long. Weighed 35 pounds (16 kg). Found in Mongolia, China. Group: Saurischia.

   Velociraptor was a member of the dromaeousaur family. Like all raptors, he had a sickle-like claw on his foot and three sharp claws on each hand. This dinosaur also had a mouth full of razor-sharp teeth.

Fossils

Since dinosaurs, as far as we know, are extinct, dinosaur fossils are the only things scientists can study. Dinosaur fossil remains have been found on every continent on earth. Robert Plot described one of the first dinosaur bones in his book *Natural History of Oxford* in 1676. The bone he found has been lost, but it was thought to have been part of a thigh bone of *Megalosaurus*.

One of the first complete fossilized dinosaur skeletons ever found was an *Iguanodon*. Over 30 individual *Iguanodon* skeletons were discovered in a Belgium coal mine in 1878.

One of the first complete skeletons ever assembled for display was a *Hadrosaurus*. It was discovered in 1850 in Haddonfield, New Jersey, and is still on display at the Academy of Natural Sciences in Philadelphia, Pennsylvania.

Since scientists study only the fossils of dinosaurs (not living specimens), and since fossils are the bones of dead things, Christians can use dinosaurs to explain the origin of death. After God created all things, including dinosaurs, He called His creation "very good" (Genesis 1:31). Death was not part of the world until Adam disobeyed God's command not to eat of the Tree of the Knowledge of Good and Evil. Once Adam disobeyed, God cursed all of creation (Genesis 3:14–19). Romans 8:22 tell us, "For we know that the whole creation groans and labors with birth pangs together until now." Creation now groans under the Curse, and death affects everything in creation.

The Flood and the Ice Age

Christians can also use dinosaurs to discuss the global Flood that occurred in Noah's day.

The global Flood may have been one of the reasons dinosaurs went extinct. Before the Flood, dinosaurs freely roamed the earth. But due to man's wickedness, God sent a global Flood that destroyed all life that was not inside the Ark. During the Flood, many of these animals and humans were buried in sediment that later hardened, thus giving us many of the fossils scientists study today.

We also need to remember that dinosaurs were on the Ark. The Bible tells us in Genesis 6:19 and 7:2–9 that two of every land-dwelling, air-breathing animal (and seven of some) were on the Ark with Noah, his wife, his sons, and their wives. So, what happened to these mighty dinosaurs?

After the Flood, these dinosaurs probably went extinct for a vareity of reasons, just as animals become extinct today. The Flood greatly changed the earth's habitat, and it may have changed it so much that many of the dinosaurs could not successfully survive the harsher environment. The post-Flood Ice Age also probably contributed to their demise.

Some of the dinosaurs that survived for a while after the Ice Age likely were referred to as "dragons." Most of these eventually died out or were killed. Other reasons for their extinction could be starvation, disease, and hunting pressure.

Conclusion

Dinosaurs and the truths that they share about God's creation, man's sin, death, the Flood, and the Ice Age can be used by Christian young people and adults to share the gospel with unbelievers. These missionary lizards uphold the authority of Scripture, and they can be powerful tools in sharing the salvation message, which should be the ultimate goal of every Christian.

As non-Christians hear the biblical explanation of dinosaurs, many have been, and will be, challenged to listen to the rest of what the Bible states. We rejoice that many have been won to the Lord using the true history of these missionary lizards.

Glossary

abiogenesis: the alleged spontaneous generation of living organisms from non-living matter

adaptation: a physical trait or behavior due to inherited characteristics that gives an organism the ability to survive in a given environment

adaptive radiation: the process of speciation as populations spread and encounter different environments

allele: any of the alternative forms of a gene that occur at a specific spot (locus) in the DNA sequence (genome) of an organism

anthropology: systematic study of the characteristics of humans through history

archaebacteria: the kingdom of prokaryotic cells excluding eubacteria (considered as a separate domain in certain classification schemes) which is alleged to be ancestral to eubacteria by some evolutionists

Archaeopteryx: extinct species of perching bird (known from fossils) with teeth, wing claws, and a bony tail

Archaeoraptor: a fraudulent fossil from China that combined the body of a bird with the tail of a dinosaur

artifact: an item or its remains produced in the past by humans; generally recovered through archaeological exploration

atheism: the belief that God, or any supreme intelligence, does not exist

Australopithecus: genus of extinct apes known from fossils found in Africa, including the infamous "Lucy"

bacteria: a group of unicellular organisms that lack a true nucleus and membrane-bound organelles; including eubacteria and archaebacteria

baramin: (see created kind)

Bible: the collection of 66 books that is the inspired Word of God; used as the authoritative source for determining truth

biblical creation: the supernatural events, occurring over 6 approximately 24-hour days, described in Genesis 1 and 2, by which God caused the formation of heaven and earth and everything in them

biblical creation model: a scientific model based on the biblical account of creation, the curse of nature brought about by Adam's sin, and the global catastrophe of Noah's Flood

big bang model: the cosmological model suggesting the universe began as a single point which expanded to produce the known universe

biology: the systematic study of the characteristics and interactions of living things

beneficial mutation: a mutation which confers a survival advantage to an organism under certain environmental conditions; usually a result of the loss of genetic information (see mutation)

catastrophism: the doctrine that changes in the geologic record are a result of physical processes operating at rates that are dramatically higher than are observed today

cell theory: a theory of biology consisting of three parts: (1) cells are the basic unit of all living things; (2) all living things are composed of one or more cells; and (3) all cells come from preexisting cells

chemistry: the systematic study of the properties and interaction of matter

clone: an organism that is genetically identical to its parent

cloning: producing a new organism using the DNA of an existing organism

compromise: Reinterpreting Scripture based on outside beliefs and developing theology around this belief. Common origins compromise positions accept the secular view of millions of years, as opposed to the global Flood of Noah. Some of these popular views are: Progressive Creation/Day Age Theory, Gap Theory, Framework Hypothesis, and Theistic Evolution.

cosmogony: a belief about the origin of the universe

cosmology: the systematic study of the structure of the universe, including its origin

created kind (baramin): the original organisms (and their descendants) created supernaturally by God as described in Genesis 1; these organisms reproduce only their own kind within the limits of preprogrammed information, but with great variation. **Note:** Since the original creation, organisms of one kind cannot interbreed with a different kind, but individuals within a kind may have lost the ability (information) to interbreed due to the effects of the Curse.

Cro-Magnon man: an extinct people group of Europe and Eastern Asia

Darwinism: a belief that all organisms have a single common ancestor that has produced all living organisms through the process of natural selection; popularized by Charles Darwin in *On the Origin of Species*

day-age theory: a compromise belief that the days of Genesis 1 are actually vast ages of different lengths; based on secular dating methods

deism: a belief in a Creator God that denies His intervention in the history of the universe since its creation

DNA (deoxyribonucleic acid): the basic molecule of hereditary information which serves as a code for the production of proteins and is common to all living organisms

eisegesis: an interpretation of Scripture that incorporates the interpreter's ideas as opposed to the actual meaning of the text (taking ideas to Scripture and reinterpreting it)

endosymbiont hypothesis: the suggestion that mitochondria, chloroplasts, and other organelles originated as bacteria that were ingested and became a part of eukaryotic cells over evolutionary time

entropy (thermodynamics): the measure of the tendency of closed systems to increase in disorder

eubacteria: the kingdom of prokaryotic cells, excluding archaebacteria (considered as a separate domain in certain classification schemes); alleged to be descended from archaebacteria by some evolutionists

evolution: all life on earth has come about through descent with modification from a single common ancestor (a hypothetical, primitive single-celled organism)

exegesis: critical interpretation of Scripture taking into account the writing style, meaning, and context of the passage (learning from what Scripture is saying)

extrapolation: inferring information outside of the range of the actual data based on trends

faith: belief in things that cannot be directly known or observed

Flood (Noah's Flood): the supernatural event described in Genesis 6–10 that covered the entire earth with water, killing all land vertebrates except those aboard the Ark built by Noah

fossil: preserved remains or traces of once living organisms

    coprolite: fossilized excrement

    included: organisms that are encased in a substance leaving the specimen virtually intact, as in amber

    living: organisms that are virtually identical to fossil organisms; often thought to have been extinct and then discovered

    mold and cast: a type of replacement fossil which includes the concave or convex impression of an organism; typical of shells and leaves

    permineralized: an organism in which the porous parts are filled with mineral deposits leaving the original superstructure intact

    replacement (mineralized): organism whose entire structure has been replaced by mineral deposits so that none of the original superstructure remains

    trace/track/micro: evidence of the activity of an organism, including tracks, burrows, root traces

fossilization: the process of preserving the remains or traces of an organism, generally by some form of petrification

framework hypothesis: a compromise belief that Genesis 1 is written in a non-literal, non-chronological way; based on secular dating methods

gap theory: a compromise belief that a vast period of time exists between Genesis 1:1 and 1:2 during which time the geologic eras can be fit

gene: a segment of DNA that codes for the production of polypeptides

gene pool: the collection of varying alleles within a population of organisms

genetics: the study of characteristics inherited by the transmission of DNA from parent to offspring

genome: the complete set of genetic material (DNA) of any cell in an organism

geocentric: using the earth as a central frame of reference

geologic column: the layers of rock that compose the crust of the earth

glacier: large mass of ice that has accumulated from snow over the years and is slowly moving from a higher place

half-life: the amount of time required for one half of the atoms of the parent isotope to decay into the daughter isotope

heliocentric: using the sun as a central frame of reference

heredity: acquiring traits by transfer of genes from parent to offspring

historical (origins) science: interpreting evidence from past events based on a presupposed philosophical point of view

hominid: extinct and living members of the family Hominidae, including modern humans and their ancestors

Homo erectus: fossils of extinct human people groups that are misinterpreted as missing links in human evolution

Homo habilis: an invalid category consisting of various ape and human fossil fragments

homologous structure: any feature that shares a common design with a similar feature in another species of organism (alleged to support common ancestry in evolutionary models)

Homo sapiens: the category that includes modern humans, Neandertals, and other extinct human groups

human: any member of the species *Homo sapiens*

humanism: a belief in mankind as the measure of all things; based on relative truth and morality and rejecting any supernatural authority

ice age: the period of glaciation following Noah's Flood during which a significant portion of the earth had a cold climate

Ice Age: when denoted in caps is referring to the biblical post-Flood Ice Age

ice cores: cores of ice that have been drilled down into a glacier

interglacial: short period of warming between glacier growth/movement that caused it to melt away

information: an encoded, symbolically represented message conveying expected action and intended purpose

interpolation: inferring information within the range of the actual data based on trends

Java man: the first fossil specimen of *Homo erectus*

Kennewick man: human remains found in Washington State in 1996

kind (see created kind)

life (biological): anything that: contains genetic information, can reproduce offspring that resemble itself, grow and develop, control cellular organization and conditions including metabolism and homeostasis, and respond to its environment **Note:** The Bible defines life in a different sense, using the Hebrew phrase *nephesh chayyah,* indicating organisms with a life spirit.

local flood: a nonscriptural compromise belief that Noah's Flood was an event confined to the Mesopotamian Valley

logic: systematic application of principles of reasoning to arrive at a conclusion

Lucy: a 40% complete fossil specimen of *Australopithecus afarensis* discovered in Ethiopia in 1974 by Donald Johanson

macroevolution: term used by evolutionists to describe the alleged, unobservable change of one kind of organism to another by natural selection acting on the accumulation of mutations over vast periods of time

mammal: any organism that has fur and nurses young from mammary glands

materialism: a belief claiming that physical matter is the only or fundamental reality and that all organisms, processes, and phenomena can be explained as manifestations or interactions of matter

metamorphic rocks: rocks that have been altered in texture or composition by heat, pressure, or chemical activity after they initially formed

microevolution: term used by evolutionists to describe relatively small changes in genetic variation that can be observed in populations

mineralization: replacement of material from an object, usually organic, with minerals that harden

mitochondrial DNA (mtDNA): small circular loops of DNA found in the mitochondria of eukaryotic cells

mitochondrial Eve: the most recent common ancestor of humans whose lineage can be traced backward through female ancestors; alleged support for the out-of-Africa hypothesis of human evolution

model: physical, mental, or mathematical representations that can be used to explain observed phenomena and make specific, useful predictions

moraines: stones, boulders, and debris that has been carried and dropped by a glacier

Mungo man: fossil human remains from Australia dated by evolutionists to 40,000 years or more

mutation: any change in the sequence of DNA base pairs in the genome of an organism

frameshift: addition or deletion of one or more nucleotide pairs in the coding region of a gene causing the triplet codons to be read in the wrong frame

deletion: removal of one or more nucleotide pairs in the DNA sequence

duplication: large segments of DNA that have been copied and inserted into a new position in the DNA sequence, possibly on different chromosomes

insertion: addition of one or more nucleotide pairs in the DNA sequence

inversion: a section of DNA that has been reversed within the chromosome

neutral: any mutation that does not effect the function of an organism

point: addition, deletion, or substitution of a single nucleotide pair in the DNA sequence

translocation: the movement of a section of a chromosome from one position to another, generally between different chromosomes

natural selection: the process by which individuals possessing a set of traits that confers a survival advantage in a given environment tend to leave more offspring on average that survive to reproduce in the next generation

naturalism: a belief denying that an event or object has a supernatural significance; specifically, the doctrine that scientific laws are adequate to account for all phenomena

Neanderthal/Neandertal: an extinct human people group with relatively thick bones and a distinct culture; disease and nutritional deficiency may be responsible for the bone characteristics

neo-Darwinism: an extension of Darwinism which includes modern genetic concepts to explain the origin of all life on earth from a single common ancestor

Noah's Flood: (see Flood)

old-earth creation: any compromise position that accepts the millions-of-years idea from secular science and attempts to fit that time into the events of Genesis 1–2

operational (observational) science: a systematic approach to understanding that uses observable, testable, repeatable, and falsifiable experimentation to understand how nature commonly behaves

organism: any cell or group of cells that exhibits the properties of life (living things) **(see life)**

paleontology: the systematic study of the history of life on the earth based on the fossil record

permineralization: the filling of cavities of an object, usually organic, with minerals which harden

petrification: processes, including mineralization, permineralization, and inclusion, which change an object, usually organic, into stone or a similar mineral structure

phylogenetic tree: diagrams that show the alleged evolutionary relationships between organisms

Piltdown man: fraudulent "prehuman" fossil consisting of the skull cap of a modern human and the jaw and teeth of an orangutan

plate tectonics: the systematic study of the movement of the plates that make up the earth's crust

uniformitarian model: based on the gradual movement of the plates over hundreds of millions of years

catastrophic model: based on rapid movement of the plates associated with Noah's Flood

polypeptide: a chain of amino acids formed from the DNA template and modified to produce proteins

presupposition: a belief that is accepted as true and is foundational to one's worldview

progressive creation: a compromise belief accepting that God has created organisms in a progressive manner over billions of years to accommodate secular dating methods

punctuated equilibrium: an evolutionary model that suggests evolution occurs in rapid spurts rather than by gradual change

radioactive decay: The breakdown of unstable nuclei of atoms releasing energy and subatomic particles

radiometric dating: using ratios of isotopes produced in radioactive decay to calculate an "age" of the specimen based on assumed rates of decay and other assumptions

> **parent isotope:** original isotope before it has undergone radioactive decay
>
> **daughter isotope:** isotope resulting from radioactive decay
>
> **half-life:** the amount of time required for one half of the parent atoms to decay into the daughter atoms
>
> **relative dating:** estimating the age of a fossil or rock layer by comparing its position to layers of known age
>
> **absolute dating:** using radiometric dating to test a specimen in an attempt to estimate its age

religion: a cause, principle, or belief system held to with zeal and conviction

RNA (Ribonucleic Acid): a molecule found in all living things that serves various roles in producing proteins from the coded information in the DNA sequence

secular: not from a religious perspective or source

secular humanism: (see humanism)

science: the systematic study of a subject in order to gain information (see also operational science and historical science)

speciation: the process of change in a population that produces distinct populations which rarely naturally interbreed due to geographic isolation or other factors

species: a group of organisms within a genus that naturally reproduce and have fertile offspring

spontaneous generation: the false belief that life can arise from nonliving matter

strata: layers of rock deposited by geologic events

theistic evolution: a compromise belief that suggests God used evolutionary processes to create the universe and life on earth over billions of years

theory: an explanation of a set of facts based on a broad set of observations that is generally accepted within a group of scientists

transitions/transitional forms: species that exhibit traits that may be interpreted as intermediate between two kinds of organisms in an evolutionary framework, e.g., an organism with a fish body and amphibian legs

uniformitarianism: the doctrine that present day processes acting at similar rates as observed today account for the change evident in the geologic record

vestigial organ: any organ that has a demonstrated reduction and/or loss of function **Note:** Vestigial organs include eyes in blind cave-fish but not organs that are assumed to have had a different function in an unknown ancestor.

virus: a nonliving collection of proteins and genetic material that can only reproduce inside of a living cell

Y-chromosome Adam: the most recent common ancestor whose lineage can be traced backward through male ancestors

Yom: one of the Hebrew words for "day" encompassing several definitions such as the daylight portion of a day (12 hours, Genesis 1:5a), a day with one evening and one morning (24 hours, Genesis 1:5b) or a longer period of time (Genesis 2:4). The context reveals which definition is in use.

Index

About the Authors

Ken Ham

Ken is the president and CEO of Answers in Genesis (USA). He has authored several books, including the best-seller *The Lie: Evolution*. He is one of the most in-demand speakers in the U.S. and has a daily radio program called *Answers...with Ken Ham,* which is heard on over 850 stations in the US and over 1,000 worldwide.

Ken has a BS in applied science (with an emphasis in environmental biology) from Queensland Institute of Technology in Australia. He also holds a diploma of education from the University of Queensland (a graduate qualification for science teachers in the public schools in Australia). Ken has been awarded two honorary doctorates: a Doctor of Divinity (1997) from Temple Baptist College in Cincinnati, Ohio, and a Doctor of Literature (2004) from Liberty University in Lynchburg, Virginia.

Jason Lisle

Jason graduated *summa cum laude* from Ohio Wesleyan University, where he double-majored in physics and astronomy, and minored in mathematics. He did graduate work at the University of Colorado, where he earned a master's degree and a PhD in astrophysics.

In graduate school, he specialized in solar astrophysics. While there, Jason used the SOHO spacecraft to investigate motions on the surface of the sun, as well as solar magnetism and subsurface weather.

He has authored papers in both secular and creationist literature, and written several books. Jason is a capable speaker and writer and is currently working as Director of Research at the Institute for Creation Research.

Georgia Purdom

Georgia received her PhD in molecular genetics from Ohio State University in 2000. As an associate professor of biology, she completed five years of teaching and research at Mt. Vernon Nazarene University in Ohio before joining the staff at Answers in Genesis (USA).

Dr. Purdom has published papers in the *Journal of Neuroscience,* the *Journal of Bone and Mineral Research*, and the *Journal of Leukocyte Biology*. She is also a member of the Creation Research Society, American Society for Microbiology, and American Society for Cell Biology.

She is a peer-reviewer for *Creation Research Society Quarterly*. Georgia has a keen interest and keeps a close eye on the Intelligent Design movement.

Andy McIntosh

Andy McIntosh is a professor (the highest teaching/research rank in UK university hierarchy) in combustion theory at Leeds University, UK. His PhD was in aerodynamics. A number of his students later worked for Rolls Royce, designing aircraft engines.

Andy has an extensive work and research background but also has interest in theological matters. His career in mathematics and science has led him to the view that the world and the universe show powerful evidence of design. As a result, he is often asked to speak on the subject of origins both in the UK and abroad.

David Menton

Dr. Menton was an associate professor of anatomy at Washington University School of Medicine from 1966 to 2000 and has since become Associate Professor Emeritus. He was a consulting editor in histology for *Stedman's Medical Dictionary*, a standard medical reference work.

David earned his PhD from Brown University in cell biology. He is a popular speaker and lecturer with Answers in Genesis (USA), showing complex design in anatomy with popular DVDs such as *The Hearing Ear and Seeing Eye* and *Fearfully and Wonderfully Made*. He also has an interest in the famous Scopes Trial, which was a big turning point in the creation/evolution controversy in the USA in 1925.

A.J. Monty White

Now chief executive of Answers in Genesis (UK/Europe), Dr. Monty White joined AiG after leaving the University of Wales in Cardiff where he had been a senior administrator for 28 years. He is a graduate of the University of Wales, obtaining his BS in chemistry in 1967 and his PhD for research in the field of gas kinetics in 1970. Monty spent two years investigating the optical and electrical properties of organic semiconductors before moving to Cardiff, where he joined the administration at the university there.

Monty is well known for his views on creation, having written numerous articles and pamphlets, as well as a number of books dealing with various aspects of creation, evolution, science, and the Bible. Monty has appeared on British television programs and has been interviewed on local and national radio about creation.

Paul F. Taylor

Paul learned to play the piano early in life and was educated at Chetham's School of Music, Manchester, England. However, an interest in science took him to Nottingham University to study chemistry, and there he graduated with a BS in 1982. He then took a year's post-graduate Certificate in Education so that he could become a schoolteacher. Paul taught science in state schools for 17 years, eventually becoming a head of department, and gained a master's degree in science education at Cardiff University.

Paul worked with AiG (UK/Europe) as a writer, speaker, and head of media and publications. He is currently working with the Creation Today ministry in Florida.

Bodie Hodge

Bodie earned a BS and MS in mechanical engineering at Southern Illinois University at Carbondale in 1996 and 1998, respectively. His specialty was in materials science working with advanced ceramic powder processing. He developed a new method of production of submicron titanium diboride.

Bodie accepted a teaching position as visiting instructor at Southern Illinois in 1998 and taught for two years. After this, he took a job working as a test engineer at Caterpillar's Peoria Proving Ground. Bodie currently works at Answers in Genesis (USA) as a speaker, writer, and researcher after working for three years in the Answers Correspondence Department.

Terry Mortenson

Terry earned a BA in math at the University of Minnesota in 1975 and later went on to earn an MDiv in systematic theology at Trinity Evangelical Divinity School in 1992. His studies took him to the U.K. where he earned a PhD in the history of geology at Coventry University.

Terry has done extensive research regarding the beliefs of the nineteenth century Scriptural geologists. An accumulation of this research can be found in his book *The Great Turning Point*. Terry is currently working at Answer in Genesis (USA) as a speaker, writer, and researcher.

Mike Riddle

As a former captain in the Marines, Mike earned a BS in mathematics and MS in education. Mike has been involved in creation apologetics for many years and has been an adjunct lecturer with the Institute for Creation Research. Mike has a passion for teaching and he exhibits a great ability to bring topics down to a lay-audience level in his lectures.

Before becoming a Marine, Mike became a US national champion in the track-and-field version of the pentathlon (in 1976). His best events were the 400 meters, javelin, long jump, and 1,500 meters. In his professional life, Mike worked for many years in the computer field with Microsoft (yes, he has met Bill Gates).

Mike Oard

Retired from the National Weather Service, meteorologist Mike Oard has researched the compelling evidence for Noah's Flood and the resulting Ice Age, and how the incredible wooly mammoth connects to biblical history.

Mike, or "Mr. Ice Age," received his MS in atmospheric science from the University of Washington. He has authored a children's book, *Life in the Great Ice Age*, and a book for teens and adults, *The Weather Book*. Mike recently wrote a semitechnical book called *Frozen in Time* for lay-readers, as well as the technical monograph *An Ice Age Caused by the Genesis Flood*.

Andrew Snelling

Andrew is currently Director of Research with Answers in Genesis (US). He received a BS in applied geology with first-class honors at the University of New South Wales in Sydney, and earned his PhD in geology at the University of Sydney for his thesis entitled "A Geochemical Study of the Koongarra Uranium Deposit, Northern Territory, Australia."

Between studies and since, Andrew worked for six years in the exploration and mining industries in Tasmania, New South Wales, Victoria, Western Australia, and the Northern Territory as a field, mine, and research geologist. Andrew was also a principal investigator in the RATE (Radioisotopes and the Age of The Earth) project hosted by the Institute for Creation Research and the Creation Research Society.

Tommy Mitchell

Tommy graduated with a BA with highest honors from the University of Tennessee–Knoxville in 1980 with a major in cell biology and a minor in biochemistry. He subsequently attended Vanderbilt University School of Medicine in Nashville, where he was granted an MD degree in 1984.

Dr. Mitchell's residency was completed at Vanderbilt University Affiliated Hospitals in 1987. He was board certified in internal medicine, with a medical practice in Gallatin, Tennessee (the city of his birth). In 1991, he was elected to the Fellowship in the American College of Physicians (F.A.C.P.). Tommy became a full-time speaker, researcher, and writer with Answers in Genesis (USA) in 2006.

Clifford Wilson

Cliff has a BA and a MA from Sydney University, a BDiv (which was postgraduate, including Hebrew and Greek) from the Melbourne College of Divinity, and a master of religious education (MRE) from Luther Rice Seminary. His PhD is from the University of South Carolina, and he has done field work in archaeology in association with Hebrew Union College in Jerusalem.

Cliff has carefully studied thousands of archaeological finds for decades and openly declares that they confirm the Bible's history. He was the founding president of Pacific International University in Springfield, Missouri. Cliff and his wife, Barbara, who also holds a PhD, have authored more than 70 books.

A Library of Answers for Families and Churches

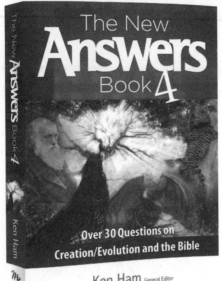

The New **Answers** Book 4

The New Answers Book 4

Over 30 Questions on Creation/Evolution and the Bible

Ken Ham *General Editor*

$14.99
978-0-89051-788-8

Over **120 Faith-Affirming Answers** to some of the Most Questioned Topics About Faith, Science & The Bible.

To help you find the answers, **Ken Ham** and the team of apologetic experts at Answers in Genesis authored *New Answers Book 1, 2, 3 and 4.*

Prepare yourself, your family, and your church to answer the questions of friends, and skeptics, and defend against the prevalent secular humanist culture that is invading our schools, government, and even the Christian community.

The New **Answers** Book

Over 25 Questions on Creation/Evolution and the Bible

Ken Ham *General Editor*

$14.99
978-0-89051-674-3

The New **Answers** Book 2

Over 30 Questions on Creation/Evolution and the Bible

Ken Ham *General Editor*

$14.99
978-0-89051-537-2

The New **Answers** Book 3

Over 35 Questions on Creation/Evolution and the Bible

Ken Ham *General Editor*

$14.99
978-0-89051-579